JOSEPH CONRAD AND ETHICS

CONRAD: EASTERN AND WESTERN PERSPECTIVES
Editor: Wiesław Krajka

VOLUME XXX

JOSEPH CONRAD AND ETHICS

Edited by
AMAR ACHERAÏOU
LAËTITIA CRÉMONA

Introduction by
AMAR ACHERAÏOU

MARIA CURIE-SKŁODOWSKA UNIVERSITY PRESS, LUBLIN
COLUMBIA UNIVERSITY PRESS, NEW YORK

2021

Cover Design
Marta and Zdzisław Kwiatkowscy
Agnieszka Muchowska

Typesetting
Agnieszka Muchowska

ISBN 978-83-227-9457-9

Publication financed by Maria Curie-Skłodowska University, Lublin

MARIA CURIE-SKŁODOWSKA UNIVERSITY PRESS
ul. Idziego Radziszewskiego 11
20-031 Lublin, Poland
tel. (81) 537 53 04
www.wydawnictwo.umcs.eu
e-mail: sekretariat@wydawnictwo.umcs.lublin.pl

Sales Department: tel./faks 81 537 53 02
e-mail: wydawnictwo@umcs.eu

TABLE OF CONTENTS

Amar Acheraïou: Introduction 1

Amar Acheraïou: Ethics and Narrative: Being, Meaning,
and Reading 17

Aileen Miyuki Farrar: Narrative Autophagy and the
Ethics of Storytelling in "Heart of Darkness" 89

Joshua A. Bernstein: Under Straining Eyes: Joseph Conrad and the Problem of "Moral Luck" 117

Thomas Higgins: "He died for the Revolution": Anarchism and Ethical Commitment in *The Secret Agent* . 145

Catherine Delesalle-Nancey: Ethics as the Secret
Agent: Dissimulation, Ethical Responsibility, and Intersubjectivity in Conrad's *The Secret Agent* 169

Laëtitia Crémona: Alfred Hitchcock's *Sabotage*: Ethics,
Politics, and Aesthetics 201

Nathalie Martinière: Reading "Heart of Darkness" with
Francis Bacon: An Ethics of Uneasiness 237

Subhadeep Ray: "After such knowledge what forgiveness?":
Nature, Community and Individual Ethics in Joseph
Conrad's "Because of the Dollars" and Adwaita Mal-
labarman's "A River Called Titas" 261

Harold Ray Stevens: The Cross of Christ as Afterthought: Killing the Christian Ethic at "An Outpost
of Progress" 291

Index of Non-Fictional Names 311

Index of Conrad's Works and Letters 317

v

ABBREVIATIONS

I. Conrad's Works

AF   *Almayer's Folly*
LE   *Last Essays*
LJ   *Lord Jim*
N   *Nostromo*
NLL   *Notes on Life and Letters*
NN   *The Nigger of the "Narcissus"*
PR   *A Personal Record*
Res   *The Rescue*
SA   *The Secret Agent*
TLS   *'Twixt Land and Sea*
TS   *Typhoon and Other Stories*
TU   *Tales of Unrest*
UWE   *Under Western Eyes*
V   *Victory*
WT   *Within the Tides*
YS   *Youth: A Narrative, and Two Other Stories*

All references to Conrad's works are to the Dent Uniform Edition (1923-28) or its reprints and other editions with identical pagination (e.g. Dent, 1946; Oxford University Press's World's Classics Edition).

II. Conrad's Letters

CL   *The Collected Letters of Joseph Conrad.* Gen. ed. Laurence Davies. 9 vols. Cambridge: Cambridge UP, 1983-2008.

Amar Acheraïou,
Montréal, Canada

Introduction

Ethics has preoccupied philosophers and thinkers for centuries. Plato and Aristotle are among the first ancient Greek philosophers to have widely dealt with ethics in *The Republic* and *Nicomachean Ethics*, and their influence on later European philosophers is immense. Since Plato and Aristotle ethics has been recurrently addressed within Western scholarly circles, and, over the last three decades, ethical issues have gained growing interest in most of the fields of research. In the humanities, this significant ethical turn was inspired by the works of Emmanuel Levinas, Michel Foucault, Jacques Derrida, and Paul Ricoeur, to name a few. These philosophers' ethical inquiries have stimulated literary critics to explore ethics in works of fiction, particularly in twentieth century literary texts. David Ellison's *Ethics and Aesthetics in the European Modernist Novel* and Lee Oser's *The Ethics of Modernism: Moral Ideas in Yeats, Eliot, Joyce, Woolf and Beckett* are two seminal studies of ethics in the fiction of key modernist writers. While they provide illuminating insights into ethical issues in the modernist works which they examine, both studies regrettably overlook, however, Joseph Conrad's fiction.

This oversight comes as a great surprise since Conrad is not only deeply engaged with ethics in his works, but his ethical perspective is also one of the densest and profoundest in twentieth-century fiction. Within Conrad scholarship, more specifically, the issue of morality has received significant critical attention.[1] However, most of the studies dealing with this topic tend to examine morality either independently from ethics or conflated and used interchangeably with ethics, as if these two distinct ontological categories were one and the same. As a result, the complex dynamics, the intricate interconnections

1

and tensions between ethics and morality, central to Conrad's ethical thought, remain widely unexplored.[2]

Joseph Conrad and Ethics rethinks the way ethics and morality articulate and relate to each other in Conrad's fiction and provides a deeper understanding of his ethical universe that sheds light on the originality as well as breadth and depth of Conrad's ethical reflection. This should help us to better grasp the underlying dynamics which sustains Conrad's ethical framework and uncover what this dialectic relationship teaches us about Conrad's own ethical position towards life and art, society and politics, truth and justice, etc. This volume is focused on these crucial interactions between the moral and ethical realms in Conrad's works. It examines the dialectical relationship of ethics and morality from a wider theoretical perspective that not only integrates these two modalities in a discussion that is not reducible to either terms, but also significantly takes into consideration the interactions and multifaceted dimension of both morality and ethics and their productive interplay.

Joseph Conrad and Ethics pivots around a fundamental Conradian ethical paradox: how to account for ethical responsibility in a world without ethical foundations and, as Conrad stated, whose aim "cannot be ethical at all" (PR 92). As it probes this essential ethical inconsistency, it examines the interconnections between ethics and morality and explores the ways in which these two ontological categories inform and contest one another. The volume offers a thorough, wide-ranging perspective on Conrad's ethical reflection in his writing that challenges and extends the scholarly discussions of his moral and ethical universe. While they navigate the slippery, conflicted terrain of ethics and morality of Conrad's fictional world, the authors bring to light the profundity of his ethical inquiry and, most importantly also, his multifarious, ambivalent position towards ethics. The themes addressed in this volume span various aspects of ethics, including the ethics of compassion and dignity, the ethics of solidarity and solicitude, transnational and planetary ethics, ethical commitment and detachment, the ethics of uneasiness and moral defamiliarization, moral obligation and ethical responsibility, the ethics of representation and storytelling, and the ethics of readership and ethical credibility.

Conrad is fundamentally concerned with the human condition in his fiction and casts a sharp critical eye on society and his fellow beings. He is also a writer with profound philosophical insights into human nature, as well as a troubled soul with deep ethical anxieties toward both existence and writing or aesthetics. The chapters of this volume are heedful of Conrad's existential anxieties and tormented ethical universe, as much as they are attentive to his sophisticated and elusive handling of ethics, his transnational sensibility, and planetary consciousness. As they discuss their own specific ethical questions, they also draw attention to the ways in which Conrad's works both resonate with and often diverge from contemporary philosophical theories on ethics, particularly on subjects like moral obligation and ethical responsibility, ethical imperatives, alterity, etc. Most of all, they delve into the ethical dilemma at the heart of Conrad's fiction: how to achieve ethical commitments in the thick of the precariousness of the human condition in which we have neither command over the circumstances, nor a solid, permanent basis for ethical responsibility.

This said, the notion of ethics, central to this volume, is a fraught and tortuous subject. It immediately raises the question of morality, since ethics and morality share common concerns and goals, not least the search for well-being and happiness that both Plato and Aristotle consider as the aim of existence.[3] Simply put, morality is a set of norms or rules governing a community to which individuals are expected to conform. Ethics, instead, is of a much convoluted and wider import. It concerns not strictly the individual's relation to his immediate community, but his distinct relation to each human being he interacts with, both within and beyond his community. This intersubjective, multi-dimensional relation inherent in ethics is not founded on mere obedience to social norms or an external coercive moral authority. It is rather the result of an independent will and an internal force that guide the individual's conduct to ethical choices and actions. Ethics, in this case, means relating responsibly to the Other, in his/her universality and radical difference.[4] It involves showing unreservedly human fellowship and answering the Other's desires and pains, as if they were our own pains and desires and this ethical responsibility, as Levinas has pointed out in *Totality and Infinity*, is not a periodic call but a permanent demand, re-activated at each encounter or dialogue with the Other. Levinas places the ethical relation above the interest of the self, which is unconditionally called to answer for the imperative ethical demands of this relation. Though critical of Levinas for having misinterpreted Martin Heidegger, Derrida fundamentally adopts the Levinasian idea of the call of the Other and argues, in turn, for an unconditional ethical imperative to answer the Other's ethical demands.[5]

Thus understood, this constant ethical imperative, stirred by the "face-to-face encounter" with the Other, is a willful, active process, not a passive, servile response to outside contingencies or moral supra-structures. It entails movement from the self to the Other that leads to deep ethical commitment to this Other's existence and well-being and, above all, to the implementation of the good for the others with whom the self interacts or enters into ethical dialogue. This dynamic impulse, made of feeling and imagination, reflection, and deliberation, suggests an ethical orientation fuelled by an active will and vital ethical demands that aim at happiness and justice, at the concordance of the self with the call of the Other. The question is: are these ethical reflections and actions fully autonomous, that is completely distinct from the moral norms regulating individuals and society, or are they connected to and inspired by this overall social morality?

The issue of boundaries between ethics and morality is, of course, hard to settle in definite terms and the debate on this problematic subject is far from being over, since ethics and morality are seen as divergent, and sometimes as interrelated and complementary. In his introduction to *The Use of Pleasure*, for example, Foucault views ethics as a part of morality, or, more precisely, as one of the three main areas of morality; at the same time, however, he tends to distinguish between "moral conduct" and "ethical conduct," "moral obligations" and "ethical obligations."[6] Gilles Deleuze, instead, makes clear-cut distinctions between ethics and morality. In a short interview with Foucault's biographer, Didier Eribon, he declares:

> the difference is that morality presents us with a set of constraining rules of a special sort, ones that judge actions and intentions by considering them in relation to transcendent values (this is good, that's bad...); ethics is a set of optional rules that assess what we do, what we say, in relation to the ways of existing involved.[7]

In this sense, an ethical action is not based on "fixed" or immutable norms, but on a fluid, free evaluation of each circumstance and relation in its uniqueness or specificity. Ricoeur similarly differentiates ethics from morality, while he also sees both as interconnected and aiming at good life and the accomplishment of the good for the others. However, as he states that ethical pursuits must sometimes go through the constraints of morality, he gives primacy to ethics over morality. He argues that in specific situations where moral norms prove impractical or wanting, morality should give way to ethics.[8] Geoffrey Galt Harpham also sees morality and ethics as interdependent, informing and contesting each other. He states that "morality [...] realizes ethics, making it ethical. At the same time [...] morality negates ethics, and needs ethics in order to be moral."[9]

The difficulty of establishing clear-cut delineations between morality and ethics is furthermore amplified by the term *ethics* itself. Derived from the Greek word *ēthikos*, which itself comes from *ethos*, *ethics* commonly means custom, character, or a set of attitudes and values; and, rather than settle the borders between morality and ethics, this semantic proliferation further blurs and problematically conflates these two ontological categories.

Whether we view morality as a rigid or closed-ended value system, characterized by "purity" and uniformity, and deem ethics fluid, multiple, driven towards alterity, and prone to self-questioning; whether we consider them autonomous or dependent on each other, the fact remains that the issue of ethics is still a contested area and will probably remain so for a long time. As a result, the various and conflicting philosophical perspectives on ethics exposed earlier unfortunately leave us with more questions than answers. Indeed, we still keep wondering about the identity of ethics and morality, about the nature of their relations to one another, about their intersections and boundaries. Are ethics and morality poles apart or connected, mutually exclusive or interdependent? Are Conrad's texts of any help in this matter? Do they provide us with a clearer picture of the nature of the relationships between ethics or morality? Above all, what does Conrad think and concretely say on these relations? Where does he stand, in fact, in this heated debate on the conflicted terrain of morality and ethics? Does he clearly distinguish ethics from morality? Is he a moralist or an ethicist, both or neither? Do his texts invite moral readings by endorsing dominant moral norms or asserting definite moral messages, or do they instead invite ethical readings by exploring the limitation of the moral norms themselves? In short, are morality and ethics so distant from each other in Conrad's fiction or are they coexistent and enmeshed? Do some Conrad's texts call for a moral reading and others for an ethical one, or are both readings equally expected?

Conrad constantly brings dialectically into play morality and ethics in his fiction, but it is often difficult for the reader to definitely delineate one from the other. Indeed, how can one, for example, easily discern morality from ethics in the conduct of the teacher of languages in *Under Western Eyes* and that of Marlow in "Heart of Darkness" and *Lord Jim*? Where does morality end in these works and where does ethics begin? What about such characters as Razumov, Kurtz or Jim? Are they to be assessed only in relation to morality or should they also be appraised by the yardstick of ethics? If so, where can we draw the line between morality and ethics in these protagonists' respective conducts? More broadly, does Conrad's fiction tend to any moral or ethical goal at all? Does he provide his readers with any moral instruction as do, for example, Henry Fielding, Laurence Sterne or Denis Diderot, who influenced his aesthetics, or does he instead challenge their ethical assumptions and expectations?[10] And what about Conrad's morality itself? Does he belong to any fixed moral tradition, as some critics claim, or is he rather the agent of a multifarious ethics which, by definition, defies single moral and ethical affiliations?

The following chapters respond, in their various ways, to these fundamental questions. As they bring to light the denseness of Conrad's handling of ethics in his fiction, they show how Conrad engages in a profound ethical inquiry that transcends Manichean and monolithic representations of both ethics and morality. The volume's approach is inter-disciplinary and blends close textual reading with elaborate, accessible theoretical discussion, alongside comparative and intertextual approaches (Conrad and Francis Bacon, Conrad and Alfred Hitchcock, and Conrad and Adwaita Mallabarman). The authors adopt a wide range of theoretical and methodological approaches that examine the multi-faceted, elusive notion of ethics in Conrad's fiction in the light of the works of Derrida, Deleuze, Ricoeur, Levinas, and Theodor Adorno – all key and influential specialists of ethics who have widely inspired the ethical turn in literary criticism and in the humanities at large. The multiple theoretical angles from which the chapters explore the ethical issues at stake combine questions of political, social, psychological, and ideological importance with aesthetic, narrative, and epistemological considerations. They submit Conrad's ethical inquiry to our contemporary understanding and assessment of the ethical questions he raises in his works, highlighting the concordances and ruptures between his own perspective on ethics and the views of Levinas, Foucault, Derrida, and Ricoeur.

The chapters are organized thematically and form an integral reflection on Conrad's overall ethical and moral outlook; they are closely interrelated and productively resonate with one another, held together by the fundamental concern of elucidating Conrad's complex, unsettling ethical universe. The thematic affinities of these chapters (ethical commitment and detachment, ethics of responsibility and alterity, ethics of storytelling and readership, etc.) and their common theoretical, social, and philosophical methodologies (theories of Levinas, Derrida, Adorno, Bernard Williams, Peter Kropotkin, Mikhail Bakunin, etc.) give this volume unity and coherence. The core structuring principle between the different chapters is their fundamental attention to the aptness and consistency with which Conrad in his works not only subjects all the spheres of existence to constant ethical scrutiny (social relations, identity politics, capitalism, imperialism, politics, ideology, ecology, etc.), but also that ethics runs through all the levels of his writing (narration or storytelling, characterization, theme, reader-response, etc.), and is profoundly planetary in scope.

The different chapters complement one another in ways that highlight not only the intersections of ethics and morality in Conrad's fiction, but also the interplay of ethics and aesthetics, ethics and narrative, and ethics and ideology. Through detailed studies of works such as "Heart of Darkness," *The Secret Agent*, *Lord Jim* and *Under Western Eyes*, the chapters probe the conflicting relationships between the individual and nature, moral individualism and humanist ideals, discourses of progress and practices of dehumanization, moral virtue and ethical disillusionment, etc. They also meticulously analyze Conrad's ethical commitment to or disengagement from these divergent discourses and reveal how his vision articulates with relation to politics, empire, globalization, ecology, and justice – prominent concerns in his fiction.

Amar Acheraïou focuses on ethics and narrative in various works, including *Lord Jim, Under Western Eyes, Nostromo*, "Heart of Darkness," *Victory*, "Amy Foster," "Karain: A Memory," and "The Secret Sharer." He provides a detailed discussion of Conrad's narrative and ethical anxieties in these works which he assesses in the light of Conrad's transnational, planetary aesthetic sensibility and ethics of representation and readership.

As he explores the ethical, aesthetic, epistemological, and ideological forces that fuel Conrad's narrative ethics in these texts, he probes the ways in which the narrative methods used uphold or question established moral doctrines or ethical frameworks. Relatedly, he highlights the enmeshment of ethics with ideology, politics, and aesthetics, as well as with identity, meaning, and reading. Acheraïou fundamentally argues that Conrad is constantly preoccupied with ethical and narrative credibility in his writing. He locates this prominent ethical anxiety in both Conrad's ethics of justification and in his narrators' attitude toward their own fictional material, as well as in their relation to their audience/readers. Acheraïou further states that through the moral dilemmas of his protagonists and narrators Conrad shows at once the necessity of ethics in human relationships and the impossibility of individual ethical fulfillment.

Aileen Miyuki Farrar pursues the discussion of narrative and ethical credibility with a focus on "Heart of Darkness." She examines Conrad's ethics of representation and storytelling in this novella and shows how Conrad uses the concept of autophagy to convey both the empire's self-devouring egoism and the self-consuming ego of Marlow's ethics of representation itself. She argues that writing and speech are problematic vehicles of ethics in this narrative, since both potentially warp knowledge and truth, while reinforcing "pernicious" ideological and moral structures. Farrar also states that the ethics of Conrad's narration in "Heart of Darkness" fundamentally lies in its circular narrative structure, which, she remarks, is suggested in the figure of the ouroboros. Farrar sees this snake as both a cannibalistically totalizing symbol and a means of generating open discourse. According to her, this symbol reflects imperial devouring egoism, embodied by Kurtz, as well as by Marlow's own consuming egotism as a narrator. Farrar further notes that Conrad invites his readers "to eat of his tale" and this eating blurs the frontiers between "beginnings and ends, heads and tails, and self and Other," while it keeps text, discourse, and (self)representation permanently open.

Joshua Bernstein deals with "moral luck" in *Under Western Eyes* and argues that Conrad does not offer a philosophical solution to the issue of moral luck, as do some contemporary philosophers, but mostly reveals the absurdity that humans face in having to be morally accountable for actions that are often outside their own making. He illustrates this human ethical dilemma through Razumov and states that the fundamental issue for Conrad in this novel is to what extent individuals should be held morally responsible for actions outside their control. As he examines Razumov's difficulty in finding moral fulfillment in a world that lacks ethical grounding, Bernstein points out the ideological and ethical implications of the narrator's repeated attempts to distance himself from his fictional material – the protagonist's diary. He demonstrates that the narrator's over-dramatization of his lack of imagination and powers of expression, alongside his overall insistence on his detachment from the story, are symptoms of ethical disengagement. They reflect this narrator's anxious desire to shy away from ethical responsibility toward his dubious narrative, by precisely presenting this narrative as not a product of his own creative powers and, thus, beyond his control and ethical responsibility.

Thomas Higgins explores the question of anarchism and ethical commitment in *The Secret Agent* and argues that this novel is a valuable text for understanding not just the ethical implications of commitment, but also the actual artistic, ideological, and political consequences resulting from lack of commitment. He also discusses the problematic issue of the writer's responsibility towards society in the light of Adorno's notion of artistic commitment, highlighting Conrad's ambivalence towards artistic engagement and responsibility. According to Higgins, Conrad is more interested in depicting the violence of anarchism, to divest anarchism of all ethical worth, than in probing and representing objectively anarchism's multi-faceted identity and fundamental ideals. He sees this unbalanced representation as a serious ethical breach to the artistic, ideological, and political neutrality that Conrad claims in his fiction, essays, and Author's Notes. Higgins also explains that Conrad in this novel exposes the emptiness of his own ethical commitment and maintains that, although Conrad insists that his novel "has no social or philosophical intention," he is far from being ideologically or politically neutral, as he proclaims. Since, by radically condemning anarchism, he issues a clear-cut political and moral verdict on anarchism and the anarchists.

Catherine Delesalle-Nancey sheds further light on the issue of ethics in *The Secret Agent*. Drawing on Derrida and Ricoeur's theories on ethics, she provides a close examination of the notions of suffering, compassion, solicitude, and responsibility. She argues that in this novel ethics appears as the true secret agent, floating freely, unhinged to any fixed allegiance, and secretly working to destabilize established systems of values and moral certainties the reader may wish to cling to. Delesalle-Nancey shows how Conrad depicts the universe in which the characters evolve as a moral wasteland. He represents the anarchists as creatures without any moral sense or ethical ideals and also dismisses the representatives of the establishment – the police, the butcher, etc. – as almost morally dubious. Delesalle-Nanccy further explores this moral nihilism and states that the absence of a fixed moral frame of reference in this novel puts readers in a precarious position and compels them into an uneasy ethical response. It calls for their solicitude and reminds them of their own human limitations and the volatility of existence, while they struggle with a world devoid of ethical foundations and with a text that keeps undermining itself.

Laëtitia Crémona pursues the discussion of ethics in *The Secret Agent* and focuses on the interrelation of aesthetics, politics, and ethics in Alfred Hitchcock's film, *Sabotage*, which she examines in the light of Conrad's ethical reflection in *The Secret Agent* from which this film is adapted. She shows how Hitchcock revisits most of Conrad's ethical concerns but adapts them to the socio-political context of his time and gives them a dramatic, global ideological and political resonance.

Crémona reveals how in *Sabotage* Hitchcock distances himself from Conrad's ethical skepticism and points out Hitchcock's moral didacticism. She argues that Hitchcock alters or adjusts his characters' moral identity and rearranges some of the elements of the plot for his own political and ethical purposes, removing or simply eluding details he considers morally suspect or detrimental to the moral sentiment he wants to convey to his audience. Crémona further demonstrates that Hitchcock uses the camera as a moral agent to direct his audience's gaze and steers them to moral reflection and ethical choices. Ultimately, she reveals how Hitchcock in *Sabotage* deceives his audience's moral expectations, by breaking the moral contract that links the filmmaker to his audience.

Nathalie Martinière explores the "ethics of uneasiness" and reads Conrad's "Heart of Darkness" through the admiring eyes of the British painter Francis Bacon. As she teases out the affinities between Bacon's paintings and Conrad's novella, she shows how these two artists' works stir sentiments of uneasiness in the audience and question their aesthetic pleasure, while they also reveal Conrad's and Bacon's problematic relation to realism. Martinière argues that Bacon and Conrad are skeptical about realistic modes of representation and both tend to "derealize" unpleasant realities to shock their audiences and induce them to face the causes of these realities' disturbing effects. While she reveals the significance of derealization as a prompt to ethical uneasiness in the works of Conrad and Bacon, she also draws attention to the crisis of language or representation in these works. She points out that language in "Heart of Darkness" is a source of uneasiness, at once incapable of adequately rendering the reality it depicts and apt to disguise distasteful or unsettling realities. This ambivalence, Martinière states, destabilizes the readers' ethical expectations and challenges their established moral norms, compelling them to make their own ethical choices in a morally bankrupt world.

Subhadeep Ray examines nature, community, and individual ethics in Conrad's "Because of the Dollars" and Adwaita Mallabarman's "A River Called Titas." Drawing on

Derrida's notion of friendship, Levinas's theory of ethical fellowship and responsibility, and Amartya Sen's views on ethics and economics, among others, he compares Conrad's and Mallabarman's treatment of the conflicting and tragic relationship between the individual, nature, and community in these two fictions. He focuses on the ethical relations these three entities engage in and shows how both authors provide a re-reassessment of the anxieties surrounding the sense of goodness underlying friendship, love, and human communion. He adopts an inter-discursive analysis of the complex theme of justice and the individual's moral struggle against changing circumstances. Ray reveals how Conrad's and Mallabarman's narratives create multiple possibilities for the self to relate ethically to the Other. He further probes the question of human fellowship, highlighting the ethics of responsibility and justice that underlies the characters' conduct towards one another. Ray concludes that Conrad's and Mallabarman's constant search for alternative meanings to both life and human conduct tends to question dominant ethical frames of representation and greedy materialist drives.

Harold Ray Stevens shifts the discussion from the secular domain of ethics to the realm of religious morality. He focuses on the symbolism of the cross in "An Outpost of Progress" and Conrad's overall attitude to religion in both his fiction and life at large. He shows how in this short story the cross is both a pervasive ethical image and is treated with caustic irony by Conrad. Stevens fundamentally argues that in "An Outpost of Progress," but also in "Heart of Darkness" Conrad refers to the denial of the Christian ethics. Meantime, he draws attention to the fact that, while Conrad dramatizes this colonial abjuration of Christian values, he also reveals his own denial of certain Christian dogmas, particularly the miracles of Christ's birth, and criticizes Christianity's "impossible standards [that have] brought an infinity of anguish to innumerable souls." Stevens further draws an analogy between Conrad's prominent use of the cross in "An Outpost of Progress" and the pervasive European relinquishment of the Christian ethic in "Heart of

Darkness." He illustrates this key ethical issue through the contrast of the final moments of the lives of Carlier, Kayerts, and Kurtz, which reveals Conrad's conflicted, ambiguous relation to religion.

NOTES

[1] For a detailed discussion of Conrad's morality, see Panichas.

[2] Roberts's essay "Conrad and the Territory of Ethics" is one of the few studies on Conrad's ethics to refer to this dialectics of ethics and morality, succinctly and usefully pointing out the specificities and interrelations of these two categories in his discusssion of *Under Western Eyes* and *Lord Jim*. There are also other interesting studies that deal with particular aspects of ethics in Conrad's fiction, athough they do not specifically address the dialectical relation between morality and ethics. See, for example, Hunter's *Joseph Conrad and the Ethics of Darwinism*, Wollaeger's *Joseph Conrad and the Fictions of Skepticism*, Hollander's "Thinking Otherwise: Ethics and Politics in Joseph Conrad's *Under Western Eyes*," Madden's "The Ethical Dimensions of 'Heart of Darkness' and *Lord Jim*: Conrad's Debt to Schopenhauer."

[3] For more insights into this classical notion of happiness, see Plato's *Republic*. For a comprehensive reading of Plato's ethics, see Irwin. See also Aristotle's *The Nichomachean Ethics*.

[4] For an extensive account on ethical responsibility, see Levinas.

[5] See Derrida.

[6] For more information on the relation of morality and ethics, see also Foucault's *Ethics: Subjectivity and Truth*; see also Habermas.

[7] Deleuze 100.

[8] See Ricoeur.

[9] Harpham 397.

[10] For more details on these specific literary influences, see Acheraïou; for more information on Conrad's literary connections with other writers, see Krajka.

WORKS CITED

Acheraïou, Amar. *Joseph Conrad and the Reader: Questioning Modern Theories of Narrative and Readership*. Basingstoke: Palgrave Macmillan, 2009. Print.

Aristotle. *The Nichomachean Ethics*. Trans. Carlo Natali. Oxford: Oxford UP, 2009. Print.

Deleuze, Gilles. *Negotiations*. Trans. Martin Joughin. New York: Columbia UP, 1995. Print.

Derrida, Jacques. *L'Ecriture et la différence*. Paris: Seuil, 1967. Print.

Ellison, David. *Ethics and Aesthetics in the European Modernist Novel: From the Sublime to the Uncanny*. Cambridge: Cambridge UP, 2001. Print.

Foucault, Michel. *Ethics: Subjectivity and Truth. The Essential Works of Michael Foucault, 1954-1984*. Vol. 1. Trans. Robert Hurley. Ed. Paul Rabinow and Robert Hurley. London: Penguin, 2000. Print.

---. *The Use of Pleasure*. Trans. Robert Hurley. London: Penguin, 1992. Print.

Habermas, Jürgen. *Justification and Application: Remarks on Discourse Ethics*. Trans. Ciaran P. Cronin. Cambridge: Polity, 2005. Print.

Harpham, Geoffrey Galt. *Getting It Right: Language, Literature and Ethics*. Chicago: U of Chicago P, 1992. Print.

Hollander, Rachel. "Thinking Otherwise: Ethics and Politics in Joseph Conrad's *Under Western Eyes*." *Journal of Modern Literature* 38.3 (2015): 1-19. Print.

Hunter, Allan. *Joseph Conrad and the Ethics of Darwinism: The Challenges of Science*. London: Croom Helm, 1983. Print.

Irwin, Terence. *Plato's Ethics*. Oxford: Oxford UP, 1995. Print.

Krajka, Wiesław, ed. *Some Intertextual Chords of Joseph Conrad's Literary Art*. Lublin: Maria Curie-Skłodowska UP; New York: Columbia UP, 2019. Print. Vol. 28 of *Conrad: Eastern and Western Perspectives*. Ed. Wiesław Krajka. 30 vols. to date. 1992- .

Levinas, Emmanuel. *Otherwise than Being or Beyond Essence*. Trans. Alphonso Lingis. Boston: Kluwer, 1981. Print.

---. *Totality and Infinity: An Essay on Exteriority*. Trans. Alphonso Lingis. The Hague: Martinus Nijhoff, 1969. Print.

Madden, Fred. "The Ethical Dimensions of 'Heart of Darkness' and *Lord Jim*: Conrad's Debt to Schopenhauer." *Conradiana* 31 (1999): 42-62. Print.

Oser, Lee. *The Ethics of Modernism: Moral Ideas in Yeats, Eliot, Joyce, Woolf and Beckett*. Cambridge: Cambridge UP, 2007. Print.

Panichas, George A. *Joseph Conrad: His Moral Vision*. Macon: Mercer UP, 2005. Print.

Plato. *The Republic*. Trans. Robin Waterfield. Oxford: Oxford UP, 1998. Print.

Ricoeur, Paul. *Soi-même comme un autre*. Paris: Seuil, 1990. Print.

Roberts, Andrew Michael. "Conrad and the Territory of Ethics." *Conradiana* 37 (2005): 133-46. Print.

Williams, Bernard. *Ethics and the Limits of Philosophy*. London: Fontana, 1985. Print.

Wollaeger, Mark A. *Joseph Conrad and the Fictions of Skepticism*. Stanford: Stanford UP, 1990. Print.

Amar Acheraïou,
Montréal, Canada

Ethics and Narrative:
Being, Meaning, and Reading

Conrad was well known both for his sophisticated narrative methods and prominent concern with philosophical ideas. Ethics is one of these fundamental ideas and in Conrad's fiction ethics and narrative structure are so inextricably linked that it is not easy to disentangle one from the other. The narrators in charge of this narrative are overly preoccupied with ethics, and their ethical perspectives are reflected in their intense involvement with the protagonists' moral dilemmas, as well as in their obsession with their own ethical identities and conflicts. This prevalent ethical self-consciousness makes ethics the essence of Conrad's narrative method itself. Narration entails representation – and structure, technique, and perspective; the way the narrator sees and relates to the world and people he describes. As such, the act of narration always consists of relations and intersubjective interactions that are also, to varying degrees, always ethical. They involve verbal and physical interaction, thought, feeling, and judgement which compel the narrator, characters, and audience into action and ethical choices.

The narrator may be compassionate, neutral, or indifferent to a character's moral predicament. Either way, in most of his interactions he often adopts a distinct ethical position through which he, positively or negatively, relates to the various characters. These ethical relations are multiple: they encompass the narrator's narrative and moral personality; his assessment of the relations and actions the characters engage in or fail to engage in; the protagonists' moral conflicts and the decisions they take to overcome these conflicts; the narrator's position *vis-à-vis* these protagonists' ethical dilemmas, as well as his ethical stance toward his audience and the response he intends to induce in this audience.

17

This chapter explores these diverse ethical relations which fuel Conrad's narrative ethics in works including *Lord Jim*, *Under Western Eyes*, *Nostromo*, "Heart of Darkness," *Victory*, "Amy Foster," "Karain: A Memory," and "The Secret Sharer." As it maps these texts' moral universe, it probes the ethical implications of Conrad's narrative methods and how these methods uphold or question established moral doctrines and ethical frameworks. Relatedly, this chapter highlights the enmeshment of narrative ethics with ideology and politics, ethics and aesthetics, as well as ethics and being, meaning, and reading.

Ethics of Being:
Identity, Moral Character, Ethical Will

The ethics of being involves the question of identity and moral character, consciousness, and conduct. Being or selfhood, as understood here, means being with oneself and the others, understanding and explaining one's existence for oneself and for the others. Trying to understand the people they interact with and wishing to be understood in return are persistent ethical preoccupations for many Conrad's characters. The word "understanding" in its polysemic ramifications (empathy, indulgence, consideration, tolerance, discernment, etc.) is of paramount importance in Conrad's fiction, and for a good reason. Conrad was misunderstood by many of his contemporary readers and critics who misjudged his works, dismissing him as a mere writer of sea and exotic tales, a label which offended him and to which he strongly objected, rightly so, for his works transcend both the notion of literary genre and aesthetic categorization. His hybrid cultural identity and dual allegiance to Great Britain and Poland were often misconstrued and never fully accepted by his fellow British citizens, nor was his Polishness for that matter, even by his close fellow writers.[1] Likewise, Conrad was misapprehended and harshly judged by several of his Polish compatriots who did not deem him patriotic enough because he chose to write in a foreign idiom,[2] did not directly represent Poland in his fiction, or plead sufficiently his country's cause.[3]

Viewed within this ideologically and politically fraught context, Conrad's characters' yearning for understanding may be seen as the expression of his own desire to be understood by his readers, by his British fellow citizens, by his Polish compatriots. This is, alas, a vain pursuit, for Conrad remained widely misconstrued throughout his life because of the nature of his fiction, his idiosyncratic ideological and ethical outlook, as well as his unwillingness to yield to narrow notions of national identity or culture. And there were sound reasons for this. Conrad was an exile who shunned nationalist, exclusive definitions of the self and belonging, just as his works and literary legacy resist both narrow literary labelling and chauvinistic appropriations. In the bulk of his fiction, indeed, he steadily demonstrates that he is a profoundly transnational writer with a manifest planetary consciousness, which is widely reflected in the global nature of his themes (trans-culturalism, imperialism, international revolutions and wars, etc.), in the impressive multi-ethnic cast of his characters, in his diverse settings that literally encompass the entire planet, as well as in his global ethical perspective on life and geopolitics. His works are mirrors of the vast, variegated existence and pull the readers in the direction of "planetarity." Justifiably so, since the ethical questions these texts raise are of a remarkably universal scope: they not only concern all cultures and places, but are also questions for all times because they hinge on the essence of existence. Conrad's planetary ethics is most eloquently conveyed in his compassion towards his fellow beings, regardless of colour, culture, or geographical location. He stated in the Author's Note to *Almayer's Folly*: "I am content to sympathize with common mortals, no matter where they live; in houses or in tents, in the streets under a fog, or in the forests behind the dark line of dismal mangroves that fringe the vast solitude of the sea" (*AF* viii).

In this statement, Conrad shows sympathy for the precarious human existence in its universal dimension. In his Preface to *The Nigger of the "Narcissus,"* he goes further in his empathetic identification with humankind to express a fundamental sense of solidarity with his common mortals on the grounds of this frail existential condition which ties his destiny to the destiny of the entire human race. He refers to

> the subtle but invincible conviction of solidarity that knits together the loneliness of innumerable hearts, to the solidarity in dreams, in joy, in sorrow, in aspirations, in illusions, in hope, in fear, which binds men to each other, which binds together all humanity – the dead to the living and the living to the unborn. (*NN* viii)

As made clear in this declaration, Conrad's planetary ethics pivots around the essence of life: dreams, joy, sorrow, solitude, illusions, etc., and the necessity of solidarity in the face of the loneliness, despair, and disillusions resulting from our precarious existence. He strongly calls for compassion, understanding, brotherhood, and lucidity about our common human destiny, while nurturing through this ethical view of humanity a fraternal sense of belonging fuelled by universal empathy and genuine solidarity.[4]

Such ethical outlook on life is remarkable and one wonders where this may come from. It is, of course, difficult to locate with absolute certainty a definite source of Conrad's global consciousness, although the Ukraine in which he grew up, a multiethnic society characterised by a tradition of multilingual authors writing in several languages, his cultural and religious background, his cultural hybridity, his navigation of the seas and oceans of the globe, and encounters with various ethnic communities worldwide must have all contributed to shaping this worldly, inclusive mindset. And it is no understatement to say that this planetary consciousness makes Conrad unique within the British literary tradition. However, while it undeniably imbues his fiction with aesthetic, philosophical, and ethical profundity which is unmatched by his British contemporary fellow writers, this universalist ethics is also one of the fundamental sources of the chronic misunderstanding that he endured throughout his career and which is widely echoed in his fiction. Several of his characters and narrators suffer from the incomprehension of the people whom they interact with, which often alienates them from their surroundings, and Yanko Gooral in "Amy Foster," who exemplifies Conrad's "indelible" foreignness, is certainly the protagonist who best illustrates this chronic misunderstanding."[5] I have dealt extensively with this character in other studies.[6] At present, I focus on Razumov in *Under Western Eyes*, Leggatt in "The Secret Sharer," and Jim in *Lord Jim*, to probe further this question of misunderstanding and the underlying search for ethical dialogue that stirs both Conrad and his protagonists and narrators.

Razumov is an orphaned young man, living in social and moral isolation, "as lonely in the world as a man swimming in the deep sea" (*UWE* 10), with no sister, brother, friends, or relations. After Victor Haldin's incursion into his rooms his "moral solitude" amplifies and so does his desire to break away from this solitude. Following this disruptive experience, Razumov explicitly craves understanding and sympathy from the people around him. He anxiously says to himself, "I want to be understood" (39), in a pressing need to strike a chord of empathy in an attentive listener and overcome his burdensome moral predicament. The teacher of languages further insists on the protagonist's desire for communion with another soul to enhance his urgent ethical necessity or desperate longing for "a word of advice, for moral support" (39). Meanwhile, he points out the obstacles in the way of the protagonist's overwhelming ethical imperative, stressing, with a perceptible streak of empathy, Razumov's extreme physical and moral solitude: "Other men had somewhere a corner of the earth – some little house in the provinces where they had a right to take their troubles. A material refuge. He had nothing. He had not even a moral refuge – the refuge of confidence" (32).

Within this starched moral landscape, in which the protagonist is trapped, Councillor Mikulin, the narrator ironically tells us, is Razumov's sole potential moral agent likely to provide the required moral support – "the only man in the world able to understand his conduct" – and supply appropriate moral recommendations (297). It is worth noting here how the moral solution the narrator proposes is locked in a huge paradox which directly leads to an ethical impasse. He at once insists on Razumov's desperate need for salvation and indicates that this salvation rests on the will of one single man, and an autocrat at that, who can certainly not be considered the best ethical agent or most suitable "moral refuge" in the world. Razumov thus remains stuck within an ontological and metaphysical deadlock, still anxiously yearning for understanding which, in his alienated condition, entails both a moral need and an ethical demand. The moral need consists of striving to find empathy in the Other – a precarious pursuit as we shall shortly see; the ethical demand, on the other hand, suggests the Other's disposition to share and feel solidarity for the burden of the person who seeks understanding – a still more elusive aspiration for the protagonist.

The ethical dilemma in which Razumov is caught is a frequent pattern in Conrad's fiction. In "The Secret Sharer," for example, this predicament is reflected in Leggatt, who is similarly in the grip of a moral strife and anxiously longs for understanding after his misadventure on the *Sephora*. Leggatt is a chief mate. He kills a man who refuses to obey orders during a fierce storm that threatens the ship and the crew's life. He is imprisoned and awaits trial but swims his way into a ship, commanded by a young captain, who hides the fugitive. Plagued by guilt, Leggatt sinks into moral solitude and is submerged with an overcoming need to communicate and be understood. To relieve his conscience, he confides in the captain and expects from this secret sharer moral recommendations and, hopefully, moral approval. He tells the captain: "'As long as I know that you understand,' he whispered. 'But of course you do. It's a great satisfaction to have got somebody to understand. You seem to have been there on purpose.' [...] 'It's very wonderful.'" ("The Secret Sharer," *TLS* 132). This statement is clearly not an elaborate ethical dialogue but a monologue of self-absolution, in which Leggatt emphatically and unilaterally insists on being understood by this captain, or moral agent, to whom he pleads his cause. Firm in his moral judgment, Leggatt further justifies himself and asserts his confidence in the moral validity of his action, which he conveys with remarkable ethical boldness, not to say presumptuous self-righteousness:

> You don't suppose I am afraid of what can be done to me? Prison or gallows or whatever they may please. But you don't see me coming back to explain such things to an old fellow in a wig and twelve respectable tradesmen, do you? What can they know whether I am guilty or not – or of *what* I am guilty, either? That's my affair. (131-32)

Leggatt expresses his resolve to face the consequences of his act and, while giving vent to this audacious ethical affirmation, he also mocks the legal system and voices his doubts about the capacity of the court of justice to understand or judge adequately his conduct. As he disqualifies the court's competence and moral worthiness, he puts forth his own ethics of justice as a substitute for this institution whose moral credentials he conspicuously questions. He unequivocally considers himself a better judge of his action, because more acquainted with the overwhelming ethical demands that led him to his burdensome decision.

Though the nature of his crime is different from that of Leggatt, Jim, in *Lord Jim,* is spurred by a similar ethical imperative to be understood after deserting the *Patna*. His effort to make sense of his act and to explain himself to others, specifically to Marlow, shows his profound desire to engage in an ethical dialogue with the Other, from whom he expects indulgence and moral relief: "I don't want to excuse myself; but I would like to explain – I would like somebody to understand – somebody – one person at least! You! Why not you?" (*LJ* 81). In this statement Conrad contrasts the ethics of explanation with the ethics of justification, giving primacy to the former. As he explicitly states here, Jim does not seek excuses for his conduct, since he seems to be moved by a profound ontological and epistemic quest, rather than by merely a moral absolution of his crime. He mostly wants to explain and make his act intelligible to his fellow beings – to Marlow and to the community of seamen, and, ultimately, to the reader from whom he expects understanding and, eventually, empathy. Jim's explanation strikes a humane chord in Marlow but leaves indifferent Brierly who unfeelingly tells Marlow to let Jim "creep twenty feet underground and stay there" (202).

Conrad in *Lord Jim* focuses on Jim's moral dilemma and dramatizes the tension between morality and ethics, obedience to moral prescriptions and pursuit of individual ethical goals. Through Brierly's moral disposition, on the other hand, he provides us with an eloquent example of an individual's mode of subjection to a rigorous moral code which this individual unconditionally recognizes and from which he gets moral validation for his statements and acts. Brierly's notion of a seaman's identity is, in this regard, widely informed by this ascetic moral system, which is founded on a fixed, inalterable sense of duty and honour, and this may largely account for his coldness and contempt for Jim. Being conditioned by a morally idealistic view of what identity is or is not, he tends to think mainly in terms of what man is supposed to be, completely ignoring the impact of circumstances on peoples' identities or moral personalities and behaviour. In short, Brierly expects individuals to unreservedly abide by the established moral norms of being, in all contexts. For him, being as one should be is, therefore, a moral obligation, an imperative to comply with the dominant moral code of subjection which alone requires or proscribes a specific kind of conduct. His entire sense of moral worth comes essentially from his subjection to this uncompromising moral system and to which he feels bound to conform. That is why he severely blames Jim for failing to honour these social moral standards and for shamefully shrinking from his professional responsibility. What he deplores most is the protagonist's incapacity to live up to the seaman's ideal of moral conduct and selfhood and which makes him morally worthless in Brierly's eyes. He replies to Marlow, "[t]he worst of it [...] is that all you fellows have no sense of dignity; you don't think enough of what you are supposed to be" (67).

A regular theme in Conrad's works, dignity is a key concept of ethics and is commonly used to refer to a person's moral identity and ethical worth. For Immanuel Kant, dignity confers on humans a fundamental moral value that exclusively derives from their sheer humanity. It is an essential universal value equally shared by all human beings regardless of their social rank, culture, or ethnic background. From Kant's perspective, therefore, to have dignity means to possess intrinsically moral worth, beyond one's birth privileges, skills, or social usefulness.[7] Brierly in the previous statement explicitly denies Marlow and Jim this shared universal moral value, which is dignity, because of their indisposition to comply with his own notion of human worth or what a person's moral identity should or should not be. And from this unforgivable failure to conform to what he sees as an absolute moral virtue follows a moral sanction, as recommended more or less explicitly by the established prescriptive moral system – professional dignity or the sea code of honour – to which Brierly and all the seamen are bound. In so far as Jim's conduct fails to conform to this code and disregards the values and rules it prescribes, he is, according to Brierly, liable to punishment, since his conduct affects the moral identity of the whole sea community. Moreover, because he considers Jim's moral defection irredeemable, he exhorts him to leave, and he does so both in compliance with the prescriptions of the sea code of honour – Jim's disappearance will preserve the honour of the profession – and from a personal need for psychological security threatened by Jim's presence. Like a sudden shockwave, Jim's desertion of the *Patna* has stirred up to the surface Brierly's former failures as a sailor and, for this very reason, he hates this negative Other, which Jim embodies in his eyes, and rejects all moral identification with him with the passion and angst of a soul dreading moral contamination. At the same time, however, being both members of the same sea community, held by a common bond of solidarity, Brierly cannot fully dissociate himself from Jim, nor is he inclined to find extenuating circumstances for his misconduct, an insoluble ethical conflict that increases his moral isolation and may have later widely contributed to his suicide.

Suicide is a persistent motif in Conrad's fiction (Brierly in *Lord Jim*, Decoud in *Nostromo*, Winnie Verloc in *The Secret Agent*, etc.), and, while it echoes Conrad's own suicide attempt in 1878, in his works suicide mostly reflects the protagonists' difficulty in living in a world which they find absurd and devoid of ethical grounding or purpose. Like all these self-destructions, therefore, Brierly's suicide is a symptom of profound existential anxieties, and carries high moral and ethical implications. Indeed, by this act, Brierly brutally shifts from the constrained domain of morality in which conduct is predetermined by fixed, unalterable moral codes, to the wider, fluid realm of ethics where actions proceed from both free ethical reflection and adjustment of individual conduct to each specific situation or relation. From this perspective, suicide is a deliberate, ethical choice rather than a moral commandment. It may mean selfishness or indifference, courage or damnation, but in Brierly's case it looks like a desperate undertaking with connotations of ethical cowardice. In a sense, Brierly dies of his incapacity to acknowledge the ethical relativity of the concepts of pride and honour. Above all, he dies of the illusory ideal image he projects into his profession and into those involved in this profession. Brierly perceives selfhood mostly as a dry, finite, and morally codified entity, stripped of instinct and emotion. This conception of selfhood, fuelled by austere, self-abnegating moral norms, is drastically limited, to say the least. For it understands human conduct in strictly rationalistic terms, as a perfect equivalence between action, the established moral prescriptions – the sea code of conduct, in this case – and the dictates of reason. Most of all, it leaves no room for productive ethical developments, which, as we know, are essentially based on dynamic, resilient relations of solidarity and mutual responsibility, as well as on permanent self-questioning and ethical discernment. That is why Brierly sees Jim's conduct as a sheer symptom of professional incompetence and moral cowardice which, in his view, results from deficient self-esteem and weakness of will.

Brierly's obdurate perception of being is expressly conveyed in the scene where he and Marlow discuss courage and selfhood, and duty and responsibility, among other things. During this encounter, Brierly completely dismisses Jim as morally worthless for failing to comply with the ideal of honour, the moral value par excellence of the maritime world, in Brierly's view. Closely considered, however, Brierly's notion of honour amounts to a stiff moral doctrine in which moral character and individual ethical worth are fully determined by the eye of the others which becomes within this prescriptive code of values the absolute judge and purveyor of moral worth.

Though less categorical, the French lieutenant's judgment of the protagonist's action also sheds significant light on the moral value of the concept of honour. The lieutenant is an emblem of courage and heroism. He has stayed for thirty hours on the *Patna* without shirking from his duty; a heroic feat that crowns him with moral authority that qualifies him to pronounce a verdict, not just on Jim's conduct but on man's moral worth in general. Yet, unlike Brierly, the lieutenant sees honour and fear as ethically relative concepts, so, although he is unsettled by Jim's conduct, he considers Jim's desertion of the *Patna* as merely an expression of the natural fear and cowardice which are in all of us: "Man is born a coward (*L'homme est né poltron*). It is a difficulty – *parbleu*! It would be too easy otherwise. But habit – habit – necessity – do you see? – the eye of others – *voilà*. One puts up with it" (*LJ* 147). The lieutenant further insists on the exogenous character of honour and its intrinsic value:

> I contended that one may get on knowing very well that one's courage does not come of itself (*ne vient pas tout seul*). There's nothing much in that to get upset about. One truth the more ought not to make life impossible. ... But the honour – the honour, monsieur! ... The honour... that is real – that is! And what life may be worth when... (148)

The French lieutenant considers man morally hollow and, in his view, which somehow echoes that of Brierly, any moral virtue a person may possess exclusively results from the external social gaze and custom, rather than from any profound individual, autonomous ethical agency. Interestingly, the lieutenant's perception of moral conduct, heroism, and honour as socially induced underlines both these concepts' overdetermined character and their relative moral significance. Marlow shows similar ethical relativity regarding fear, bravery, and honour, which echoes Conrad's own ethical relativism. His ethical expectations, however, are brutally blown off when he enquires about the motive behind the French lieutenant's heroic conduct. He is filled with disappointment when the lieutenant informs him that his action has been induced by the sense of honour alone: "Hang the fellow! He had pricked the bubble," protests Marlow, disillusioned (148). Marlow expects a profound ethical incentive behind the lieutenant's remarkable action, but finds instead self-referential, dry morality, with the shady, elusive concept of honour as its cornerstone. Although as a seaman Marlow, and Conrad too in this respect, regards honour highly, in this statement he clearly distances himself from the zealous versions of honour and their moral prescriptions propounded in this narrative by characters like Brierly or Chester.

Through Marlow, on the one hand, and Brierly and Chester, on the other, Conrad contrasts two conflicting codes of morality and ethics, to highlight both their interplay and the difficulty in reaching any satisfactory or definite ethical judgement or meaning on life and human conduct. Brierly and Chester are two inflexible moral agents, and both adhere, to varying degrees, to a version of selfhood or moral personality that is enclosed within a stiff, coercive system of values, based on punishment and reward, inclusion and exclusion. In contrast, Marlow appears as a dynamic ethical subject, steadily questioning these two characters' reductive understandings of honour and selfhood, alongside the type of individual moral character they entail. Like Socrates who, in Plato's Socratic Dialogues, refers to renowned specialists, including two eminent generals of the Peloponnesian War, Laches and Nicias, to discuss courage, Marlow summons two seasoned seamen – the French lieutenant and Brierly – to enlighten him on the questions of courage, cowardice, and honour. And just as Socrates leads his distinguished specialists to admit their own limitations in the subject of their expertise, so, too, Marlow consistently challenges these two seamen's moral ideas, particularly those of Brierly, to reveal their inadequacy.

During their entire discussion, Brierly obstinately holds to his exclusive, close-ended conception of courage and honour, while Marlow displays an ethical framework with an open, ever-extending space, where the individual's conduct is susceptible to change and improvement, prone to self-examination and redemption. He embraces an elastic, profounder sense of selfhood, understood both as being with oneself and with others in reciprocal relations of answerability and ethical responsibility. This ethical frame is founded on frankness, understanding, compassion, and identification with the plight of the Other – Jim in this case. That is why, unlike Brierly, whose idea of selfhood is too rigid to extend fellowship to the protagonist in the name of human weakness, Marlow unconditionally shows sympathy to Jim and considers him as "one of us," despite his misconduct (78, 93). He even commends Jim for facing the consequences of his failure – for accepting to withstand the "eye of others" (147), and "be alone with his loneliness" (171). Marlow further praises Jim for willing to confront his ethical fallibility and to bravely cast a self-questioning inward look. He states with admiration: "and indeed very few of us have the will or the capacity to look consciously under the surface of familiar emotions" (222). Like Marlow who, in "Heart of Darkness," praises Kurtz for his courage to say the unsayable, Marlow in this statement assigns Jim's achievement to his ethical fortitude or what he calls "that inborn ability to look temptations straight in the face" (*LJ* 43).

Marlow sounds like Conrad in this overall reflection on moral judgement, on surface and depth, on superficial seeing and deep self-introspection. In these various statements, Marlow draws attention to the extent to which ethics and gaze are intricately linked, and does so to underscore the value of the inward look in assessing the ethical value of a person's self and actions. The gaze is a fundamental means of assessing ethical worth in *Lord Jim* and, generally, in Conrad's fiction. In contrast to Brierly, Marlow, as we have seen, does not irredeemably condemn Jim as ethically worthless on the grounds of his moral weakness. Rather, he acknowledges the protagonist's human fallibility, while also extolling the merits of his ethical gaze or the courage to look into his undesirable inmost self.

The ethical gaze, the inward look evoked above, involves both will and consciousness, thanks to which Jim acquires, in Marlow's eyes, the status of a worthy ethical agent who accepts to face boldly his condition instead of skimming through the surface of existence "gazing with clear unconscious eyes," (342) as do most people. This remarkable willingness to look deeply inward, Marlow suggests, imbues Jim with ethical depth that distinguishes him from the literalistic, myopic multitude, including Brierly, whose strict dependence on ossified conventional notions of selfhood or moral identity ties their gaze to the surface of things and people. It is obviously Brierly and individuals with a similar mindset that Marlow has in mind when he declares: "It's extraordinary how we go through life with eyes half shut, with dull ears, with dormant thoughts. Perhaps it's just as well; and it may be that it is this very dullness that makes life to the incalculable majority so supportable and so welcome" (143). Indifference to alterity, as reflected in Brierley's attitude toward Jim, strict observance of rigid moral norms, and moral individualism, Marlow implies, may both lead to ethical myopia, which causes the individual to go through life with "eyes half shut, with dull ears, with dormant thoughts" (143). Three sensory faculties are mentioned here: seeing, hearing, and thinking – and all three are fundamental means of communication and ethical perception. Yet, all three faculties are, in the case of Brierly, equally stunted by the inflexible moral doctrine by which he abides. This doctrine prevents him from precisely seeing the ethical value of Jim's acknowledgement of his failure, as does Marlow with Jim in this novel, or, as we shall shortly see, Marlow with Kurtz in "Heart of Darkness" or the teacher of languages with Razumov in *Under Western Eyes*.

Solidarity, Trust, Ethical (Mis)understanding

Like *Lord Jim, Under Western Eyes* pervades with moral and ethical considerations. It relates with sustained pathos the dialectical interplay of morality and ethics and brings to light the tension between individual ethics and state morality. Early in the narrative the narrator firmly states that his main ambition is to convey Russia's "moral conditions" (*UWE* 67) and describes this country as a ruthless, despotic political system, founded on a morality of compulsion and coercion. Russia is a place of

> moral corruption [...] where the noblest aspirations of humanity, the desire of freedom, an ardent patriotism, the love of justice, the sense of pity, and even the fidelity of simple minds are prostituted to the lusts of hate and fear, the inseparable companions of an uneasy despotism. (7)

Despite Russia's profound moral corruption, the politicians who serve this autocracy present their system as a progressive moral force, inherently good, if not goodness itself. They take their native land's benevolence for granted and expect their fellow countrymen to unquestionably embrace its ideological and moral precepts as universal truths.

This is roughly the moral and emotional landscape in which Razumov evolves and this landscape is of a clearly totalitarian nature: it expects a flawless compliance of the individual's thoughts and actions with the moral disposition of the state. This stringent moral demand makes the very idea of individual ethical will irrelevant and, in any case, a daring undertaking with foreboding consequences. Razumov is an invisible and insignificant component of this Russian autocratic moral vacuum. His moral character and conduct being moulded by this totalitarian moral force, any social achievement to which he may aspire is premised on complete obedience to the autocratic ideological and moral norms. Besides, Razumov's moral identity is not just overdetermined, it is also precarious and, so, too, is the steady life he apparently enjoys. Both this frail moral identity and existence are brusquely thwarted forever by the intrusion of the revolutionary Haldin into his life. Haldin kills Mr. de P— and seeks refuge in Razumov's lodging.

This scene is of the utmost importance not only for its dramatic intensity, but also for being the ethical matrix that fuels most of the other ethical concerns in the novel. Razumov's first accepts to go and see Ziemianitch to help Haldin as the latter advised. He journeys through a frigid, snowy landscape to find this man and the narrator provides an eloquent description of Razumov's contact with this landscape.

> It was a sort of sacred inertia. Razumov felt a respect for it. A voice seemed to cry within him; "Don't touch it!" It was a guarantee of duration, of safety, while the travail of the maturing destiny went on – a work not of revolutions with their passionate levity of action and their shifting impulses – but of peace. What is needed was not the conflicting aspirations of a people, but [...] a man – strong and one! (33)

Razumov feels a mystic respect for this blanket of snow, which embodies, in his eyes, autocratic Russia with its moral guarantee of "safety and duration." His ethical dilemma stirred by Haldin's visit is still intense, but at the end of this statement it seems settled, and we see his ethical choice finally cast on autocracy or – "a man – strong and one" – rather than on revolution – "the conflicting aspirations of a people." Razumov's endorsement of autocracy is further reinforced in the narrator's following declaration: "But absolute power should be preserved – the tool ready for the man – for the great autocrat of the future. Razumov believed in him. The logic of history made him unavoidable" (35).

Here, Razumov provides a moral justification for the *raison-d'être* of the autocratic system, which later paves the way for his betrayal of Haldin to Prince K— and Councillor Mikulin, who arrest this revolutionary and enlist Razumov in the service of autocracy as a secret agent. These autocrats (mis)interpret Razumov's act as a sign of fidelity to the autocratic regime, or, more exactly, as a perfect correspondence of this protagonist's "moral personality" with the moral doctrine of the autocracy.

The narrator hates autocracy, although he does not particularly appear overly shocked by Razumov giving in his fellow student to this appalling regime. Rather, he readily sympathizes with his moral predicament and justifies the ethical validity of this protagonist's betrayal on the grounds of universal human weakness.[8]

We see how Conrad plays again on the chord of ethical relativity in this scene to resist absolute moral prescriptions. The teacher of languages embodies in this specific case a relativist ethicist who deems Razumov's action ethically viable on the grounds that, in his view, this act proceeds not from a ruthless motivation but from a basic natural human response to fear and to external forces threatening our survival. His argument is, of course, philosophically sustainable if interpreted only through the perspective of the human condition and ethics of self-preservation. It is less persuasive, however, when gauged in the light of the ethical significance of the concept of betrayal itself. Betrayal connotes boundless egoism, violence, and indifference to the fate of others, which makes it therefore difficult to justify on ethical grounds. The betrayer completely disregards his fellow beings by placing his own interest and self-preservation before and above everyone else's; and this fundamentally questions the very essence of ethical relationships, based on reciprocity and solidarity between the self and others. Betrayal may also put into deadly risk the life of another person, as does the protagonist here, which is ethically even more objectionable.

We should not forget that Razumov is under no direct or immediate life-threatening menace to give up his fellow countryman and cause his death. Haldin has reassured him that he met no one on the stairs and nobody saw him enter his rooms. Daphna Erdinast-Vulcan rightly pointed out that Razumov is "trapped in a situation he has neither initiated nor planned," and argued on this premise that the protagonist could not be easily held responsible for his action because he is not free: "if we are not free, how can we be made accountable for our actions?"[9] As Erdinast-Vulcan remarks here, ethical responsibility is circumstantial, and it is, certainly, much easier

for individuals living in a free country to account for their
actions since their conduct is induced not by coercion but by
free will and choice. It is, nonetheless, dangerous to attempt to
justify irresponsible conduct by assuming that because we live
in an oppressive society we should feel less accountable for our
actions or lay full responsibility for our actions on the coercive
structures of power of this society. In that case, why should we
condemn, for example, the actions of those who collaborated
with fascist and Nazi regimes and caused the death of millions
of people? After all, these men and women lived in extremely
oppressive regimes; many of them committed their horrors
out of ideological and political convictions, which they thought
morally justified, others out of fear or cowardice, and some
others from sheer interest and indifference to the plight of their
victims. Whatever their motives and the circumstances, in the
end all these people acted knowingly and, most of the time,
with no remorse for the horrors in which they participated.

Like these collaborators, Razumov certainly lives in a society
where freedom of choice is severely curtailed; nevertheless, he
still possesses freedom of conscience of which he is the sole
master. Thus, no matter how oppressed, helpless, or terrified he
may feel in the face of the mighty shadow of autocracy gliding
menacingly over his precarious existence, Razumov remains
widely accountable for his action because he acted consciously,
out of free will and after sustained ethical deliberation in which
he rationally justified both the moral rightness of his own action
and the moral validity of the autocratic system itself. And this
action is doubly destructive, since in deliberately choosing to
give up Haldin to the police Razumov does not just destroy this
undesired revolutionary Other, who threatens his interests, but
also destroys himself. Because of this selfish act, he definitively
loses control over both his existence and moral personality,
along with the semblance of truth this former existence had in
his own eyes:

> The true Razumov had his being in the willed, in the determined
> future – in that future menaced by the lawlessness of autocracy – for

autocracy knows no law – and the lawlessness of revolution. The feeling that his moral personality was at the mercy of these lawless forces was so strong that he asked himself seriously if it were worth while to go on accomplishing the mental functions of that existence which seemed no longer his own. (*UWE* 77-8)

Authenticity and truth are key ethical concepts in Conrad's fiction, particularly in works like *Under Western Eyes* and "Heart of Darkness." Of course, Conrad is suspicious about the ethical validity of both concepts and often represents in his writing the failure of his protagonists' or narrators' search for truth and authenticity. In both "Heart of Darkness" and *Under Western Eyes* Conrad also consistently represents the manipulation of authenticity and truth by some of his characters and narrators, such as Marlow in "Heart of Darkness" or the teacher of languages and the autocrats in *Under Western Eyes*. In the latter work, more specifically, on which I focus here, Conrad tends to dramatize through these manipulations of truth and authenticity the gulf separating politics from ethics, a recurrent theme in his writings.

In *Under Western Eyes* Razumov is in the thick of this extensive ethical manipulation and, with Haldin's unfortunate intrusion into his existence, he may be said to have definitively lost his foothold on any veneer of truth he may have previously pinned his faith to. By his solicitation or ethical demand, Haldin robs Razumov of his "true" and promising self, or what Razumov considered as an authentic existence, fully devoted to his studies and social promotion, and condemns him to a life of lies and deception. Ironically, as in the encounter between Razumov and Mikulin, the entire dramatic situation between Haldin and Razumov also stems from a basic mutual misunderstanding. Razumov misunderstands Haldin's visit, thinking that his fellow student has merely come for a little talk. Although he considers this visit ill-timed, he offers Haldin hospitality, inviting him to share a smoke with him. Haldin, on the other hand, mistakes Razumov's plain hospitality for a sign of friendship and even brotherhood – he calls him "brother" three times (16, 19, 24). In fact, Haldin tragically misreads the whole of Razumov's moral character. He effusively tells his host: "We are not perhaps in exactly the same camp. Your judgement is more philosophical. You are a man of words, but I haven't met anybody who dared to doubt the generosity of your sentiments. There is a solidity about your character which cannot exist without courage" (15). Haldin further praises Razumov's "strong character" and expresses admiration for his "reserve" (15), which he (mis)interprets as a sign of reliability. Razumov is, of course, flattered by this encomium, but his delight quickly wears off when Haldin informs him that it is he who killed Mr. de P–; a devastating news which ruins forever Razumov's hopes of winning the silver medal.

Significantly, in this important exchange between Haldin and Razumov, Conrad seems to cast doubt on the very essence of ethical relations as articulated by contemporary philosophers, notably Emmanuel Levinas, Jaques Derrida and Paul Ricoeur. Since the ethical call of the Other, that is Haldin's request, is not only rejected by Razumov, but its very *raison d'être* also seems undermined, as this call for compassion and solidarity becomes a source of misunderstanding rather than of ethical fulfilment or harmony. The moral absurdity of the whole situation lies, in fact, in this core ethical misunderstanding: Razumov does not even understand why Haldin solicits his assistance in the first place. He hardly knows him, and when he asks for explanation, Haldin self-assuredly answers: "Confidence," a word which "sealed Razumov's lips as if a hand had been clapped on his mouth" (19).

The term *confidence*, used emphatically by Haldin to account for his ethical demand on Razumov, implies a degree of intimacy or friendship and reciprocity of feelings. Yet, in this specific encounter the ethics of confidence is emptied of its ontological substance and reduced to a one-way process. It is just Haldin who blindly confides in Razumov and expects him to show him solidarity in the name of mutual confidence, Razumov's good heart, and of their presumed common revolutionary ideals, while Razumov refuses to reciprocate to this ethical call, dismissing the solidarity and confidence into which he is compelled as being morally unfounded. In a sense, Haldin is both ignorant of and indifferent to Razumov's ethical sensibility and self-interest, although he paradoxically presents his crime as a vital common good that profits both to active revolutionaries like himself and to Razumov whom he wrongly assimilates to a revolutionary sympathizer. Firm in his conviction, he stresses the political importance of his act and naively tells Razumov that his crime is a worthy sacrifice, committed to make room for the exercise of advanced minds like Razumov who are called to "help to build" the country sometime in the future: "Men like me are necessary to make room for self-contained, thinking men like you" (19). After enhancing the political significance of his act, Haldin provides Razumov with a moral justification, presenting the murder of Mr. de P— as ethically valid or immune to blame because this man is, in his view, the incarnation of moral corruption – the destroyer of truth and progress: "You suppose that I am a terrorist, now – a destructor of what is. But consider that the true destroyers are they who destroy the spirit of progress and truth, not the avengers who merely kill the bodies of the persecutors of human dignity" (19).

Conrad in this scene shows with scathing lucidity the dramatic ethical consequences to which misunderstanding can lead. Throughout this ironic situation, he highlights the extent to which Haldin tragically fails to see that Razumov is not a man of feelings or revolutionary ideals, as this fervent revolutionary fantasizes, but an egoistic, independent mind ruled solely by the power of intellect and self-interest. Haldin does not realize that Razumov feels no human fellowship for him and scoffs his social and political ideals. Above all, he tragically overlooks that the ethical responsibility he expects from Razumov has no place in the latter's ontological framework and coldly cerebral vision of existence: "There must be a moral bond first. All a man can betray is his conscience. And how is my conscience engaged here; by what bond of common faith, of common conviction, am I obliged to let that fanatical idiot drag me down with him?" (37-38). Razumov is presented here as an emblem

of moral individualism, as this protagonist defines his self not
in terms of its ethical relation to another being, but in terms of
this self's relation to its own moral agency. Razumov's extreme
subjectivation of his ontological identity amplifies his moral
being and, like Jim or Kurtz, places him above and beyond alterity
or external ethical agencies in relation to which individual
moral identity shapes itself. Levinas states that "the ethical
relation takes place in an immediate realm where the relation
to or encounter with the other is antecedent to knowledge
and brings with it the burden of responsibility to the other."[10]
Razumov disregards this Levinasian ethical relation, in words
that sound like a more or less explicit translation of Conrad's
vision of ethical encounters. He completely rejects, in the
name of free will and freedom of choice, the solidarity into
which Haldin compels him, and offers an implacable rational
explanation of his betrayal couched in an ethical affirmation
that makes his decision, though not easily endorsable, at least
ethically understandable. This ontological mindset, which
excludes alterity from its frame of reference, has its logic that
Razumov translates in these plain terms: since, in his firm
conviction, there exists no moral bond, or prior agreement
of any sort between him and Haldin, he does not see why he
should feel any ethical responsibility for this man who ruined
his life. Razumov further questions the very ethical validity of
his betrayal by literally dismissing the notion of betrayal itself
as superfluous, arguing that self-betrayal, or the betrayal of
one's conscience, is the sole betrayal for which a man can be
accountable.

    This moral individualism, crude and intense as it were,
is perfectly attuned to Razumov's chilling rationalism and
perspective on existence and human relationships. It is
important to point out, however, that his ethical detachment
from his fellow beings is not absolute. While he powerfully
rejects systematic or unconditional forms of ethical relations,
he argues for a commitment to another type of relation based
on conscience and clear moral bonds and choices. Razumov
sounds here like Conrad's mouthpiece, through whom Conrad

tends to question both Levinas' universalist ethics of relation and Kant's moral universalism. And what Conrad's protagonist says in this novel is that one should be able to freely choose whom to ethically relate with, and this choice must be entirely grounded in reason and shared ethical values and understanding, rather than in some unconditional universalist moral condition. Thus, for him, ethical action, as an unconditional act of solidarity and responsibility of the self for the Other, is redundant, in the absence of a common moral connection which, in his perception, should precede all ethical relations. In other words, Razumov implies that ethical responsibility cannot be bestowed unconditionally, but granted (s)electively, and accorded only to those we share moral bonds with, or to relations based on volition and mutual moral consent.

Razumov's characteristic reflection in this intense ethical dialogue carries a distinctly Conradian undertone, as hinted earlier, and sounds like a diluted form of nihilist ethics which, without completely excluding all moral grounding of existence or human relations, nonetheless reduces the essence of ethical relationships to their simplest expression. It is on the grounds of this nihilist ethics that Razumov minimizes the ethical implication of his betrayal and questions the validity of the notion of betrayal itself. He even pushes his ethical egotism further to mock the idea of unconditional ethical responsibility towards the Other, by ironically claiming his responsibility for Haldin just after betraying him. "I am responsible for you," he ruthlessly tells Haldin (60).

This statement is a glaring parody of ethical responsibility itself, as articulated by Levinas, Ricoeur and Derrida. Razumov crudely eschews relations that unqualifiedly bind the self to the Other, in favour of an individualistic ethics based exclusively on reason, will, and shared moral values. Once again, Razumov's suspicion of transcendent ethical relations echoes Conrad's own skepticism not just about ethical relations, but also about the validity of ethics itself – more exactly, the futility to see the world and human relations in ethical terms. Conrad declared in *A Personal Record*: "The ethical view of the universe involves us at last in so many cruel and absurd contradictions, where the last vestiges of faith, hope, charity, and even of reason itself, seem ready to perish, that I have come to suspect that the aim of creation cannot be ethical at all" (*PR* 92). It is not clear which "cruel" and "absurd" contradictions Conrad refers to. What is yet obvious is his forthright assertion of the irrelevance of ethics on the grounds of these contradictions. Conrad, in fact, doubts the very relevance of ethics itself, on the assumption that the world is not created for an ethical purpose. In his view, this fundamental deficiency, de facto, renders the very notion of ethics worthless, superfluous. From this premise, Conrad goes on to state, in a markedly Nietzschean undertone, that to view the world in ethical terms is absurd, since the world itself is absurd and is not designed for ethical aims.[11] Furthermore, as he questions the world's ethical foundation, Conrad also doubts the ethical nature of humankind itself. He harbours what sounds like a profound existential disenchantment in which individuals are left to fend alone for their ethical survival in a world not meant for ethics in the first place. This may widely account for Conrad's protagonists' incessant ethical meanderings. In most of his novels and short stories these protagonists constantly drift and waver between an endless ethics of struggle and a precarious, desperate striving for an ethics of mutual solidarity and human fellowship, which often proves limited, if not simply illusory. Conrad is a pessimist, and yet his grim ethical outlook occasionally allows for faint glimmers of redemption, as Razumov's experience suggests.

Ethical Redemption, Moral Worth

Razumov's ethical redemption is achieved late in the narrative and it comes at a high price. It has first begun by Razumov admitting to himself that in betraying Haldin it is his conscience he betrayed: "In giving Victor Haldin up, it was myself, after all, whom I have betrayed most basely" (*UWE* 361). He seems to have finally understood the ethical implications of his act, although this ethical conscience seems to be triggered by self-interest or his awareness of having harmed his moral worth, rather than by the damage he inflicted on Haldin. After having firmly denied sharing any moral bonds with Haldin, Razumov thus, willingly or not, slips into an ethical relationship with this character, by ultimately acknowledging moral connections. He feels ethically responsible for Haldin, who now becomes his mirror image – his guilty conscience, without, nonetheless, going as far as to politically identify with Haldin. He unflinchingly states: "I am not converted [...]. No! I am independent" (361-62). Razumov reasserts his independent spirit, as he adamantly keeps at bay Haldin's revolutionary ideals, in compliance with his, and Conrad's, distance from and suspicion of revolutions.[12]

Razumov's final admission that his betrayal of Haldin is self-betrayal constitutes a significant ethical twist. At this stage, he performs a decisive action to assuage his conscience and engages in a morally approved conduct, and, in doing so, he literally acquires the status of a sovereign ethical agent. This important ethical conversion, wherein Razumov radically shifts from an obstinately rational ethics to an instinctual ethics, is especially reflected during his meeting with Haldin's sister, Natalia, an emblem of beauty, sincerity, and authenticity. Razumov is in love with Natalia Haldin and it is her exceptional beauty and outstanding moral virtues that have stirred his decision to confess his betrayal of her brother to her and to the revolutionaries. He states: "You were appointed to undo the evil by making me betray myself back into truth and peace" (358). He shortly adds with similar confessional verve: "You fascinated me – you have freed me from the blindness of anger and hate – the truth shining in you drew the truth out of me" (361). These statements underline the ethical power of love and its capacity to merge moral sensibilities and blend the interests of the self with the ethical imperatives of the Other. In contact with Natalia, Razumov experiences a brutal ethical awakening that painfully liberates him from his moral blindness and reconnects him with truth. The question is: what ethical worth to assign to Razumov's confession.

In "The Foundation of Ethics," Arthur Schopenhauer defines "actions of moral worth"[13] as acts which are undertaken only in the "absence of all egoistic motivation," since "the moral significance of an action can lie only in its reference to others."[14] Conrad read and was influenced by Schopenhauer's ideas on will and individual consciousness.[15] From Schopenhauer's perspective, Razumov's final conduct is an act of minor or insignificant ethical worth, for it is motivated by his selfish passion for Natalia Haldin, rather than by lofty altruistic pursuits. Razumov's confession does not go unpunished. Nikita bursts his eardrums and Razumov stoically endures this punishment in belated acceptance of responsibility for his act. The scene of the confession at Laspara's house is of high ethical significance. It forms a cathartic moment of ethical truth, in which Razumov finally sheds his former false self with its burdening ideological and moral deceptions. He states: "To-day, of all days since I came amongst you, I was made safe, and to-day I made myself free from falsehood, from remorse – independent of every single human being on this earth" (*UWE* 368). Razumov finally reconciles himself with truth and thus acquires ethical worth in his own eyes and in the eyes of the narrator – eventually also, in those of the reader. The narrator admiringly states:

> how many of them would deliver themselves up deliberately to perdition (as he himself says in this book) rather than go on living secretly debased in their own eyes. How many? [...]. And please mark this – he was safe when he did it. It was just when he believed himself safe and more – infinitely more – when the possibility of being loved by that admirable girl first dawned upon him, that he discovered that his bitterest railings, the worst wickedness, the devil work of his hate and pride, could never cover up the ignominy of the existence before him. There's character in such a discovery. (380)

In terms echoing Marlow's commendation of Jim's moral courage, the teacher of languages acclaims Razumov's remarkable ethical undertaking which, as we have seen, is acquired at the price of deafness. The deafness inflicted on Razumov is a kind of symbolic death, since it cuts him off from verbal communication with the others. It is also a birth into a new and more authentic form of relation with the others, free from the dissimulating powers of language or voice. Conrad seems to suggest here that ethical relations are built not just on language or verbal communication, but also on empathetic imagination and instinct, since speech, discourse, and eloquence, even in their most idealistic form, are no guarantee of authentic ethical relations. In fact, in Conrad's fiction both ideal statements and eloquence are ethically suspect. They are either vehicles of deception and manipulation, or oppression and horrors – often both. The moral personalities and conducts of Charles Gould and Holroyd in *Nostromo* and Kurtz in "Heart of Darkness" provide an eloquent illustration.

Thought, Action, Ethics: Ethical Skepticism

In *Nostromo*, Conrad relates the effects of American and European imperialism on the Sulaco population in terms that set thought, action, and ethics in a productive dialectical relation. This contrast of the ethics of thought and ethics of action is showcased through Martin Decoud and Dr. Monygham, on the one hand, and Charles Gould and Holroyd, on the other. Decoud and Monygham embody a range of important ethical concerns that echo in Conrad's writing: philosophical and ethical detachment, skepticism, cynicism, etc. They are emblems of ethical detachment, *par excellence*, observing the world with cold, skeptical eyes. Monygham had a "misanthropic mistrust of mankind" (N 432) and boasts a philosophical view of the world free of emotion and sentimentalism. He is also endowed with a "habit of sceptical, bitter speech" and emphatically claims to detach his opinions, desires, and actions from all spiritual or idealistic value (45). Decoud, similarly, scorns sentiments and asserts attaching no "sentimental basis for his action," and does not "endow [his] personal desires with a shining robe of silk and jewels," as does Gould (218).

Both Decoud and Monygham show utter contempt for humankind and place their respective thoughts and actions beyond and above ethics, thus shutting themselves out to the ethical demands of those they interact with. They take life literally, as a succession of facts and impassive statements, and reject ethical idealism and any attempt to assign an "idealistic meaning to concrete facts" (219). Decoud is even more extreme in his skepticism and takes his "habit" of scorning empathy and ethical commitment "to a point where it blinded him to the genuine impulses of his own nature" (153). Like Dr. Monygham, Decoud, too, shuns the transcendent ethical framework and ethical optimism of Levinas, as he is not only blind to the interests and call of the Others, but also blind to the demands of his own ethical self.

If in art or aesthetics skepticism may be a "tonic" of artistic creation, as Conrad declared in a letter to John Galsworthy, it goes differently in life where it may become a source of alienation and self-destruction, as suggested by Decoud's fate on the Isabel islands.[16] Decoud, who mostly relies on rational powers to guide his life and actions, dies in complete solitude, from a drastic lack of ethical inner force that may have enabled him to overcome his moral isolation. Lacking faith in both himself and his fellow beings, Decoud is "not fit to grapple with himself single-handed" (N 497). The overwhelming darkness of the Isabel islands, in which he is helplessly trapped, has triumphed over his intellectual vanity and ethical cynicism. He dies of skepticism and contempt for sentiment, which shield him not just from the simple pleasant moments of life, but also from the very essence of his being. The narrator states: "After three days of waiting for the sight of some human face, Decoud caught himself entertaining a doubt of his own individuality" (497).

In the overpowering solitude of the jungle Decoud contemplates his mental and physical deterioration without the power to act, lacking, as it were, inner ethical will. Ultimately, he perishes from want of alterity – from the absence of that human face he despised throughout his existence, and which he drastically needed at this moment of absolute loneliness. There is manifestly a great deal of Conrad in Decoud's ethical outlook, not least his propensity to skepticism, pessimism, and, most of all, suspicion of ethical idealism. While through both Monygham and Decoud Conrad highlights the moral nihilism prominent among most of his characters, through Decoud specifically he also draws attention to the dialectical relationship between intelligence and ethics and suggests two important things: first, that intelligence without ethics is worthless and potentially destructive. Second, that an individual, whatever his intellectual detachment or contempt for his fellow beings, cannot fully cut off himself from ethical relations.

One of the hopeful examples of such rare, productive ethical relations in Conrad's fiction is to be found in the protagonist of *Victory*, Axel Heyst. Like Decoud, Heyst is a detached character who is described living an absolute solitary life, "not conscious of either friends or of enemies" (V 90). He is a symbol of ethical elusiveness, as suggested in the following statement: "In this scheme he had perceived the means of passing through life without suffering and almost without a single care in the world – invulnerable because elusive" (90). However, although Heyst lives in an isolated place which looks like a "moral desert" (80), he is, unlike Decoud, not an ethical island, but a man of exemplary humanity, imbued with goodness and sense of fellowship. He lends money to Morrison, whom he knows only by sight and through the usual islands gossip, out of sheer empathy for a fellow being in difficulty. Heyst does not expect any privilege or profit in return, performing an ethical gesture that looks like an end in itself rather than a means to some individual gain or self-gratification. Like Marlow who, in *Lord Jim*, prides himself on always seeing "merely the human being" during his encounters, Heyst in *Victory* noticeably puts the human factor first, as he mostly perceives through Morrison's predicament the vulnerability of a fellow being with whom he shares a common human condition. In this respect, his action is both an act of solidarity and an ethical resistance to the indifference and ruthlessness of existence; in other words, an instance of pure instinctive ethics, in which the self unconditionally responds to the ethical demands of the Other and is fully devoted to the interests of that Other – Morrison, in this case – to the detriment of its own interests.

In contrast to Heyst, Decoud in *Nostromo* drastically lacks this vital inner ethical force which has enabled Heyst to project himself into the plight of his fellow beings despite his rational detachment from his surroundings. Further still, Decoud despises instinct or sentiment with religious fervour, although, finally, he ironically becomes sentimental himself and, on the brink of death, he begins to feel the urgent and "sudden desire to hear a human voice" (*N* 301), from which, formerly, he has obstinately shut off himself. Significantly, in this extreme moral despair, Decoud longs for the ethical encounter with the voice that might release him from this hopeless condition; he expresses a kind of metaphysical desire for a master that would completely take care of his destiny. However, this desperate wish for human communion or an intersubjective dialogue with a significant Other at this final breath of his existence sounds like a belated admission of his – and generally man's – incapacity to fully evade meaningful ethical engagements with his fellow beings. Mikhail Bakhtin reminds us that our identity draws its stability and permanence from its ethical relation to alterity:

> Cutting oneself off, isolating oneself, closing oneself off, those are the basic reasons for the loss of self [...]. To be means to communicate [...] [m]an has no internal sovereign territory; he is all and always on the boundary; looking within himself he looks in the eyes of the other or through the other.[17]

Without human presence and ethical substance, Decoud helplessly sees his individuality dissolve into nothingness. His suicide is the result of the ethical inefficiency of his intelligence in the face of the absolute moral solitude of his condition on the Isabel islands. What Conrad seems to further suggest through this character's tragic fate is that when intellect and will are stripped of ethics they become instruments of moral isolation, unhappiness, and self-destruction.

The Colonial Ethos: Efficiency, Ideals, Lies

Gould and Holroyd showcase another morally significant dimension of the dynamic tension of thought and action, and action and ethics in this narrative, a central theme in Conrad's fiction.[18] Both characters share a thirst for material interests and imbue their activities with moral idealism. Right from the start, Gould readily states his ambition to turn the mine he inherited from his father into a moral force or, more precisely, to transform what he saw as "an absurd moral disaster" into a "moral success" (N 66):

> What is wanted here is law, good faith, order, security. Anyone can declaim about these things, but I pin my faith to material interests. Only let the material interests once get a firm footing, and they are bound to impose the conditions on which alone they can continue to exist. That's how your money-making is justified here in the face of lawlessness and disorder. [...] A better justice will come afterwards. (84)

Responsible ethical action rests on a combination of foresight, reason, and feeling, as well as on will and aptness to assess and choose rightly. The ethical force and significance of an action largely stem from this dynamic synergy without which action becomes either fruitless or a shallow performance. In the above statement, Gould presents his project of rebuilding the San Tomé mine as a progressive undertaking meant to uplift morally and materially the inhabitants of Sulaco. Gould is a colonial archetype, in both his rational projections and moral pretences. His discourse remarkably mimics and absorbs the Enlightenment's universalist ethics of humanization that nineteenth-century's colonialist discourse appropriated and used to morally justify imperialism. In this hackneyed colonial discourse, morality and material interests, empire and ethics go hand in hand and promise an ideal world of justice and human development. Holroyd, the financer of the mine and Gould's ally, reinforces Gould's moral doctrine by further enhancing the spiritual value of work which, according to him, is what provides meaning or moral worth for existence and human undertakings: "Things seem to be worth nothing by what they are in themselves. I begin to believe that the only solid thing about them is the spiritual value which everyone discovers in this own form of activity" (318). Viewed in the light of Gould's and Holroyd's actions in Sulaco, this bombastic moral doctrine of work, of course, soon turns out to be empty – a shady moral smokescreen behind which these two imperialist characters hide their insatiable cupidity. It is sheer colonialist propaganda which makes these characters' pompous moral declarations sound as a caricature of the empire's self-proclaimed ideals of development, justice, and moral elevation of the colonized.

Gould and Holroyd are extraordinary actors in every sense of the word and in *Nostromo* ethics and performance or theatricality are intricately linked. The empire itself, as embodied by Gould and Holroyd, appears mainly as a stage for the dramatization of colonial ethics or lack thereof. For Gould, ethics amounts to a show, much like Nostromo's actions, done more for the glorification of the protagonist's ego than for the community's well-being. And like Jim or Razumov, Gould's ethical framework, too, is unstable, elusive, subject to the changing circumstances. In the main, Gould treats ethics as a mere commodity, dependent on interest and market fluctuations, and which he pragmatically invests in or withdraws from according to material opportunities. When the mine grows into a monster devouring the lives of the miners and his wife calls him back to his initial ideal, Gould entirely overlooks the former moral principles in which he grounded his activity. He replies to his wife's inquiry: "I thought we had said all there was to say a long time ago. There is nothing to say now. There were things to be done. We have done them; we have gone on doing them. There is no going back now" (207). Gould simply considers ethics or ethical inquiries out of place, and the narrator enhances this character's moral insularity, stating: "He seemed to dwell alone within a circumvallation of precious metal, leaving her outside with her school, her hospital, the sick mothers, and the feeble old men, mere insignificant vestiges of the initial inspiration" (222). Gould retreats from the province of morals and abandons the realm of ethical action to his wife. He walls himself in an inaccessible fortress of material interests, cut off from ethics, while his wife dwells in an ethical bubble, fanning alone the embers of their former common moral ideals. She is busy with her schools and hospitals, selflessly devoting herself to the poor and needy.

Charles Gould's ethical defection shows how material interests have triumphed over ethics or, more precisely, how the transformation of the mine into an insatiable source of profit has made ethical reflection irrelevant. It indicates, above all, that for Gould ethics has no place in business, since it is either completely useless or harmful to his material interests. As Conrad highlights through Gould's conduct the fraught relationship between business and ethics, he especially points out the difficulty of introducing ethics into the greedy, profit-driven field of business. Meanwhile, he draws attention to the fact that when business is left to its own pursuits it cannot be ethical, because the sirens of material interests are stronger than the call or ethical imperatives of the Other (the colonized workers in general). This said, Gould has, by no means, renounced all ethical pretensions forever. At the end of the novel, when he is forced by political circumstances to make choices, he firmly justifies his decision to stay in Sulaco on moral grounds, invoking ethical responsibility for his workers: "we have brought mankind into it, and we cannot turn our backs upon them to go and begin a new life elsewhere" (209).

Gould thus pragmatically mobilizes ethics in the service of material interests, mimicking in this way the ideals of the Enlightenment, while ruthlessly engaging in ecological destruction and dehumanization. Conrad seems to suggest through his protagonist that in the mouths of colonialists, ethics amounts to a mere word, a subterfuge to justify selfish materialist pursuits. Gould boasts lofty ethical ideals, but, deep down, his action is mostly stirred by a merciless utilitarian ethics with self-interest as its sole goal. As most of Conrad's characters, Gould is in the thick of an ethical paradox, and through this character's moral contradictions Conrad highlights both the individuals' need for moral virtues, in order to assign ethical value to their actions, and their inability to live up to their ethical ideals. He widely discredits the colonial work ethics Gould and Holroyd represent by showing that the spiritual value these characters pin to their actions is a mere hoax. Since in Sulaco the activities of the mine tend to increase the population's suffering and alienation, rather than contribute to their well-being or moral elevation.

Conrad's mocking of the colonialist work ethic in *Nostromo* is taken to its extreme in "Heart of Darkness." Empire prides itself on efficiency and progress. In this novella, the ethics of efficiency and progress, represented by Kurtz and the chief accountant, boils down to an empty shell. The very notion of colonial activity itself connotes ethical emptiness, as most of the activities undertaken in the (unnamed) Congo where the story is set amount either to an absurd practice, performed for no clear material purpose, or to a means of exploitation and subjection with selfish materialist interests as its higher end. The brick maker no longer produces bricks and Kurtz's idea of work rhymes with exploitation and boundless profit.

Kurtz embodies imperialism in its extreme version. He comes to Africa for purely materialist pursuits: to make money in order to marry his Intended. Marlow insists, however, that Kurtz is not only of fine artistic sensibility but arrived in Africa equipped with "moral ideas of some sort" ("Heart of Darkness," YS 88) and further refers to him as a humanizing ethical force or "an emissary of pity, and science, and progress" (79). It is this symbol of universalization that Marlow comes to meet in Africa in an expedition which takes the shape of both an epistemic pursuit and an ethical quest. He sets out on his journey and expects the moral values of progress and enlightenment to be implemented by Kurtz on the African continent, but when he arrives there he discovers exploitation, murder, and moral decadence, which reveals a gulf between the empire's idealistic pretences and real practices.[19] Kurtz's insatiable hunger for ivory and material success has gradually eroded his moral dispositions and turned him into an abject imperialist ruthlessly exploiting the African populations. Ethics and space are closely interconnected in this novella, and Kurtz's abjectness is often ascribed to his incapacity to adapt his moral ideals to the African continent's overwhelming powers of darkness. Throughout his journey, Marlow anticipates Africans to be cannibals and Africa a dark, ethical wasteland. Yet, his ethical expectations are brutally unsettled when, for example, he realizes that the thirty starving black men on his steamboat remarkably refrain from eating the five Europeans aboard or devouring each other. Marlow both admires and is deeply disconcerted by this outstanding ethical self-discipline. All the more so as his preconceived ethical framework does not foresee such a prospect.

Marlow sporadically shows us flickers of morality in this heart of darkness, as in the previous example, but, overall, he depicts Africa as mostly a moral wilderness. In his presentation, the (unnamed) Congo is neither an ethical place, nor a place for ethics. In fact, it is not even a space where ethics is relevant. The reason is that since in colonial representations Africa is considered as being completely outside – and beneath – the European moral framework, it is dismissed by Western colonialists as an ethical void, in much the same way as the African continent is deemed a land without history. The strangeness of this landscape and its people, the European characters' physical and moral disorientation all reinforce Africa's ethical bareness. Marlow is bewildered by the shapes, sounds, and signs bursting chaotically into his senses. He is constantly shown groping anxiously in this disconcerting environment for bearings and for ways to relate ethically to the obscure, threatening otherness he encounters – the Africans as well as the African landscape itself. His emphasis on obscurity, mist, and vagueness indicates the inadequacy of his epistemic, cultural, and ethical models in assessing this alien environment and its inhabitants. It also reinforces the image of Africa as a moral void, expressly rendered in Marlow's description, and which is highly significant from a colonialist perspective. Imperial ideology is a sophisticated multi-layered discourse which rests on basic myths and a simplistic morality, in order to validate empire. So, by denying, for example, all ethical foundations to these African societies, by stressing the colonized peoples' presumed backwardness and lack of humanity, the colonizers tend to morally justify the exploitation and dehumanization of these populations.

Conrad powerfully conveys this colonial epistemic and moral arrogance in Kurtz's abject methods, as well as in the conduct of the Company's chief accountant. This accountant is an emblem of colonial ethical blindness and stands for crude inhumanity and decay of Western civilization.[20] He is indifferent not only to the predicament of the radical Others – the African workers dying only a few feet away from his house – but also to the familiar Other, the "invalid agent," whose groanings in the adjacent room, "distract [his] attention." Marlow further derides the chief accountant, by drawing attention to this servant of empire's absurd efforts to keep up an impeccable appearance amidst chaos and death:

> I respected the fellow. Yes; I respected his collars, his vast cuffs, his brushed hair. His appearance was certainly that of a hairdresser's dummy; but in the great demoralization of the land he kept up his appearance. That's backbone. His starched collars and got-up-shirt-fronts were achievements of character. (68)

The chief accountant's absurd neatness of dress and appearance indicates that European civilisation in the African colonies is at best a farcical show. His complete indifference to otherness, on the other hand, reveals the extent to which empire is no place for ethical considerations. And it is so because colonialism, as a fundamentally capitalist pursuit, is, in essence, beyond and above ethics, since it is mainly fuelled by material quests and hunger for profits, which are incompatible with ethical ideals. That is why even characters such as Kurtz, who come to the colony equipped with moral values, soon see these values dissolve into the prevalent colonial moral darkness. Kurtz is a fallen icon of universalization, that is of the Enlightenment's ideals – rationalism, progress, and the humanization of the universe – that nineteenth-century's colonial ideology incorporated into its discourse to justify colonizing non-European countries. During his ethical encounter with the Other – the Africans – Kurtz is clearly not motivated by a universal humanizing ethics as should normally be a moral agent of "pity" and "progress" such as himself. Rather, like Charles Gould, he embodies a despotic subject stirred by an ethics of mastery and a blind will to power whose goal is the dehumanization and destruction of Africans and their continent (slavery, massacre of elephants, rape, etc.).

Marlow provides a detailed picture of Kurtz's abject conduct in Africa in a narrative that blends condemnation and atonement. His ethical insights into the colonial horrors reach a culminating point at the end of the narrative where he comes face to face with Kurtz and hears his voice for the first time. This is an important ethical moment – the ethical core of the novella, in fact, in which the dying Kurtz pronounces a verdict on his actions. Against all expectations, this unsettling protagonist recognizes his cruelty in what sounds like a brutal awakening from a long ethical torpor. Marlow calls this epiphanic instant "the supreme moment of complete knowledge" because it constitutes the culminating point of his epistemic as well ethical quest (149). In this climactic ethical encounter, Marlow praises Kurtz's courage for pronouncing this judgment which he emphatically calls a "moral victory" (151). The question is: is this ultimate ethical awakening a mere rhetorical or intellectual manoeuvre through which Kurtz deceitfully seeks to relieve his soul, or a genuine ethical impulse?

Marlow informs us that Kurtz's "intelligence was perfectly clear" (144), while "his soul was mad" (145). This suggests that Kurtz's final moral statement is the product not of a deep ethical incentive but of pure cerebration and eloquence; in short, an exercise of reason and will, rather than the feat of the heart and instinct. If so, the moral courage Marlow admires in Kurtz may then, at best, appear as a "moral victory" with limited ethical worth. The reason is that Kurtz's moral verdict is mostly directed to himself and to the familiar Other – Marlow, not to the radical African Others. This is a serious ethical issue since these Africans are the first victims of Kurtz's horrors and also the essential alterity without which Kurtz's moral judgment may amount to an empty ethical shell. The same may be said of Razumov's and Jim's final ethical pronouncements, discussed earlier. They, too, are suspect, because they are driven by egoistic incentives, intended for self-healing rather than for universal human fellowship and deep ethical relations with the Others.[21]

Knowledge, Truth, Ethical Credibility

The question of moral worth and ethical credibility, evoked with relation to Kurtz, is a central concern in Conrad's works and encompasses all the aspects of his aesthetics, starting with representation or narrative method. In Conrad's works, the narrative ethics is governed by a set of ontological and epistemic values by which the narrators are intended to abide. Among these ethical narrative virtues, reliability, objectivity, and humanity stand out as fundamental qualities required for narrators to qualify as narratively and ethically credible. Conrad is constantly preoccupied with his narrators' reliability and this narrative reliability is intricately connected to ethical credibility, or more precisely the first largely rests on the second. In many works including *Victory*, "Amy Foster," "Karain," "Heart of Darkness," *Lord Jim*, and *Under Western Eyes*, the narrators are obsessed with their own narrative credibility and that of the voices feeding their narratives, to the point of almost becoming burdensome. In *Victory*, for example, the anonymous narrator refers to his narrative trustworthiness, while also insisting on the credibility of the ancillary narrative voices fuelling his narrative. He describes Davidson as a sincere, objective, genuinely kind, and remarkably humane individual. This high moral profile increases Davidson's ethical worth and, by the same token, the narrator's own narrative trustworthiness.

Similarly, in "Amy Foster" Doctor Kennedy is presented by the frame narrator as a credible narrative voice, gifted with a "penetrating power of [the] mind," "an intelligence [...] of

a scientific order," and "unappeasable curiosity" ("Amy Foster,"
TS 106). He also possesses broad knowledge of life and world
cultures and wrote papers on the flora and fauna of remote,
unfamiliar regions. Furthermore, he inspires trust because
he has "the talent of making people talk to him freely, and an
inexhaustible patience in listening to their tales" (106). Finally,
Kennedy is endowed with a humane outlook which leads him
to view compassionately the ethnic difference of the persecuted
ship-wrecked protagonist – Yanko Gooral. Throughout, he
displays narrative moderation and ethical relativity, describing
the cultures of Yanko and the Colebrook community as both
poles apart and morally equal. However, Kennedy's narrative
credibility is eroded at the end of the story, where he attempts to
find extenuating circumstances for the Colebrook community's
racism towards Yanko. For, by suggesting that the local
inhabitants' racism is mostly grounded in fear, ignorance, and
lack of imagination and sensitivity, he engages in a redemptive
ethics intended to lighten the racial burden on his fellow
villagers' shoulders.

In "Heart of Darkness," Marlow's narrative profundity
is emphasized from the outset by the frame narrator and
throughout the story Marlow is centrally concerned with his
representation and narrative reliability, as much as with search
for knowledge and truth – both about Kurtz's actions and the
imperial system he represents. Marlow discovers this much
sought-after truth when he finally meets Kurtz, but he strangely
does not seem to feel the ethical demand to disclose it to the
protagonist's Intended. He unashamedly tells the Intended that
Kurtz is a loved and admired "universal genius" (YS 154) and
the "last word he pronounced was – your name" (161).

Marlow's lie raises complex ideological and ethical issues
and, once more, brings to the fore another key Conradian
paradox: can we lie and still preserve our ethical worth, or more
specifically, is Marlow's lie ethical or unethical? Does it bolster
or impair his narrative and ethical trustworthiness? Is it a form
of betrayal to his ethical principles or an expression of human
fellowship? Marlow's ethical framework in this narrative is

a blend of conventional Christian morality and secular humanist ethics. Throughout, he stands on the cusp of morality and ethics, moving from one to the other with relative ease. His meeting with the Intended is a moment of prominent ethical significance and, in this scene, Marlow draws our attention to the face of the Intended, with a particular focus on her eyes: "This fair hair, this pale visage, this pure brow, seemed surrounded by an ashy halo from which the dark eyes looked out at me. Their glance was guileless, profound, confident, and trustful" (157).

As in *Lord Jim*, gaze and ethics are closely linked in this statement in which Marlow presents the Intended's eyes as mirrors of ethics, reflecting her sorrows and dreams, her confidence and faith. The Intended's despondent, imploring glance in particular, on which Marlow focuses in this momentous "face-to-face encounter," has a strong effect on Marlow and seems to exert an ethical call on his compassion, to which he is summoned to respond. And, indeed, overcome with "a feeling of infinite pity" (161), Marlow answers this ethical demand by what looks like a basic form of Christian compassion performed for the good of another grieving soul. However, this moral support comes at the price of lies that, Marlow emphatically tells us, he hates with religious fervour, because he believes "there is a taint of death, a flavour of mortality in lies – which is exactly what I hate and detest in the world – what I want to forget" (82).

We are yet again in the midst of another Conradian paradox: disliking lies and still lying, seeking truth and hiding this truth from those who are entitled to it. To say the least, Marlow's lie constitutes a serious infringement to his moral principles and leaves us with this nagging question: is this lying sheer hypocrisy on Marlow's part, sophistry, cynicism, or complete unconsciousness? Whichever! The fact remains that Marlow lies to the Intended and does so both unselfishly and selfishly: he lies not to burden the shoulders of the grief-stricken widow with further sorrow, as well as to spare himself the trouble of having to disclose appalling truths to this innocent, mournful soul. Marlow hits two birds with one stone. As he lightens the load on the Intended, he also spares his conscience the trouble of having to unveil awful truths to someone who is indisposed to hear them. Meantime, he magnanimously thinks that this woman and, all women for that matter, should be protected from the harsh realities of empire and thus have their benevolent ignorance of the world preserved. He contemptuously states: "Oh, she is out of it – completely. They – the women I mean – are out of it – should be out of it. We must help them to stay in that beautiful world of their own, lest ours gets worse" (115). Marlow's disdain for women is at its crudest here and his lie to the Intended is a flagrant affirmation of his patriarchal arrogance and sense of intellectual superiority over this woman and the female world she embodies.

Overall, Marlow's lie is an ethical shield that serves a highly moral purpose. It comforts and helps the naïve, heart-broken woman to preserve her ideal image of the man she loves, while it also secures her psychological and moral balance. Above all, it safeguards her from the empire's abuses and atrocities of the man she loves, as mentioned earlier. Still, no matter how soothing it may be for the Intended, this lie constitutes, in the end, a fundamental ethical rupture that affects the core of Marlow's ethics of representation and position towards the notion of truth – a valuable tenet in his ethical framework. Throughout the narrative, Marlow consistently presents himself as the voice of ethics and truth unveiling to us the lies and horrors of empire, insisting that his discourse is "the speech that cannot be silenced" (97). Yet, at the final scene this bold ethical promise to speak freely (the truth) fades, and Marlow resorts to this unexpected, blatant lie that widely discredits him as a truth revealer and makes every ethical statement he claims suspect. This leaves us pondering: if Marlow can so easily lie to the Intended why shouldn't he lie to us, readers as well, and, in this case, why should we assign any ethical worth to his account? Why should we believe his thoughts, opinions, and feelings? Why should we, at all, take his ethics of sympathy and fellowship toward Africans at face value?

In speaking so admirably of Kurtz to the Intended, in enhancing the moral value of this protagonist's final statement,

or "moral victory" (151) as Marlow calls it, it is ultimately his
ethical authority that Marlow undermines. It is important to
underline that Marlow fundamentally functions in this text as
an ethical filter, not to say a diligent censor, and his position
toward Kurtz's verdict is a blend of religious complacency and
ethical cynicism. So, unless one really sees Kurtz's verdict from
a purely religious perspective – sin, confession, absolution – it
would, indeed, make little sense to realistically consider this
verdict a moral victory. The reason is simple: Kurtz is an abject
character who has betrayed both morality and ethics – both
his moral and ethical obligations – by engaging in actions so
abominable that make us doubt his very humanity. Kurtz's
conduct being beyond ethics and morality altogether, his final
confession has, therefore, little ethical worth. It is, at best, sheer
religious hypocrisy that Marlow presents to us as a revolutionary
ethical awakening. Marlow, we recall, has begun his tale of
darkness on the *Nellie* as a Buddha, but ends it as a surrogate
priest, listening with pious devotion to Kurtz's confession
and absolving his guilty conscience. Thus, with remarkable
evangelical complacency, he expediently rehabilitates Kurtz
both in the Intended's eyes and, implicitly, in the eyes of the
audience back in England. However, the moral authority with
which he sanctions Kurtz's ultimate judgment of his conduct
proves hollow and ethically questionable. It is tainted by his
final lie to the Intended, which irredeemably discredits him as
a trustworthy narrative voice and as an ethical agent. By this lie,
therefore, Marlow betrays not only his own moral convictions,
but also his ethical commitments to his audience, by uncaringly
breaching his initial moral pact with this audience, especially
with the implied reader embodied by the Intended and who
symbolically stands for the British audience.

From a postcolonial perspective, on the other hand, Marlow's
lie, which, as made clear, widely undermines his ethical
integrity, also makes him complicit with the imperial ideology he
criticizes, which further questions his status as a viable ethical
agent and critic of empire. Marlow, who has throughout stood
for an objective, humane ethical voice, and the locus of truth

and moral probity, finally turns into a liar and proponent of the imperial lie he steadily condemns, and which is symbolized by Kurtz and crystallized in the colonial proclaimed ideals or the "idea at the back of it" (51).

The idea of colonialist discourse as a lie, conveyed in Marlow's concluding statement to the Intended, is recurrent in many Conrad's works, including "Karain: A Memory," where the anonymous narrator, Hollis, and Jackson feed the naïve Karain with lies or myths of the phantasmagoric Western world which he craves. Karain implores the three Englishmen to relieve him of his haunting memories, begging them to take him to England, in a discussion that re-enacts the myth of the colonizer as the redeemer of the backward, superstitious colonized peoples. "We felt as though we three had been called to the very gate of Infernal Regions to judge, to decide the fate of a wanderer coming suddenly from a world of sunshine and illusions" ("Karain: A Memory" *TU* 45). Note the ethics of healing here, as Hollis' attempt to relieve Karain of his tormenting ghosts makes him appear as a spirit healer grappling with a mad soul. The three Englishmen present themselves as enlightened, rational and moral agencies, in charge of freeing Karain and the East he represents from its superstitions and moral backwardness. Ironically, the moral superiority these characters claim is a farce, since they try to dispel Karain's ghosts not with rational or lofty ethical means, but through deception. In answer to Karain's fervent plea to be taken to England and provided with a "charm," Hollis produces his Jubilee sixpence, after opening the box containing, among other things:

> Amulets of white men! Charms and talismans! Charms that keep them straight, that drive them crooked, that have the power to make a young man sigh, an old man smile. Potent things that procure dreams of joy, thoughts of regret; that soften hard hearts, and can temper a soft one to the hardness of steel. Gifts of heaven – things of earth… (48)

Here, Conrad mocks the power of money by showing the charm it exerts on people and its corruptive potential. Hollis further enhances Karain's curiosity and admiration for England, but,

ironically, the picture that he provides Karain with is contrived,
made of inventions rather than authentic details.

> He multiplied questions; he could never know enough of the Monarch
> of whom he spoke with wonder and chivalrous respect – with a kind
> of affectionate awe [...]. We had to invent details at last to satisfy his
> craving curiosity; and our loyalty must be pardoned, for we tried to
> make them fit for his august and resplendent ideal. (13)

The three Englishmen rely on deceitful inventions to maintain
the idyllic image of imperial England in Karain's admiring eyes.
Once again, Conrad shows how colonial morality, enthroned
in the empire's discourse of progress and justice, is a sham,
constantly wavering between a lie and a hoax. Conrad further
rails the three Englishmen's ethical cynicism by revealing that
their apparent moral project of uplifting the backward Karain is
underpinned by greedy commercial interests: arms smuggling.
Behind their moral ideals of enlightenment and advancement
lie, therefore, sheer material pursuits, which, as shown through
both Gould's and Kurtz's conduct, do not tally with ethics.

Narrative and Ethics of Human Fellowship: Feeling, Listening, Seeing

The ethical and ideological inconsistencies, prominent in
"Heart of Darkness," "Karain: A Memory," and "Amy Foster,"
are also recurrent in *Lord Jim*, and so is Marlow's preoccupation
with narrative and ethical trustworthiness in this novel.
The anonymous narrator presents Marlow as being equipped
with unquestionable epistemic and ethical standards. He is
a retired seaman with a remarkable experience of life at sea
and a deft reader of human character. He is, above all, humane,
a feature that Marlow consistently reiterates to underline his
ethical trustworthiness. Marlow's humanity cannot, of course,
be doubted. From the outset he readily establishes an ethical
connection with Jim: "'OH YES. I attended the inquiry, he
would say', 'and to this day I haven't left off wondering why
I went. I am willing to believe each of us has a guardian angel,

if you fellows will concede to me that each of us has a familiar devil as well'" (*LJ* 34). The words "angel" and "devil" clearly set the moral tone of the relation between Marlow and Jim, and throughout Marlow appears as a "guardian angel" playing the devil's advocate in Jim's case. Marlow further strengthens his moral bonds with Jim by seeing him as his younger self[22]:

> a youngster of the sort you like to see about you; of the sort you like to imagine yourself to have been; of the sort whose appearance claims the fellowship of these illusions you had thought gone out, extinct, cold, and which, as if rekindled at the approach of another flame, give a flutter deep, deep down somewhere, give a flutter of light... of heat! (128)

Marlow is chagrined by Jim's desertion of the *Patna* which disrupts the moral code that binds this young seaman to the sea community. However, he still considers the protagonist as part of the community despite his misconduct. The previous statement consolidates, indeed, the moral ties between these two men, by presenting their relation as a profound ethical connection characterized by human fellowship and remarkable reciprocity which, as we have seen previously, are drastically missing in the ethical encounter between Razumov and Haldin in *Under Western Eyes*. While he insists on the reciprocity of their relation, Marlow also points out that this relation proceeds not from any moral obligation, but from a deliberate ethical choice, which, he stresses, is also mutual. He has chosen Jim as the object of his affection, Marlow emphatically informs us, as much as he has been chosen by Jim who has "singled [him] out" from the "insignificant multitude" at the court of justice: "I felt a gratitude, an affection, for that straggler whose eyes had singled me out, keeping my place in the ranks of an insignificant multitude. How little that was to boast of, after all!" (334).

This mutual attraction, which has a strong moral connotation here, is the prompt which has triggered this ethical relation between Marlow and Jim. Marlow's compassion and solidarity for Jim further lead him to ethical responsibility for the protagonist: "It was tragic enough and funny enough in all conscience to call aloud for compassion, and in what was

I better than the rest of us to refuse him my pity?" (129).
Marlow justifies his conduct towards Jim by making his
compassion or pity for this young man appear as a fundamental
natural ethical demand, difficult to resist or reject. His ethics
of pity is expressed in various ways and has both a humanist
undertone and a charitable Christian resonance. He helps
Jim to find work; he provides him with moral comfort at the
Malabar Hotel that allows him to put into words his moral
predicament. In this scene Marlow talks mainly to prompt Jim
to unburden himself and establish with him a relation of mutual
trust. If the gaze is a source of reciprocal human fellowship
between Marlow and Jim at the court of justice, at the Malabar
Hotel it is the ear which fundamentally fulfills this function.
The ethics of listening, the disposition to lend a compassionate
ear to a soul in grief, acquires great significance in this scene
and Jim vigorously draws our attention to the soothing power
of Marlow's attentive ear: "'You are an awful good sort to listen
like this,' he said. 'It does me good. You don't know what it is to
me. You don't…words seemed to fail him'" (128).

Marlow's solidarity with Jim is a case of strong ethical
engagement that sets him apart from the community of seamen.
His efforts to reintegrate Jim to this community, his wish to mend
an essential broken chain of solidarity, despite the protagonist's
betrayal of the ethics of this community, are a strong ethical
gesture. They sharply contrast Marlow with characters like
Chester or Brierly, who stiffly comply with an ethics of natural
justice – the law of the strongest and bravest – which makes
them insensible to Jim's failing. Marlow's consistent empathy
for Jim is a strong disavowal of these characters' ethics of natural
justice.[23] So, while Chester bluntly dismisses Jim as "no good,"
or morally worthless, and, therefore, not "one of us," Marlow
powerfully asserts his close ties to the protagonist and firm
adherence to the ethics of solidarity, out of the conviction that
"we exist only in so far as we hang together" (223).

Here, Marlow acknowledges that the individual self builds in
relation to the alterity which shapes this self and permanently
redefines it. He thus questions the moral individualism of Chester

and Brierly, in solidarity with a fallen fellow seaman and, above all, in the name of a universal human weakness, or shared humanity, which recalls the teacher of languages' ethical justification of Razumov's betrayal of Haldin. It is on the grounds of this ethics of human fellowship, which values feeling and ethical inner worth, that Marlow grants a second chance to Jim. His opponents, who are governed by stringent moral dogmatism, provide instead, as previously mentioned, no room for second chances or redemptive possibilities. Marlow's unconditional ethics of forgiveness, which demands of him to listen compassionately and look with clement eyes to Jim's immoral conduct, reinforces his ethical credibility and, by the same token, his narrative trustworthiness. Incidentally, through his compassion for Jim and overall humanity and altruism, Marlow ultimately seeks to induce the reader to a compassionate relation with the protagonist.

Marlow's main concern throughout this narrative is to make sense of Jim's conduct and ethical dilemma, resorting to an ethics of justification, frequent among several of Conrad's protagonists and narrators: Marlow's incessant justifications in *Lord Jim* and Jim's self-justifications, Razumov's moral justification of his betrayal of Haldin, Leggatt's assertion of his moral superiority over the court of justice, etc. All these moral validations echo, in various ways, Conrad's own ethics of justification conveyed in the Author's Note to *The Secret Agent*, where he declared: "The true motive of my selection lies in quite a different trait. I have always had a propensity to justify my action. Not to defend. To justify" (*SA* viii).

Marlow in *Lord Jim* both strongly justifies Jim's action and does so rather defensively, especially at the court of justice. His overall ethical approach is not horizontal, nor fully vertical, but fragmented and labyrinthine and, on the whole, relatively consistent with his narrative ethics. This is perceptible in the way he opposes his own method of inquiry to that of the court. Marlow seeks to make sense of Jim's act by summoning reason and fact, as well as the psychological, ethical, and philosophical dimension of this act. The court of justice instead relies exclusively on fact and on the consequences of Jim's act, thus widely overlooking the questions of internal incentive or motives. Like Leggatt in "The Secret Sharer," Marlow distrusts this legal institution and condemns its proceedings which, in his view, "had all the cold vengefulness of a death sentence" (*LJ* 158). He particularly criticizes this institution's focus on sheer externals and horizontal meaning and, above all, for neglecting the human aspect of this affair which he considers valuable. In the process, he steadily reasserts his humanity, knowledge of sea life, and capacity for moral discernment to further distinguish his approach from that of the court: "I have met so many men [...] and in each case all I could see was merely the human being. A confounded democratic quality of vision which may be better than total blindness, but has been of no advantage to me, I can assure you" (94). Marlow affirms his ethical pre-eminence over the judicial system. He prides himself on his "democratic quality of vision," which enables him to see Jim's ethical dilemma as unique. The court, which lacks such discernment, deems instead Jim's situation a case among others weighed only in the light of fact and evidence.

Duality, Self-referentiality, Romantic Ethics

Marlow's narrative ethics is noteworthy for its dynamic nature and distinction from the moral doctrine and insular modes of identification embodied by the court of justice, Chester or Brierly. Throughout Marlow consistently portrays himself as an emblem of humanity, free of egoism, and profoundly inclined to altruism; in short, as a remarkable ethical agent devoted to his fellow beings and spurred by an ethics of compassion which he presents as a natural and unavoidable ethical demand. A close look at his overall relation to his narrative suggests, however, that this ethics of compassion is not as disinterested as Marlow wants us to believe, but tainted with selfishness to the extent of becoming self-referential. All the more so as he does not really see Jim as a completely distinct, autonomous self or total exteriority, but rather as his younger alter ego. His sympathy and pity for Jim are, therefore, also self-sympathy and self-pity; his devotion to Jim is devotion to himself. Similarly, just as Marlow wishes the reader to show compassion for Jim's moral conflicts, he also wants this reader to sympathize with his own predicament as a narrator struggling to grasp the protagonist's elusive moral character. In other words, Marlow nurtures close ethical bonds with Jim because he egoistically recognizes in this protagonist his own "youthful illusions." At times, he also ethically distances himself from Jim for the same narcissistic demands: "I was aggrieved against him, as though he had cheated me – me! – of a splendid opportunity to keep up the illusion of my beginnings, as though he had robbed our common life of the last spark of its glamour" (131). The word "aggrieved" is highly significant for both its emotional and ethical undertones. Marlow feels at once angry and offended, upset and wounded by Jim's misconduct, since he, again, sees Jim as a part of himself – a sort of secret sharer – who shunned decent ethical conduct of which Marlow is a noble representative. His grief for Jim is again self-grief, an egocentric sentiment intended for the preservation of the ideal moral self embodied by Marlow and marred by Jim's unethical behaviour. Ironically, Jim, too, engages in a self-referential form of connection with the Bugis.

In Patusan, Jim regains confidence in himself and a good name, as he tells us, which increases his self-esteem and ethical worth in his own eyes. He becomes the master of his destiny, reborn as a mythic figure with remarkable powers. Marlow speaks highly of Jim's ethical transformation. He presents him as a progressive, humanizing force, equipped with a liberal, non-coercive discourse, living happily and harmoniously among free and equal participants, where everyone understands and respects the perspective of the others, while also projecting themselves into the world of their fellow members. A collective ethical ideal seems to emerge from these interlocking perspectives into which Jim is integrated and holds the community together in a spirit of sharing and solidarity. However, we soon realize that these ethical encounters are not as fulfilled as Marlow seems to suggest, since Jim finally turns out to be a questionable moral authority who, like Gould or Kurtz, is stirred by an ethics of mastery or a will to power that is indifferent to the Bugis' ethical demands. While his regained self-esteem obviously relieves him of his former anxieties and grants him psychological security, it is finally overcome by his "exalted egoism" (416) and morphs into vulgar self-love which leads him to see the Bugis as mostly a means of self-gratification. He selfishly subjects these populations to his own narcissistic needs and colludes with Brown's Machiavellian designs, which later causes his own destruction and the disruption of the Bugis community. Despite his apparent devotion and sense of responsibility towards the Bugis, therefore, Jim fundamentally remains "a supreme egotist," driven mostly by "the preservation of his own self-image,"[24] and thus ignoring, like Gould or Kurtz, the moral ideals which are supposed to guide his actions and ethical choices in Patusan.

In "Heart of Darkness," Kurtz, we recall, is the quintessence of egocentrism, as suggested in his famous statement "My Intended, my ivory, my station, my river, my –" (YS 116), and this excessive egoism blinds him to the people around him and leads him to ruthless conduct. In Lord Jim, too, as we have seen, Marlow refers to Jim's "exalted egoism" (LJ 416) that blinds him to the interests of the Bugis. Through both Kurtz and Jim Conrad highlights the destructive effects of unbridled egoism or what may be called an excessive romantic ethics, which takes the self and its needs and desires as an end. Like Kurtz in "Heart of Darkness," Jim's devouring ego is the source of his ethical blindness, and just as he is blind to the Bugis' interests and well-being, he is also blind to Gentleman Brown's horrid intentions.

Jim is, in many respects, an imperial agent and, once more, Conrad draws our attention to the failure of empire or its representatives to live up to the Enlightenment's rational ideals of progress and humanization of the universe, since the progressive, humanitarian discourse Jim promotes in Patusan fits a (colonial) dominant discourse of progress, whose goal is not to humanize the Other – the Bugis – or fulfill their ethical demands, but to appropriate their myths and symbols to better dominate them. Consequently, Jim's words are not vehicles of shared practice or common ethical destiny, but means to glorify his own self-image and place the interest of the self above and beyond the ethical imperatives of the Other. In terms of ethics, therefore, his discourse, like that of Gould or Kurtz, is shallow and tautological since it refers only to itself and to the needs and desires of the ego. His actions, too, are of little ethical worth, as they do not seek the good in itself or the happiness of the Bugis but are essentially stirred by overwhelming selfish incentives.

Conrad seems to indicate through Jim's ethically deficient conduct the incapacity of ethics to triumph over the overpowering structures of egoism and romantic perceptions of the self. Ultimately, Jim's romantic ethics of being inexorably leads to the deception of both his ideal self and the Others because the ego always exceeds its own representations, as much as it places itself above and beyond the happiness and ethical demands of the Other. That is why Jim may be said to have finally failed both morality (the sea code of honour and solidarity) and ethics (the confidence the Bugis placed in him – the "profound, rare friendship between brown and white" – between Jim and Dain Waris (261). Ironically, by shunning both his moral obligation and ethical commitment, by betraying Jewel, Dain Waris and, generally, the Bugis, Jim lamentably fails as an ethical agent, but triumphs as a romantic subject.

To hark back to Marlow's dubiousness as ethical agent, it is important to point out that Marlow is not as excessively egoistic or romantic as Jim, although his dramatized narrative self-consciousness betrays a romantic sense of narrative identity, in which ethical self-centredness, reflected in his attitude toward the protagonist, dovetails with narrative self-centredness. In "Heart of Darkness," as we have seen, Marlow is highly self-conscious, always directing our attention to his mode of narrative and cultural and epistemic disorientation.[25] He emphatically tells the reader "I don't want to bother you much with what happened to me personally" ("Heart of Darkness," YS 51), and still the bulk of his tale is about his own personal experience in Africa – his journey, what he saw,

and his encounter with Kurtz. Marlow in *Lord Jim* displays
a similar propensity to self-dramatization or ego-telling. He is
so narratively self-conscious that he tends to lead the reader
to focus more on his own bewilderment about Jim's conduct
than on the protagonist's predicament. He confesses to the
reader: "I am telling you so much about my own instinctive
feelings and bemused reflections," although this awareness
does not prevent him from this narrative prolixity (*LJ* 224).
As we shall shortly see, however, neither Marlow in *Lord Jim*
nor Marlow in "Heart of Darkness" matches the narrator of
Under Western Eyes, regarding narrative self-centredness. The
question is how we, readers, can make sense of Conrad's texts
amidst such dense, thwarted narrative and ethical elusiveness,
and, ultimately, what kinds of meaning(s) are to be drawn from
these narrators' ethics of representation?

Ethics of Reading and Meaning: Self-centredness, Self-denial, Ethical Impartiality

In Conrad's fiction the ethics of meaning builds around the
dense, elusive narrative ethics and it is intertwined with the ethics
of reading. In the main, this reading and sense-making ethics
mostly consists of the narrators' attitudes towards both their
own representations and their audiences. Conrad's narrators,
as pointed earlier, constantly seek to establish close connections
with their narratees and readers, in the hope of drawing their
interest and compassion. They often set up more or less explicit
moral pacts with these audiences and employ a host of narrative
devices including direct modes of address such as apostrophe,
intense visual effects (gestures, theatricality, etc.), hyperbole,
narrative self-consciousness, ruse, and deception.[26]

In *Under Western Eyes* the teacher of languages widely resorts
to these different devices to win his audience's sympathy and
collaboration. His narrative self-consciousness, for example,
suggested from the outset, is maintained throughout with such
intensity that his presence becomes overwhelming despite
his over-dramatized detachment. In this text, in fact, Conrad

goes a step further in his concern with narrative ethics and, more particularly, in his obsession with narrative and ethical credibility. Representation and ethics are closely connected in *Under Western Eyes*, and the issue of the narrator's credibility consists of two levels. It relates both to the nature of the fictional material this narrator uses and to his relation to this material and to his audience/reader. Right from the outset, he stresses the authenticity of Razumov's diary to showcase its epistemic value. Meantime, he presents himself as a mere mediator of Razumov's story, which he claims to faithfully convey to the reader. This rhetorical precaution aims to bring into focus the narrator's ethical detachment or objectivity, in order to convince his audience of his narrative trustworthiness. He states: "The very words I use in my narrative are written where their sincerity cannot be suspected" (*UWE* 214). The narrator's consistent concern with authenticity and objectivity echoes Conrad's anxious preoccupation with ethical impartiality. He writes in the Author's Note to *Under Western Eyes*:

> My greatest anxiety was in being able to strike and sustain the note of scrupulous impartiality. The obligation of absolute fairness was imposed on me historically and hereditarily, by the peculiar experience of race and family, in addition to my primary conviction that truth alone is the justification of any fiction which makes the least claim to the quality of art or may hope to take its place in the culture of men and women of its time. I had never been called before to a greater effort of detachment: detachment from all passions, prejudices and even from personal memories. (viii)

Conrad's insistence on his "scrupulous impartiality," "absolute fairness," and "truth" as "the justification of any fiction" is an anxious attempt to reassure his readers of his ethical impartiality in a particularly vexed subject, Russia, that Conrad is known to objectively hate and dismiss as an absolute force of negation.[27] What is especially compelling about Conrad's handling of narrative ethics in this novel is his narrator's tendency to assert his narrative and ethical trustworthiness mostly through a sustained ethics of denial:

To begin with I wish to disclaim the possession of those high gifts of
imagination and expression which would have enabled my pen to
create for the reader the personality of the man who called himself,
after the Russian custom, Cyril son of Isidor – Kirylo Sidorovitch –
Razumov. (3)

The ethics of denial is a recurring narrative motif in Conrad's
fiction, and in *Under Western Eyes* it constitutes the teacher
of languages' privileged mode of representation and the
cornerstone of the overall narrative ethics. In this novel, the
narrator vigorously denies having imagination and the power
of expression: his apparent goal is to underline his narrative
humility, in order to elicit his audience's attention and
compassion. As made clear in the previous statement, the
narrator's ethics of denial revolves around the status of language
and writing, and, through this device, he paradoxically aims to
enhance his narrative aptitudes and ethical worth, rather than
to undermine them. The narrator's alleged linguistic deficiency
justifies his use of Razumov's diary as the fount of his narrative.
His presumed lack of imagination, on the other hand, tends to
emphasize his supposed faithful rendering of the protagonist's
story, while it also props up his presumed ethical impartiality
and thus narrative reliability. This ethics of denial is a highly
convenient design for the teacher of languages, as well as for
Conrad's representation of the Russian characters and politics
in this text.[28] Basically, it enables the narrator to make assertions
about Russia's politics and moral character, without openly
committing himself, since the material on which his story is
based is supposed to be a faithful rendering of a journal written
by a Russian citizen – Razumov. Most of all, this ethics of denial
forms the backbone of the ethics of reading, or, more precisely,
the bait through which the narrator intends to hook his reader.
    Conrad is obsessed with audience, as we know, and this
obsession is reflected in the teacher of languages' constant
attempts to set up a close relation with the reader. Right from
the start, he emphatically draws his audience's attention
to his narrative identity, by dramatizing his linguistic and
creative inadequacies, in a consistent appeal to the audience's

compassion. To further emphasize his narrative humility, objectivity, and ethical credibility, the teacher professes complete incomprehension of the Russian character, sharply contrasting the West, with which he morally identifies, to the East embodied by Russia from which he distances himself. He further compares himself to "a traveller in a strange country" (169) to underline his alienation from his fictional universe and insists on his Western cultural identity or mindset to mark the Russians as radical Others. This is suggested in his repeated use of the terms "Western" and "Occidental," whenever he refers to Russian politics or moral landscape. Meanwhile, he pragmatically includes the reader in this ethnic affiliation – "we Occidentals" "to us Europeans of the West" (105, 109) – and insistently claims that his story is written for Western readers. By stressing these common cultural roots and shared moral values with his West European readers, the narrator obviously hopes to lead them to see Russia through the same moral lens:

> I wanted to bring it forward simply to make what I have to say presently of Mr. Razumov's presence in Geneva, a little more credible – for this is a Russian story for Western ears, which, as I have observed already, are not attuned to certain tones of cynicism and cruelty, of moral negation, and even of moral distress already silenced at our end of Europe. (163-64)

Aesthetics and ethics are intricately linked in *Under Western Eyes*, and generally in Conrad's fiction, and the teacher of languages steadily stresses his detachment from his fictional material to better reinforce his narrative trustworthiness. While these distancing manoeuvres and relentless self-justifications are intended to highlight his moral respectability as a member of a civilized, democratic country, they also reveal his uneasiness toward the world he describes. Conrad wrote in a letter to E. V. Lucas dated 6 October 1908 that "An author is not a monk" (*CL* 4: 137).

The teacher of languages is not, of course, Conrad, although he shares with his creator several prejudices against Russia. He is nonetheless widely moralistic despite his many disclaimers and in numerous instances he clearly speaks and behaves like a monk. He describes all the major Russian characters as being morally flawed and expects the reader to emulate his occidental prejudices about these characters and their country. Apart from Natalia Haldin, who is a marginal character, there is no Russian character of any significant ethical worth for the reader to identify with. Despite his repeated claims to ideological and ethical detachment, therefore, the teacher proves, in practice, a potent moral authority, judging and unequivocally condemning Russia and the Russians. His treatment of Russia and the Russians as a monolithic block; his absolute stigmatisation of the Russian moral character, which often verges on caricature, obviously reveals his moral bias and widely discredits the ethical credibility he self-proclaims. The eagerness with which he tends to disclose to the reader "truths" about Russia and draw an exhaustive moral and ideological portrait of this country further reinforces this bias. He states that some words used in Razumov's journal contain essential truths, if not the very truth about this country that he wishes his readers to be acquainted with. And this truth lies in the word *cynicism*, which, the narrator remarks, is the emblem of the Russian spirit.

The word *cynicism* is of the utmost significance, since, according to the narrator, it constitutes Russia's defining moral trait. Ironically, this word, used to qualify Razumov's and most of the Russian autocrats' personalities and conduct, may also be fittingly applied to the narrator's narrative and ethical identity itself. We can readily see, indeed, that the teacher of languages does not live up to his vaunted ideals of objectivity or ethical neutrality. Rather, throughout the narrative he is a prominent voice of morality, reproving one set of values while reaffirming the moral superiority of others. By emphasizing his common cultural roots and shared moral values with the reader, by dismissing Russia and the Russians as morally worthless, the teacher blatantly undermines most of his previous statements on narrative ethics, not least his ethical impartiality. He asserts with unflinching confidence sweeping and categorical judgements on both Russia and the West, in order to consolidate his Western moral identity and implicitly induce the readers to moral mimeticism, hoping to persuade them to embrace his views on the Russian moral character. He describes the West as ordered, democratic, and enlightened, while he dismisses Russia as despotic and benighted, and its political system absurd and cruel: "To us Europeans of the West, all ideas of political plots and conspiracies seem childish, crude inventions for the theatre or a novel" (*UWE* 109).

For the teacher of languages Russia and the Russian moral identity are not only abhorrent but also beyond understanding. Because Russia is, in his view, outside the Western ideological and moral compass, as is Africa for Marlow in "Heart of Darkness" or the Malay tropical nature for the anonymous narrator and his two fellow Englishmen in "Karain: A Memory." Through this process of moral defamiliarization, the teacher tends to enhance his own (Western) moral supremacy and thus ethical credibility, while dismissing Russia as an absolute moral darkness. Like Conrad, the teacher of languages is anxiously striving to secure his Western reader's interest and ethical commitment. And as he insists on being a reliable voice of the democratic, enlightened, and benevolent Occident relating to Western readers the story of Russia's obscurity, violence, and decadence, the teacher presents himself as "a helpless spectator" (336) of this absolute Eastern moral darkness unfolding before his Western eyes; and he does so to win his reader's empathy. This moral alienation of which he emphatically complains is reflected in his description of the first encounter between Razumov and Natalia Haldin: "they seemed brought out from the confused immensity of the Eastern borders to be exposed cruelly to the observation of my Western eyes. And I observed them. There was nothing else to do" (346).

As in *Nostromo*, *Lord Jim*, or "Karain: A Memory," in *Under Western Eyes*, too, ethics and theatricality are intricately linked. This is suggested in the previous statement and highlighted throughout the narrative via the teacher of languages' insistence on eyes, observation, and performance, in its various guises. The Russian politicians are described as performers in a sordid

play of violence and crime, and Russian politics is compared
to "an obscure drama." Once more, the teacher of languages
reiterates his distance from the events and characters better
to buttress his presumed ethical impartiality. The problem with
this narrator, though, is that he tends to affirm and deny what/
who he is or is not with such hyperbolic fervour that leads us to
suspect the sincerity of his statements. The core of this problem
lies in his ethics of denial itself through which, as mentioned
earlier, he seeks, in truth, to increment rather than diminish
his narrative skills and ethical credibility. His general aim is
to induce readers into a sympathetic identification with him
and, ultimately, lead them into active collaboration in the story.
In other words, the teacher mainly seeks to appear unpretentious
and thus congenial in his readers' eyes to better appeal to their
sympathy and understanding. This is an honourable goal, of
course, although the ethics of self-depreciation this narrator
uses to this effect appears dubious, as his devaluing rhetoric
finally turns out to be an oblique affirmation of his powers of
representation, rather than a genuine expression of narrative
modesty.

Significantly, the teacher's ethics of affirmation is also just
as suspect. For instance, his previous claim to being completely
detached   from   "passions,"   "prejudices,"   and   "personal
memories," intended to shore up his apparent ethical impartiality,
is sharply contradicted by his overt and abundant denigration
of the Russian characters whom he describes as being cruel,
dogmatic, prolix, cynical, mystic, childish, incomprehensible,
etc.; a depiction that connotes an ideological and moral
involvement in the material he relates. Another evidence of his
moral and ideological connivance with the fictional material lies
in the strong likelihood of his having edited the protagonist's
diary. He states: "On looking through the pages of Mr. Razumov's
diary I own that a 'rush of thoughts' is not an adequate image.
The more adequate description would be a tumult of thoughts
– the faithful reflection of the state of his feelings" (24). In
this statement, the teacher explicitly refers to his interference
with the content of Razumov's journal, by replacing words or

phrases he deems inadequate with more appropriate ones. We might as well rightly suspect other edits he does not disclose to us. More significant still, the narrator's editorial intrusion into the diary is compounded by sweeping, Manichean political views which further dent his claim to ethical impartiality. For instance, he considers democracy morally superior to autocracy, and, meantime, widely criticizes the bulk of the political systems – autocracy, revolution, and liberal democracy – in a way that smacks of pessimism and political conservatism that echo Conrad's own views. If all forms of government are equally rotten, as the narrator states, then any action or hope for social and political improvement seems pointless. The world and the people within it are inexorably caught in a permanent ethical impasse, doomed to a life of pessimism, inaction, and moral darkness, no matter their efforts. The teacher of languages states that "the spirit of Russia is the spirit of cynicism" (67). If cynicism is the key moral feature of the Russian character, as the narrator claims, we may then reasonably state that this narrator's own narrative method itself is also tainted by cynicism.[29] His blunt dismissal of autocracy, liberal democracy, and revolution as equally worthless sounds, in this respect, like crude cynicism, and anyone who lived in a system equivalent to Russian autocracy will readily find the teacher's perspective both cynical and dangerously mistaken. In any case, for the reader such pessimistic perspective must be as mystifying as is the teacher's overall relation to both his fictional material and to his audience.

The Reader as Writer:
Collaboration, Manipulation, Moral Didacticism

Conrad catered for an elite readership and his works suffered from lack of popularity, as a result of this elitist bias.[30] He also considered the reader as a dynamic force in the production of textual meaning. Conrad wrote to R. B. Cunninghame Graham in a letter dated 5 August 1897: "To know that you could read me is good news indeed – for one writes only half the book; the

other half is with the reader" (*CL* 1: 370). We wonder which
half of the book is left for the reader to write in *Under Western
Eyes*. Manifestly, the narrator in this novel overtly attempts
to engage in an ethical dialogue with his reader, whom he
perceives as a potential collaborator he tries to win over. Given
the narrator's narrative and ethical distortions, however, it is
perhaps not half the book that reader should write or re-write,
but the entire book. The narrator at once vigorously calls on
the reader's understanding and empathy, and consistently
deceives and manipulates this reader's affections and outlook,
and these ethical warps are not a particularly reliable source of
collaboration. Interestingly, the ethical inconsistencies of the
teacher of languages vividly recall Marlow's ethical perspective
in "Heart of Darkness." And as with Marlow's lie in "Heart
of Darkness," in *Under Western Eyes*, too, we are faced with
the same nagging question regarding the teacher's narrative
distortions: are his deceptions ethical or unethical? Can they
be considered morally objectionable or as necessary lies,
undertaken for higher aesthetic and readerly ends?

This remains an open question, so does the teacher's success
or failure in his efforts to entice his audience. It is difficult to
say with absolute certainty whether this unsettling narrator has
achieved his goal. What we may confidently state instead is that
Conrad has unmistakably failed to secure the much-coveted
compassion of his reading public, as he himself acknowledged
in the Author's Note to this novel: "*Under Western Eyes* on
its first appearance in England was a failure with the public,
perhaps because of that very detachment" (*UWE* viii). Perhaps
more than detachment, it is the narrator's obtuse rhetorical
schemes that constitute a serious impediment for readers.
Clearly, the novel's topic is too obscure and daunting for the
(average) reader. Besides, the narrator's perspective on his
fictional material turns out to be not as sincere and ethically
reliable as he wants his readers to believe.[31]

As in *Under Western Eyes*, in *Lord Jim*, too, the relation
between narrator and narratee/writer and reader occupies
centre stage and sheds light on Conrad's overall anxious

concern with audience. Obviously, this relation is presented in less dramatic terms in *Lord Jim*, but the narrator is equally preoccupied with narrative and ethical credibility. Although Marlow also sometimes complains of having no imagination (*LJ* 223) and of his difficulty in understanding the protagonist, he is, overall, different from the teacher of languages in both narrative approach and ethical perspective. The teacher of languages, as pointed out, self-deprecates his narrative aptitudes, and professes ethical detachment to increase his credibility. Marlow, instead, adopts a narrative method made of both self-valorization (emphasis on his humanity and knowledge of the world he describes) and self–questioning (admission of his limits as observer and narrator). Moreover, although tortuous and confusing at times, Marlow's position toward both his characters and fictional material is comparatively less ethically suspect.

From the outset, as we have seen, Marlow straightforwardly asserts his ethical position toward both Jim and the moral issues triggered by his misconduct. He unambiguously expresses compassion, solidarity, and strives to understand and justify Jim's conduct, both rationally and ethically. As Marlow in "Heart of Darkness," the narrator in *Victory* or the teacher of languages in *Under Western Eyes*, Marlow in *Lord Jim* also takes narrative and ethical reliability very seriously, as shown in his insistence on his humanity and knowledge of both the world and the moral personality of the characters he depicts. In terms of narrative representation, Marlow alternates authorial confidence and epistemic indeterminacy, suggested in his (dramatized) limited and fragmented perspective, narrative ambivalence, vagueness, and elusiveness. These various devices complement and blend with each other, to finally converge into an ethics of uncertainty[32] – Marlow's privileged mode of representation through which he intends to secure the reader's interest, collaboration, and, ultimately, compassion towards the protagonist. This ethics of uncertainty encompasses three fundamental faculties: seeing, knowing, and understanding. It consists of a set of epistemic and ethical filters through which Marlow opens the texts' ethical possibilities while avoiding definite moral meanings. Throughout, he insistently confesses to his readers his limitations in all three faculties, humbly and strategically, admitting his limited knowledge and informing them of his incapacity to clearly see and understand Jim who, despite numerous efforts, remains a "nameless shade," "an insoluble mystery" (393). Meanwhile, he assigns this narrative deficiency to his lack of imagination: "As to me, I have no imagination (I would be more certain about him to-day, if I had)" (223). It is worth noting here that although Marlow is frustrated by not seeing distinctly or understanding Jim, he remains strongly bonded to him. Marlow even explicitly states that it is this very incomprehension itself that stimulates him to strengthen his ethical bonds with Jim: "I cannot say I had ever seen him distinctly [...] but it seemed to me that the less I understood the more I was bound to him in the name of that doubt which is the inseparable part of our knowledge" (221).

Conrad suggests through Marlow's statement that incomprehension or mystery, silences and blanks are stimuli for ethical relations rather than a hindrance: they urge us to inquire and find out more about the Other, to know and understand the Other's anxieties and needs. That is what Marlow does with the elusive Jim and his repeated admission of his incomprehension and narrative doubts and inadequacies paradoxically serves as both a narrative spur and a significant ethical prompt. As he enhances his narrative modesty and thus ethical authenticity through this deft rhetorical device, he fundamentally also seeks to educe the audience's sympathetic identification with his challenging representation of the protagonist's story, while eagerly inviting this audience to actively participate in the story and "fit the pieces" of this "fragmentary" narrative in order "to make an intelligible picture" (343).

As in most of Conrad's works, narrative is entwined with ethics in *Lord Jim*, and the meaning or ethics of this text seems to waver between the words of the narrator/author and the ethical commitment of the reader. Like Conrad who expects the reader to write the other half of the book, Marlow in this narrative also conceives of reading and sense-making as a collaborative creative endeavour involving narrator, text, and reader. And faithful to Conrad's elitist outlook, the audience Marlow has in mind is both intellectually competent to stitch the fragments into a comprehensible whole, and humane enough to sympathize with both the protagonist's human frailty and the narrator's epistemic and narrative inadequacies. This ideal audience is embodied by the "privileged man" (337), also called "the privileged reader" (351), who is singled out to hear the last word of Marlow's tale.

This privileged man is entrusted with a packet that contains letters and Marlow's message to him. We notice that Marlow's decision to trust his material to this man proceeds from a shared sense of human fellowship. He tells the privileged man: "I don't suppose you've forgotten," goes on the letter. "You alone have showed an interest in him that survived the telling of his story" (338). With this final narrative twist, Marlow seals forever the story's ethical and epistemic fate: "That was all then – and there shall be nothing more; there shall be no message, unless such as each of us can interpret for himself from the language of facts, that are so often more enigmatic than the craftiest arrangement of words" (340).

Marlow expects the – privileged – reader to be both an active generator of meaning and a dynamic, conscientious ethical agent, called to position responsibly himself toward the protagonist and the ethical issues at stake. In this, Marlow appears as both a liberal ethicist and a disguised moralist. After a steady, unambiguous ethical commitment to the protagonist's predicament combined with a strong desire to draw the readers into his tale, which sounds at times like moral canvassing, he ends his narrative letting the readers freely make their ethical decisions about the meaning of the story and the ethical issues at stake – honour, courage, cowardice, betrayal, compassion, ethical responsibility, etc.

Ethical relations, as Marlow indicates through his compassion for Jim, are acts of fellowship and solidarity. The interpretative and ethical effort he demands of his readers is similarly an

instance of solidarity. This makes the overall act of reading
as framed in this novel a collective undertaking in which the
reader's epistemic, sensory, and ethical faculties of perception
are involved. In the main, for Marlow, the ethics of reading
means reading together, or, more precisely, seeing, hearing,
thinking, and sensing together,[33] in the same way as the ethics
of being entails seeing, hearing, thinking, and feeling together
with the Other. So, just as ethical being is seeing and feeling
beyond the self, ethical reading, too, is reading beyond the
surface of words and meanings, of thoughts and emotions, as
Conrad suggests in this book.

If at the novel's end Marlow leaves his readers to see and
decide for themselves, throughout the narrative, however,
he has, directly or indirectly, induced them to see with him
and together reach a common understanding of the moral
dilemma he exposes to them, in the hope of securing the
much-needed complicity of his audience's ear and gaze. In his
Preface to *The Nigger of the "Narcissus"* Conrad declared that
his main aesthetic ambition is to make the reader see, with
all the aesthetic, epistemic, and moral didacticism involved in
this statement.[34] In his final declaration, Marlow expresses his
willingness to see with his readers after he has extensively told
and shown them what to see. In this specific case, *seeing with*
means for Marlow having the readers empathize and show
ethical responsibility for Jim in the name of human frailty
and solidarity with the human condition. Thus, while Marlow
does not exactly tell the readers what ethical stance to adopt,
he nonetheless wishes them to share his ethical sympathies,
in keeping with Conrad's aesthetic and moral didacticism,
suggested in his ethics of seeing in the Preface to *The Nigger
of the "Narcissus."*

Conrad is, of course, not a moralist in the sense that Henry
Fielding, Denis Diderot or Laurence Sterne, who inspired
him, could be. He is not either an absolute nihilist or social
Darwinist, or, for that matter, a heartless, cynical sceptic, as are
some of his characters. Rather, he is a fundamentally relativist
ethicist with a clear, intransigent eye on his fellow beings' moral

contradictions and precarious ethical aspirations. While he does not offer definite answers to his protagonists' ethical dilemmas in any of his works, he nonetheless attempts to understand and often justifies their conducts, without, yet, suggesting either resolution of these moral predicaments or the possibility of achieving ethical fulfillment. In most of his texts, he stages the moral drama of the human condition in its multi-faceted complexity and keeps it eternally open, in compliance with his split ethical consciousness and love of paradox, ambiguity, vagueness, and irresolution. That is why Conrad's ethical framework is both an ethics of paradox(es) and a paradoxical ethics. And one of these essential paradoxes lies precisely in the fact that Conrad questions the relevance of ethics, in a world he considers devoid of ethical foundations and ethical purpose; meantime, he asserts the humans' need for ethical relations in the name of a wider planetary ethics of fellowship that embraces the frailty of the human condition in its universal breadth.

NOTES

[1] In an interview with Marian Dąbrowski, Conrad referred to the controversial issue of Poland's absence from his works, arguing: "English critics – and after all I am an English writer – whenever they speak of me they add that there is in me something incomprehensible, inconceivable, elusive. Only you can grasp this elusiveness, and comprehend what is incomprehensible. That is Polishness. Polishness which I took from Mickiewicz and Slowacki. My father read Pan Tadeusz aloud to me and made me read it aloud. [...] Later I liked Slowacki better. [...] Il est l'âme de toute la Pologne, lui" (Dąbrowski 199).

[2] Conrad defended his use of English as his medium of writing against his detractors. In the Author's Note to A Personal Record, he wrote: "The truth of the matter is that my faculty to write in English is as natural as any other aptitude with which I might have been born. I have a strange and over-powering feeling that it had always been an inherent part of myself. English was for me neither a matter of choice nor adoption [...]. If I had not written in English I would not have written at all" (PR v-vi). For more information on the influence of Polish language and literary tradition on Conrad's works, see Morf; Busza; Krajka, "The Past Moribund Legacy of Polishness"; Kurczaba; Najder.

[3] In an article entitled "A Pole or an Englishman?" Wiktor Gomulicki complained about the lack of Polishness in Conrad's works, declaring: "How

much happier we would be to find Polish traits in Conrad's works! But this is more difficult; in fact well-nigh impossible" (194). Indeed, apart from "Prince Roman," which directly refers to Poland's history, Conrad has never explicitly represented his native country in his fiction. Nevertheless, the image of Poland, as I have demonstrated in "The Shadow of Poland," is diffused in Conrad's fiction where "it takes the shape a "haunting shadow," or a lingering "echo that permeates the narrative" (56, 49). Conrad responded to his Polish critics in his letters, arguing that he was writing fiction not history books: "I do not write history, but fiction, and I am therefore entitled to choose as I please what is suitable in regard to characters and particulars to help me in the general impression I wish to produce" (Jean-Aubry 1: 77).

⁴   For a detailed discussion of the notion of *planetarity*, see Spivak.

⁵   In "Amy Foster," Yanko Gooral's stigmatized cultural and ethnic difference echoes the view of some of Conrad's contemporary fellow writers, such as H. G. Wells, who spoke of Conrad's "ineradicable" or "implacable" foreignness. Other terms like "Oriental" were also used by Ford Maddox Ford, Richard Curle, Henry Newbolt, and Jessie Conrad to describe Conrad. Jessie Conrad once referred to her husband as an "almost Oriental aristocrat" (Meyers 136). Rudyard Kipling similarly pointed out Conrad's un-Englishness, stating: "When I am reading him [...] I always have the impression that I am reading an excellent translation of a foreign author" (Meyers 209).

⁶   See Acheraïou, *Joseph Conrad and the Reader*, specifically the chapter on British reception, 49-66.

⁷   See Kant.

⁸   For further insights into the notion of betrayal in *Under Western Eyes,* see Delesalle-Nancey. For a discussion of ethics and politics in this novel, see Carabine; Hollander; Panichas.

⁹   Erdinast-Vulcan 95.

¹⁰   Levinas 56.

¹¹   For more information on Nietzsche's influence on Conrad, see Butte.

¹²   Conrad may have been disenchanted by revolutions after Poland's numerous failed attempts to overthrow the Russian oppressor. He strongly expressed his doubts about revolutions in both his essays and fiction. In "Autocracy and War," for example, he criticized the French Revolution which he dismissed as mostly a means of violence and a source of moral and intellectual degradation: "The degradation of the ideas of freedom and justice at the root of the French Revolution is made manifest in the person of its heir; a personality without law or faith, whom it has been the fashion to represent as an eagle, but who was, in truth, more like a sort of vulture preying upon the body of a Europe which did, indeed, for some dozen of years, very much resemble a corpse" (*NLL* 86). In *Under Western Eyes* Conrad's anti-revolution sentiment pervades the narrative and is reflected in his narrator's depiction of revolutionary characters such as Peter Ivanovitch and Sophia Antonovna. The narrator caustically calls the first the "great author of the revolutionary gospels" (*UWE* 148) and "the arch-priest of Revolution" (210), while he describes the second

as "the true spirit of destructive revolution" (261). The narrator further labels Haldin a "sanguinary fanatic" (34) and equates revolution with tyranny, stating that Razumov's life has been destroyed by "Haldin's revolutionary tyranny" (82). Conrad's view on revolutions is certainly best rendered in the following statement where the narrator gives vent to his disillusionment about revolutionary ideals: "A violent revolution falls into the hands of narrow-minded fanatics and of tyrannical hypocrites at first. Afterwards comes the turn of all the pretentious intellectual failures of the time. Such are the chiefs and the leaders. You will notice that I have left out the mere rogues. The scrupulous and the just, the noble, humane, and devoted natures; the unselfish and the intelligent may begin a movement – but it passes away from them. They are not the leaders of a revolution. They are its victims" (134).

[13] Schopenhauer 140.

[14] Schopenhauer 142.

[15] For more details on this influence, see Panagopoulos; Madden.

[16] In this letter of 11 November 1901, Conrad wrote: "One must explore deep and believe the incredible to find the few particles of truth floating in an ocean of insignificance. [...] You want more scepticism at the very foundation of your work. Scepticism, the tonic of minds, the tonic of life, the agent of truth – the way of art and salvation" (CL 2: 359). For other insights into the issue of skepticism in Conrad's works, see Wollaeger.

[17] Bakhtin 311-12.

[18] For more information on this dialectical ethics of thought and action in Nostromo, see Acheraïou, "Action is consolatory."

[19] In a similar vein, Watt argued that the society "Heart of Darkness" depicts is "so widely and deeply fissured by its contradictions between its pretenses and its realities" (235).

[20] For additional insights into the ethics of dehumanisation in this novella, see Romanick Baldwin.

[21] For a detailed discussion of the notions of otherness/alterity, see Acheraïou, "Nina and Nedjma"; Krajka, Various Dimensions of the Other; Sewlall; Tenenbaum.

[22] The notion of duality is a recurrent theme in Conrad's fiction. Leggatt in "The Secret Sharer" is a mirror-image figure who carries some of the young skipper's "shadow," Razumov is perceived as a younger version of the teacher of languages, Lingard in Almayer's Folly as Almayer's idealised self, etc. The motif of the double may be seen as a symptom of a split ethical consciousness, which often leads the characters to existential crisis, ethical inconsistencies, skepticism, etc. For further details, see Batchelor's discussion of the motif of the double in Under Western Eyes and Lord Jim (181-82).

[23] The ethics of natural justice is, for example, eloquently expressed in Plato's Socratic Dialogues where it is embodied by Callicles; see Irwin. In contemporary criticism, the ethics of natural justice equates what is commonly referred to as social Darwinism. On Conrad and Darwinism, see Hunter.

[24] Roberts 142.

²⁵ For other insights into self-consciousness, see Hawthorn.

²⁶ See Acheraïou, *Joseph Conrad and the Reader*; Lothe; Szittya.

²⁷ In "Autocracy and War" Conrad wrote: "Prince Bismarck has been really complimentary to the useful phantom of the autocratic might. There is an awe-inspiring idea of infinity conveyed in the word *Néant* – and in Russia there is no idea. She is not a *Néant*, she is and has been simply the negation of everything worth living for. She is not an empty void, she is a yawning chasm open between East and West; a bottomless abyss that has swallowed up every hope of mercy, every aspiration towards personal dignity, towards freedom, towards knowledge, every ennobling desire of the heart, every redeeming whisper of conscience" (*NLL* 100).

²⁸ For an extensive discussion of Conrad's representation of politics in his works, see Hay.

²⁹ For a detailed study of Conrad's narrative methods, see Lothe.

³⁰ *Under Western Eyes* is manifestly addressing an elite reader, as Kermode; Higdon; and Greaney pointed out. Furthermore, the three critics refer to the reader of *Under Western Eyes* as a "victim" or "scapegoat" of the narrator's various rhetorical ruses and ironies. I think that the notion of victim should be understood in two ways. The reader is obviously a victim of the narrator's rhetorical manipulations and deceptions, but the narrator, too, is a victim of his own self-dramatization that ultimately undermines his narrative and ethical credibility, as shown in this chapter. For a further discussion of Conrad's elitism and relation to readership, see also Acheraïou *Joseph Conrad and the Reader.*

³¹ In other contexts it is "foreignness" or Polishness that Conrad invoked to account for the commercial failure of some of his works. Expressing his disappointment about *The Secret Agent*, he declared: "*The Secret Agent* may be pronounced by now an honourable failure. It brought me neither love nor promise of literary success. I own that I am cast down. I suppose I am a fool to have expected anything else. I suppose there is something in me that is unsympathetic to the general public [...]. Foreignness I suppose" (*CL* 4: 9-10).

³² The ethics of uncertainty, prominent in *Lord Jim*, echoes Conrad's artistic anxieties which, he remarked, arose from his shift from the simple artistic phase of *Almayer's Folly* and *An Outcast of the Islands* to what he called the sophisticated period of his later works. In a letter to E. L. Sanderson dated 21 November 1896, Conrad wrote: "Gone are, alas! those fine days of *Alm: Folly* when I wrote with the serene audacity of an unsophisticated fool. I am getting more sophisticated from day to day. And more uncertain!" (*CL* 1: 139).

³³ By "sensing" I mean here both *making sense* and *feeling*.

³⁴ "My task which I am trying to achieve is, by the power of the written word to make you hear, to make you feel – it is, before all, to make you *see*. That – and no more, and it is everything" (Preface, *NN* x).

WORKS CITED

Acheraïou, Amar. "'Action is Consolatory': The Dialectics of Thought and Action in *Nostromo*." *Nostromo: Centennial Essays*. Ed. Allan H. Simmons and J. H. Stape. Amsterdam: Rodopi, 2004. Print. *The Conradian*.

---. *Joseph Conrad and the Reader: Questioning Modern Theories of Narrative and Readership*. Basingstoke: Palgrave Macmillan, 2009. Print.

---. "Nina and Nedjma: The Tension between the Pure and the Murky." *L'Époque conradienne* 28 (2002): 85-96. Print.

---. "The Shadow of Poland." *A Return to the Roots: Conrad, Poland and East-Central Europe*. Ed. Wiesław Krajka. Boulder: Social Science Monographs; Lublin: Maria Curie-Skłodowska U; New York: Columbia UP, 2004. 47-70. Print. Vol. 13 of *Conrad: Eastern and Western Perspectives*. Ed. Wicsław Krajka. 30 vols. to date. 1992- .

---, and Nursel Içöz, eds. *Joseph Conrad and the Orient*. Boulder: East Europen Monographs; Lublin: Maria Curie-Skłodowska UP; New York: Columbia UP, 2012. Print. Vol. 21 of *Conrad: Eastern and Western Perspectives*. Ed. Wiesław Krajka. 30 vols. to date. 1992- .

Bakhtin, Mikhail. *Art and Answerability: Early Essays of Mikhail Bakhtin*. Trans. Vadim Liapunov. Ed. Michael Holquist and Vadim Liapunov. Austin: Texas UP, 1990. Print.

Batchelor, John. *The Life of Joseph Conrad: a Critical Biography*. Oxford: Blackwell, 1994. Print.

Busza, Andrzej. "Conrad's Polish Literary Background and Some Illustrations of the Influence of Polish Literature on His Work." *Antemurale* 10 (1966): 109-247. Print.

Butte, George. "What Silenus Knew: Conrad's Uneasy Debt to Nietzsche." *Comparative Literature* 41 (1989): 155-69. Print.

Carabine, Keith. "'No Action is Simple': Betrayal and Confession in Conrad's *Under Western Eyes* and Ngugi's *A Grain of Wheat*." *Conrad at the Millennium: Modernism, Postmodernism, Postcolonialism*. Ed. Gail Fincham and Attie De Lange with Wiesław Krajka. Boulder. Social Science Monographs; Lublin: Maria Curie-Skłodowska U; New York: Columbia UP, 2001. 233-71. Print. Vol. 10 of *Conrad: Eastern and Western Perspectives*. Ed. Wiesław Krajka. 30 vols. to date. 1992- .

Dąbrowski, Marian. "An Interview with Joseph Conrad." 1917. Najder, *Familial Eyes* 196-201.

Delesalle-Nancey, Catherine. "Underground Explosion: The Ethics of Betrayal in *Under Western Eyes* and Malcolm Lowry's *Under the Volcano*." *The Conradian* 36.2 (2011): 79-94. Print.

Erdinast-Vulcan, Daphna. "The Subject-in-Process: The Question of Ethics in *Under Western Eyes*." *The Conradian* 36.2 (2011): 95-105. Print.

Gomulicki, Wiktor. "A Pole or an Englishman?" 1905. Najder, *Familial Eyes* 193-96.

Greaney, Michael. *Conrad, Language, and Narrative*. Cambridge: Cambridge UP, 2001. Print.

Hawthorn, Jeremy. *Joseph Conrad, Language and Fictional Self-Consciousness*. London: Arnold, 1979. Print.

Hay, Eloise Knapp. *The Political Novels of Joseph Conrad: A Critical Study*. Chicago: U of Chicago P, 1963. Print.

Higdon, David Leon. "'His Helpless Prey': Conrad and the Aggressive Text." *The Conradian* 12.2 (1987): 108-21. Print.

Hollander, Rachel. "Thinking Otherwise: Ethics and Politics in Joseph Conrad's *Under Western Eyes*." *Journal of Modern Literature* 38.3 (2015): 1-19. Print.

Hunter, Allan. *Joseph Conrad and the Ethics of Darwinism: The Challenges of Science*. London: Helm, 1983. Print.

Irwin, Terence. *Plato's Ethics*. Oxford: Oxford UP, 1995. Print.

Jean-Aubry, Georges. *Joseph Conrad: Life and Letters*. Vol. 1. London: Heinemann, 1927. Print.

Kant, Immanuel. *Groundwork for the Metaphysics of Morals*. Ed. and trans. Allen W. Wood. New Haven: Yale UP, 2002. Print.

Kermode, Frank. "Secrets and Narrative Sequence." *Essays on Fiction 1971-1982*. By Kermode. London: Routledge, 1983. Print.

Krajka, Wiesław. "The Past Moribund Legacy of Polishness? The Case of Joseph Conrad." *East-Central European Traumas and a Millennial Condition*. Ed. Zbigniew Białas and Wiesław Krajka. Boulder: East European Monographs; Lublin: Maria Curie-Sklodowska U; New York: Columbia UP, 1999. 19-40. Print.

---, ed. *Various Dimensions of the Other in Joseph Conrad's Fiction*. Lublin: Maria Curie-Skłodowska UP; New York: Columbia UP, 2020. Print. Vol. 29 of *Conrad: Eastern and Western Perspectives*. Ed. Wiesław Krajka. 30 vols. to date. 1992- .

Kurczaba, Alex S., ed. *Conrad and Poland*. Boulder: East European Monographs; Lublin: Maria Curie-Sklodowska U; New York: Columbia UP, 1996. Print. Vol. 5 of *Conrad: Eastern and Western Perspectives*. Ed. Wieslaw Krajka. 30 vols. to date. 1992- .

Levinas, Emmanuel. *Otherwise than Being or Beyond Essence*. Trans. Alphonso Lingis. Boston: Kluwer, 1995. Print.

Lothe, Jakob. *Conrad's Narrative Method*. Oxford: Clarendon P, 1989. Print.

Madden, Fred. "The Ethical Dimensions of 'Heart of Darkness' and *Lord Jim*: Conrad's Debt to Schopenhauer." *Conradiana* 31 (1999): 42-62. Print.

Meyers, Jeffrey. *Joseph Conrad: A Biography*. London: Murray, 1991. Print.

Morf, Gustav. *The Polish Heritage of Joseph Conrad*. London: Sampson Law, 1930. Print.

Najder, Zdzisław, ed. *Conrad under Familial Eyes*. Trans. Halina Carroll-Najder. Cambridge: Cambridge UP, 1983. Print.

---. *Conrad's Polish Background: Letters to and from Polish Friends*. Trans. Halina Carroll. London: Oxford UP, 1964. Print.

Panagopoulos, Nic. *The Fiction of Joseph Conrad: The Influence of Schopenhauer and Nietzsche*. New York: Lang, 1998. Print. Vol. 12 of *Anglo-American Studies*.

Panichas, George A. *Joseph Conrad: His Moral Vision*. Macon: Mercer UP, 2005. Print.

Roberts, Andrew Michael. "Conrad and the Territory of Ethics." *Conradiana* 37 (2005): 133-46. Print.

Romanick Baldwin, Debra. "The Horror and the Human: The Politics of Dehumanization in *Heart of Darkness* and Primo Levi's *Se questo è un uomo*." *Conradiana* 37 (2005): 185-204. Print.

Schopenhauer, Arthur. "The Foundation of Ethics." *On the Basis of Morality*. By Schopenhauer. 1841. Trans. E. F. J. Payne. Indianapolis: Bobbs-Merrill, 1965. Print.

Sewlall, Harry. "'A Story of a Magnificent Savage': Interrogating Alterity in 'Karain: A Memory.'" Acheraïou and Içöz 113-32.

Spivak, Gayatri Chakravorty. *Death of a Discipline*. New York: Columbia UP: New York, 2003. Print.

Szittya, Penn R. "Metafiction: The Double Narration in *Under Western Eyes*." *English Literary History* 48.4 (1981): 817–40. Print.

Tenenbaum, David. "The Continental Divide: Ethics and Alterity in Conrad's Lingard Trilogy." Acheraïou and Içöz 133-56.

Watt, Ian. *Conrad in the Nineteenth Century*. Berkeley: U of California P, 1979. Print.

Wollaeger, Mark A. *Joseph Conrad and the Fictions of Skepticism*. Stanford: Stanford UP, 1990. Print.

Aileen Miyuki Farrar,
Nova Southeastern University,
Fort Lauderdale, FL, USA

Narrative Autophagy and the Ethics
of Storytelling in "Heart of Darkness"

Jean-Paul Sartre states in "Intentionality," "to know is to eat."[1] In travel accounts of the long nineteenth century, ranging from Olaudah Equiano's *The Interesting Narrative* (1789) and Mungo Park's *Travels in the Interior Districts of Africa* (1799) to Sir Henry Morton Stanley's *Through the Dark Continent* (1878) and Henry Rider Haggard's *King Solomon's Mines* (1885), fiction and nonfiction storytellers had an obligation to legitimize their narratives and thereby uphold the guarantee of honest consumerism. Travel narratives could demonstrate this through their cr/edibility; that is, the narrators' promise that their product is safe to consume, the act of consumption potentially taking the shape of a shared meal ensuring no poisoned food or, as is the case in Joseph Conrad's "Heart of Darkness," cannibalism. By making himself the subject of the tale he purports, a storyteller demonstrates that his food is edible, his narrative credible, and he trustworthy. In Conrad's "Heart of Darkness," Self is the food of memoir, a means of literary and philosophical realism that captures not absolute moral truths but the significance of discourse. Marlow, the authorial persona, fulfills the travel narrative imperative with a myth of autophagy that not only confronts the challenges of authenticating an egotistical Self but explores the ethics of representation and storytelling.

Many critics have noted what F. R. Leavis distinguished as Marlow's "adjectival insistence,"[2] some remarking that for one so talkative, he seems to say distressingly little.[3] As T. S. Eliot remarks, "Mr. Conrad has no ideas, but he has a point of view, a 'world,' it can hardly be defined, but it pervades his work and is unmistakable."[4] This nebulosity makes pinpointing Conrad's ethical concerns simultaneously more and less problematic. With more yet less to ascertain, the ubiquitous concern repeatedly addressed in Conrad's novels – colonialism and the confrontation between the "civilized" and "savage" – risks feeling agonizingly abstract. Chinua Achebe famously reads Marlow's longwinded loquacity as ultimately silencing and misrepresenting African bodies:

> It is clearly not part of Conrad's purpose to confer language on the "rudimentary souls" of Africa. In place of speech they made "a violent babble of uncouth sounds." They "exchanged short grunting phrases" even among themselves. But most of the time they were too busy with their frenzy.[5]

Achebe claims that Conrad is a "thoroughgoing racist" who has thoughtlessly promoted a thesis-antithesis foil for Africa and England while conveniently insulating himself from condemnations and hiding behind a framed narrative.[6]

Achebe's aggressive denunciation raises serious concerns, leading many critics to ask whether or not the novella dehumanizes Africans, and responses are typically complex. Some, such as Masood Ashraf Raja, have plumbed Conrad's corpus, especially the Malay novels, and come to the conclusion that Achebe's critique would be inconsistent with Conrad's other works. Debra Romanick Baldwin, likewise, refuses to easily dismiss Marlow's struggle in confronting his prejudices and instead favors perceiving that process as a collective challenge to readers to examine that which binds humanity together.[7] Others have dissected Achebe's premises and Conrad's language, again underscoring the slipperiness of Conrad's "Heart of Darkness." Analyzing the messiness of the term *racism*, Peter Firchow concludes that the novella technically is "no more than weakly racist [against Africans] [...] for it recognizes [the Africans'] difference from Europeans as a separate race but does not suggest an essential superiority," albeit it implies a "temporary cultural superiority."[8] Whereas certain phrases in the novella have been incendiary for Achebe, other critics have found those same words optimistic. Marlow's identification of "kinship" between him and his helmsman or the description of his crew as, "Fine fellows – cannibals – in their place" ("Heart of Darkness," YS 119, 94), are ambiguous enough to support readings of the text as both dehumanizing[9] and potentially humanizing.[10]

From Achebe's stance, even if Marlow is not guilty of "strong racism," as Firchow sates, i.e. even if the most racist attitude about the book is that there is a preference for the English over other Europeans or that the Europeans appear more brutal than the Africans,[11] the unfortunate irony in the face of Marlow's interminable and indeterminable utterances is that the Africans remain, in Achebe's view, largely silent "backdrops."[12] As Achebe remarks, the Africans only speak to affirm the horrors of Africa, to suggest open cannibalism and announce Kurtz's death.[13] In this way, it may be maintained that the Africans are mere accessories to the European craving for validation to distinguish them from the "savage" Other. Achebe demands responsible representation. The question is: does Conrad's novella practice ethical storytelling?

Ethics of Storytelling

Is it possible to represent an Other, whose experiences are not the same as the Self, without reducing the Other to an object? As long as one perceives ontology as a totality of Other and Self, a zero-sum equation where the two subjectivities may merge to form one absolute objectivity, such representation is not possible. Viewing the Africans as a Saidian projection of the Occidental Self, where Other is Self, or as a Hegelian thesis-antithesis and complementary body limits the identity of the Other as not-Self. It is Self-reliant ontologies like these that become problematic in postcolonial readings since representations of the Other will only ever be representations of the Self. Within this framework, one may turn to postmodern critics like Donna Haraway who interrogates the power dynamics of *articulation* (speaking for oneself) and *representation* (speaking for Others): "Where we need to move is not 'back' to nature, but *elsewhere*, through and within an artifactual social nature."[14] Haraway explodes the totalistic *logos* of Self-Other in order to locate an allochronic and allotopic condition for those "inappropriate/d others" who do not fit in the dominant Western ideology of binaries.[15] In this way, defining the Other is not internal to the Self but external and relational, i.e. not binary but cosmic. As Marlow says, "meaning [...][is] not inside like a kernel but outside, enveloping the tale which brought it out [...] as a glow brings out a haze" ("Heart of Darkness," YS 48). Haraway's claim that humans must move "elsewhere" rather than "back" is similar to Jacques Derrida's in *The Animal That Therefore I Am (More to Follow)*, where he deconstructs the anthropocentric metanarrative associated with Genesis by arguing that it is the human who "follows" the animal forward in both evolution and phenomenology.[16] The finite ideology of modern binaries must give way to the infinitude of multi-directionality and polyvocality. In short, an ethical representation of the Other cannot happen within a totalistic *logos* but it can exist in a postcolonial, posthuman, or poststructuralist *ethos* and exploration of ontology.

The nineteenth century was a time of totalizing *logos*-based ethics that emphasized traditionally non-ethical concepts, such as pleasure and utility, to explain social relations and obligations. Darwinian evolutionary theory gave rise to Social Darwinism and aesthetic Naturalism. These excused at best and exalted at worst the framing of human behaviors not as altruistic, as was valued by pre-Modernist humanism, but as an economy of egos and self-fulness, a redundancy of individual consciousnesses competing to fulfill their wants and needs. As Herbert Spencer, extrapolating from Darwinian theory in his *Principles of Biology* (1864), popularly declares, all is a "survival of the fittest." In the years preceding Conrad's "Heart of Darkness," Thomas H. Huxley, "Darwin's bull-dog," furthered the conversation, arguing in his seminal lecture, "Evolution and Ethics" (1893), that it would be with ease that humans slip back into their atavistic selves; society is in a constant state of struggle against its animal nature. Obverse to Darwin's optimistic conception of progressive evolution, Spencer's and Huxley's skepticism sharpened the bleak *fin-de-siècle* anxiety of degeneration and belief in a greedy "dog-eat-dog" world. Allan Hunter finds traces of direct engagement with these views in "Heart of Darkness." Most notably, Marlow's opening lines – "I was thinking of very old times, when the Romans first came here, nineteen hundred years ago – the other day [...] darkness was here yesterday" (49) – echo the whimsy of Huxley's Prolegomena, added to the first publication of "Evolution and Ethics": "It may be assumed that, two thousand years ago, before Caesar set foot in Southern Britain, the whole countryside visible from the windows of the room in which I write was in what is called 'a state of nature.'"[17] While Huxley and Marlow both operate from the same national history, Huxley locks society indoors, where one may hunker down and safely peer out upon the long-distant past and human primitive state. On the other hand, Marlow locates human "savagery" recently, only "yesterday," situating wild humanity and social humanity in close proximity, implying that there can be no backsliding when all human conditions are omnihistorical. As the steamboat navigates up the Congo, Marlow suspects he is "travelling back to the earliest beginnings of the world," because as Conrad's novella makes clear, the past is not past at all but constantly made present ("Heart of Darkness," YS 92.) "Heart of Darkness" consistently reminds readers of this with its haunted recollections and framed narrative form.

A recollection of Self is not the same as a representation of Other. Emmanuel Levinas insists that an Other is essential to ethical living. It is in the Levinasian giving of oneself that Conrad locates his ethical responsibility as an author. Before Derrida and Haraway expanded ethics into the nonhuman domain, Levinas set the foundation for confronting ontological imperialism. He pinpoints the fallacies of a totalistic *logos* that identifies the Other as Self, notably comparing this "I am I" ipseity to the "famous serpent grasping itself by biting onto its tail."[18] This vision of the imperialistic, or self-revolving and

self-consuming, ouroboros will be significant in this argument
as a metaphor for discoursing on ethical living, responsible
representation, and social duty. For the moment, it is important
to note that Levinas submits the ouroboros as an antithetical
condition of ethical being.

As mentioned above, social existence necessitates recognition
of an Other who must remain always and absolutely Other,
or not subsumable to the Self. This equal power of the Other
can be threatening.[19] Thus, while Marlow's evident laboring
over cultural biases may be discomfiting, it is his struggle
that is ultimately encouraging. Encounters with those who
are wholly separated from his Self disables Marlow from fully
understanding his situations, explaining the repeated aporetic
gaps in his narrative: whether the drums "meant war, peace, or
prayer, *we could not tell.* [...] The prehistoric man was cursing
us, praying to us, welcoming us – *who could tell?*" ("Heart of
Darkness," *YS* 95-96; emphasis added). It is the Europeans'
misunderstanding of the Africans that leads to hostilities. The
Dane whom Marlow replaces at the beginning of the narrative
had imagined himself slighted over only two hens yet ends
up dead in the subsequent "scuffle with the natives" (53).
To get the carriers to simply carry his corpulent companion,
Marlow attempts an energetic speech in English complete
with commanding gestures, only to find his companion later
unceremoniously ditched in a bush (72). Upon guardedly
throwing overboard the corpse of his loyal helmsman without
consulting any others, Marlow finds he has scandalized both
Africans and Europeans (120).

The Other who has the sovereignty to oppose the Self will
always implicate struggle, but the most ultimate struggle is
the one for life. Resistance comes not from the body but from
the face. Levinas explains the face "expresses itself. The face
brings a notion of truth"; it is the "idea of the other in me" while
recognizing the complete autonomy of the Other from "me";
it is the "primordial expression" that imposes one's common
vulnerability, the imperative: "You shall not commit murder."[20]
This forceful entreaty is loudly stamped upon the silence of

every African face recounted in Marlow's story, compelling
him to respond. In Matadi, Marlow is affronted by starving
and sunken eyes, "enormous and vacant," prompting him to
offer a biscuit ("Heart of Darkness," YS 66). He encounters
this hungry face over and over. On the river, he is rattled by
the visage, "fierce and steady," that leaps from the gloom and
multiplies into many, swarming "naked breasts, arms, legs,
glaring eyes" attacking his steamboat (110). Outside Kurtz's
home, he is sickened by the symbolic heads on sticks: "they
were expressive and puzzling [...] food for thought and also
for the vultures" (130). The memory of his dying helmsman,
whom he purportedly valued more than Kurtz, haunts him:
"his lustrous and inquiring glance enveloped us both. I declare
it looked as though he would presently put to us some question
in an understandable language; but he died without uttering
a sound" (112). The helmsman's craving becomes Marlow's
craving as their shared experiences render him skeptical and
searching. Gazing upon the glittering "stillness on the face"
of the immense river, Marlow's thoughts become restless and
open-ended:

> "What were we who had strayed in here? Could we handle that dumb
> thing, or would it handle us? I felt how big, how confoundedly big,
> was that thing that couldn't talk, and perhaps was deaf as well. [...]
> Do you see the story? Do you see anything? It seems to me I am trying
> to tell you a dream – making a vain attempt, because no relation
> of a dream can convey the dream-sensation, that commingling of
> absurdity, surprise, and bewilderment in a tremor of struggling revolt
> [...]." He was silent for a while. (81–82)

Marlow's questions evolve in short order from those focusing
on self-preservation to those concerned with conveying
representation, finally collapsing into Conrad's most expressive
utterance: silence, a freedom from one's egotism. The gaze
of Marlow's helmsman, of his audience, of Conrad, and of
Conrad's readers are each the same; in the silence there is not
a *need* that the Other must fulfill – for the Self is complete on its
own (as is the Other) – but a *desire*. Just as the Other hungers,
it feeds, surrendering not power and control, but granting

freedom and potentiality. As Levinas states, "To recognize the Other is to recognize a hunger. To recognize the Other is to give."[21] While it might be argued that Marlow ultimately swallows the imperial line, creating a closed narrative that refuses recognition of the Other, Conrad supplies an open and generous one, inviting social discourse.

To write the novella, Conrad drew from his own experiences as an employee in 1890 of the newly formed *Société Anonyme Belge pour le Commerce du Haut-Congo* in the Congo Free State. His experiences haunted him, inspiring visceral writings including a journal, "The Congo Diary" (1890), the short story "An Outpost of Progress" (1897), the novella "Heart of Darkness," the essay "Geography and Some Explorers" (1924), and a multitude of references in letters. The strength of his memories is so impressive that, as many have noted, readers are able to identify the setting even though Africa and the Congo are never named, the Congo only appearing as "the big river." Africa left a physical imprint on Conrad as well. Allan Simmons suggests that it was Conrad's poor health, precipitated by his six months in Africa, that contributed to his decision to abandon prospects of a livelihood at sea in favor of a career in writing informed, yet unformed, by his experiences in Africa.[22]

Conrad's writings circumnavigate his experiences, and this apparent serpentine approach is central to his philosophy of how writing should perform. Just as Achebe criticizes Conrad for writing irresponsibly, Conrad felt frustrated with his contemporaries. In "A Glance at Two Books," he is incisive against the "national English novelist" who far from realizing his writing as "an achievement of active life by which he will produce certain definite effects upon the emotions of his readers" instead presents "an instinctive, often unreasoned, outpouring of his own emotions" (*LE* 132). He claimed the novelist "has no such clear conception of his craft," i.e., no conception that writing should be "an enterprise as much as the conquest of a colony" (132). It is not the emotion that Conrad condemns but the incompleteness with which one articulates subjectivity. In his letters, he instructs another ex-seaman and aspiring writer, Edward Noble (1857-1941), to "give yourself up to your emotions (no easy task)":

> [to] treat events only as illustrative of human sensation – as the outward sign of inward feelings [...] you must squeeze out of yourself every sensation, every thought, every image – mercilessly [...] you must search them for the image, for the glamour, for the right expression. (*CL* 1: 252)

Prescient of Levinas's ethics of generosity, what Conrad envisions is an utterly total giving of oneself. In a letter dated 28 October 1895, he states: "You must do it so that at the end of your day's work you should feel exhausted, emptied of every sensation and every thought, with a blank mind and an aching heart, with the notion that there is nothing – nothing left in you" (252).

This seemingly esoteric self-abnegation grounds the "truth" towards which Conrad strives, not in representation of an objective reality – such is impossible – but in "situated knowledges," to borrow a term from Haraway, that is just as factual as history. In comments on Henry James, published in *The North American Review*, Conrad observes:

> Fiction is history, human history, or it is nothing. But it is also more than that; it stands on firmer ground, being based on the reality of forms and the observation of social phenomena, whereas history is based on documents and the reading of print and handwriting – on second-hand impression. Thus fiction is nearer truth. [...][A] novelist is a historian, the preserver, the keeper, the expounder of human experience.[23]

Reminiscent of an Aristotelian perspective, Conrad favors fiction over history. However, while Aristotle's preference is justified by the ability of literature to universalize and thus access the grander truths of an outer, material reality, Conrad does not wish to delimit lived experience but to plumb it further for interstitial expressions of reality between the Self and Other.

The Problematics of Literary Cannibalism

While the novella in its entirety indicts imperialism, Conrad entirely gives of himself through a complex irony exploring Marlow's ignorance, showcasing a European's nationalistic preconceptions, as well as skepticism towards imperial ideology. Marlow often unwittingly reveals the grotesque ideality of imperialism, i.e., the concurrence of benevolent rhetoric alongside ignoble dehumanization. At first, he appears to concede that taking away land from those with a "different complexion or slightly flatter noses" is "not a pretty thing," but he quickly undermines any potential good in this statement by sagely insisting that "[w]hat redeems it is the idea only [...] and an unselfish belief in the idea" ("Heart of Darkness," YS 51). He continues to consistently critique imperial endeavors, such as the building of the railway, only when they appear to have "no [...] moral purpose" while increasingly revealing his limitations (87). He exposes a racist myopia in his surprise that the Africans on his steamboat are strangers to the area further inland, even though "their homes [are] *only* eight hundred miles away" (102-03; emphasis added), and he finds little contradiction in the alarming account of the "gentle," "quiet" Dane who "whacked the old nigger mercilessly" because he needed to assert his "self-respect" (54). In short, Marlow fails to comprehend the many inconsistencies in his thinking. Most fundamentally, he fails to recognize how he mirrors those he critiques. He judges the Russian for his continued devotion to Kurtz even though Kurtz thanklessly threatened his life over ivory (130). Meanwhile, Marlow continues to defend Kurtz and lie for him (e.g., to the Intended) after discovering that Kurtz ordered the attack on the river that led to the tragic death of his helmsman. The dream of conquest silhouetted in the novella is a dangerously puerile one, fueled by boys delighted in coloring maps, as Marlow did in his youth (52), and sustained by common men who have thoroughly fashioned their minds and bodies after the ideology of that map, like the Russian whose harlequin dress quite significantly echoes the parti-colored dream (122).

Conrad's authorial giving of oneself combats imperial selfishness, but self-sacrifice is not the same as generosity. In fact, it is the myth of paternal benevolence, or the pretense of self-sacrifice within imperial rhetoric, that the novella ousts as reprehensibly totalizing and cannibalistic. To be clear, as David Gill notes, not all types of cannibalism appear to be the target of Conrad's criticism.[24] While many have interpreted Kurtz's "unspeakable rites" (118) to indicate the taboo ritual of cannibalism, others like Firchow point out that cannibalism in the novella is not "unspeakable" at all.[25] Typical of Conrad's elusive style, the word *cannibalism* appears only twice, both times describing the twenty Africans hired as crewmembers for Marlow's steamboat, but Marlow goes into some detail explaining his cannibal crew's alternate diet of rotten hippo meat and marveling at their unexpected "restraint" (94). What makes Kurtz's metaphorical and potentially real acts of cannibalism objectionable is that they serve no social purpose. He does not cannibalize as a last resort to survive nor is his cannibalism part of cultural rituals that contribute to social bonds. His is gratuitous and, as the heads on stakes facing the house demonstrate, circumscribed and self-feeding.

While Kurtz's intentions distinguish him from Marlow's crew, cannibalism as a trope remains blindly, and in this sense potentially irresponsibly, all-consuming. Its semantics are indiscriminately promiscuous. In "Heart of Darkness," language, in general, evades clarity. Such ambiguity impresses upon audiences the duplicitous nature of imperial rhetoric. As Marlow observes, names such as Gran' Bassam and Little Popo are a "sordid farce acted in front of a sinister black-cloth" (61), and although starstruck by Kurtz, even Marlow expresses incredulity when he hears that the beheaded Africans were supposedly "rebels" (132). Words, just like stories, risk appearing stubbornly categorical. Kurtz naming the Africans "enemies, criminals, workers," and "rebels" is evidence of an inequitable monologic rhetoric (132). Similarly, the cannibal trope has been appropriated for colonial purposes. Harry Sewlall, echoing Achebe's concerns with Conrad, explains that the historical assignation of cannibalism as an "ontological category" contributed greatly to the justification of imperial rule.[26] Rather than consider foreign cultures for "who" they were, imperialism superciliously designated "what" they were: good or bad. Cannibalism finds its place in these discourses of difference and identity and has been used over the centuries to negatively label a gamut of "Others," invoking colorful ideas of evilness, witches, head-hunting, bestiality, werewolves, and vampires.[27] Thus the trope has historically served as a pretense for annihilating subjugated peoples, such as Jews, Catholics, and slaves.[28] In "Heart of Darkness," the use of cannibalism becomes ambiguous when it serves a dual purpose of justifying Kurtz's imperial ego, at the same time that it gives shape to Conrad's indictment against totalizing imperialism. The act of cannibalism aptly mirrors the colonizer's projected appetite to acquire capital and commodities and to assimilate the "Other" into the "Self."[29] As Spencer fiercely asserts in a letter to Moncure Conway on 17 July 1898, European imperialism is quite simply "social cannibalism."[30]

Kurtz headlines as an enigmatic cannibal. Kurtz, the man into whom "All Europe contributed to the making," the "universal genius" who might have been a musician, painter, journalist, or politician, whose beloved Intended faithfully awaited his return, is surrounded by the paraphernalia of barbarism (117, 154). The ghoulish trophies ornamenting the perimeter of Kurtz's home suggest head-hunting, which in the nineteenth century was associated with cannibalism,[31] and while Marlow parochially accepts cannibalism amongst the Africans, speaking freely of their habits, cannibalism in European circles would have been, as William Arens explains, one of the two most "unspeakable" taboos for Victorians (the other being incest).[32] Even if Kurtz has not literally partaken of human flesh, Marlow perceives that he is Spencer's "social cannibal," embodying Conrad's critique of brute society and selfish man.[33] Yet Marlow also imagines that Kurtz has been figuratively cannibalized. Dark Africa has swallowed Kurtz whole. He describes Kurtz's balding forehead as an ivory ball; [the wilderness] had caressed him, and – lo! – he had withered; it had taken him, loved him, embraced him, got into his veins, consumed his flesh, and sealed his soul to its own by the inconceivable ceremonies of some devilish initiation. (115)

Africa has rent his mask, exhuming the grotesque ideality of imperial benevolence which he embodies. Kurtz, "on the stretcher, opening his mouth voraciously, as if to devour all the earth with all mankind," articulates the imperial ego (155). Much like the gleaming, somber "polished sarcophagus" Marlow finds upon observing the Intended's grand piano (156), both forehead and piano keys in their polished brilliance are pretenses of pristine English virtue although both confess culpability in the consumption of Africa and its resources, namely the bodies of the workforces in the grove of death and ivory. Thus, as Marlow troops further into the forests, he notes the heavy silence, not because Africans have no language or cannot speak, but because they have been steadily cleared out by colonial companies: "The people had vanished. Mad terror had scattered them" (54).

In other canonical framed narratives featuring wanderers compelled to tell a story – e.g. Samuel Taylor Coleridge's "The Rime of the Ancient Mariner" (1798) and Mary Shelley's *Frankenstein* (1818) – the main speaker, whether he is conscious of it or not, is making a confession. What is Marlow confessing? Such a question implies that Marlow has a sense of responsibility, something that he has failed to do that he knows inwardly is right and that continues to eat away at his conscience. He speaks obliquely of this guilt, framing it in the context of his duty as steamboat captain:

> I managed not to sink that steamboat on my first trip. [...] Imagine a blindfolded man set to drive a van over a bad road. I sweated and shivered over that business considerably, I can tell you. After all, for a seaman, to scrape the bottom of the thing that's supposed to float all the time under his care is the unpardonable sin. No one may know of it, but you never forget the thump – eh? A blow on the very heart. You remember it, you dream of it, you wake up at night and think of it – years after – and go hot and cold all over. (94)

What is the unseen and haunting "thump" beneath the smooth surface of the river? What compels Marlow to return to the Congo after witnessing "The horror!" (149)?

The Ouroboros: Taking and Giving Oral Narratives

As mentioned above, Conrad plunges Marlow back into the Congo in a writerly act of self-giving to counter the all-consuming ideology of colonialism. Writing or re-presenting the narrative is essential. However, this is not without complications. Writing is not always a responsible answer. Plato famously excoriates literature as promoting false representations of ideal truths and thus corrupting youths. While Conrad is writing long after Plato, modern philosophers were still debating the place of representation in society. Immanuel Kant's "Copernican turn" at the end of the eighteenth century rejects the notion that truths come from without, spurring a revolution in metaphysical thought that emphasizes self-representation, or representation of knowledge that revolves around the Self rather than reflects the external world. This modern representation is limited by the subject's relation with something other than itself, which means that knowledge is not simply present but must be re-presented in relation to that other thing. No longer is there an objective ground for justifying human behavior, and thus it is in this limitation that representation must become responsible, or self-aware. Each representation separates the Self from the world and easily backslides into a forgetfulness that the representation – e.g., divine law, cultural tradition, or human right – originates with the Self, or humans. Thus, the Darwinian and Naturalist perspectives that unravel Kurtz and ultimately Marlow, may be linked to a *logos*, or reified logic, unrecognized representations of our selves. As will be further discussed, it is Marlow's continual idealization of Kurtz and his inability to recognize the limits of representation that likewise delimit Marlow's self-recognition, just as Kurtz reifies imperialism and thus alienates himself from his Self.[34]

Critics including Raymond Williams and Edward Said

have noted Conrad's preferences for speech over writing as a form of more responsive representation.[35] This kind of claim participates in the seminal speech-writing debate between those like Levinas, who argues that speech is a more immediate manifestation of knowledge than writing, and others like Derrida, who undermines the speech-writing hierarchy. For Levinas, speech represents mental experiences while writing represents the symbols used in speech, thus being two-degrees separated from the intended meaning. Meanwhile, Derrida argues that speech is just as reliant on another set of signs as writing.

For Conrad, while word-of-mouth exchanges carry promises of speech communities, storytelling, and sharing, all means of reaching the mass readership, writing limited him to "cold, silent, colourless" print ("Autocracy and War," *NLL* 83). Likewise, in "Heart of Darkness," writing baffles Marlow. On Kurtz's report for the International Society for the Suppression of Savage Customs, Marlow remarks:

> It was eloquent, vibrating with eloquence, but too high-strung, I think. Seventeen pages of close writing he had found time for! But this must have been before his – let us say – nerves, went wrong, and caused him to preside at certain midnight dances ending with unspeakable rites [...]. But it was a beautiful piece of writing. The opening paragraph, however, in the light of later information, strikes me now as ominous. [...] The peroration was magnificent, though difficult to remember, you know. It gave me the notion of an exotic Immensity ruled by an august Benevolence. It made me tingle with enthusiasm. This was the unbounded power of eloquence – of words – of burning noble words. (YS 117–18)

"Ominous" yet "eloquent" and "immens[e]," despite Kurtz's terrifying postscript scribbled at the bottom of the report – "Exterminate all the brutes!" (118) – Marlow coolly critiques its slight bombast then fawns over the sublime effects. He even aids in perpetuating Kurtz's monologic untruths by tearing off the incriminating postscriptum before handing over the report to the Company solicitor, a manipulation that would not have been possible if Kurtz had delivered the information orally himself.

At the same time, Marlow equally manipulates facts when speaking. It might be said that one of his haunting crimes is lying, and his prevarications have drawn wide critical attention as a symbol of cultural decay in Europe, as a cordon separating the domestic from global affairs, or even an act belying potential redemption.[36] In his greatest lie, Marlow erases Kurtz's final words, "The horror! The horror!", and instead comforts the Intended: "The last word he pronounced was – your name" (161). As with his censoring of Kurtz's manuscript, the choice he makes here not only attempts to realize Kurtz's unconsummated ideal intentions but cowardly denies the blurring of Kurtz's embodied Self (the atavistic past) with the ego of intentions (the future potential magnate and artist), reinforcing false social values. He is wholly unable to articulate the "unspeakable rites" Kurtz participated in, and at the same time, he is stricken dumb by Kurtz's elocution: "I am trying to account to myself for – for – Mr. Kurtz – for the shade of Mr. Kurtz. This initiated wraith from the back of Nowhere honoured me with its amazing confidence before it vanished altogether. This was because it could speak English to me" (117). The power of Kurtz's oral being becomes a thing in itself, an allusion to divinity and the biblical "Word" more present and real than his corporeal or embodied Self. Lived speech outweighs the effaced Kurtz of Africa, and the spoken voice overrides the dead letter. Thus, Marlow never corrects the Intended's perception of Kurtz and guiltily agrees as she confides, "His words, at least, have not died" (160), leaving Marlow with the spectral memory that becomes Conrad's text: "He was just a word for me. I did not see the man in the name any more than you do" (82).

Both writing and speech within the plot of "Heart of Darkness" are problematic languages of ethics. Both potentially distort knowledge and reinforce pernicious social constructs. Thus, lying on its own cannot be the unseen "thump" propelling Marlow to recollect his story. The ethics of Conrad's narration lie not in the mode of expression or degrees of separation but in the circular narrative structure. As suggested above, this ouroboros form risks being cannibalistically totalizing but it may also generate open discourse. At the start of Marlow's story, he notes: "I like what is in the work, – the chance to find yourself. Your own reality – yourself, not for others – what no other man can ever know. They can only see the mere show, and never can tell what it really means" (85). One's representation can only ever be responsible to oneself, in which case the "show" is not the end goal but the "work." The work Conrad puts readers through is boundless and thus liberating, transforming the trope of imperial cannibalism into an act of autophagous narration.

Simmons observes that Marlow's tale begins *in medias res* – "And this also"[37] – then proceeds in a spectacularly circular fashion. Marlow's story opens and closes on the *Nellie* in the Thames estuary; his quest begins and ends with Europe; he journeys up and down the Congo River; the tides ebb and flow; and so forth.[38] This seemingly inescapable circularity belies the insatiable ouroboros of imperial egotism. The snake as symbolic of consuming selfishness has a long history in Western culture. Plato's *Timaeus*, one of the earliest written records of the ouroboros, paints the creature as a Creator who has "no need of eyes when there was nothing remaining outside him to be seen,"[39] similar to Marlow's depiction of Kurtz as a "weak-eyed devil" unable to see beyond himself. As a "flabby, pretending" being of "rapacious and pitiless folly" (65), Kurtz also alludes to the myth of the Bosom Serpent, demonstrated by Nathaniel Hawthorne's short story, "Egotism; or, The Bosom-Serpent" (1843) as an animal that "take[s] up residence in a vital organ, occasionally in the heart but more frequently somewhere in the gastrointestinal tract [...] and steals the host's food, causing great suffering and sometimes even death."[40] As Kurtz embodies devouring egotism, Marlow's tale reinscribing Kurtz becomes a tale reconfiguring Marlow's own consuming egotism. He purports to tell a story void of himself – "I don't want to bother you much with what happened to me personally" ("Heart of Darkness," *YS* 51) – but the narrative becomes nothing but Self: how he went to Africa, what he saw, and how he met

Kurtz. As he was blind to Kurtz's fatal *logos,* Marlow is blind to his own egotistic *ethos.*

The ouroboros authenticates Marlow's narrative but not his "Truth." As a trope, the cannibal serpent delimits a totalizing reality; as narrative form, the serpent feeds infinitely. In describing the moment that inspired him to pilot steamboats, Marlow discovers that the Congo River "resembl[es] an immense snake uncoiled, with its head in the sea, its body at rest curving afar over a vast country, and its tail lost in the depths of the land" (52). This Great World Serpent encircles the Earth with its tail clasped in its jaws. As a creature made of water, the fluid tail of the snake is able to follow the course of rivers around the world until it meets the mouth of the Congo, or the mouth of the snake, once again.[41] Staring at a map, Marlow realizes, "steamboats! Why shouldn't I try to get charge of one? [...] The snake had charmed me" (53). Marlow childishly suggests that the Congo River – Africa – invited him, releasing him from imperial culpability, but more accurately, the scene should be understood as underscoring his juvenile dream and mature hunger for glory. He has swallowed the imperial tale of glamorous expeditions and exploration. However, as an ouroboros, the river also equips Marlow with a tale (tail) of validation: "Between us there was, as I have already said somewhere, the bond of the sea. Besides holding our hearts together through long periods of separation, it had the effect of making us tolerant of each other's yarns – and even convictions" (45-46). The infinitude of the ever-revolving world serpent invites polyvocality. The river itself invites Marlow to speak. As mentioned above, the "stillness" and "immensity" of its face provokes not just a self-awareness but social awareness. The menacing river and sea demand interconnection, "kinship" even, like that which Marlow found with the helmsman.

In fictional and autobiographical travel accounts, storytellers have an obligation to legitimize their narratives. In his Author's Note to *Youth: A Narrative, and Two Other Stories,* Conrad claims that "Heart of Darkness" is "authentic," and only "pushed a little (and only very little) beyond the actual facts

of the case for the perfectly legitimate" (YS xi). Establishing
authenticity was imperative in these texts as they were often
used to further advancements in science and natural history.
Travel narratives could demonstrate their legitimacy through
their cr/edibility, or autophagous narration. This convention
is evident early in the nineteenth century when Olaudah
Equiano describes in his autobiography, *The Interesting
Narrative*, a seller's routine allegorizing the African ritual for
storytelling. In the ritual, the seller proffers a narrative of his
ethos. He wishes to say he is a trustworthy salesman, and to
prove this, he subjects himself to his own narrative, kissing his
comestible products all around to show that he has not lied and
the food is not poisoned.[42] By making himself the subject of the
tale he purports and showing that his food is edible, he confirms
his honesty and demonstrates that he is a credible salesman.
Nonfiction travel narratives popularly enact this validation
ritual by directly transforming the narrator into a comestible
product whose reliability is associated with the narrator's
cr/edibility. For instance, in Sir Henry Morton Stanley's
Through the Dark Continent, Stanley's narrative of cr/edibility
depends not on a starving Africa that symbolically eats away at
his English identity but on a veracious continent that means to
gorge on Stanley and his men. The Africans cry, "Meat! meat!
Ah! ha!" spotting Stanley's crew, and when the Africans do
not devour them, the narrative exemplifies in real terms the
kind of story that sensationalizes itself to appeal to consumers
while failing to completely prove its cr/edibility.[43] It is the kind
of text that threatens to poison audiences with recriminatory
falsehoods. Similarly, Marlow confuses himself with his own
stalwart story of Africa-wild/Europe-civilized conceptions
when he realizes that his cannibal crewmembers are not as
unrestrained as he initially believed them to be.

    The imperial lie cannot nourish the people because it
remains parsimoniously in the mouth of colonists. Those
in Conrad's Congo nursed upon the monologic ideality of
colonialism sicken or die. The Africans at the grove "fed on
unfamiliar food," i.e., the stuff of imperialism, suffer disease and

starvation (66). Kurtz, the most avaricious imperial, repeatedly falls ill, finally succumbing to the folds of death only once he has realized, as Marlow describes it, "that supreme moment of complete knowledge," which unfortunately may only entail the overwhelming certitude of that which is most finite – Death (149). The ouroboric ego thus becomes a conveyor of brute vocabulary, articulating the "unspeakable," taking its own tail (tale) in its mouth, and forming what Derrida calls *la clôture*, a logocentric closure that delimits and enslaves audiences in their own created myths. When Kurtz's, "horror!" leaves his mouth wide, it is with the yawning implication that his voice has little of value and meaning, offering only a hollow ideal that deprives, exploits, and eats the Other. Likewise, Marlow's ego, failing to englobe totality, digests nothingness, bound close by a self-absorbed *logos* of selfhood. Shrinking from the task of disrupting the Intended's vision of Kurtz and thus Kurtz's beloved image of the imperial Lady Justice, Marlow becomes ironically complicit in the furtherance of imperial apathy and injustice.[44]

The speech act is thus often brutish. Marlow's lie to the Intended aims to actualize his purported project of selflessness when in fact he acts self-lessly, or without moral conviction and selfhood, cyclically re-presenting the "benevolent" *logos* of Kurtz rather than authentically articulating his Self. Like a Derridean animal, Marlow bites his tongue in hostility, confusion, or shame. The imperial narrative is thus both consumed and consuming. At the beginning of his account, Marlow shuddered at the prospect of injustice, claiming that to lie is to eat rot, as if eating something dead: "There is a taint of death, a flavor of mortality in lies" (82). The link between death and storytelling is in the cannibal mouth. Upon hearing of Kurtz's passing, Marlow continued sedately with his dinner, resolutely and loyally imbibing an affirmation of European normalcy and upholding appearances. The greatest crime, to tell oneself a story, self-cannibalizes. It removes one from public discourse and sustains a condition of perpetual metaphysical hunger. It is this – Marlow's reinforcement of a selfish ego – that eats away at his inmost conscience. He falls ill immediately following this dinner: "And then they very nearly buried me" (150). The primary narrator closes the narrative comparing Marlow to an idol (i.e., Buddha). Just as Kurtz fascinated Marlow, Marlow charms the primary narrator, and in a train of cyclical autophagous acts, they each consume and reproduce the tales of the Others while searching for an idol-self to reingest in what has become the moral vacuums of themselves, trapped in *la clôture*. One might reframe this phenomenon in Althusserian terms of ideology: the primary narrator, Marlow, and Kurtz cyclically reproduce imperial labor (e.g., harvest ivory and recruit additional laborers) motivated by their pursuit of an Ideal-I.

In a metaphysics of equal ipseity between selves and others, there can be no single, absolute Truth because there is no lack of truth, truth not being Other.[45] Thus, conversation is necessary for a just existence. As Levinas states, "[i]f truth arises in the absolute experience in which being gleams with its own light, then truth is produced only in veritable conversation or in justice."[46] The ethical purpose of storytelling is not to deliver onto audiences a finite conclusion but to liberate by initiating discourse. Conrad's framed narrators and the infinite, ouroboric continuity with which Kurtz's, Marlow's, and the primary narrator's stories are perpetuated by Conrad and readers sustain this open discourse, and this is evident in the lively conversation that continues to be had in interpretations of the novella.

As travel narratives became more publicized, literature, like Conrad's "Heart of Darkness," reveals a disturbing obsession not with the apprehension of ingesting foreign contaminants but with the fear of being consumed. Eating and consumption are subjects that emerged as central themes in much nineteenth-century British literature as a result of real concerns at the time regarding adulteration of foods. The first Adulteration of Foods Acts and amendments in the 1860s and 1870s sought to criminalize food tampering, including diluting portions to increase yields or disguising

spoiled products.[47] From quotidian dinner parties and soup
kitchens to sensational explorations of appetite in texts like
Thomas de Quincey's *Confessions of an English Opium
Eater* (1821), Christina Rossetti's "Goblin Market" (1862),
and Bram Stoker's *Dracula* (1897), eating became central
to the nineteenth-century British perception of morality
and identity: "Tell me what you eat, and I shall tell you what
you are" quips gastronomist Jean Anthelme Brillat-Savarin
in *The Physiology of Taste* (1825). However, on an imperial
level, growing fears of vulnerability and degeneration led to
literature that tested the permeable boundaries of individual
and national bodies. Portrayals of the mouth became a site of
dialogic exchange, and the Self became open to dangerous
impurities. Observing this, critics situate Victorian society's
growing awareness of health and regimes in the imperial
body's need to define the Self through proper regulation
of appetite and differentiation from rapacious Eastern
and African savages, sparking tremendous trends towards
vegetarianism and other diets.[48]

The representational structure of Conrad's ouroboros begs
the question: Are humans giving or are they being given (given
away as well as given something)? In short, self-cannibalism
is not only de(con)structive. In capitalized letters, Derrida
concludes his critique of Levinas, "*En ce moment même dans
cet ouvrage me voici*," with the word, "*BOIS*," an imperative
to give to the Other, to offer drink and nourish the Other:
"I WEAVE MY VOICE SO AS TO BE EFFACED THIS TAKE
IT HERE I AM EAT – APPROACH – IN ORDER TO GIVE
HIM/HER [*LUI*] – DRINK [*BOIS*]."[49] The capitalized typeface
is the author's interruption of the ego, to entwine with the
Other, and break the Other's fast. It is a giving of oneself,
a decomposition or analysis of Self, allowing oneself to be
generously consumed. While Marlow and Kurtz never willingly
give of themselves, Conrad's narrative invites readers to
drink and eat of the many decomposed *logos*, from Marlow's
scuttled steamer and dismantled biases to Kurtz's collapsed
mental state and breakdown of humanist values. As readers

interrogate the text, they perform this deconstructive *clôtural* reading, a close reading rather than a closed reading, no longer operating only within a finite totality of logocentric closure, but outside, "enveloping the tale which brought it out only as a glow brings out a haze, in the likeness of one of these misty halos that sometimes are made visible by the spectral illumination of moonshine" ("Heart of Darkness," YS 48). Thus, more than a responsibility of "communicat[ing] incommunicability," as Julian Wolfrey argues,[50] Conrad invites readers to eat of his tale, envelop it, and thereby enact the erasure of beginnings and ends, heads and tails, Self and Other, within and without the text's increasingly accumulating raconteurs from Kurtz and Marlow to the unnamed narrator, Conrad, and finally readers. In "Heart of Darkness," Conrad ensures that there can be no end to ideologies, for self-representation must never be whole but remain perpetually open (and) mouthed.

NOTES

[1] Sartre 382.
[2] Leavis 204.
[3] Greaney 58.
[4] Eliot 297.
[5] Achebe 8.
[6] Achebe 3-4, 10.
[7] Romanick Baldwin 200, 203.
[8] Firchow 11.
[9] Achebe 11, 7
[10] Acheraïou, "Ethics and Horror," 61; Gill 11.
[11] Firchow 12.
[12] Firchow 12.
[13] Achebe 9.
[14] Haraway 89-90.
[15] Haraway 69.
[16] Derrida 17–18.
[17] Qtd. in Hunter 18.
[18] Levinas 37.
[19] Levinas 38.
[20] Levinas 50-51, 199.
[21] Levinas 75.

Aileen Miyuki Farrar

[22] Simmons 15-16.
[23] Conrad 589.
[24] Gill 1.
[25] Firchow 123.
[26] Sewlall 170.
[27] Arens 139-46.
[28] See Kilgour 5; Phillips 119; Guest vii.
[29] Phillips 185-90; Said, *Orientalism* 250; Kilgour 5; Slemon 163.
[30] Spencer 410.
[31] Sagan 36-37.
[32] Arens 146.
[33] As Conrad famously wrote to Cunninghame Graham on 8 February 1899, "Man is a vicious animal [...]. Society is essentially criminal" (*CL* 2: 159).
[34] For a comprehensive history and analysis of modern representation from Kant to Foucault, see Colebrook.
[35] Williams 140; Said, *The World, The Text* 94.
[36] Acheraïou, *Rethinking Postcolonialism* 147.
[37] Simmons 105.
[38] Simmons 18.
[39] Plato 452.
[40] Bennett 4.
[41] Images of the ouroboros date back to ancient Egypt and depict a snake, worm, or dragon curled in the shape of a circle with its tail in its mouth, hence the name *ouroboros* which means "devouring its own tail." The ouroboros, being inherently paradoxical in nature, has been diversely interpreted as an alternatingly and simultaneously positive and negative symbol for classical themes including regeneration and destruction; the unity of good and bad; and complete totality of all. See Charlesworth 155-56.
[42] Equiano 43.
[43] Stanley 1805.
[44] For further discussion of *la clôture*, see Critchley.
[45] Levinas 61.
[46] Levinas 71.
[47] Wood 17-24.
[48] Norcia 253; Lee 185.
[49] Qtd. in Critchley 108.
[50] Wolfrey 163.

WORKS CITED

Achebe, Chinua. "An Image of Africa: Racism in Conrad's *Heart of Darkness.*" *Hopes and Impediments: Selected Essays.* By Achebe. New York: Anchor, 1988. 1-20. Print.

Acheraïou, Amar. "Ethics and Horror in *Heart of Darkness.*" *Critical Insights.* Ed. Robert C. Evans. New York: Salem P, 2019. 49-71. Print.

---. *Rethinking Postcolonialism: Colonialist Discourse in Modern Literatures and the Legacy of Classical Writers.* Basingstoke: Palgrave Macmillan, 2008. Print.

Arens, William. *The Man-Eating Myth: Anthropology and Anthropophagy.* Oxford: Oxford UP, 1979. Print.

Bennett, Gillian. *Bodies: Sex, Violence, Disease, and Death in Contemporary Legend.* Jackson: UP of Mississippi, 2005. Print.

Brillat-Savarin, Jean Anthelme. *The Physiology of Taste: Or Meditations on Transcendental Gastronomy.* Trans. M. F. K. Fisher. Ed. Bill Buford. New York: Vintage, 2009. Print.

Charlesworth, James. *The Good & Evil Serpent: How a Universal Symbol Became Christianized.* New Haven: Yale UP, 2010. Print.

Colebrook, Claire. *Ethics and Representation: From Kant to Post-structuralism.* Edinburgh: Edinburgh UP, 1999. Print.

Conrad, Joseph. "Henry James: An Appreciation." *The North American Review* 203, 1 Apr. 1916: 585-91. Print.

Critchley, Simon. *The Ethics of Deconstruction: Derrida and Levinas.* West Lafayette: Purdue UP, 1999. Print.

Derrida, Jacques. *The Animal That Therefore I Am (More to Follow).* Trans. David Wills. Ed. Marie-Louise Mallet. New York: Fordham UP, 2008. Print.

Eliot, T. S. "Kipling Redivivus." *Athenaeum* 9 May 1919: 297-98. Print.

Equiano, Olaudah. *The Interesting Narrative of the Life of Olaudah Equiano, Or Gustavus Vassa, the African. The Interesting Narrative and Other Writings.* 1789. Ed. Vincent Carretta. New York: Penguin, 2003. Print.

Firchow, Peter. *Envisioning Africa: Racism and Imperialism in Conrad's "Heart of Darkness."* Lexington: UP of Kentucky, 2000. Print.

Gill, David. "The Fascination of the Abomination: Conrad and Cannibalism." *The Conradian* 24.2 (1999): 1-30. Print.

Greaney, Michael. *Conrad, Language, and Narrative.* Cambridge: Cambridge UP, 2002. Print.

Guest, Kristen, ed. *Eating Their Words: Cannibalism and the Boundaries of Cultural Identity.* Albany: State U of New York P, 2001. Print.

Haraway, Donna. "The Promises of Monsters: A Regenerative Politics for Inappropriate/d Others." *The Haraway Reader.* New York: Routledge, 2004. 63-124. Print.

Hunter, Allan. *Joseph Conrad and the Ethics of Darwinism: The Challenges of Science.* London: Helm, 1983. Print.

Kilgour, Maggie. *From Communion to Cannibalism: An Anatomy of Metaphors of Incorporation.* Princeton: Princeton UP, 1990. Print.

Leavis, F. R. *The Great Tradition.* Harmondsworth: Penguin, 1983. Print.

Lee, Michael Parrish. *The Food Plot in the Nineteenth-Century British Novel.* Basingstoke: Palgrave Macmillan, 2016. Print.

Levinas, Emmanuel. *Totality and Infinity: An Essay on Exteriority*. Trans. Alphonso Lingis. Dordrec ht: Kluwer, 1991. Print.

Norcia, Megan. "The Imperial Food Chain: Eating as an Interface of Power in Women Writers' Geography." *Victorian Literature and Culture* 33.1 (2005): 253-68. Print.

Phillips, Jerry. "Cannibalism qua Capitalism: The Metaphorics of Accumulation in Marx, Conrad, Shakespeare and Marlow." *Cannibalism and the Colonial World*. Ed. Francis Barker, Peter Hulme, and Margaret Iversen. Cambridge: Cambridge UP, 1998. 183-203. Print.

Plato. *Timaeus*. *The Dialogues of Plato*. Ed. and trans. Benjamin Jowett. Vol. 3. Oxford: Clarendon P, 1892. 339-516. Print.

Raja, Masood Ashraf. "Joseph Conrad: The Question of Racism and Representation of Muslims in his Malayan Works." *Postcolonial Text* 3.4 (2007): 1-13. Print.

Romanick Baldwin, Debra. "The Horror and the Human: The Politics of Dehumanization in *Heart of Darkness* and Primo Levi's *Se Questo' è un uomo*." *Conradiana* 37 (2005): 185-204. Print.

Sagan, Eli. *Cannibalism: Human Aggression and Cultural Form*. New York: Harper, 1974. Print.

Said, Edward. *Orientalism*. New York: Vintage, 1979. Print.

---. *The World, the Text, and the Critic*. Cambridge: Harvard UP, 1983. Print.

Sartre, Jean-Paul. "Intentionality: A Fundamental Idea of Husserl's Phenomenology." *The Phenomenology Reader*. Trans. Joseph P. Fell. Ed. Dermot Moran and Timothy Mooney. New York: Routledge, 2002. 382-84. Print.

Sceats, Sarah. *Food, Consumption, and the Body in Contemporary Women's Fiction*. New York: Cambridge UP, 2000. Print.

Sewlall, Harry. "Cannibalism in the Colonial Imaginary: A Reading of Joseph Conrad's 'Falk.'" *Journal of Literary Studies* 22.1-2 (2006): 158-74. Print.

Simmons, Allan. "Reading *Heart of Darkness*." *The New Cambridge Companion to Joseph Conrad*. Ed. J. H. Stape. Cambridge: Cambridge UP, 2015. 15-28. Print.

Slemon, Stephen. "Bones of Contention: Post-colonial Writing and the 'Cannibal' Question." *Literature and the Body*. Ed. Anthony Purdy. Amsterdam: Rodopi, 1992. 163-78. Print.

Spencer, Herbert. "To Moncure D. Conway: 17 July 1898." *Life and Letters of Herbert Spencer*. Ed. David Duncan. London: Methuen, 1908. 410. Print.

Stanley, Henry Morton Sir. *Through the Dark Continent*. 1878. *The Longman Anthology of British Literature*. Vol.2. Ed. David Damrosch. Harlow: Longman, 2003. 1803-10. Print.

Williams, Raymond. *The English Novel from Dickens to Lawrence*. New York: Oxford UP, 1970. Print.

Wolfrey, Julian. *Deconstruction. Derrida. Transitions*. New York: St. Martin's P, 1998. Print.

Wood, Laura. "Sweet Poison: Food Adulteration, Fiction and the Young Glutton." *Food, Drink, and the Written Word in Britain, 1820-1945*. Ed. Mary Addyman, Laura Wood, and Christopher Yiannitsaros. New York: Routledge, 2017. 17-37. Print.

Joshua A. Bernstein,
University of Southern Mississippi,
Hattiesburg, MS, USA

Under Straining Eyes:
Joseph Conrad and the Problem of "Moral Luck"

In 1976, Bernard Williams, the British moral philosopher, writing in *The Aristotelian Society Supplementary*, asked a question that would ultimately challenge several hundred years of moral philosophy. Imagine, he writes in "Moral Luck," that a fictional painter, whom he calls "Gauguin," chooses to abandon his family and reside on a desert island so that he can pursue his dream of painting. If he fails in the effort, we deem him irresponsible. But if he succeeds and becomes a timeless painter, Williams says, we tend to deem his sacrifice negligible. Yet the irony is that Gauguin's success as an artist depends, in large part, on factors beyond his control, such as how his work is received. Therefore, Williams asks, is it possible that our moral assessments of people's actions depend in part on factors beyond their control?[1]

Writing in the *Stanford Encyclopedia of Philosophy*, Dana Nelkin summarizes the "problem of moral luck," as it has come to be called. One of the dilemmas, she explains, is that "reasoning suggests that it is impossible to morally assess anyone for anything" if we assume that people should only be judged for situations that are fully within their grasps. At stake, she adds, are not only our conventional notions of morality, but also our very systems of law and punishment.

Sixty-five years before Williams published his article, Joseph Conrad posed a similar scenario in his 1911 novel, *Under Western Eyes*. Razumov, the protagonist, flees his native Russia and retreats to an island in Geneva, where, like Gauguin, he pursues an expressive path, in this case recounting his life in a diary. He has also made a tremendous sacrifice in coming, having fatally betrayed his classmate to the Czarist authorities.

117

Indeed, much of the book hinges on whether Razumov's choice should be seen as morally correct. Although the novel is often treated as one of Conrad's "political novels," the narrator explains that his purpose is the "rendering" of "the moral conditions ruling over a large portion of this earth's surface" (*UWE* 67). As the narrator provides the reader with a moral canvas of Russia, he also unravels Razumov's moral character, showing how the protagonist is enmeshed in his country's moral conditions. In fact, Razumov is aware of his social vulnerability and believes that "his moral personality was at the mercy of these lawless forces" (77), so much so that he contemplates suicide. While Razumov's scenario isn't entirely parallel to Gauguin's – his quest is largely one of self-preservation, rather than artistic fulfillment – the question Conrad poses is the same: to what extent can we judge Razumov for moral actions outside his control?

Indeed, what a close reading of *Under Western Eyes* suggests is the degree to which Conrad presciently anticipates the debate over what we now call "moral luck." Yet, rather than offering one philosophical solution to the problem, as contemporary philosophers like Williams have tried,[2] Conrad seems to bask in the absurdity that humans are forced to make sense of a world in which they are held morally accountable for decisions outside their own making. This is important, because while many critics, such as Owen Knowles, Rachel Hollander, Barbara DeMille, and Michael Lackey, have tried to position Conrad ethically, often through the lenses of Arthur Schopenhauer, Friedrich Nietzsche, or Emmanuel Levinas, none of the major criticism thus far has discussed him in terms of "moral luck."[3] Other writers, including Thomas Hardy, Jane Austen, and Geoffrey Chaucer, have proven relevant to the topic.[4] Yet the omission of Conrad would seem rather glaring, given that he, perhaps more than any writer of the twentieth century, wrestles with what Williams calls "the superficial concept" of "responsible agency."[5] One of the central ironies of *Under Western Eyes* is that Razumov feels "menaced by" and ultimately assumes responsibility for a "complicity forced upon him," as he calls it in admitting his role to the revolutionists (366). In fact, this question – of whether humans are responsible for moral choices that are "forced upon" them – underlies many of his novels' protagonists, from the brooding Winnie Verloc, whose family has become entangled in the antics of her husband, to the guilt-afflicted Lord Jim, who has found himself implicated in a ruinous act of betrayal while at sea. Exploring Conrad's concern with "moral luck" is also helpful for reinterpreting the contemporary philosophical debate, especially in differentiating between what Thomas Nagel has called the four different kinds of "moral luck" – resultant, causal, circumstantial, and constitutive.[6] Of these four kinds, I argue, Conrad places particular emphasis on the fourth, reflecting, more than anything, what Conrad believes is the primacy of character, even in a morally inscrutable world.

"Moral Luck": A Primer

The concept of "moral luck" has roots in ancient philosophy, as Roger Crisp explains, as well as in works by Adam Smith and, more recently, Joel Feinberg.[7] The contemporary debate is commonly associated with a series of exchanges between Williams and Nagel, where they grapple with an apparent contradiction in our everyday thinking about moral responsibility. We tend to believe that luck can accord a person more praise or blame for an action. To cite an example that Nagel uses, if two equally reckless drivers set out in their cars, and one happens to hit and kill a crossing pedestrian, while the other encounters no one, we tend to blame the pedestrian-killing driver more than the non-killing driver. Yet the only difference between the two drivers is luck.[8] Blaming one driver more than the other seems to contradict another widely held belief: that people should only be blamed or praised on account of situations for which they are fully responsible.

This principle, which has come to be called the "Control Principle," would seem on its face to be irreconcilable with many of the everyday moral assessments we make, such as that of the reckless drivers, or, to cite Williams' example, Gauguin. While one could certainly question the particulars of these examples – Nelkin, for instance, asks whether artistic success could ever justify Gauguin's abandoning his family – the basic point remains: our moral judgments often seem to fly in the face of our other otherwise generally held belief that individuals are morally responsible only for that which they control.

In his initial response to Williams, Nagel distinguishes between four different kinds of moral luck.[9] The first, resultant luck, centers on the outcomes of choices and describes scenarios such as the aforementioned drivers and Gauguin. In these cases, the perceived moral responsibility of an agent depends on consequences outside her/his control. The second kind, causal luck, which is sometimes seen as "redundant" or bracketed as part of the larger problem of free will,[10] refers to situations where an agent's choices are "determined by antecedent circumstances," as Nagel puts it.[11] In these cases, moral actions are caused by prior events and thus outside an agent's control. The third kind, circumstantial luck, describes the conditions in which an agent finds herself/himself, rather than the outcomes of her/his actions. An example Nagel gives includes a Nazi collaborator who happens to have been born into a time and place that compels her/him to commit morally atrocious acts.[12] The fourth kind, constitutive luck, pertains to the character traits of an agent, as well as her environmental influences, upbringing, genes, and other internal factors she does not choose.

As Nelkin explains, the basic problem for philosophers is how to reconcile the Control Principle, or the belief that people should be judged only for situations they control, with the everyday judgments we make, many of which seem to involve moral luck. Philosophers tend to respond by either denying the existence of moral luck or the Control Principle altogether or by adopting some combination of the two. Others accept or deny particular kinds of moral luck, employ counterfactual strategies, question agent-causation, or take other approaches.[13] The debate itself is enormously complicated and beyond the scope of this essay. Nevertheless, if Williams, among others, is right, and "morality itself cannot be rendered immune to luck,"[14] it is hard to think of a writer more concerned with the vagaries of fate – and their implications for moral introspection – than Conrad, whose protagonist, Razumov, finds his "moral personality" at "the mercy" of "lawless forces" (*UWE* 77).[15]

"Just a Man":
The Moral Landscape of *Under Western Eyes*

Under Western Eyes has long been regarded as one of Conrad's most personal novels, an assessment fueled, in part, by its subject matter, the tale of a disaffected Eastern European émigré, and, in part, by the facts surrounding its composition. Most scholars agree that Conrad suffered "a complete mental breakdown" while writing it, as his wife, Jessie, attested.[16] His anxiety stemmed, to some extent, from mounting debts to his agent, J. B. Pinker, with whom he quarreled bitterly, and, partly, from crippling health ailments, including influenza, delirium, and a painful case of gout. According to Jessie, Conrad even spoke aloud with his characters in Polish after writing them.[17] While some of the saga behind the novel remains speculative – it is unclear, for example, if Conrad really intended to burn the manuscript, as he threatened Pinker with doing – it is true, as Zdzisław Najder remarked, that novel might have "caused him more anguish than anything else he ever wrote."[18]

Marking roughly the end of Conrad's "middle period," whose works would become his most acclaimed, and the third in his trilogy of "political novels," following *Nostromo* (1904) and *The Secret Agent* (1907), *Under Western Eyes* has long proved baffling to critics, with many divided on its meaning and intent. An early reviewer, writing in the *Pall Mall Gazette*, counted it among Conrad's "best work" but thought Haldin's "crime merited the swift and degrading execution that was its punishment." Readers after the Russian Revolution of 1917 tended to regard the novel as prophetic, though the book, like most of Conrad's major works, sold poorly at the outset, causing

him much consternation. Ironically, it was later reissued and
well received in Russia after the Revolution. As Peter Mallios
explains, the novel also enjoyed something of a renaissance in
the West during the Cold War, highlighting, as it purportedly
did, the perils of Russian "tyranny."[19] Conrad himself probably
and unwittingly contributed to that perceived Russophobia,
writing in his letters, for example, that Russian literature
was "repugnant to me, hereditarily and individually" and that
Dostoevsky – against whose novel, *Crime and Punishment*
(1866), *Under Western Eyes* is often read – was "too Russian
for me" (*CL* 7: 615; 5: 70).[20]

For the most part, *Under Western Eyes* continues to be
read in primarily political terms,[21] a reading spurred in part
by Conrad's own admission, in a 1911 letter to his friend
Edward Garnett, that the novel was "concerned with nothing
but ideas, to the exclusion of everything else" (4: 489).
This is, of course, an exaggeration because the novel also
teems with individualized characters and feelings. Conrad's
statement is, in all likelihood, a defensive retort, and one that
should probably be regarded as truthfully as the narrator's
claims to be faithfully recounting a diary. Conrad's letter was
sparked by Garnett's unsigned review in *The Nation* in which
he lauded the novel but suggested that it depicted "Russian
types." In his Author's Note to the novel, Conrad dismisses the
notion that the novel arose from any anti-Russian enmity:

> The various figures playing their part in the story also owe their
> existence to no special experience but to the general knowledge
> of the condition of Russia and of the moral and emotional reactions of
> the Russian temperament to the pressure of tyrannical lawlessness,
> which, in general human terms, could be reduced to the formula
> of senseless desperation provoked by senseless tyranny. What I was
> concerned with mainly was the aspect, the character, and the fate
> of the individuals as they appeared to the Western Eyes of the old
> teacher of languages. (*UWE* viii)

Aside from the irony that Conrad's afterward only furthers the
insinuation that he is depicting Russian types, or "temperaments,"
as he calls them, what is perhaps most revealing is Conrad's

interest in "moral" examination: how Russians cope or react to the "senseless tyranny" around them, and how that experience is transmuted or distilled through the eyes of a foreign observer. Thus, Conrad's focus, it becomes clear, is both ethical and epistemic, a combination that, as we will see, surrounds current quandaries of "moral luck" and perhaps helps to explain, at least in part, the novel's multifarious reception. An early, unsigned review in the *Morning Post* in 1911, for example, calls the novel "a study in remorse, mainly moving from within, but also affected by external forces of personality."[22] Another unsigned review, this one published two days later in the *Westminster Gazette*, finds Razumov far less beholden to external forces:

> He has a strange detachment from all the minutiae of existence, a disregard for what we call comfort. He is wrapped in the contemplation of his own moral action, and this not because he has been placed by Fate in an extraordinary position, but because he is a Russian.[23]

If both reviews treat Razumov, to varying degrees, as an embodiment of Russianness, or a type, Richard Curle's review in the *Manchester Guardian* that week is more personal, highlighting the "awakening of [Razumov's] conscience" and ascribing to Conrad a growing interest in human psychology.[24] Curle actually faults the novel for that reason, deeming it imitative of Henry James.[25] For each of these reviewers, not least of all Garnett (despite Conrad's objection), *Under Western Eyes* is as much about Razumov as it is about any conflict of nations. And for each, the question remains whether Razumov emblematizes Russia or finds himself morally entrapped by it.

Conrad's admission to Garnett, along with his 1920 afterword, also need to be seen in the context of what was a very tumultuous time in Conrad's life, perhaps his most vexing. Two years after the novel's release, Bertrand Russell recounted visiting Conrad at Capel House: "Then he talked a lot about Poland, & showed me an album of family photographs of the [18]60's – spoke about how dream-like all that seems, & how he sometimes feels he ought not to have had children, because they have no roots or traditions or relations."[26] While Russell's account is not without question,[27] Conrad's alleged remarks closely parallel a passage in *Under Western Eyes*, where Razumov, having discovered the revolutionary assassin Haldin in his room, responds to his request for help:

> Did it ever occur to you how a man who had never heard a word of warm affection or praise in his life would think on matters on which you would think first with or against your class, your domestic tradition – your fireside prejudices?... Did you ever consider how a man like that would feel? I have no domestic tradition. I have nothing to think against. My tradition is historical. What have I to look back to but that national past from which you gentlemen want to wrench away your future? Am I to let my intelligence, my aspirations towards a better lot, be robbed of the only thing it has to go upon at the will of violent enthusiasts? You come from your province, but all this land is mine – or I have nothing. No doubt you shall be looked upon as a martyr some day – a sort of hero – a political saint. But I beg to be excused. I am content in fitting myself to be a worker. And what can you people do by scattering a few drops of blood on the snow? On this Immensity. On this unhappy Immensity! (*UWE* 61)

Arguably here more than anywhere else, Conrad articulates the thematic focus of the novel: Razumov's quest to find moral fulfillment in a world that lacks moral sense – an "immensity," as he puts it, stained by the blood of "violent enthusiasts." Whereas Haldin comes from a closely knit circle and enjoys familial support, Razumov, an orphan, has only Russia as a whole to depend on, a vague concept to which he can only historically relate.

While one can and should resist the impulse to read Razumov as entirely reminiscent of Conrad, it is hard not to see him as one of Conrad's most personal characters and *Under Western Eyes* as his most "autobiographical" book, as David R. Smith noted.[28] Like Razumov, Conrad was orphaned at an early age, his father having been imprisoned on account of revolutionary activity and subsequently contracting tuberculosis, from which he and Conrad's mother later died. Similar to Razumov, Conrad also fled his homeland as a late-teenager, opting for a life in the merchant marines and eventually settling in various parts of Great Britain. As Jeffrey Meyers explains in his biography, Conrad nurtured a "lifelong guilt" at having chosen to live abroad rather than return to his homeland and follow his father's revolutionary path.[29] Thus, when Conrad bemoans his lack of "roots" to Russell (assuming that account is correct), he not only reveals his discomfort in Britain – a discomfort he would feel throughout his life – but also echoes the sentiment of Razumov, who declares himself "just a man" (61), and one without "tradition" or "prejudice." The discomfort Conrad felt throughout his life was also, in large part, due to his being considered by many of his British contemporaries, including Virginia Woolf, as a foreigner, despite his having spent most of his life in Great Britain.[30]

The question, then, for the novel, and perhaps for Conrad himself, is how, or to what extent, humans should be judged for moral actions outside their grasps. It is no more Razumov's fault that he becomes the unwitting accomplice of the Czar's violent repression than it is Conrad's fault he could not return to his homeland. Razumov's own life becomes in jeopardy after the assassination, a fact he freely admits.[31] For Conrad, Najder explained, returning to his homeland would have subjected him to lengthy and dangerous conscription, if not persecution on account of his father's anti-Czarist agitation.[32] Moreover, like Gauguin in Williams' example, neither Razumov nor Conrad could foresee the ultimate effects of their choice to leave their native lands. Although he was obviously unable to control the circumstances prompting his exile, Conrad remained guilty throughout his life for leaving his native land, a guilt that undoubtedly tormented him and reflects the central question of moral luck: to what extent do we blame one for a choice that is not entirely of one's accord? Thus, it is worth reinterpreting these choices, especially Razumov's, in the light of moral luck, particularly the four kinds that Nagel describes.

"Some Unforeseen Event": Resultant Luck

In surveying the first kind of moral luck, "resultant," Nelkin explains that one related question is how, or whether, we can ultimately know an agent's true intentions when fortune intervenes. She cites as an example two attempting murderers, one of whom misses her target, the other of whom succeeds. We tend to deem the successful killer more culpable – hence the legal distinction between murder and attempted murder, with the former carrying a severer punishment – even though the only difference between the two attempts could be luck. (In one common variant on this example, the unsuccessful murderer sneezes, causing her to miss). Nelkin, drawing on what Andrew Latus has called the "epistemic argument,"[33] points out that we can assess with more certainty the successful murder's intentions, whereas the one who missed (or sneezed) remains opaquer in her motives. After all, she might well have wished to miss, however subconsciously.

Interestingly, the same issue of scrutinizing intent amidst unforeseen results emerges in *Under Western Eyes*, especially in so far as Razumov's motives in betraying Haldin – and later confessing to the act – remain a perennial mystery to both the narrating teacher of languages and the reader. After fleeing Haldin, who has sought out his help in escaping, for instance, Razumov contemplates whether to betray him:

> What is betrayal? They talk of a man betraying his country, his friends, his sweetheart. There must be a moral bond first. All a man can betray is his conscience. And how is my conscience engaged here; by what bond of common faith, of common conviction, am I obliged to let that fanatical idiot drag me down with him? On the contrary – every obligation of true courage is the other way. (37-38)

The major ethical question raised in this statement revolves around betrayal, and Razumov clearly distinguishes between betraying others or outside moral agents (one's country, friends, or "sweetheart") and betraying one's self. Razumov in this statement argues that for the first type of betrayal to have any ethical validity there must first be a moral bond between the betrayer and betrayed. Razumov, as he sees it, has no such moral bond, so the only possible betrayal is of his own conscience. The opposition between these two ethical dimensions is important and should be probed further in connection with the notion of moral luck.[34]

On the one hand, the narrative concludes that Razumov feels little in the way of attachment to Haldin or anyone else. Razumov's only obligation, it would seem, is to himself and his own sense of moral right and wrong. On the other hand, the narrating teacher of languages also confesses at the start of the novel that he has "no comprehension of the Russian character" (4). This is one more strategic distancing narrative device or ruse from the narrator to evade moral responsibility for the numerous prejudices about Russia seeping through his narrative. By confessing his ignorance of the Russian character, he seeks to convince the reader that this prejudiced view of Russia is not of his own making, but innocently and faithfully drawn from the protagonist's dairy itself. Wondering "why Mr. Razumov has left this record behind him," the narrator cites his "inscrutable motives" and attributes to him "a mysterious impulse of human nature" (4-5). At other points, the narrative ascribes to Razumov a clearer motivation – self-preservation – and attempts to relay his internal thoughts: "Do I want his death? No! I would save him if I could – but no one can do that – he is the withered member which must be cut off. If I must perish through him, let me at least not perish with him, and associated against my will with his sombre folly" (36). Here, Razumov engages in an intense ethical discussion with himself over Haldin's fate. Finally, however, he rejects all ethical bonding or solidarity with Haldin and justifies this moral disengagement on the grounds that Haldin is unsavable. In short, Haldin does not pose an ethical obligation, in Razumov's eyes, because he has become "withered" or removed from society. In a sense, Razumov concocts an elaborate ethical justification for betraying him and seems to find validation for his action in Haldin's "somber folly," or moral blindness.

Indeed, as the narrative progresses, the reader comes to realize that the narrating teacher of languages is hardly a disinterested observer, nor a detached, objective narrator, as he claims. He harbors prejudices against what he sees as the Russian character and mindset, while pretending to report objectively to the reader what is stated in Razumov's diary, which he consistently edits and adapts to his narrative and moral goals. He also competes with Razumov for Natalia's affection, for whom he acknowledges the "warmth of [his] regard" (164). In Geneva, Razumov even lashes out at the narrator directly, calling him "the devil himself in the shape of an old Englishman" (360) and asking: "What have you to do with any confounded circumstances, or with anything that happens in Russia, anyway?" (186). Razumov goes as far as to remind him and, by extension, the reader: "I am not a young man in a novel" (185-86), which adds what Penn R. Szittya has called a "metafictive" component[35] and immediately calls into question both the veracity of the narrator's account and his claim to be relaying a "record."[36] To some extent the line even echoes the narrator's own initial assertion that "words [...] are the great foes of reality" (3). Thus, the question that Latus and other philosophers ask – namely, whether we can ever know an agent's underlying intentions, much less appraise "the strength of her commitment" to an "action"[37] – is inseparable from the broader question in Conrad of narratological truth: whether the narrator himself can be trusted, and what exactly a novel is doing in pretending to relay underlying emotional truths.[38]

Certainly, opacity of character and unreliability of narrative are well-established themes in Conrad's works.[39] Yet both are important in exploring Razumov's moral considerations, especially in betraying Haldin, because they call into question whether the narrator, reader, or anyone else could faithfully recount, much less discern, the truth of Razumov's intentions.[40] While he claims to enter into a kind of "moral solitude" (39), which is almost Kantian or deontic in its sense of autonomous moral introspection, Razumov also begins to hold a more consequentialist view. After having fatally betrayed Haldin, for instance, Razumov has persistent visions of his roommate, whose "phantom" he cannot escape (302): "whenever he went abroad he felt himself at once closely involved in the moral consequences of his act" (299). Here the moral turnout, or results of his deed, acquire a metaphysical presence in the form of Haldin's ghost, "a moral specter infinitely more effective than any visible apparition of the dead" (299-300). Where this moral consequentialism becomes most apparent to Razumov is in fleeing the apartment with Haldin after having learned of the assassination, a point at which Razumov wavers: "Razumov envied the materialism of the thief and the passion of the incorrigible lover. The consequences of their actions were always clear and their lives remained their own" (78). Stranded in his own "moral solitude," Razumov is very much torn between his own internal sense of right and wrong, coupled with fear for his safety, and his outward concern for the results of betraying Haldin, none of which, to be sure, remains clear to him, the narrator, or reader.

"The Crazy Fate": Causal Luck

Another major problem in discerning Razumov's motives and indeed the novel's moral outlook is that it is unclear to what extent Razumov controls his own fate. Upon learning of Haldin's involvement in the assassination, Razumov muses almost comically, "There goes my silver medal!" and reflects on the fact that "his life [is] being utterly ruined by this contact with such a crime," as if fate itself were the culprit (16). This sense of fatalism also comes to underlie Razumov's assessment of his own future. After betraying Haldin, for instance, Razumov wonders how far he dictates the terms of his life:

> The true Razumov had his being in the willed, in the determined future – in that future menaced by the lawlessness of autocracy – for autocracy knows no law – and the lawlessness of revolution. The feeling that his moral personality was at the mercy of these lawless

forces was so strong that he asked himself seriously if it were worth
while to go on accomplishing the mental functions of that existence
which seemed no longer his own. (77-78)

To the extent Razumov is at the "mercy of these lawless forces,"
the narrative asks the same question that Nagel poses in his
discussion of "causal luck": "how can one be responsible even
for the striped-down acts of the will itself, if they are the product
of antecedent circumstances outside of the will's control?"[41]
For Nagel, the question of causal luck is ultimately one of free
will: namely, how can moral agents be held accountable if their
actions are unwilled or outside their own volition? While Nagel
does not answer the question directly, his argument bears
tremendously on Razumov, especially in so far as he operates
in what he – or at least what the narrator – perceives to be
a "willed" and "determined future" (*UWE* 77).

      Indeed, where this sense of fatalism first registers with
Razumov is in learning of Haldin's involvement in the
assassination, the point at which Razumov comically foresees
his own fate:

> He stared in dreary astonishment at the absurdity of his position.
> He thought with a sort of dry, unemotional melancholy; three years
> of good work gone, the course of forty more perhaps jeopardized –
> turned from hope to terror, because events started by human folly
> link themselves into a sequence which no sagacity can foresee and
> no courage can break through. Fatality enters your rooms while your
> landlady's back is turned; you come home and find it in possession
> bearing a man's name, clothed in flesh – wearing a brown cloth coat
> and long boots – lounging against the stove. It asks you, "Is the outer
> door closed?" – and you don't know enough to take it by the throat and
> fling it downstairs. You don't know. You welcome the crazy fate. "Sit
> down," you say. And it is all over. You cannot shake it off any more. It
> will cling to you forever. Neither halter nor bullet can give you back the
> freedom of your life and the sanity of your thought... (83-84)

Here, the narrative explicitly contrasts the "freedom"
Razumov desires with the "sequence" of "events started by
human folly." Presumably, the initial "folly" is that of the
conspirators, not Razumov. Yet the word "folly" is telling. For

one, it echoes Haldin's initial request of help from Razumov, where Haldin offers to wear a "false beard" in making his escape and parodies Proverbs: "Let a fool be made serviceable according to his folly" (Prov. 26:4:81). Secondly, it mirrors Razumov's later discussion with the narrator, who asks him if Haldin might have been betrayed as a result of "some unforeseen event" or "the folly or weakness of some unhappy fellow-revolutionist." Razumov, afraid of being found out, can only reply "bitterly": "Folly or weakness" (*UWE* 193). In so doing, however, Razumov also hints at his own underlying weakness – his inability to "take" Haldin "by the throat and fling [him] downstairs," as he only half-humorously reflects. More broadly, Razumov's remark about "weakness" signals the larger transformation occurring within him: the realization that he may, in fact, be culpable for Haldin's death, even if the betrayal was compelled by "lawless forces," or what he calls "the absurdity of his position."

Thus, central to the question of Razumov's responsibility is the very question Nagel asks: can or should humans be responsible for unwilled acts? In the case of Razumov, it is debatable whether he, or anyone else in the novel, is in full control of his future, especially when, as the narrator puts it, "fatality enters your [room]." At the same time, one begins to wonder if the narrator's account is disingenuous and, by extension, attributing to Razumov a sense of "fatality" in effort to clear his name, especially after realizing that Natalia's affection for both him and the narrator is lost.

"The Sorrows of Your Miserable Life": Circumstantial Luck

No less important than the consequences of Razumov's betrayal and the role played by fate in this regard are the "confounded circumstances" in which he finds himself, as Razumov aptly terms them. Indeed, one of the persistent themes of the novel is the way one's lot in life shapes one's behavior, including the moral choices one makes. Sophia

Antonovna, for instance, recounts to Razumov the plight of her revolutionary father:

> What had society to say to him? Be submissive and be honest. If you rebel I shall kill you. If you steal I shall imprison you. But if you suffer I have nothing for you – nothing except perhaps a beggarly dole of bread – but no consolation for your trouble, no respect for your manhood, no pity for the sorrows of your miserable life. (262)

The passage reflects a common theme in Conrad's writings, the corruption of society, which he voices in a letter to Cunninghame Graham: "Society is essentially criminal. It is so because, taken as a whole, man is *un animal méchant* ('a vicious animal')" (*CL* 2: 159). For Sophia Antonovna in this passage, and largely for Conrad, as well,[42] society is fundamentally incongruous with ethics. It forces individuals into obedience and submission, it imprisons and kills them, but it is incapable of offering them empathy, respect or consolation. In short, society represents the antithesis of good behavior.

The irony in this conversation is that Razumov, unbeknownst to Sophia Antonovna, has found himself in the exact plight she has described. If he submits to the authorities and relays to Mr. de P— the truth about Haldin's involvement, Razumov is destined to suffer regret, not to mention a life lived in isolation abroad, as he does. Should he "rebel" and keep Haldin's deed secret, he would, as he sees it, be accused and eventually deported or hung, much like Sophia Antonovna's father. The double bind,[43] characteristic of Conrad's characters – here one thinks of Nostromo, faced with the choice of placating his European masters in Sulaco or appeasing a peasantry he has come to despise – reflects Conrad's essentially fatalist view: the impossibility of achieving moral clarity in a morally inscrutable world.

How, then, should one hold a character like Razumov responsible? In her discussion of "moral luck," Nelkin extends the "epistemic argument" to circumstantial luck. Citing Nagel's example of a Nazi collaborator, she imagines an émigré counterpart (a German who is forced to move to Argentina for business in 1929). Nelkin asks if the two – the collaborator and the non-collaborating émigré – can be compared, since the only difference between them is situational luck. Citing the work of Norvin Richards, she explains that

> we do judge people for what they would have done, but [...] what they do is often our strongest evidence for what they *would have done*. As a result, given our limited knowledge, we might not be entitled to treat the counterpart in the same way as the Nazi sympathizer, even though they are equally morally deserving of such treatment.[44]

Thus, in this account, circumstances, like consequences, should affect our judgments of agents, just not the treatments they deserve.

Interestingly, in depicting Natalia, Razumov's foreign-born counterpart and chief love interest by the end, Conrad presents a scenario that is remarkably similar to Nagel's two German-born counterparts. Leading up to his confession to Natalia, Razumov even compares himself with her, implying that since living "abroad" she has developed a romanticized view: "you have given yourself up to vain imaginings while I have managed to remain amongst the truth of things and the realities of life – our Russian life – such as they are" (*UWE* 345). He compares his "cruel" outlook with her "pure heart which had not been touched by evil things" (359) and explains: "I have had the misfortune to be born clear-eyed. And if you only knew what strange things I have seen! What amazing and unexpected apparitions!" (345).

Central to the novel is the contrast between the idyllic life of Geneva and the violent terrain of Saint Petersburg, with all the "cynicism and cruelty" it bears, as Christopher GoGwilt has shown.[45] Yet the irony is that Natalia, hardly the "pure heart" that Razumov envisions, opts to hand over his diary to the narrator at the end and, in so doing, reveals the full scope of Razumov's misdeeds, as well as her involvement with him. Her own motives here are debatable. On one level, she is impressing upon the teacher of languages the truth of her connection with Razumov, rather than him, thereby fending off his advances. Indeed, she tells the teacher "rather abruptly" that she's "decided to leave it with you. I have the right to do that. It was sent to me. It is mine," she adds, as if underscoring her authority (376). On another level, she is laying bare the full record of events and, in so doing, exposing the inanity of the conspirators, who hailed Razumov as a revolutionary, demonized Ziemianitch, and valorized figures like Peter Ivanovitch, the "great feminist."

This irony is important, not only because numerous critics have overlooked the complexity of Natalia's character,[46] but also because at the novel's end she reveals herself to be the moral counterpart to Razumov: while he grows more idealistic,[47] admitting his misdeeds, righting his "conscience," and, in so doing, "[giving himself] over to [the] vain imaginings" he formerly decried, she ultimately grows more cynical, rejecting him, along with the narrator and the conspirators, in favor of a solitary life. Thus, if Richards – and the "epistemic argument"– are correct, and we judge moral actors on the basis of "what they do" more than "what they *would have done*,"[48] it is fair to ask whether Natalia, had she been in Razumov's shoes, would have protected a conspirator like Haldin, rather than betray him, even if it came at her expense. After all, by the end of the novel, she foregoes the comforts of Geneva and effectively forsakes her wellbeing to move to Russia and devote herself to its "overcrowded jails" and "bereaved homes," as Sophia Antonovna explains (*UWE* 378). Of course, Natalia's motivations, much like Razumov's, remain enigmatic and filtered through an outsider's view, raising the question, as Richards also asks, of whether we can assess them in full.

"There's Character in Such a Discovery": Constitutive Luck

Perhaps the deepest question, then, for both Razumov and Natalia is whether their misfortune, their tragic and bifurcated destinies, finally stems from external twists of fate or from qualities endemic to them as individuals. The narrative, which, again, remains questionable as a source of authority, expounds at length on the protagonist's personality and traits, along with "the peculiar circumstances of Razumov's parentage, or rather of his lack of parentage" (26). Razumov reiterates this humble background, however sardonically, when Peter Ivanovitch accuses him of having ulterior motives: "'To be sure my name is not Gugenheimer,' [Razumov] said in a sneering tone. 'I am not a democratic Jew. How can I help it? Not everybody has such luck. I have no name, I have no....'" Attempting to ingratiate himself further, Ivanovitch addresses Razumov by his patronymic, to which Razumov replies: "I have no father. So much the better. But I will tell you what: my mother's grandfather was a peasant – a serf" (208). To some extent, the question of inherited wealth (or poverty) is as much a matter of circumstantial luck as it is constitutional. Nevertheless, what is clear is that Razumov, irrespective of his origins, is playing off Ivanovitch's suspicions, even deploying anti-Semitic tropes, to help conceal his own role. Although the narrator frequently reminds the reader that Razumov has only his Russianness to embrace, and while Ivanovitch naively comes to accept that, welcoming him as "one of us" (210), the truth of Razumov's attachments remains unclear, as does his value-scheme. In fact, one might claim that Razumov, more than anyone in the novel, ends up embracing a "democratic" ethos in so far as he self-sacrificingly clears Haldin's name, as well as Ziemianitch's, while disclosing his role to the revolutionists.

In fact, where Razumov's character traits and constitution become most determining of his fortune is in his confession to the revolutionists, which immediately hastens his demise. Sophia Antonovna even lauds him for the effort and compares him implicitly with Ivanovitch, whom she serves. "How many of the revolutionists," she asks:

> would deliver themselves up deliberately to perdition (as he himself says in that book) rather than go on living, secretly debased in their own eyes? How many?... And please mark this – he was safe when he

did it. It was just when he believed himself safe and more – infinitely more – when the possibility of being loved by that admirable girl first dawned upon him, that he discovered that his bitterest railings, the worst wickedness, the devil work of his hate and pride, could never cover up the ignominy of the existence before him. There's character in such a discovery. (380)

Notably, Sophia Antonovna, who has devoted her life in service to a fraud in Ivanovitch, admires Razumov's conviction and attributes it partly to the genuine affection he feels for Natalia (Razumov's unexpected confession is a highly significant narrative moment, which unsettles the novel's overall ethical structure. Sophia Antonovna admires Razumov's admission of his guilt, which she sees as an exceptional act of moral courage. Interestingly, this statement echoes Marlow's admiration of Kurtz's courage in admitting his own horrors in "Heart of Darkness"). When Sophia Antonovna confides to the narrator at the end that Ivanovitch has married a peasant girl in Russia and become an "inspired man" (382), she even implies that Razumov has altered the views of the misogynist (Ivanovitch) and prompted him to feel real love, as well as devotion. Of course, it is entirely possible that Sophia Antonovna is being sarcastic, especially in conversing with the narrator, whom she otherwise distrusts and regards with "hard" and "brilliant black eyes" (379). In any case, the supreme irony is that by the end of the novel, Razumov has embraced the truly revolutionary spirit, forsaking everyone and everything to repent, while Peter Ivanovitch, the "Arch-Revolutionist," has settled into a comfortable, domesticated role.

Clearly, the difficulty in assessing Razumov's character – and the extent to which it underlies his fate – is that he changes throughout the book. The one constant feature, however, seems to be his willingness to undergo a moral reckoning, ultimately precipitating his confession. Where Dostoevsky's Raskolnikov could be said to harbor spiritual views, resulting in a kind of Christian redemption by the end, [49] Razumov, by contrast, embarks on a secular path, [50] and, if anything, enters "perdition," as he calls it. Michael John DiSanto, among others, reiterates this point, arguing that where "Dostoevsky's idea" of "confession leads to salvation, Conrad reveals that the confession, at least potentially, leads to damnation."[51]

Towards a "Pure Heart":
Conrad's Take on Moral Luck

Most importantly, the "character" Razumov displays, as Sophia Antonovna calls it, presages an important point in the contemporary debate over moral luck. In his 1976 article, Williams outlines a concept called "agent-regret," which "a person can feel only towards his own past actions (or, at most, actions in which he regards himself as a participant)."[52] In the case of the pedestrian-killing driver, Williams argues, "there is something special about his relation" to the killing, even if "it was not his fault."[53] For Williams, this "agent-regret" helps underscore the point that morality, as commonly understood, is inherently flawed (and would best be replaced with what he calls a system of ethics, although a few different communities). For other philosophers, such as Susan Wolf, this notion of agent-regret forms the basis for expecting moral actors, such as the pedestrian-killing driver, to adopt a degree of self-blame, even when they are not entirely at fault. As Nelkin explains,

> Wolf argues that there is a "nameless virtue" which consists in "taking responsibility for one's actions and their consequences" [...]. It is the virtue of taking responsibility in some sense for the consequences of one's actions, even if one is not responsible for them. In some ways it is akin to the virtue of generosity in that it "involves a willingness to give more...than justice requires."[54]

Of course, Wolf's approach is not without criticism. Darren Domsky, for example, finds it "intolerable," insisting that "we do not want the [unlucky agents] merely to blame themselves; we want them to recognize that they deserve to be blamed, even though we also believe that they cannot deserve to be."[55]

Regardless of which approach is more "tolerable" or in keeping with human practice, what is noteworthy is that Razumov, in sounding his confession, displays Wolf's notion of a "nameless virtue." Having retreated to a little island in Geneva named after Jean-Jacques Rousseau, he writes in his diary to Natalia: "In giving Victor Haldin up, it was myself, after all, whom I have betrayed most basely. You must believe what I say now, you can't refuse to believe this. Most basely. It is through you that I came to feel this so deeply" (*UWE* 361). For Razumov, the assumption of responsibility for Haldin's death, even if it was partially outside of his own doing or the result of "fatality," becomes a way of settling his own conscience. In fact, as in Wolf's description of the pedestrian-killing driver, Razumov, despite accepting fault, is not entirely blamed for the affair. Much to the narrator's "surprise," Sophia Antonovna explains that after Razumov's confession, the conspirators "visited" him in Russia: "He is intelligent. He has ideas.... He talks well, too" (379). She even notes that Razumov's punishment – his deafening – was unintentional and only sprang from Nikita's treachery (380).

Where Razumov perhaps differs from Wolf's ideal agent, however, is that his assumption of responsibility comes on the heels of a failed romance, prompting the question of whether his "virtue" is self-induced or inculcated through his relationship. Indeed, if anyone is perceived to be virtuous in the novel, it is Natalia, whom the narrator twice describes as "generous" (192, 193), echoing Wolf's term. While Natalia's motives, as explained, are more complicated than that which the narrator allows, the question Conrad asks through her – and it is very much pertinent to the approaches Williams and Wolf take – is whether love, or "the virtue of generosity," can nurture a kind of reckoning, or help to induce a form of self-regret, especially in a person like Razumov, who initially feels no regret or otherwise attributes his acts to "fatality." If "generosity," as Wolf explains it, entails "a willingness to give more – more time, more money, more love, more lenience, more, in one way or another, of oneself than justice requires," it is hard to imagine a better exemplar than Razumov, who confesses his betrayal, as Sophia Antonovna admits, "just when he believed himself safe."

What Conrad teaches us, then, about moral luck is that the self-blame Wolf extols and which Razumov arguably exhibits can come about externally through an act of inspiration, or the "tenderness" Natalia shows him (*UWE* 351). This is crucial, because while Razumov remains a "puppet of his past" (362) and at "the mercy" of "lawless forces," it is ultimately character – Natalia's "pure heart" – that engenders his confession, impelling him to "truth and peace" (358). While critics like Domsky assail Wolf's approach, asking, "what reason can morally unlucky agents have to start their self-blaming,"[56] perhaps Razumov himself gives a clue when he confesses to Natalia, however morosely, "It is through you that I came to feel this so deeply" (*UWE* 361). Lawless forces, indeed.

NOTES

[1] Williams and Nagel 117-22.

[2] See Williams; Enoch and Marmor.

[3] One exception is Daniel Brudney who, in discussing *Lord Jim*, mentions "moral luck" in a footnote (279n33), though in reference to broader issues in moral philosophy.

[4] For a discussion of "moral luck" in Hardy, see Larson (*Ethics and Narrative* 64-70; "When Hope Unblooms"); Zhang. For "moral luck" in Austen, see Larson (*Ethics and Narrative* 64-65); Hopkins. For "moral luck" in Chaucer, see Mitchell.

[5] Williams and Nagel 126.

[6] Nagel, *Mortal Questions* 60.

[7] See Crisp 1; Adam Smith; Feinberg.

[8] Williams and Nagel 140-41.

[9] Williams and Nagel 140.

[10] See Latus, "Moral Luck."

[11] Nagel, *Mortal Questions* 60.

[12] Williams and Nagel 145-46.

[13] For a counterfactual approach, see Hanna; for one involving agent-causation, see Clarke.

[14] Williams and Nagel 116.

[15] For more information on Conrad's fatalist view of existence, see Phillips; Bohlmann.

[16] See Blackburn 192.

17 Jessie Conrad 140-44.
18 Najder 409.
19 Mallios 167.
20 For more details on the influence of Dostoevsky on *Under Western Eyes*, see Knowles, "Literary Influences" 39-40; Carabine 64-96.
21 Richard Niland, for example, reads *Under Western Eyes* in terms of "betrayal, political commitment and conspiratorial revolutionary opposition in Russian society and politics" (38). One exception to the primarily "political" readings of the novel is George A. Panichas, who, while ceding the novel's political elements, finds it more concerned with unlocking moral discovery.
22 Sherry 232.
23 Sherry 234.
24 Sherry 230.
25 Sherry 230.
26 Griffin 461.
27 For more details on the relationship between Conrad and Russell, see Knowles, "Joseph Conrad and Bertrand Russell."
28 David Smith vii.
29 Meyers 10-11.
30 For more information on Conrad's sense of alienation, see chapter on "Conrad and Englishness" in Acheraïou.
31 As is discussed later in this essay, Razumov, in deciding whether to betray Haldin, for instance, concludes that both of them are doomed, reflecting: "If I must perish through him, let me at least not perish with him" (*UWE* 36).
32 Najder 41.
33 Latus "Moral and Epistemic Luck."
34 For more information on the issue of betrayal in *Under Western Eyes*, see Delesalle-Nancey; Erdinast-Vulcan.
35 Szittya 838.
36 Szittya 5.
37 Nelkin.
38 For further insights into the narratological truth and the narrator's reliability/unreliability in *Under Western Eyes*, see Szittya; Acheraïou, especially the chapter on *Under Western Eyes*.
39 Lothe offers perhaps the most definitive account of narrative complexity in *Under Western Eyes*, including the "problem of narrative reliability," as he puts it (68).
40 In assessing *Under Western Eyes*, for example, Christopher Cooper reminds us that "the interpretation of the morality of any given action depends also on the morality of the interpreter" (104). Likewise, Amar Acheraïou argues that the novel "attempts to establish a close, complex relationship with the reader through a marked narrative self-consciousness and techniques of reader manipulation," techniques that he locates in Sterne's *Tristram Shandy*, among other works (109). Acheraïou also notes that Conrad eschews the "didacticism" of Sterne, allowing for a kind of readerly engagement (150).

[41] Williams and Nagel 146.

[42] Certainly, the conventional wisdom in Conrad studies has been to regard him as distrustful of society. Ian Watt, for example, characterized "Heart of Darkness" as presenting a society "so widely and deeply fissured by its contradictions between its pretenses and its realities" (235), a view undoubtedly shared by Marlow. For Watt, the novella was "Conrad's most direct expression of his doubts about the foundation of human thought and action" (252). One notable exception to this view of Conrad-as-pessimist, however, is Andrew Roberts, who offers an interesting interpretation of *Under Western Eyes*, seeing in it an "ethics of the other" (142), wherein Razumov, through his gradual discovery of an "obligation to Haldin," begins to display a "Levinasian conception of an ethical responsibility" (143). Roberts is careful to point out that an "ethics of the other" is hardly an endorsement of society as such (145). The question also remains whether an "ethics of the other," whether applicable to Conrad or not, could translate into any larger social vision or societal project of the sort Conrad generally abhorred.

[43] Nicole Rizzuto also uses the term "double bind" to describe Razumov's predicament, though with reference to his specific choice of whether to confess his deeds to the revolutionists (72).

[44] Nelkin.

[45] GoGwilt 163.

[46] Thomas Moser, for instance, saw Natalia as "little more than a speaker of noble sentiments" (95); and Lissa Schneider-Rebozo regards Natalia as a "peg" and "pivot" for the plot, an assessment fueled in part by Conrad's own use of those terms to describe Natalia in an apologetic letter to Garnett's sister (40-41). Carola M. Kaplan, in contrast, highlights the "power, autonomy, and clear-sightedness that characterize Natalia," arguing that "her moral authority, along with that of her mother, Sophia, and Tekla [...] undermines Razumov's plan to deceive and betray her" (274).

[47] Allan Hunter, among others, hints at Razumov's growing idealism when he writes: "The determination to believe in no consoling delusions that marked Razumov throughout the novel have been subverted. His honesty has become venerable in itself" (239). More broadly, Hunter explores Razumov's thinking in the light of evolutionary ethics.

[48] Nelkin.

[49] Irving Howe, among others, discussed the Christian element of redemption in Dostoevsky.

[50] Compare, for instance, Sonia's admonition in *Crime and Punishment* – "You turned away from God and God has smitten you" (Dostoevsky 424) – with Sophia Antonovna's remark in *Under Western Eyes*: "a belief in a supernatural source of evil is not necessary; men alone are quite capable of every wickedness" (*UWE* 151).

[51] DiSanto 153.

[52] Williams and Nagel 123.

[53] Williams and Nagel 124.

142 Joshua A. Bernstein

[54] Nelkin, quoting Wolf.
[55] Domsky 451.
[56] Domsky 452.

WORKS CITED

Acheraïou, Amar. *Joseph Conrad and the Reader*. Basingstoke: Palgrave Macmillan, 2009. Print.

"Betrayal." *The Pall Mall Gazette* 11 Oct. 1911. [n/a]. Print.

Blackburn, William, ed. *Joseph Conrad: Letters to William Blackwood and David S. Meldrum*. Durham: Duke UP, 1958. Print.

Bohlmann, Otto. *Conrad's Existentialism*. Basingstoke: Palgrave Macmillan, 1991. Print.

Brudney, Daniel. "*Lord Jim* and Moral Judgment: Literature and Moral Philosophy." *The Journal of Aesthetics and Art Criticism* 56 (1998): 265–81. Print.

Carabine, Keith. *The Life and the Art: A Study of Conrad's* Under Western Eyes. Amsterdam: Rodopi, 1996. Print.

Clarke, Randolph. "Agent Causation and the Problem of Luck." *Pacific Philosophical Quarterly* 86 (2005): 408–21. Print.

Conrad, Jessie. *Joseph Conrad and His Circle*. London: Jarrolds, 1935. Print.

Cooper, Christopher. *Conrad and the Human Dilemma*. London: Chatto, 1970. Print.

Crisp, Roger. "Moral Luck and Equality of Moral Opportunity." *Aristotelian Society Supplementary Volume* 91 (2017): 1–20. Print.

Delesalle-Nancey, Catherine. "Underground Explosion: The Ethics of Betrayal in *Under Western Eyes* and Malcolm Lowry's *Under the Volcano*." *The Conradian* 36.2 (2011): 79-94. Print.

DeMille, Barbara. "Cruel Illusions: Nietzsche, Conrad, Hardy, and the 'Shadowy Ideal.'" *Studies in English Literature* 30 (1990): 697–714. Print.

DiSanto, Michael John. *Under Conrad's Eyes: The Novel as Criticism*. Montreal: McGill-Queens UP, 2009. Print.

Domsky, Darren. "There Is No Door: Finally Solving the Problem of Moral Luck." *The Journal of Philosophy* 101 (2004): 445–64. Print.

Dostoevsky, Fyodor. *Crime and Punishment*. 1866. Trans. Constance Garnett. New York: Collier, 1917. Print.

Enoch, David, and Andrei Marmor. "The Case against Moral Luck." *Law and Philosophy* 26 (2007): 405–36. Print.

Erdinast-Vulcan, Daphna. "The Conradian Subject-in-Process: The Question of Ethics in *Under Western Eyes*." *The Conradian* 36.2 (2011): 95-105. Print.

Feinberg, Joel. "Problematic Responsibility in Law and Morals." *The Philosophical Review* 71 (1962): 340-51. Print.

Garnett, Edward. "Mr. Conrad's New Novel." *The Nation* 21 Oct. 1911. [n/a]. Print.

GoGwilt, Christopher. *The Invention of the West: Joseph Conrad and the Double Mapping of Europe and Empire*. Palo Alto: Stanford UP, 2005. Print.

Griffin, Nicholas, ed. *The Selected Letters of Bertrand Russell*. Vol.1: *The Private Years 1884-1914*. New York: Routledge, 2013. Print.

Hanna, Nathan. "Moral Luck Defended." *Noûs* 48 (2014): 683-98. Print.

Hollander, Rachel. "Thinking Otherwise: Ethics and Politics in Joseph Conrad's *Under Western Eyes*." *Journal of Modern Literature* 38.3 (2015): 1-19. Print.

Hopkins, Robert. "Moral Luck and Judgment in Jane Austen's *Persuasion*." *Nineteenth-Century Literature* 42 (1987): 143–58. Print.

Howe, Irving. "Dostoevsky: The Politics of Salvation." *The Kenyon Review* 17.1 (1955): 42–68. Print.

Hunter, Allan. *Joseph Conrad and the Ethics of Darwinism*. London: Helm, 1983. Print.

Kaplan, Carola M. "Beyond Gender: Deconstructions of Masculinity and Femininity from 'Karain' to *Under Western Eyes*." *Conrad in the Twenty-First Century: Contemporary Approaches and Perspectives*. Ed. Carola M. Kaplan, Peter Mallios, and Andrea White. New York: Routledge, 2004. 267–79. Print.

Knowles, Owen. "Joseph Conrad and Bertrand Russell: New Light on Their Relationship." *Journal of Modern Literature* 17.1 (1990): 139–53. Print.

---. "Literary Influences." *Joseph Conrad in Context*. Ed. Allan Simmons. Cambridge: Cambridge UP, 2009. Print.

---. "'Who's Afraid of Arthur Schopenhauer?': A New Context for Conrad's 'Heart of Darkness.'" *Nineteenth-Century Literature* 49 (1994): 75–106. Print.

Lackey, Michael. "The Moral Conditions for Genocide in Joseph Conrad's 'Heart of Darkness.'" *College Literature* 32 (2005): 20–41. Print.

Larson, Jil. *Ethics and Narrative in the English Novel, 1880–1914*. Cambridge: Cambridge UP, 2001. Print.

---. "When Hope Unblooms: Chance and Moral Luck in the Fiction of Thomas Hardy." Center for the Study of Ethics in Society Papers. Western Michigan University. Nov. 2001. Web. <http://scholarworks.wmich.edu/ethics_papers/59>. 7 March 2021.

Latus, Andrew. "Moral and Epistemic Luck." *Journal of Philosophical Research* 25 (2000): 149–72. Print.

---. "Moral Luck." *The Internet Encyclopedia of Philosophy*. Ed. J. Feiser. A Peer-Reviewed Academic Resource. 2001. Web. <www.iep.utm.edu/moralluc/>. 7 March 2021.

Lothe, Jakob. *Conrad's Narrative Method*. Oxford: Oxford UP, 1989. Print.

Mallios, Peter. *Our Conrad: Constituting American Modernity*. Palo Alto: Stanford UP, 2010. Print.

Meyers, Jeffrey. *Joseph Conrad: A Biography*. New York: Cooper Square, 2001. Print.

Mitchell, J. Allan. "Romancing Ethics in Boethius, Chaucer, and Levinas: Fortune, Moral Luck, and Erotic Adventure." *Comparative Literature* 57 (2005): 101–16. Print.

Moser, Thomas. *Joseph Conrad: Achievement and Decline.* Hamden: Archon, 1966. Print.

Nagel, Thomas. "Moral Luck." *Moral Luck.* Ed. Daniel Statman. Albany: State U of New York P, 1993. 57-71. Print.

---. "Moral Luck." *Mortal Questions.* By Nagel. Cambridge: Cambridge UP, 1979. Print.

Najder, Zdzisław. *Joseph Conrad: A Life.* Trans. Halina Carroll-Najder. Rochester: Camden, 2007. Print.

Nelkin, Dana K. "Moral Luck." *The Stanford Encyclopedia of Philosophy.* Ed. Edward N. Zalta. Summer 2019 Edition. 26 Jan. 2004. Substantive revision 19 Apr. 2019. Web. <https://plato.stanford.edu/archives/sum2019/entries/moral-luck/>. 7 March 2021.

Niland, Richard. "The Political Novels." *The New Cambridge Companion to Joseph Conrad.* Ed. J. H. Stape. Cambridge: Cambridge UP, 2015. Print.

Panichas, George A. *Joseph Conrad: His Moral Vision.* Macon: Mercer UP, 2005. Print.

Phillips, Temple. "The Fatalism of Joseph Conrad." *America* 68.8 (1942): 213-14. Print.

Rizzuto, Nicole. *Insurgent Testimonies: Witnessing Colonial Trauma in Modern and Anglophone Literature.* Oxford: Oxford UP, 2015. Print.

Roberts, Andrew M. "Conrad and the Territory of Ethics." *Conradiana* 37 (2005): 133–46. Print.

Schneider-Rebozo, Lissa. *Conrad's Narratives of Difference.* New York: Routledge, 2003. Print.

Sherry, Norman. *Conrad: The Critical Heritage.* New York: Routledge, 1973. Print.

Smith, Adam. *The Theory of Moral Sentiments.* 1759. Ed. D. D. Raphael, A. L. Macfie. Indianapolis: Liberty Fund, 1982. Print.

Smith, David R, ed. *Joseph Conrad's* Under Western Eyes*: Beginnings, Revisions, Final Forms.* Hamden: Archon, 1991. Print.

Szittya, Penn R. "Metafiction: The Double Narration in *Under Western Eyes.*" *English Literary History* 48 (1981): 817–40. Print.

Watt, Ian. *Conrad in the Nineteenth Century.* Berkeley: U of California P, 1979. Print.

Williams, B. A. O. "Postscript." *Moral Luck.* Ed. Daniel Statman. Albany: State U of New York P, 1993. 241-47. Print.

---, and T. Nagel. "Moral Luck." *Aristotelian Society Supplementary Volume* 50 (1976): 115–52. Print.

Wolf, Susan. "The Moral of Moral Luck." *Philosophic Exchange* 31.1 (2001): 4-19. Print.

Zhang, Chengping. "Moral Luck in Thomas Hardy's Fiction." *Philosophy and Literature* 34 (2010): 82-94. Print.

Thomas Higgins,
Villanova University,
Villanova, PA, USA

"He died for the Revolution": Anarchism and Ethical Commitment in *The Secret Agent*

In "Commitment," Theodor W. Adorno writes: "The committed work of art debunks the work that wants nothing but to exist; it considers it a fetish, the idle pastime of those who would be happy to sleep through the deluge that threatens us – an apolitical stance that is in fact highly political."[1] Adorno's condemnation of apolitical art, of art that is not committed, constitutes a moral critique of bourgeois aestheticism and of the theory of "art for art's sake," which considers that art serves no didactic, moral, or political function. Joseph Conrad's work is as well known for its stylistic prowess and historic importance to the so-called canon of Western Literature, as it is for the questions it raises about artistic commitment and the writer's responsibility towards society. In his essay "An Image of Africa: Racism in Conrad's 'Heart of Darkness,'" Chinua Achebe famously condemned "Heart of Darkness" and called Conrad a "thoroughly bloody racist."[2] For Achebe, literature is a medium of social and political change. A strong advocate of *"une littérature engagée,"* Achebe is an "organic intellectual" who rejects the Western notion that "art should be accountable to no one, and need[s] to justify itself to nobody except itself." He concludes on this premise that any "good" story or novel should have a "message," a "use" and a "purpose" and "serve a down-to earth necessity."[3] Conrad, by contrast, is a writer who embraces the notion of an autonomous, politically neutral art.

Conrad's 1907 novel *The Secret Agent* is a valuable text for understanding not just the ethical implications of commitment, but also the actual consequences a lack of commitment can bring about, and through which the "idle pastime" of fiction can become all-too real. While the novel takes anarchist violence as its subject, it is far more interested in portraying anarchism as inherently violent, than it is in investigating its founding principles or ideals. However, according to Conrad's contemporary, Peter Kropotkin, a noted Russian scientist and anarchist, actual anarchism is committed to an ethics of mutual aid, anti-authoritarianism, and human freedom. In *Living Without Domination: The Possibility of an Anarchist Utopia*, Samuel Clark sees *The Secret Agent* as a text which marginalizes anarchism, particularly through the Professor's expression of "pathological hatred for everything with calculated violence."[4] In contrast to Conrad's portrayal of anarchists, Clark argues that such violent figures were largely "in the minority, their activity [...] confined to the period between 1890 and 1930 (particularly in France and the United States)."[5] As he points out that "many other anarchists repudiated their actions," Clark also highlights that "few political positions can claim that no one has ever committed violence in their names."[6] In his essay "Analytical Anarchism: Some Conceptual Foundations," Alan Carter claims that anarchism should "be regarded as a form of [...] political egalitarianism."[7] He argues that anarchist opposition to the state cannot be confounded with opposition to society, therefore anarchism must not "be confused with a rejection of all the rules that a society might need – for example, moral rules. In fact, most anarchists are highly moral."[8] If anarchism can thus be understood as a political ideology grounded in an ethical obligation to society, then it is necessary to reconsider *The Secret Agent* for its narrow representation of anarchist violence. This essay considers to what extent an author is responsible for representing the truth behind fiction. In Conrad's case, how does one tally the author's ironic and dismissive representation of anarchists with anarchism's well-documented moral framework, as well as with the lived experience of those who sought and continue to seek, through opposition to the state, a society freed from violent oppression? To do so, I approach Conrad's text by revisiting both its publication and reception histories, as well as reading its fictional representation of historical events alongside contemporary accounts of the Greenwich Observatory bombing of 1894. Ultimately, I will show that it is important not only to restore both anarchism's historical representation and the circumstances surrounding French anarchist Martial Bourdin's death, but also to demonstrate the extent to which Conrad's novel fails in its obligation to society via "an apolitical stance that is in fact highly political."[9]

Since its publication, some critics have interpreted *The Secret Agent* as a novel intent on accurately portraying anarchists and their revolutionary tactics, while others argued that it is a novel which lampoons and critiques both anarchists and the state. In *Joseph Conrad among the Anarchists: Nineteenth Century Terrorism and "The Secret Agent,"* David Mulry notes that while Conrad's "political sympathies regarding anarchist terror are much disputed, [...] the dominant critical stance seems to be that he is conservative and treats the anarchists scornfully."[10] He contrasts Richard Curle's 1914 text *Joseph Conrad: A Study* with Irving Howe's *Politics and the Novel,* published in 1957.[11] Curle describes Conrad's anarchists as "a curious group" whose de facto leader, the Professor, is "an extremist who believes in destruction simply for itself," seemingly taking Conrad's representation at face value.[12] Contrastingly, Howe wholeheartedly condemns Conrad's treatment of anarchism.[13] Mulry argues this suggests "that not to treat the subject of anarchism and anarchists seriously does [them] a disservice [...] and ultimately undermines the novel's grasp and scope."[14] In his 1997 essay "Joseph Conrad's *The Secret Agent* as a Moral Tale," George A. Panichas claims that "Conrad's novel [...] particularly illustrates not only his moral universality but also his moral indictment of the betrayal of order, which a civilized society needs for its existence."[15] Whereas Panichas contends that "Conrad has no sympathy for anarchists," Jakob Lothe declares that "authorial attitude to the characters varies, ranging from the scorn and contempt of the narrator's descriptions of some of the anarchists to the sympathy and pity characteristic of his portrayal of Stevie."[16]

Despite the novel's irony, and despite letters written during the process of composing and publishing the novel, in which Conrad claims not to take anarchist violence very seriously at all, the book has become – as this essay will show – a source for terrorists, law enforcement, and the press alike, all of whom have repeatedly manipulated Conrad's lack of commitment to their own ends. Blurring the line between fiction and reality even further, Conrad adapts the character Stevie from the historical figure Bourdin, whose name has managed to survive both despite, and, as this paper argues, as a direct result of Conrad's intentions.[17] Conrad records his vision of anarchism's lack of commitment to humanity, but his distant irony exposes the emptiness of his own ethical commitment, as do his letters, which display his strong desire to see the novel increase his standing as a serious, respected artist.

Writing to his fellow-novelist, John Galsworthy on 12 September 1906, a full year before *The Secret Agent*'s publication, Conrad admits that he "had no idea to consider Anarchism politically – or to treat it seriously in its philosophical aspect: as a manifestation of human nature in its discontent and imbecility" (*CL* 3: 354). We find in a letter written on 7 November 1906 to Algernon Methuen, the publisher of *The Secret Agent*, that Conrad did not condone the description of his novel printed on posters to advertise its serialization in the U.S.: "A Tale of Diplomatic Intrigue and Anarchist Treachery," claiming that the story is "a fairly successful (and sincere) piece of ironic treatment applied to a special subject – a sensational subject if one likes to call it so." He further states that "[the novel] is based on the inside knowledge of a certain event in the history of active anarchism. But otherwise it is purely a work of imagination. It has no social or philosophical intention" (371). Interestingly, there is something of Conrad's disdain of anarchism in Chief Inspector Heat's attitude toward anarchism, most potently exemplified in the figure of Stevie, himself a mentally disabled individual who struggles to assimilate into British society:

> Truth to say, Chief Inspector Heat thought but little of anarchism. He did not attach undue importance to it, and could never bring himself to consider it seriously. It had more the character of disorderly conduct; disorderly without the human excuse of drunkenness, which at any rate implies good feeling and an amiable leaning towards festivity. As criminals, anarchists were distinctly no class – no class at all. And recalling the Professor, Chief Inspector Heat, without checking his swinging pace, muttered through his teeth: "Lunatic." (SA 96-97)

Despite claiming that the novel "has no social or philosophical intention," in aligning his own view with that of a government official, Conrad casts a sincere political judgment on anarchism, while also issuing a moral verdict on the anarchists whom he dismisses as social scum – a "classless" gang of violent, ruthless "criminals."

In a letter written on 6 May 1907 to J. B. Pinker, his literary agent, Conrad describes his forthcoming novel as "a distinctly new departure in [his] work" and admits he is anxious that "[p]reconceived notions of Conrad as sea writer will stand in the way of its acceptance," in the process, hoping to "strik[e] a blow for popularity" (CL 3: 434-35). In a follow-up letter, responding again to Pinker, Conrad remarks on 18 May 1907 that he

> would try to reach [popularity] not by sensationalism but by means of taking a widely discussed subject for the text of my novel. Apart from religious problems the public mind runs on questions of war and peace and labour. I mean war, peace, labour in general not any particular way or any particular form of labour trouble. (439-40)

In a letter written again to Pinker on June 1st, he clarifies the novel's title to be "THE SECRET AGENT. A Simple Tale" and once more insists that he does not "want the story to be misunderstood as having any sort of social or polemical intention" (446).

Conrad's desire for ideological neutrality likely stems from an overarching obsession with readership and popularity. In *Joseph Conrad and the Reader*, Amar Acheraïou explains that while "following the commercial failure of his works Conrad occasionally claimed that he did not want to be popular [...] [he] strove unremittingly for literary and commercial success" throughout his career.[18] According to Acheraïou, *The Secret Agent*, a novel with which Conrad sought to capitalize upon both "his compatriots' anxiety over national identity" and the contemporary trend toward a domestic literature, failed to achieve the popularity he desired: "[D]espite its evident concern with the threats of anarchism and republicanism on English society, *The Secret Agent's* focus on the local was apparently not profound enough to arouse English readers' deep sympathies."[19] Reading this alongside Conrad's complex relationship with his readership offers another explanation for the novel's failure to reach a wide audience upon publication. Acheraïou argues that Conrad, like many of his fellow Modernists, simultaneously disparaged the average reader while addressing his texts to an ideal, elite readership.[20] Just as he both craves and eschews popularity, Conrad at once rejects and welcomes his readers. This need for distance perhaps explains why, for Acheraïou, Conrad "almost never addresses his readers directly [...] instead [articulating his relation to the audience] around a gamut of theoretical and narrative devices subtly orchestrated by his primary narrators."[21] In *Conrad's Narrative Method*, Lothe states that "Conrad's fiction exhibits intricate modulations of distance,"[22] and, with regard to *The Secret Agent*, in particular, distance functions attitudinally "in the sense that the authorial narrator obviously approves neither of anarchy nor of anarchist activity."[23] Ultimately, Lothe argues,

> one effect of the irony [needed to establish this authorial distance] is to reinforce the reader's impression of the narrator's need for distance from the characters described. And, in a complex way, this need of the narrator's distance can be seen as reflecting Conrad's need for distance from the fictional reality of *The Secret Agent*.[24]

By distancing himself from readership, narrator, and his fictional universe, Conrad tends to create an atmosphere in which a lack of authorial commitment not only contributes to the novel's commercial failure, but also ensures *The Secret Agent* will be read as a highly political novel despite Conrad's stated neutrality.

It is also important to point out that Conrad seems to have been worried about the reception of his text as "sensational," rather than as a serious novel that sought to deal with "a widely discussed subject" (*CL* 3: 439-40). While one may argue that Conrad is simply being coy here, his claims comply, nonetheless, with the novel's highly ironic treatment of anarchists. In the text itself, a creation which must, to some degree, escape its author's beliefs and intentions the very moment it is released to the reading public, there is something to be gained in understanding how the text has been received. Namely, we must look to the debates it has generated throughout the twentieth and twenty-first centuries, as well as to the damage it inflicts on the French anarchist historical figure Bourdin.

On Thursday, 14 February 1894, Bourdin died when the bomb he was carrying accidentally exploded in Greenwich Park. The event caused a national uproar at a time of heightened paranoia over anarchism and dynamite attacks in Great Britain and in Europe, and added to an ongoing debate in the House of Commons regarding the government's immigration policies, specifically its willingness to grant asylum to foreign revolutionaries. Mulry points out that the bombing, "a *cause célèbre* in its day," "was the first anarchist bombing, or explosive act of anarchist 'propaganda by deed,' to take place on British soil during the era of bombs in the latter part of the nineteenth century."[25] The effect of the Greenwich bombing, according to Mulry, was to drastically "shift the political landscape in England":

> The English press, which had been largely forgiving of European dissidence (especially Slavic rebellion against Tsarist autocracy), and had espoused the idea of England as a refuge for men of ideas and principled exiles from autocratic cruelties, began to conflate Fenian activities with anarchist, communist, and socialist protest. The political distinctions were increasingly moot for an anxious public.... For Conrad and his readers, through the end of the

nineteenth century and the beginning of the twentieth, alarming
reports of dynamite activity linked to anarchist revolt had come to
be commonplace in the news from the continent, as is evident in
a leader in *The Times*, rounding up the news of 1894, the year of the
Greenwich bombing (which occurred early, on the 15th of February),
where political terroristic acts feature prominently in the annual
review of events.[26]

Rather than raise awareness and sympathy for the anarchist
cause, it seems that the Greenwich bombing contributed to
a culture of fear and anxiety within British public, increasingly
wary of threats both foreign and domestic. It is perhaps
unsurprising, then, if the English press's conflation of dissenting
political ideologies is reflected in Conrad's novel, especially
in its simplistic and caricatured portrayal of anarchists and
foreigners. Although *The Secret Agent* critiques and mocks the
British state as well, by feeding into generalizations, anxieties,
and most clearly disparaging representations of anarchist
dissenters and radicals, the novel is far from being politically
neutral, as Conrad contends.

To return to the historical event, while much speculation over
Bourdin's motives and the facts surrounding the Greenwich
explosion abounded for several weeks following the event, no
indisputable consensus has ever been established.[27] Outside of
Conrad's novel, the Greenwich bombing and Martial Bourdin
have entered the popular consciousness numerous times. T.
S. Eliot mentions Bourdin–despite misspelling his name–in
his 1929 *Ariel Series* poem "Animula": "For Boudin, blown
to pieces."[28] To date, *The Secret Agent* has been adapted into
film three times – Hitchcock's *Sabotage* (1936); a feature
film starring Bob Hoskins and Patricia Arquette (1996);
and a three-part BBC series (2016).[29] Following the BBC
adaptation, *The Guardian* published on 5 August 2016 a blog
by Rebekah Higgitt on Bourdin and the "real story" behind the
Greenwich Observatory Bombing.[30] Several scholarly articles
have connected Bourdin to Conrad's novel.[31] In "Kaczynski,
Conrad, and Terrorism," James Guimond and Katherine
Kearney Maynard report that FBI agents "had begun reading

The Secret Agent carefully even before Kaczynski was identified as a suspect, and the agency had consulted a number of Conrad scholars in the hopes of discovering more about the Unabomber's mentality and identity," themselves referencing Serge Kovaleski's *Washington Post* article published on 9 July 1996: "1907 Conrad Novel May Have Inspired Unabomb Suspect." They also write, again citing Kovaleski, that

> [Kaczynski's] parents had Conrad's collected works in their home, that Kaczynski himself had told them in a 1984 letter from Montana that he was "reading Conrad's novels for about the dozenth time," and FBI agents revealed that Kaczynski may have used "Conrad" or "Konrad" as his alias three times when he stayed at a hotel in Sacramento, where he presumably mailed his bombs.[32]

The Secret Agent would become, according to Judith Shulevitz, "[i]n the aftermath of the attacks of September 11 [...] one of the three works of literature most frequently cited in the American media."[33] In his 2005 book chapter "Reading *The Secret Agent* Now: The Press, the Police, and the Premonition of Simulation," Peter Lancelot Mallios reveals that "[d]uring the past three years, *The Secret Agent* has been referenced over a hundred times in newspapers, magazines, and online journalistic resources across the world."[34] There are certainly reverberations of Cesare Lombroso's criminal anthropology, which influenced Conrad's character descriptions,[35] within discourse that sought to typify terrorists as Muslim and Arab in the aftermath of 9/11. In one case, an author made a direct comparison between the Professor and Osama bin Laden less than a month after the attack, describing both figures as violent ideologues dedicated to death and destruction. Robert Harris, an English novelist, wrote a column for the *Daily Telegraph* titled "Forget Islam: bin Laden is no more than a spoiled rich kid." In his very first paragraph, Harris compares Osama bin Laden to the Professor, whom he confuses with Ossipon, and continues quoting from Conrad's novel throughout the column. He concludes with an ominous warning:

> If you want to understand Osama bin Laden and his Al-Qa'eda
> organization, my advice is to put the newspapers aside for a while
> and get hold of a novel published in 1907. *The Secret Agent* [sic]
> by Joseph Conrad describes the activities of a small group of state-
> sponsored terrorists, plotting an atrocity against a world-famous
> building – in this case, the Greenwich Observatory.[36]

Curiously, Harris describes bin Laden as "a 21st-century religious fanatic" motivated, like the Professor, by "a vast rage against the all-powerful Western world," while also suggesting the reader to "[s]et aside his religion and his race" to consider him as "a recognisable type in history," made untypically monstrous by the technological sophistication and openness of the modern world he so despises."[37] Like Conrad, he attempts to divest his violent terrorist of all ideological commitment while describing him in terms suggesting that his hatred is grounded in opposition to progress, modernity, and Western democracy – in other words, he pressuposes the invalidity of the ideology allegedly represented by the figure in question. It would almost seem that Harris is Conrad's "ideal reader," despite confusing the names of two of the novel's characters. In any case, it is clear that Conrad's depiction of anarchist violence in Victorian England was easily and swiftly transposed onto the discourse regarding bin Laden's involvement in the attacks on 9/11. *The Secret Agent* has survived as much for its topical relevance as for its transition into a political narrative through consistent readings which determine Conrad's novel to be a text that is committed in its portrayal of the anarchists' actions and motives. In much the same way, Bourdin's story, whether Conrad intended it or not, survives because of its transition to fiction.

To see the stakes involved in the formation of a narrative, we need look no further than the February 16th, 1894 edition of *The Times*, which likely served as source material for Conrad's fictionalization of the Greenwich Bomb Outrage. On page 5 of the broadsheet, in an article titled "Explosion in Greenwich Park," it describes the events of the previous day in graphic detail:

> Last evening an explosion was heard by a keeper of Greenwich
> Park on the hill close to the Royal Observatory. Proceeding thither
> he found a respectably-dressed man, in a kneeling posture, terribly
> mutilated. One hand was blown off and the body was open. The
> injured man was only able to say, "Take me home," and was unable to
> reply to a question as to where his home was.[38]

Comparing this to Conrad's description of Stevie's death, we
find some telling differences. It is a constable, not a keeper,
who discovers the body, though the constable does tell Chief
Inspector Heat that he "sent a keeper to fetch a spade" to
"scrap[e]" Stevie's remains from the ground (*SA* 87). Unlike
Bourdin, Stevie dies instantaneously, a detail Conrad seems to
have adapted for his novel. The importance of this comparison,
however, is to show that Conrad both adopts and magnifies
violent details of mutilation straight from the British press.
Toward the end of *The Times*' "Explosion in Greenwich Park,"
in a passage which reprints the *Central News Agency's* report
on the explosion, Bourdin's death is treated sensationally:

> Walking along the main avenue lined with great trees on both sides, he
> reached the top of the hill, near the Observatory. Across the pathway
> the roots of the older trees protrude through the gravel, and it may
> be assumed that, it now being quite dusk, the man stumbled and fell,
> with the result that the infernal machine or machines which he was
> carrying exploded on his own person. It is possible that at the last
> moment, remembering the Observatory was a Government building,
> he decided to expend his explosives against it [...]. The first to arrive
> found a man half crouching on the ground. His legs were shattered,
> one arm was blown away, and the stomach and abdomen were torn
> open [...]. The pockets of the unknown contained papers in French
> and English which showed conclusively that he was an Anarchist and
> a trusted man in the party; but they did not satisfactorily establish
> his identity [...]. That the man was a foreigner is placed beyond
> doubt....[39]

Once again, the constable's account echoes a contemporary
report – he "announce[s] positively" to Chief Inspector Heat
that Stevie "[s]tumbled against the root of a tree and fell, and
that thing he was carrying must have gone off right under

his chest" (*SA* 89). In fact, it is almost as if Ossipon were holding this very edition of *The Times* in the basement of the Silenus Restaurant, quoting its contents to the Professor in the stillness left in the pause of a player piano. We find yet more gory details here, "shattered" recalling Stevie's "fragments," the "cannibal feast" consumed by an eager public in the news. The last portion of the *Central News'* report speaks volumes regarding popular British discourse of the Victorian era on the "nonassimilable." While Conrad's novel mocks British paranoia and distrust of foreigners, especially those from the continent – something a Polish-born writer must have known firsthand – it is crucial to ask why he chose to leave out this most important detail in forming the character of Stevie.[40] Why did he go to such great lengths to ensure the accuracy of his account of the Greenwich Bomb Outrage, only to portray Stevie as a disabled British subject and not as the French anarchist Bourdin was known to be? It must be asked whether such an erasure renders Conrad complicit, or at least negligent, in his treatment of xenophobia and political unrest in *fin-de-siècle* England. Although Conrad was considered an outsider in the British writers' circles and suffered personally from xenophobia, he was, according to Acheraïou, "an outsider with a strong commitment to his adopted country" who sought to overcome "obstacles in the way of his acceptance by the insular British literary establishment and the British reading public."[41] In failing to condemn the xenophobic political atmosphere of his adopted country, Conrad commits himself to a national ideal which will never fully accept him. Despite stating his desire to avoid sensationalism in *The Secret Agent*, Conrad's violent portrayal of anarchism and assimilation of racist and xenophobic attitudes constitutes a failure of the artist's ethical commitment to humanity.

While the actual moment of Stevie's death does not appear in the novel, it is alluded to in a manner consistent with Conrad's vision of anarchism as nihilistic and dependent upon sensationalist violence. He describes Stevie's remains, which Chief Inspector Heat goes to the morgue to investigate, as:

"a sort of mound–a heap of rags, scorched and bloodstained, half concealing what might have been an accumulation of raw material for a cannibal feast" (*SA* 86). This language echoes the scene following Ossipon's conversation with the Professor, as the anarchist steps out into the streets of London:

> In front of the great doorway a dismal row of newspaper sellers standing clear of the pavement dealt out their wares from the gutter. It was a raw, gloomy day of the early spring; and the grimy sky, the mud of the streets, the rags of the dirty men, harmonized excellently with the eruption of the damp, rubbishy sheets of paper soiled with printers' ink. The posters, maculated with filth, garnished like tapestry the sweep of the curbstone. The trade in afternoon papers was brisk, yet, in comparison with the swift, constant march of foot traffic, the effect was of indifference, of a disregarded distribution. (79)

As Stevie's body transforms into the narrative told by the press, his blood turns to ink, and his fragments become fragments of text upon the "rubbishy sheets of paper soiled with printer's ink" sold "from the gutter." Disregarded in life, he is disregarded in death, too, sold and told only, perhaps, as the "swift, constant march of foot traffic" continues undisturbed. Reading this passage alongside Conrad's letters, and in light of his lack of political commitment and stated interest in improving his reputation as a writer, it is important to ask whether the novel itself is such "a disregarded distribution." Adding to this the novel's complicated historical reception, it becomes necessary to consider that the novel sensationalizes the very material – anarchism and revolutionary violence targeting state property – it sets out to fictionalize in an apolitical manner.

Just as we find hints of Conrad in Chief Inspector Heat's view of anarchism, the anarchists themselves, in their nihilistic and amoral obsession with violence, also capture Conrad's inadvertent sensationalism as well as his lack of commitment as a novelist. Discussing the bombing at Greenwich Park, Ossipon and the Professor initially fail to recognize that one of the Professor's bombs – a symbol and mechanism of anarchist violence – was the cause of Stevie's death:

"I am afraid I'll have to spoil your holiday for you, though. There's a man blown up in Greenwich Park this morning."

"How do you know?"

"They have been yelling the news in the streets since two o'clock. I bought the paper, and just ran in here" [...]

He pulled the newspaper out. It was a good-sized rosy sheet, as if flushed by the warmth of its own convictions, which were optimistic. He scanned the pages rapidly.

"Ah! Here it is. Bomb in Greenwich Park. There isn't much so far. Half-past eleven. Foggy morning. Effects of explosion felt as far as Romney Road and Park Place. Enormous hole in the ground under a tree filled with smashed roots and broken branches. All round fragments of a man's body blown to pieces. That's all. The rest's mere newspaper gup. No doubt a wicked attempt to blow up the Observatory, they say. H'm. That's hardly credible." (70-71)

As the Professor recites the newspaper's report, he refuses to believe the narrative it presents him with, even though it is the truth. Here, he reveals a lack of commitment to his own supposed cause, failing to recognize that this was the same bomb he gave to Verloc – himself a secret agent attempting to frame the anarchists for an attack planned by the government.[42] When he finally realizes that the bomb was likely supplied by the Professor, Ossipon angrily asks if he is "really handing [his stuff] over at large like this, for the asking, to the first fool that comes along?'" to which the Professor smugly replies: "'Just so! The condemned social order has not been built up on paper and ink, and I don't fancy that a combination of paper and ink will ever put an end to it, whatever you may think'" (71). The Professor fails to realize the power of ideology, of the control of the press, in believing that his bombs are somehow more effective tools for disseminating and disrupting narratives. In fact, he seems to overlook altogether that a bomb attack is only powerful if it makes the headlines. While Conrad's anarchists reject writing in favor of symbolic acts of violence, the cultural relevance of Conrad's own text – no doubt exacerbated by his apolitical, uncommitted authorial stance – makes a case for the power of narrative. If this proves anything, it is perhaps that no art is apolitical (even when it openly claims to be so, as does Conrad's writing), that every aesthetic stance is an ethical one as well. If Conrad's anarchists deal solely in nihilistic violence, and if this reflects the author's own position more than does anarchism itself, then we must look to how anarchists in Conrad's time articulated their ideology.

Kropotkin was perhaps the most prolific and notable proponent of anarchism of the late-nineteenth and early-twentieth centuries. His writing provides a valuable counter-narrative to Conrad's vision of anarchism as nihilistic and violent. In "Anarchism," an entry written by Kropotkin for the 11th Edition of *Encyclopaedia Britannica* (1910), he defines the ideology as

> [T]he name given to a principle or theory of life and conduct under which society is conceived without government – harmony in such a society being obtained, not by submission to law, or by obedience to any authority, but by free agreements concluded between the various groups, territorial and professional, freely constituted for the sake of production and consumption, as also for the satisfaction of the infinite variety of needs and aspirations of a civilised being.[43]

While this statement gives a succinct summary of Kropotkin's vision of anarchist social organization, his most compelling work is where he uses his background in natural science to situate anarchism within evolutionist discourse, specifically regarding the ethical nature of humanity. In "The Place of Anarchism in Socialistic Evolution," a speech delivered by Kropotkin in Paris in 1886 and printed in *Le Révolté* in May of the same year, he argues for an anarchist morality grounded in mutualism and opposed to authority and compulsion:

> [Anarchist morality] is the morality of a people which does not look for the sun at midnight – a morality without compulsion or authority, a morality of habit. [...] Men are certainly not to be moralised by teaching them a moral catechism: tribunals and prisons do not diminish vice; they pour it over society in floods. [...] A morality which has become instinctive is the true morality, the only morality which endures while religions and systems of philosophy pass away.[44]

If anarchist morality is "a morality of habit," then it can be learned by all and practically instituted. In this way, Kropotkin suggests, anarchism will promote and foster morality without the threat of punishment. Kropotkin's understanding of habit comes directly from his knowledge of natural history, and is consistent with his overall vision of mutual aid, not mutual struggle, as the foundation of human nature. In "Mutual Aid: An Important Factor in Evolution," an essay published in Emma Goldman's *Mother Earth* in June 1914 summarizing his larger work *Mutual Aid: A Factor in Evolution,* Kropotkin describes the connection between anarchism and evolutionary biology:

> At first received with distrust, the idea that mutual aid and mutual support represent an important factor in the progressive evolution of animal species seems to be accepted now by many biologists. [...] At the same time it begins to be recognised that the struggle for life *within* the species has been exaggerated and that *mutual aid is*, to say the least, *as much a fundamental principle in Nature as mutual struggle*; while for *progressive evolution* it is without doubt the most important of the two.[45]

As such, Kropotkin not only provides a vision of anarchism grounded in the science of human life and behavior which supports an anarchist morality, but also guards that vision against arguments that anarchism is inherently violent, as Conrad's portrayal of anarchists tends to do. The final paragraph of the novel finds the Professor leaving the Silenus beer-hall, having met with Comrade Ossipon one last time. While Ossipon is overcome with despair following the murder and suicide of Verloc and his wife, the Professor remains spiteful and unaffected, a nihilist until the end:

> And the incorruptible Professor walked, too, averting his eyes from the odious multitude of mankind. He had no future. He disdained it. He was a force. His thoughts caressed the images of ruin and destruction. He walked frail, insignificant, shabby, miserable – and terrible in the simplicity of his idea calling madness and despair to the regeneration of the world. Nobody looked at him. He passed on unsuspected and deadly, like a pest in the street full of men. (*SA* 311)

This inhuman, hateful figure displays an attitude toward humanity that bears no resemblance to Kropotkin's vision of anarchist morality and to a social order grounded in mutual respect and agreement. The Professor disdains the very future Kropotkin hopes to build. This is not only Conrad's last word on anarchism, but the very last scene in the novel. Despite his wish to remain apolitical and avoid sensationalism, Conrad views anarchism as a violent ideology devoid of ideals and ethical responsibility; a vision which is, in fact, starkly contradicted by Kropotkin's progressive version of anarchism, based on social equality and human solidarity.

Where critics, among whom we can count Conrad, would claim that anarchists do nothing but perpetuate acts of violence against the state, it is important to present what anarchists actually thought about violence as a means to political ends. For Kropotkin, violence – although necessary for revolution – is always secondary to anarchism's promotion of human productivity: "All belongs to everyone! And provided each man and woman contributes his and her share of labour for the production of necessary objects, they have a right to share in all that is produced by everybody."[46] Kropotkin understands that revolution will be necessary in order to achieve a society "in which each individual will be able to give free rein to his inclinations, and even to his passions, without any other restraint than the love and respect of those who surround him."[47] Though such an "ideal will not be attained without violent shocks," its goal is not the violence itself, but the achievement of its moral vision. Placing Bourdin's act of violence against state property into this ends-means model of ethics, we might ask whether this act, which had no victim other than the bomber himself, negates the moral ends of anarchism. In the case of Conrad's novel, Stevie's death appears to be nothing more than a meaningless act, devoid of political significance. His death, which is barely registered, is merely one violent circumstance in a novel rife with violence and depravity. The reader is told that Verloc will "take Stevie into the country himself, and leave him all safe with Michaelis" (SA 189). When they leave, Conrad describes Stevie's expression as "proud, apprehensive, and concentrated, like that of a small child entrusted for the first time with a box of matches and the permission to strike a light" (189). Winnie Verloc is initially unaware that Stevie has any connection to the bombing, and the reader is told that she was "alone longer than usual on the day of the attempted bomb outrage in Greenwich Park" (190). In a few short, barely noticeable paragraphs, Stevie disappears from the text.

In stark contrast both with Stevie's lonely, dehumanizing death and with Conrad's depiction of anarchism and anarchists as morally hollow, the public outpouring of grief following the death of Bourdin shows a community committed to resistance and meaning. Among the Max Nettlau Papers in the International Institute of Social History's online archive, there is a scanned copy of Bourdin's memorial card.[48] Along with posthumous images of Bourdin, this memorial card was widely distributed amongst anarchists following his death. The day of his funeral, on 23 February 1894, saw several violent anti-anarchist protests, and a raucous crowd of over one thousand attended his interment in St. Pancras cemetery in Finchley.[49] The memorial card is scanned in black and white, though it may have been colorful in its original. It depicts three angels perched on top of what appears to be a grave or mausoleum, the face of which is inscribed with text. Aside from information on Bourdin's burial location and the name and address of the undertaker, the card reads "In Loving Memory of MARTIAL BOURDIN. Who was killed by the Bursting of a Bomb in Greenwich Park on February 15th, 1894."[50] The centerpiece of the memorial card is a brief verse that reads as follows:

Spurning the name of a slave,   Time shall not rob him of fame;
Fearless of gaol or of grave,   Hating the Tyrant, and game
Fighting for Freedom he gave,   in the spirit that rings in his name
His life in the Revolution.   He died for the Revolution.[51]

This verse seeks to immortalize Bourdin as both martyr and hero; it claims for him an active role in revolution, one that seems to respond directly to the press's portrayal of his death as both a meaningless accident and a failed anarchist bombing.

For anarchists, however, Bourdin is a fearless source of inspiration for their cause, and his death is neither meaningless nor accidental, but an act of revolutionary violence. This is the figure they memorialized, the life they mourned.

What do we make of *The Secret Agent* as a novel valued by terrorists and law enforcement officials alike, as a text that has time and again escaped Conrad's avowed apoliticism? If Stevie is the morally ambiguous, ultimately empty center of a novel that foregoes its commitment to politics in favor of irony, and if Conrad's anarchists are no more than caricatures of figures such as Kropotkin, who promoted a morality grounded in principles of peace and justice, then perhaps it is possible to claim that no text can remain apolitical, that there can be no aesthetics without ethics. Critiquing Jean-Paul Sartre's view of commitment, articulated in *What is Literature?*, Adorno states that

> For Sartre the work of art becomes an appeal to the subject because the work is nothing but the subject's decision or nondecision. He will not grant that even in its initial steps every work of art confronts the writer, however free he may be, with objective requirements regarding its construction. Confronted with these demands, the writer's intention becomes only a moment in the process.[52]

Beyond intent, Conrad's novel stands as a record not just of Bourdin's life and death, but of anarchism's commitment to morality. It is, of course, impossible, reckless even, to claim that an author bears complete responsibility for how his work will be read, received, and used over time. However, when an author foregoes ethical commitment altogether, choosing instead to remain apolitical, it is crucial that scholars or critics should attempt to right the record, in this case to portray anarchism and anarchists as they were in Conrad's time, and not as Conrad imagined them to be, or wished them to be seen by his readers. It is fitting for the novel to end with the Professor – the architect of the destruction and depravity which is the heart of the text – disappearing down a crowded street, "averting his eyes from the odious multitude of mankind" (*SA* 311).

As Acheraïou notes, Conrad himself "held disparaging views of the general public throughout his life, denying them a capacity for discernment, skepticism, and intelligence – qualities that he regarded highly."[53] Despite distancing himself from his anarchist characters, Conrad ironically provides the perfect illustration of an author who fails to commit himself ethically in his work. It is clear, however, that where the author would rather disappear without a trace, having made no clear ideological claims, is precisely where readers return, time and again, not just for answers, but for the meaning they see fit to make.

NOTES

[1]   Adorno 240.
[2]   Achebe 8.
[3]   Achebe 19.
[4]   Clark 2.
[5]   Clark 2.
[6]   Clark 2.
[7]   Carter 231.
[8]   Carter 232.
[9]   Adorno 240.
[10]   Mulry 11.
[11]   Mulry 10.
[12]   Curle 137.
[13]   Howe 97-100.
[14]   Mulry 104.
[15]   Panichas 143-44.
[16]   Lothe 252.
[17]   While many critics have made the connection between Bourdin and *The Secret Agent*, Mulry provides exhaustive historical detail on Conrad's source material. It is important to note, however, that Conrad never explicitly mentions Bourdin, merely referring to him in his Author's Note as "a man blown to bits for nothing even most remotely resembling an idea, anarchistic or other" and, second-handedly, as "'half an idiot'" (*SA* x). So, the fictional Stevie is only loosely based on Conrad's knowledge of the historical Bourdin.
[18]   Acheraïou 128.
[19]   Acheraïou 59.
[20]   Acheraïou 128-29.
[21]   Acheraïou 123.
[22]   Lothe 13.
[23]   Lothe 234.
[24]   Lothe 234.

[25] Mulry 1.

[26] Mulry 5-6.

[27] See Gibbard.

[28] Eliot 101-02. Eliot was proficient in French and in 1917 he wrote six poems in French, four of which were subsequently published (see Ackroyd). His misspelling of Bourdin's name was perhaps not accidental. As Acheraïou pointed to me in his e-mail letter of 5 May 2020, *boudin* means a type of sausage in French. Eliot may have used this derogatory term in contempt for Bourdin and anarchist violence in general.

[29] "Sabotage" (1936). "The Secret Agent" (1996). "The Secret Agent" (2016). See Internet Movie Database (IMDb).

[30] See Higgitt.

[31] See Guimond and Kearney Maynard; Mallios; Mulry; Panagopoulos.

[32] Guimond and Kearney Maynard 4.

[33] See Shulevitz.

[34] Mallios 347.

[35] Rochelle L. Rives describes how Conrad simultaneously employs and mocks Lombroso's pseudoscientific racism to caricature the features of the novel's anarchist characters (98-99). She describes physiognomy as "a specific hermeneutic system designed to categorize human expression according to specific character traits, which then often take on moral or ethical connotations," a system exploited by Lombroso in the development of his theory of criminal anthropology (98).

[36] Harris.

[37] Harris.

[38] The Times Digital Archive.

[39] The Times Digital Archive.

[40] The British political attitude toward foreigners during Conrad's composition of *The Secret Agent* was overwhelmingly hostile. According to Helena Wray, the Aliens Act 1905, which came into effect in Britain on 1 January 1906, "was the first attempt to establish a system of immigration control upon entry" (302). The Act "was the consequence of agitation around Jewish immigration into Britain, as well as of a broader hostility towards other nationalities including Europeans" (308).

[41] Acheraïou 50.

[42] Although a full analysis of Conrad's treatment of government in *The Secret Agent* is outside the scope of this essay, it is important to note that, though Conrad treats both government officials and anarchists with disdain in this novel, I believe that the historical reception of the novel as committed in its vilification of anarchism and in its accurate portrayal of terroristic violence shows that Conrad's critique of the state is less palpable.

[43] Kropotkin 163.

[44] Kropotkin 125.

[45] Kropotkin 677.

[46] Kropotkin 119.

[47] Kropotkin 126.

[48] Nettlau (1865-1944) was a German historian and anarchist who helped found the London-based Freedom Press, an anarchist periodical, in 1886. The International Institute of Social History, founded in 1935, is a Dutch organization dedicated to research on the global development of work and labor relations. See IISH.

[49] See Gibbard.

[50] Nettlau 3167.

[51] Nettlau 3167.

[52] Adorno 244.

[53] Acheraïou 129.

WORKS CITED

Achebe, Chinua. "An Image of Africa: Racism in Conrad's 'Heart of Darkness.'" *Hopes and Impediments: Selected Essays, 1965-87*. By Achebe. Oxford: Heinemann, 1988. Print.

Acheraïou, Amar. *Joseph Conrad and the Reader: Questioning Modern Theories of Narrative and Readership*. Basingstoke: Palgrave Macmillan, 2009. Print.

Ackroyd, Peter. *T. S. Eliot: A Life*. New York: Simon, 1984. Print.

Adorno, Theodor W. "Commitment." *Can One Live After Auschwitz?: A Philosophical Reader*. Ed. Rolf Tiedemann. Stanford: Stanford UP, 2003. 240-58. Print.

Carter, Alan. "Analytical Anarchism: Some Conceptual Foundations." *Political Theory* 28 (2000): 230-53. Print.

Clark, Samuel. *Living Without Domination: The Possibility of an Anarchist Utopia*. Burlington: Ashgate, 2007. Print.

Curle, Richard. *Joseph Conrad: A Study*. Garden City: Doubleday, 1914. Print.

Eliot, T.S. "Animula." *Selected Poems*. By Eliot. New York: Harcourt, 1988. 101-02. Print.

Freedom. "History." *Freedom Press*. Web. <https://freedompress.org.uk/history/#>. 27 Feb. 2019.

Gibbard, Paul. "Bourdin, Martial (1867/8–1894), Anarchist." *Oxford Dictionary of National Biography*. Oxford UP. 3 Jan. 2008. Web. 27 Feb. 2019. <http://www.oxforddnb.com/view/10.1093/ref:odnb/9780198614128.001.0001/odnb9780198614128-e-73217>.

Guimond, James, and Katherine Kearney Maynard. "Kaczynski, Conrad, and Terrorism." *Conradiana* 31 (1999): 3-25. Print.

Harris, Robert. "Forget Islam: bin Laden is no more than a spoilt rich kid." *Daily Telegraph*. 9 Oct. 2001. Web. <https://www.telegraph.co.uk/comment/4266193/Forget-Islam-bin-Laden-is-no-more-than-a-spoilt-rich-kid.html>. 11 March 2021.

Higgitt, Rebekah. "The real story of the Secret Agent and the Greenwich Observatory bombing." *The Guardian*. 5 Aug. 2016. Web. <https://www.theguardian.com/science/the-h-word/2016/aug/05/secret-agent-greenwich-observatory-bombing-of-1894>. 27 Feb. 2019.

Howe, Irving. *Politics and the Novel*. New York: Horizon P, 1957. Print.

IISH. "About IISH / International Institute of Social History." *International Institute of Social History*. Web. <https://iisg.amsterdam/en>. 27 Feb. 2019.

Internet Movie Database (IMDb). "Sabotage (1936)." Web. <https://www_imdb_com/title/tt0028212/?ref_=nv_sr_5?ref=nv_sr_5>. 12 Dec. 2020.

---. "The Secret Agent (1996)." Web. <https://www.imdb/com/title/tt0117582/?ref_=nv_r_2?ref_=nv_sr_2>. 12 Dec. 2020.

---. "The Secret Agent (2016)." Web. <https://www.imdb.com/title/tt1902046>. 12 Dec. 2020.

Kropotkin, Peter. *Direct Struggle Against Capital: A Peter Kropotkin Anthology*. Ed. Ian McKay. New York: AK P, 2020. Print.

Lothe, Jakob. *Conrad's Narrative Method*. Oxford: Oxford UP, 1989. Print.

Mallios, Peter Lancelot. "Reading *The Secret Agent* Now: The Press, the Police, the Premonition of Simulation." *"The Secret Agent"*. Ed. Richard Niland. New York: Norton, 2017. 294-310. Print.

Mulry, David. *Joseph Conrad among the Anarchists: Nineteenth Century Terrorism and* The Secret Agent. New York: Palgrave Macmillan, 2016. Print.

Nettlau, Max. "3167. Bourdin, Martial. 1894. (Cover, large size A3)." *Max Nettlau Papers*. International Institute of Social History (IISH). Web. <https://search.iisg.amsterdam/Record/612364>. 27 Feb. 2019.

Panagopoulos, Nic. "False Flag at Greenwich: 'Bourdin's Folly,' the Nicoll Pamphlet, and *The Secret Agent*." *Conradiana* 48 (2016): 1-24. Print.

Panichas, George Andrew. "Joseph Conrad's *The Secret Agent* as a Moral Tale." *Modern Age* 39 (1997): 143-52. Print.

Rives, Rochelle L. "Face Values, Optics as Ethics in Joseph Conrad's *The Secret Agent*." *Criticism: A Quarterly for Literature and the Arts* 56 (2014): 89-117. Print.

Shulevitz, Judith. "Chasing After Conrad's *Secret Agent*." *Slate*. 27 Sept. 2001. Web. <https://slate.com/culture/2001/09/chasing-after-conrad-s-secret-agent.html>. 27 Feb. 2019.

The Times Digital Archive. "Explosion in Greenwich Park." *The Times*, 16 Feb. 1894: 5. Web. <http://tinyurl.galegroup.com.ezp1.villanova.edu/tinyurl/9EA5m1>. 27 Feb. 2019.

Wray, Helena. "The Aliens Act 1905 and the Immigration Dilemma." *Journal of Law and Society* 33 (2006): 302-23. Print.

Catherine Delesalle-Nancey,
Université Jean Moulin – Lyon 3,
Lyon, France

Ethics as the Secret Agent: Dissimulation, Ethical Responsibility, and Intersubjectivity in Conrad's *The Secret Agent*

Reading Joseph Conrad's *The Secret Agent* is a rather bleak and upsetting experience. The reader is not only confronted with three violent deaths, but he/she is also presented with a range of miserable and uninviting characters in a drab, misty London described by the Assistant Commissioner as "a slimy aquarium from which the water had been run off." Whichever narrative thread is privileged, that of the anarchists or "the domestic drama" – the two being intricately interwoven – it is difficult to find a single flicker of hope in the whole story. The novel ends on two anarchist survivors, Comrade Ossipon – nicknamed the Doctor   and The Professor, the former "walk[ing] disregarded [...], [haunted by] *'this act of madness and despair,'*" and the latter "calling madness and despair to the regeneration of the world. Nobody looked at him. He passed on unsuspected and deadly, like a pest in the street full of men" (*SA* 311): this is a dismal ending for a dismal tale. Although here the Professor, as a true anarchist, calls for the regeneration or a possible improvement of the world based on new values, and although Winnie Verloc, after murdering her husband, claims herself "a free woman," suggesting liberation from a patriarchal model and the advent of "the new woman," neither statement holds its promise. The bomb designed by the Professor misses its target, the Greenwich Observatory, and results in the violent blasting of an innocent simple-minded boy, while Winnie falls into the grip of a self-serving womanizer who betrays her and drives her to suicide. Even the central action of the novel, which brings together the anarchist plot and the domestic drama, is underpinned by a perverse and distorted logic. Since, as Véronique Pauly notes, the planned bombing is an anti-terrorist act which creates chaos to restore order.[1] Indeed, Mr. Vladimir's aim in attacking an emblem of science is to cause enough terror to stir the lethargic English middle classes into actively fighting anarchism. Such a chaotic world offers no sense of morality or moral values to hold onto, so to talk of ethics in *The Secret Agent* may appear as a paradoxical endeavour.

Yet, precisely because this novel does not provide a fixed moral frame of reference and also because of its ironic treatment of event and character – oscillating between "pity and scorn" and "carried right through to the end" – as Conrad remarks in his Author's Note, it forces the reader into an uneasy ethical response. In *Oneself as Another*,[2] Paul Ricoeur distinguishes between morality and ethics: for him, ethics is teleological and constitutes the aim to which each individual conduct tends, while morality is the articulation of this aim in prescriptive social norms.[3] He also states that the ethical purpose of life is self-esteem whereas compliance with social norms produces self-respect. Ricoeur further argues that, when faced with an aporetic situation in which moral norms lead to practical dead ends, the ethical aim should guide the norm, and self-esteem be resorted to when no certain norm can guarantee self-respect.[4] Seen in this light, morality thus appears as a limited form of ethics. I would argue that *The Secret Agent*, like most of Conrad's novels, places the reader in a selfsame aporetic moral situation, which ultimately calls for an ethical stance. As Marlow reminds his listeners in "Heart of Darkness":

> how can you imagine what particular region of the first ages a man's untrammelled feet may take him into by the way of solitude – utter solitude without a policeman – by the way of silence – utter silence, where no warning voice of a kind neighbour can be heard whispering of public opinion? These little things make all the great difference. When they are gone you must fall back upon your own innate strength, upon your own capacity for faithfulness. (*YS* 116)

Could not this "capacity for faithfulness" be related to Ricoeur's self-esteem which, he says, is the ethical equivalent to self-interpretation in narratives of the Self – "the interpretation of ourselves mediated by the ethical evaluation of our actions" – that, consequently, is equally subject to contradiction and controversy?[5] *The Secret Agent*, with its absence of any stable moral ground, induces conflicting interpretations in the reader, which ultimately compel him/her to an ethical standpoint. Ethics implies a permanent questioning of both existence and the Self in situations involving conflicting interests and moral standpoints that prevent any easy ethical positioning. *The Secret Agent* permeates with such conflicting moral situations and ethics appears in this morally fraught universe as the true secret agent in the novel. For it has no fixed allegiance, it secretly works to destabilize any simple unproblematic system of values the reader may be tempted to hold onto, and remains elusive, subject to constant reassessment. Meantime, ethics, as a transcendent mode of interaction, forms the foundation of the relations between the Self and Other. As such, it calls for solidarity and responsibility – responsibility for one's own interpretations and choices, responsibility for oneself and the Other. For Ricoeur, as for Levinas, the individual must have the capacity to respond to the demand of the Other, and self-esteem is intimately related to our capacity to care for the other, to our openness to the Other.

Both Ricoeur and Levinas consider intersubjectivity essential to self-esteem and to ethics, although Ricoeur insists on reciprocity, while Levinas' face-to-face encounter with the Other implies external transcendence, an injunction to the Self from an absolute Other. Ricoeur endorses Levinas' assertion that there can be no Self without another Self that exhorts it to responsibility. However, he claims that for this command to be heard, the dissymmetry introduced by the injunction must somehow be compensated for, in order not to break the giving/receiving dialectic of the exchange. Ricoeur places "solicitude," or "benevolent spontaneity" at the heart of his ethics[6]:

"Self-esteem is said to arise from a primitive reciprocity of spontaneous, benevolent feelings, feelings which one is also capable of directing toward oneself, but only through the benevolence of others."[7] The issue of responsibility is central in *The Secret Agent*, and Stevie's horrible death elicits both response to the Other and solicitude. The tragic event around which the plot revolves and the investigations this event leads to prompt a range of actions that involve the responsibility of various characters. The novel significantly opens on a sequence of transference of responsibility: "Mr. Verloc, going out in the morning, left his shop nominally in charge of his brother-in-law. [...] Mr. Verloc cared but little about his ostensible business. And, moreover, his wife was in charge of his brother-in-law" (*SA* 3). Of course, as a secret agent, Mr. Verloc is also in charge of missions for which his employers wish, by no means, to be held accountable. This shows how the transference of responsibility, in fact, often leads to the leaders and order-givers shying away from their responsibility by not directly assuming the consequences of their own decisions. Within this endless transference of responsibility recurring throughout the novel, the reader stands last in line. He/she is dismally, even helplessly, contemplating the abject universe depicted in the narrative, but complete detachment from or indifference to the events and characters' moral conflicts is not an open option for him/her. For by his/her very face-to-face encounter with the text he/she involves himself/herself in the tale. And because of this epistemic involvement the reader cannot evade the responsibility for his/her own reading. The darkness of the text becomes the darkness of the reader's world. And this darkness is felt by the reader as a radical Other which at once challenges his/her perceptions and may inspire in him/her some sort of solicitude. There is a form of intersubjective ethics in the interaction between the text and the reader in this narrative and this may be seen as a call for an ethical reading of Conrad's novel – a call paradoxically stirred by the bleak, elusive moral character of the narrative itself. This intersubjective ethics involving reader and text will be addressed in detail at the final part of this essay. The first part is mainly concerned with showing how this novel flouts and even negates any notion of morality. The second closely examines the relationships between the characters and reveals how these relationships seem to preclude any true exchange with the Other, in both the various injunctions they submit to and in the solicitude and sympathy the characters may feel for Others.

Failing Moral Norms

As Chief Inspector Heat observes when he is slightly destabilized by his chance meeting with the Professor – the true anarchist whose deathly logics of utter destruction and sacrifice he cannot comprehend – it is the moral support of the multitude that gives meaning to his life and actions as a guardian of social peace and order:

> Chief Inspector Heat [...] stepped out with the purposeful briskness of a man disregarding indeed the inclemencies of the weather, but conscious of having an authorized mission on this earth and the moral support of his kind. [...] The consciousness of universal support in his general activity heartened him to grapple with the particular problem. (96)

Yet the distinction between order and disorder, defender of the law and criminal is not so clear-cut, as the Professor points out: "'The terrorist and the policeman both come from the same basket. Revolution, legality – counter moves in the same game; forms of idleness at bottom identical'" (69). And indeed, Chief Inspector Heat himself, without his superior knowing, uses Verloc as an informer on the anarchists, turning a blind eye to "his business of a seller of shady wares" and protecting the shop where he sells pornography and clandestinely receives fellow anarchists. Besides, Inspector Heat's superior, the Assistant Commissioner, does not share his subordinate's faith in the regulating moral power of the multitude: "The near presence of that strange emotional phenomenon called

public opinion weighed upon his spirits, and alarmed him by
its irrational nature" (99). When in his solitary walk in the
streets of London, enveloped in "murky, gloomy dampness,"
he enters a dingy Italian restaurant with an atmosphere of
"fraudulent cookery," his identity seems to dissolve, as though
a confrontation with men's baser instincts entailed a loss
of moral and social identity: "In this immoral atmosphere
the Assistant Commissioner, reflecting upon his enterprise,
seemed to lose some more of his identity" (148).

The characters of *The Secret Agent* certainly do not run
the risk of losing their identities, since they are already mere
caricatures, each defined by a set of recurring traits that
encapsulate them. The Assistant Commissioner is regularly
presented as foreign, slender with angular features, and
as having a profound aversion for the English foggy rainy
weather and office work; a portrait which contrasts with Chief
Inspector Heat's stalwart and vigorous vitality, his indifference
to weather, his Norse moustache and his simple faith in his
professional mission. As for their superior, Sir Ethelred, he
is either referred to as "the great Personage" or "[t]he deep-
-voiced Presence," "The Personage on the hearthrug" and
even as "the great and expanded personage, expanding a little
more" (139). As he talks with the Assistant Commissioner, the
paranomasia, in its stuttering, somehow belies this presumed
grandeur. The narrator's insistent use of capital letters is
a parody of this character's self-importance and condescending
behaviour, which is reflected in his insistence on not wanting
to be bothered with details. The man is attended by a "smooth-
faced young man," "the young private secretary (unpaid)" (135),
"the volatile and revolutionary Toodles" whose revolutionary
politics stop at his social privileges. Thus, the representatives
of law and order, those supposed to be the upholders of moral
norms, become the butt of the narrator's Dickensian irony and
cannot but elicit an amused smile from the reader. Virginia
Woolf's statement that each character in Charles Dickens is
somehow turned into a gargoyle perfectly fits the way Conrad
handles characterization in *The Secret Agent*.[8]

This is also true of the narrator's portrayal of the anarchists, each with his own oddities and nickname. The Professor is "the dingy little man in spectacles" (62), whose determination and self-confidence are as strong as his physique is frail, and whose desire to exterminate all the world is symbolized in "the fierce glitter of his thick glasses" (309). At the other end of the character-type spectrum stands Michaelis – "the ticket-of-leave apostle" (48) who, with his "round, hard hat," "round head," "round and obese body" (51), and "candid blue eyes," is "a grotesque incarnation of humanitarian passion" (108). He is a pathetic "humanitarian sentimentalist," a former convict and now a drawing-room revolutionist kept by a rich lady. His optimistic "laissez-faire" – which gradually evolves into the utopian dream of "a world planned out like an immense and nice hospital, with gardens and flowers, in which the strong are to devote themselves to the nursing of the weak" (303) – can hardly stand as a valid moral aim. Nor can, for that matter, the scientific utopia of Comrade Ossipon who "was free from the trammels of conventional morality – but he submitted to the rule of science" (296–97). A follower of Cesare Lombroso, The Doctor is repeatedly said "to gaze scientifically,"[9] at Stevie first, and later at Winnie, to read the signs of degeneracy in their physical appearances. The gaze of the womanizer, with his "Apollo-like ambrosial head," is just as predatory as that of the pseudo-scientist, for he lives on women's generosity. And yet "the robust anarchist," whom Winnie ironically calls "her saviour," is eventually condensed into one emotion: fear,[10] which shows in his "pale ghastly face," "like a fresh plaster-cast of himself" (293). The venomous and moribund Karl Yundt, self-named "the terrorist" – old, bald, toothless with "a wisp of a white goatee" and limbs "deformed by gouty swellings" (42) – completes the wretched anarchists' catalogue. Insistent, and at times literally grotesque, bodies seem to prevent any form of uplifting idealism, as is clearly reflected in the Verloc household.

Indeed, flesh seems ubiquitous in the domestic arrangement of the Verlocs. From the outset, Winnie is described as having "a full, rounded form" which, part of her charm, made her attractive to Mr. Verloc, while her mother is a "stout, wheezy woman, with a large brown face" and "swollen legs" (6). They are respectively the daughter and widow of a licensed victualler. Mrs. Verloc, once in love with a young butcher, is seen on several occasions presenting a roast to her husband, the last tragic meal leading to Verloc's turning into a carved piece of meat. As we shall shortly see, this image echoes, of course, Stevie's dislocated body, "raw material for a cannibal feast" (86) in Chief Inspector Heat's words. Prior to this, as the word cannibalistic is uttered by Yundt, Stevie is described as "swallow[ing] the terrifying statement with an audible gulp" (51). The sonority of the word *swallow* is close to that of the verb *wallow*. And the latter word, itself mimetic in its soft sonorities and specular form, is repeatedly associated with Mr. Verloc and is an emblem of his indolence, laziness, and unkempt appearance: he has "an air of having wallowed, fully dressed, all day on an unmade bed." Mr. Vladimir blames this man for his portliness. Verloc is further described as "undemonstrative and burly in a fat-pig style," with "the air of moral nihilism" (13), and although he boasts a powerful voice, it is almost always associated with the adjective "husky," with its double meaning of hoarse and bulky. The two meanings come together when he is eventually compared to a seal: "He paused, and a snarl lifting his moustaches above a gleam of white teeth gave him the expression of a reflective beast, not very dangerous – a slow beast with a sleek head, gloomier than a seal, and with a husky voice" (257). The narrator's irony is scathing: "He was in a manner devoted to [his idleness] with a sort of inert fanaticism, or perhaps rather with a fanatic inertness" (12). This chiasmic structure emphasizes the character's entrapment in his idleness and thus highlights his moral worthlessness.

The body is a site of inter-subjective connections, and yet, in this novel, flesh precludes transcendence. Both Mr. and Mrs. Verloc, for instance, remain on the surface of things, unable to perceive anything beneath or beyond this superficial reality: "It was a tacit accord, congenial to Mrs. Verloc's incuriosity and to Mr. Verloc's habits of mind, which were indolent and secret. They refrained from going to the bottom of facts and motives" (245). Winnie Verloc's "constitutional indolence" matches her husband's, and her silent motto is that "things do not stand much looking into" (177). Her face is repeatedly said to be "unfathomable," "blank," as she stonily stares with her big eyes wide open or her "steady incurious gaze." The first time she appears, "her unfathomable indifference" and her being a woman deter a young man from buying pornography. He buys ink instead at an extortionate price, only to throw it in a gutter: Winnie seems to thwart male fantasy and is, at the same time, susceptible to trigger writing which yet fails to capture the character, and eventually boils down to a few lines in newspapers: "[Ossipon's] revolutionary career [...] was menaced by an impenetrable mystery – the mystery of a human brain pulsating wrongfully to the rhythm of journalistic phrases. '... *Will hang for ever over this act.* ... It was inclining towards the gutter ... *of madness or despair...*'" (310–11). In his Author's Note, Conrad claims that Winnie is the true heroine of the story. This is a problematic statement, especially after she kills her husband in an outburst of passion and declares herself a free woman, only to become enslaved to Ossipon, "her savior," in what looks like a parody of sentimental novels. This mysterious woman remains blind to Ossipon's true motives, ironically placing "her grateful confidence in his protecting strength." Thus, Conrad's "true heroine" is not spared his irony; nor is the heroine's mother, who is yet the only character to be described as astute and heroic[11] when she decides to sacrifice herself for her destitute son and join an alms-house: she only asks for some of her own furniture, "the Foundation which, after many importunities, had gathered her to its charitable breast, giving nothing but bare planks and cheaply papered bricks to the objects of its solicitude" (154). This really sounds like Dickensian irony, except that the Victorian confident moral frame of reference has been replaced with Conradian ubiquitous undermining doubt.

Typically Conradian also is the kernel of horror that lies at the heart of this novel, or rather the absent centre which reverberates throughout, threatening society's order and norms. The scene of Stevie's exploding with the bomb he was carrying is conspicuously absent, the reader being presented first with the terrible results of this explosion and then with the events that lead to it. If the bomb fails to destroy Greenwich, a symbol of universal time, it blows up, however, the novel's chronology, as several critics have underlined.[12] The centrifugal core of energy that dismantles Stevie's body also fragments the text, as is made obvious by the way Ossipon first relates, in broken sentences, the news he read in the paper:

> Ah! Here it is. Bomb in Greenwich Park. There isn't much so far. Half-past eleven. Foggy morning. Effects of explosion felt as far as Romney Road and Park Place. Enormous hole in the ground under a tree filled with smashed roots and broken branches. All around fragments of a man's body blown to pieces. That's all. (70-71)

Despite the attempts to circumscribe the appalling fragmentation, the outcome remains vain, and this futile endeavour foreshadows that of the local constable: "'He's all there. Every bit of him. It was a job'" or again "'Well, here he is – all of him I could see. [...] Look at that foot there. I picked up the legs first, one after another. He was that scattered you didn't know where to begin'" (89). Nothing can restore any kind of integrity and stop the disintegration at work. The shock wave pursues its deathly work, reaching first Mr. Verloc, then his wife. Horror strikes at the very basis of society, as the father[13] symbolically eats off Stevie's remains:

> The piece of roast beef, laid out in the likeness of funeral baked meats for Stevie's obsequies, offered itself largely to his notice. And Mr. Verloc again partook. He partook ravenously, without restraint and decency, cutting thick slices with the sharp carving knife, and swallowing them without bread. (253)

This is somehow the implementation or re-enactment of an earlier metaphor when Chief Inspector Heat, another representative of the symbolic Law, observes Stevie's mangled body: "And meantime the Chief Inspector went on peering at the table with a calm face and the slightly anxious attention of an indigent customer bending over what may be called the by products of a butcher's shop with a view to an inexpensive Sunday dinner" (88). This is a cruel irony: Stevie, the somehow literal by-product of a butcher,[14] is offered to the knife of a foster-father by his real father and/or his motherly sister.[15] The family nucleus, the first social unit, is shattered, and the image of a Cronos-like figure eating his own children reveals a disruption and inversion of time, as the past destroys the future. After murdering Verloc Winnie makes a striking confusion between the blood dripping from the carving-knife planted in his chest and the clock's ticking: "a sound of ticking growing fast and furious like the pulse of an insane clock" (265). This confusion is further evidence that the attack on Greenwich has, in fact, been effective, annihilating the very foundations of society. Since, although Stevie's innocence and infinite compassion for all living creatures are repeatedly underlined, his oversensitiveness, simple mindedness, and inarticulateness prevent his being a Christ-like figure, and Verloc's last supper is but a parodic version of the Eucharist.[16] No regenerated world is born from this sacrifice which comes about accidentally as Stevie stumbles on a root.

Incidentally, this unexpected event, which defies logic and puzzles everybody, exposes all the lies, misunderstandings, and deceptions that have so far been secret or hidden. This reveals how fragmented society is beneath the superficial veneer. Mr. Verloc's acting among the anarchists as a spy for a foreign Embassy and an informer for the police comes to light, as does Chief Inspector Heat's private arrangement with Verloc. The Assistant Commissioner's bias towards Michaelis as a friend of his wife's lady-friend is also disclosed and runs against Chief Inspector Heat's desire to accuse Michaelis, in order to deflect attention from the frightening Professor, thus betraying a latent animosity and rivalry between the two men. Such is the case as well among the anarchists, who surreptitiously feel contempt for each other. Winnie's secret motive to marry Verloc – her plan to provide through this union care for her crippled mother and dumb brother – is eventually laid bare, as is the fictitious love relationship between Winnie and her mother: "Winnie had been a good daughter because she had been a devoted sister. Her mother had always leaned on her for support. [...] Now that Stevie was dead the bond seemed to be broken" (269-70). As for Stevie's affection for Verloc, it proves to be the outcome of his sister's and mother's schemes:

> Of these sentiments [his father's anger, the lodgers' irritability and Mr. Verloc's sorrow], all easily provoked, but not always easy to understand, the last had the greatest moral efficiency – because Mr. Verloc was *good*. His mother and his sister had established that ethical fact on an unshakable foundation. They had established, erected, consecrated it behind Mr. Verloc's back, for reasons that had nothing to do with abstract morality. And Mr. Verloc was not aware of it. (175)

The overinsistence on morality and ethics here works as an antiphrasis, as both morph into self-interest. Finally, the extent of Ossipon's villainy and unscrupulousness in his dealing with women reaches its height when he abandons Winnie and steals her money. Manifestly, with Stevie's death, the fabric of society falls into pieces. Winnie's feeling of utter loneliness at the end of the novel when she realizes that "Nobody would miss her in a social way" is widely shared. Anyway, in the end every character is moved by self-concern and has little interest in or curiosity for Others. Because of her "distant and uninquiring acceptance of facts," Winnie fails to appreciate her mother's self-sacrifice in leaving for the alms house. And when he presents the Verlocs to Sir Ethelred as "'[a] genuine wife and a genuinely, respectably, marital relation,'" the Assistant Commissioner is only moved by a narcissistic desire to preserve his self-image.[17] The antiphrastic use of "genuine" thus applies both to the marriage of the Verlocs and to that of the Assistant Commissioner, as well as to his own assertion or discourse. Genuineness seems to lose all meaning in such a society where truth is subservient to self-interest. In this, *The Secret Agent* looks like a kaleidoscopic picture of disparate, fragmented, and elusive subjective positions, hinged to no clear judgement or definite ethical frame of reference. As David Prickett writes: "Conrad's recurrent insistence on isolation implies a tendency to self-interest, a condition arising out of the inescapably subjective position of the individual."[18]

All the characters in this novel seem to be living in parallel worlds that do not communicate with each other, each sealed in their own preoccupations. The third-person omniscient narrator gives us access to the characters' personal thoughts and to their idiosyncrasies. This is true of the interviews between Mr. Vladimir and Verloc, Chief Inspector Heat and the Assistant Commissioner, the Assistant Commissioner and Sir Ethelred, Winnie and her mother. However, this is nowhere more apparent than in the last scene between Mr. and Mrs. Verloc. Here, Verloc rambles on about his being sorry for what happened, the reasons that led him to ask Stevie to take the bomb, the danger he was, and still is in, and his forgiving Winnie for bringing the police in their home because of the label she left on Stevie's coat. Winnie, instead, is locked up in her grief, haunted by the image of Stevie's mangled body. She is obsessed with Verloc's taking the boy away from her to lead him to his death, and with his breaking the terms of their tacit marriage contract. The conspicuous repetition of adverbs like "magnanimously" and "excusably" applied to Verloc – which are set against Winnie's ominous silence and bodily pain; "the effect of a white-hot iron drawn across her eyes; [...] her heart, hardened and chilled into a lump of ice" (*SA* 241) – all emphasize the unbridgeable gap between the two spouses. The narrator ironically states: "He wished only to put heart into her. It was a benevolent intention, but Mr. Verloc had the misfortune not to be in accord with his audience" (250). With characters so engrossed in themselves and blind to the Others, the intersubjectivity essential to Levinas' and Ricoeur's concepts of ethics proves problematic, and so, too, are the notions of responsibility or solicitude for the Other.

Viewed in this light, the world of *The Secret Agent* seems not only deprived of moral norms, but also of any form of ethics.

Perverted Relationships to the Other

In *The Secret Agent*, most relationships look more like business arrangements than true involvement with the Other. Characters are mere pawns in the hands of their fellow beings, who manipulate them to serve their own aims. This is manifest in the Verlocs' marriage. The narrator insists on Mr. Verloc's misguided belief that he is loved for himself and shows how this belief blinds this character to his wife's true motives and feelings. For Winnie, the marriage is merely a transaction: she agrees to be a good wife in exchange for Verloc's taking "a crippled mother and a crazy idiot of a boy," complete with their furniture, in the bargain. Hence her reaction at Stevie's death: "He would want to keep her for nothing." One of the terms being unfulfilled, the contract is null: "This woman, capable of a bargain the mere suspicion of which would have been infinitely shocking to Mr. Verloc's idea of love, remained irresolute, as if scrupulously aware of something wanting on her part for the formal closing of the transaction" (259). The Verlocs' shady transactions, on which the novel opens, can be seen as emblematic of the exchanges between people. The giving/receiving reciprocity is unsound:

> But Mr. Verloc knew his business and remained undisturbed by any sort of *aesthetic* doubt about his appearance. With a firm, steady-eyed impudence [...], he would proceed to sell over the counter some object looking obviously and scandalously not worth the money which passed in the transaction: a small cardboard box with apparently nothing inside, for instance, or one of those carefully closed yellow flimsy envelopes, or a soiled volume in paper covers with a promising title. (4-5; my emphasis)

In this fool's game, much goes unspoken and appearances are deceptive; ordinary and insignificant relationships conceal deeper duplicitous motives. Ethics, as well as aesthetics, are doubtful.

The world of *The Secret Agent* does not seem to harbour the intersubjectivity essential to Levinas' and Ricoeur's ethics, the trust and the capacity to respond to the demand of the Other which fosters self-esteem. Faces pervade the novel, calling to mind Levinas' face-to-face encounter with the Other. In their various interactions, the characters keep scrutinizing each other's faces in order to detect a sign that would give them a clue to their respective states of mind. If this experience often proves unsettling, it seldom results in a character acknowledging responsibility for the Other. *The Stanford Encyclopedia of Philosophy* identifies several stages in Levinas' concept of the face-to-face encounter:

> First, the onset of the other – as the expression of the face – interrupts our free activity (and willing) and calls us to account for ourselves. (*Totality and Infinity* 198, 291). [...] Second, in thereby responding, the subject approached by the other engages in an act that opens the possibility of dialogue. The unfolding of dialogue expands the social relationship, and Levinas argues that social life preserves a residuum of the initial "ethical" encounter with the face. Intersubjective dialogue entails conversation, teaching, and at a more general level, literary or philosophical discourse. (*Totality and Infinity* 51, 57, 251–52, 295).[19]

In *The Secret Agent,* the call or the face-to-face encounter becomes literal. Throughout the narrative, Verloc, Chief Inspector Heat, and the Assistant Commissioner are all called to answer for their actions. As the man in charge of the police, the Assistant Commissioner must account for his service's failure to prevent the bomb explosion, and he manages to deflect Sir Ethelred's dissatisfaction by persuading him of Heat's unsound method in keeping a private agent. He administers this reproof to Chief Inspector Heat in an interview which increasingly turns sour, as the Chief Inspector comes to understand that there must be some secret motives to his superior's animosity:

> He had discovered in this affair a delicate and perplexing side, forcing upon the discoverer a certain amount of insincerity. [...] He felt at

the moment like a tight-rope artist might feel if suddenly, in the
middle of the performance, the manager of the Music Hall were to
rush out of the proper managerial seclusion and begin to shake the
rope. Indignation, the sense of moral insecurity engendered by such
a treacherous proceeding joined to the immediate apprehension of
a broken neck, would, in the colloquial phrase, put him in a state.
(SA 116)

Because, for personal reasons, the Assistant Commissioner will
not have Michaelis bothered, he challenges his subordinate's
methods. On the other hand, Heat has his own unspoken reasons
for accusing Michaelis: his reluctance to presently deal with the
dangerous Professor, "the perfect anarchist." Both characters
scrutinize each other's face in mutual assessment, and their
surface conversation rests on secret, unsafe, and shifting
grounds, which precludes the possibility of an open, genuine
dialogue. This kind of injunction from an Other within these
two characters' face-to-face encounter creates insecurity and
fear – especially for the Inspector – instead of ethical epiphany.
An even a stronger fear arises when Verloc is summoned to the
foreign Embassy by Mr. Vladimir, who violently questions his
efficiency as a secret agent in the present as in the past and
threatens to dismiss him.

The scene relating this heated interaction focuses on voice,
gaze, and face: Mr. Vladimir's "round and clean-shaven face" –
so pleasing to the ladies – is an enigma, as its innocence sharply
contrasts with his cruelty: "But there was no trace of merriment
or perplexity in the way he looked at Mr. Verloc. [...] he had with
his smooth and rosy countenance the air of a preternaturally
thriving baby that will not stand nonsense from anybody" (19).
His inquisitive gaze and abrupt questioning critically assess
Verloc's corpulence and his laziness and challenges the reason
of his very existence. Verloc, on the other hand, vainly tries
to prove his worth through a display of the power of his voice
which he can modulate to stir up people. But eventually he
is reduced to silence, as the dialogue between the two men
gradually turns into a self-complacent monologue wherein
Mr. Vladimir glosses the advent of a new form of terrorism.

Like Inspector Heat, Verloc is utterly destabilized by fear, a "sensation of faintness running down [his]legs" (28-29). Back home, he does *preserve a residuum of the initial encounter*, but in the shape of Mr. Vladimir's haunting face:

> And suddenly the face of Mr. Vladimir, clean-shaved and witty, appeared enhaloed in the glow of its rosy complexion like a sort of pink seal impressed on the fatal darkness. The luminous and mutilated vision was so ghastly physically that Mr. Verloc started away from the window, letting down the venetian blind with a great rattle. Discomposed and speechless with the apprehension of more such visions, he beheld his wife re-enter the room and get into bed in a calm, business-like manner which made him feel hopelessly lonely in the world. (57)

If the encounter haunts Verloc, it is certainly not for its social benefits. Since it entails no conversation, no *expanding social relationship;* it only begets feelings of utter solitude and moral isolation. Rather than stir up an epiphanic self-questioning, this face-to-face encounter, therefore, generates anxiety, injustice, and a desire for revenge. In the end, these various face-to-face encounters are merely a parody of ethical encounters and subsequently lead to the most unethical act in the novel: the manipulation of an innocent boy that leads to the most horrible death. It is this act of blind destruction that Verloc is finally called to answer for through Winnie's silent, blank, undecipherable face, and which causes him to justify himself, without, however, acknowledging full responsibility for this abominable deed. Winnie is also summoned through her vision of Stevie's face, but her immediate ethical response is to stab her husband to death: "Mrs. Verloc closed her eyes desperately, throwing upon that vision the night of her eyelids, where after a rain-like fall of mangled limbs the decapitated head of Stevie lingered suspended alone, and fading out slowly like the last star of a pyrotechnic display" (260). Refusing to take full responsibility for one's actions and transferring instead this responsibility to others is a widespread practice in *The Secret Agent*: during their conversation, or rather parallel monologues, Verloc reminds Winnie that she has her share of

responsibility in her brother's death, since she is the one who
urged him to take Stevie with him on his walks:

> Strike me dead if I ever would have thought of the lad for that
> purpose. It was you who kept on shoving him in my way when I was
> half distracted with the worry of keeping the lot of us out of trouble.
> What the devil made you? One would think you were doing it on
> purpose. "[...] Don't you make any mistake about it: if you will have it
> that I killed the boy, then you've killed him as much as I." (257–58)

Once again, we are in the presence of a cruel and multi-sided
irony: Winnie's plan to protect her brother, by making him
indispensable to her husband, leads to his death, and the verb
"shove" dismally recalls the shovel used to retrieve Stevie's
body fragments. The phrase "Strike me dead," on the other
hand, is, of course, unintentionally proleptic. Winnie does not
only feel hatred and resentment for her husband. She also
blames her mother for leaving them and causing her to shove
Stevie in Verloc's hands. In turn, Verloc blames Mr. Vladimir
for forcing him to take the boy on this deathly mission, as he
could not find anybody crazy enough to accept such a job, and
he eventually blames poor Stevie himself: "If only that lad had
not stupidly destroyed himself!" (253). Likewise, Ossipon holds
the Professor responsible for providing a bomb to just anybody,
and the Assistant Commissioner imputes the terrible accident
to Chief Inspector Heat's private decision to use Verloc as
an informer and protect him. Chief Inspector Heat seems to
internalize this reproach, which creates a kind of schizophrenic
dissociation between Chief Inspector Heat and Private Citizen
Heat when he visits Verloc: "Private Citizen Heat murmured:
'What's coming out?' [...]. This appeal to old acquaintance
must have been extremely distasteful to the Chief Inspector"
(209). As for Winnie, she refuses to take responsibility for
the murder of her husband and considers herself a passive,
helpless victim of overwhelming circumstances: "'Haven't you
guessed what I was driven to do?'" (282) she tells Ossipon.

Responsibility for the Other, and the solicitude that,
according to Ricoeur, should come with it, appear out of reach

for this novel's characters, because no character is concerned with the well-being or fate of the others. However, Ricoeur identifies another end on the spectrum of the giving/receiving dialectic of solicitude which he calls *suffering*. According to him, *suffering* is the reverse of injunction, since, in the case of injunction, Ricoeur contends, the scale is tipped in favour of receiving, as one is called to responsibility by an Other, while in *suffering*, giving is prominent since one offers the Other one's sympathy.[20] The dissymmetry in each case can be compensated for by *giving* acknowledgement of the superiority of the Other that calls me to responsibility, and by *receiving* from the suffering Other an intimation of my own vulnerability. As seen previously, no acknowledgement of the superior knowledge of the Other who calls me to responsibility can be found in the various injunctions present in the novel's plot. On the other hand, within this sordid tale, we may also wonder whether *suffering* could not paradoxically be the gateway to ethics.

Stevie's cognitive impairment and his being born with a "vacant droop of his lower lip" both made him a victim of his father's violence and stirred his sister's and mother's sympathy towards him. This young boy is a significant site of morality. He is mentally enfeebled but endowed with an intense moral sense which often verges on oversensitivity. He is shaken by "the dramas of fallen horses, whose pathos and violence induced him sometimes to shriek piercingly in a crowd" (9) and takes everything at face value. The narrator remarks that stories have the power to work "his compassion to the pitch of frenzy." The intensity of his emotions "rob[s] him of the power of connected speech" and leaves him with stammering broken sentences. The episode of the cab-drive is a good illustration. Unnerved by the extreme misery of the horse and the cabman, Stevie is overcome with mute compassion:

> "Poor! Poor!" stammered out Stevie, pushing his hands deeper in his pocket with convulsive sympathy. He could say nothing; for the tenderness to all pain and all misery, the desire to make the horse happy and the cabman happy, had reached the point of a bizarre longing to take them to bed with him. And that, he

knew, was impossible. For Stevie was not mad. It was, as it were, a symbolic longing; and at the same time, it was very distinct, because springing from experience, the mother of wisdom. Thus when as a child he cowered in a dark corner scared, wretched, sore and miserable with the black, black misery of the soul, his sister Winnie used to come along, and carry him off to bed with her, as into a heaven of consoling peace. Stevie, though apt to forget mere facts, such as his name and address for instance, had a faithful memory of sensations. To be taken into a bed of compassion was the supreme remedy, with the only one disadvantage of being difficult of application on a large scale. (167-68)

Stevie sympathetically identifies with these two suffering creatures and wishes to take them with him home and soothe their pain. However, the narrator soon draws attention to the limitations of this naïve character's universal empathy by pointing out the impossibility of applying compassion on a large, global scale. Clearly, Stevie is totally absorbed in his compassionate feelings and sensations, although he is unable to articulate them into thoughts and lacks discrimination, as is contrapuntally reflected in the narrator's elaborate prose. His natural and indiscriminate empathy precisely makes him an easy prey to unscrupulous people like Mrs. Neale who plays on Stevie's sensitivity to extort money from him.

This episode shows how his frustrating inability to act may turn into violence: "In his inability to relieve at once Mrs. Neale's 'little 'uns' privations, he felt somebody should be made to suffer for it" (185). The narrator highlights this ingrained character trait:

> Supremely wise in knowing his own powerlessness, Stevie was not wise enough to restrain his passions. The tenderness of his universal charity had two phases as indissolubly joined and connected as the reverse and obverse sides of a medal. The anguish of immoderate compassion was succeeded by the pain of an innocent but pitiless rage. (169)

As Josiane Paccaud-Huguet pointed out in "Winnie Verloc's Secret Passion" the carving knife Stevie holds up after hearing the anarchists talk of cannibalistic capitalism is a disquieting proleptic detail.[21] Stevie's extreme solicitude turns compassion into pathos and then into violence. In his simple apprehension of the world, every evil must be ascribed to a culprit: "Somebody, he felt, ought to be punished for it – punished with great severity. Being no sceptic, but a moral creature, he was in a manner at the mercy of his righteous passions" (172). This naïve morality inevitably leads to melodrama; it cannot, therefore, be considered as a persuasively ethical position.

As for Winnie's compassion for Stevie, it is marred by her tendency to view him more as an object than as a subject. He is said to "ha[ve] been for so many years an object of care and fears" (59). Likewise, her mother sees her son as a burden: "And there was always the anxiety of his mere existence to face" (39). With disquieting ambivalence, she seems to assimilate Stevie to refuse: "For he was difficult to dispose of, that boy" (8). The two women agree on Stevie's having always been a source of anxiety, yet they relentlessly compete for his possession: "'He was much more mine than mother's. I sat up nights and nights with him on my lap [...]. And then – He was mine, I tell you...'" (275). This objectification of Stevie, whom Winnie can easily manipulate by playing on his feelings because of his blind trust in his beloved sister, is not compatible with a genuine ethical sympathy: giving is, in this case, superficial and, furthermore, it is impossible to receive anything from a mere object. Neither Winnie nor her mother can see in the young boy a reflection of their own fragile humanity. Finally, Winnie seems impervious to solicitude, as well as to remorse: she remains unmoved by the sight of Verloc's inert body "who was less than nothing now." Her only thought is to escape the gallows and her desperate love of life makes her even forgetful of Stevie's fate, although she claims he was "what there was of the salt of passion in her tasteless life" (174). The reciprocity necessary to the ethical dimension of solicitude is absent. For Ricoeur, within an ethical exchange, the esteem of the Other as oneself and the esteem of oneself as the Other are one. It is precisely this kind of ethical esteem that Winnie's suicide belies at the end of the narrative. And on the level of the plot, this flouts the very notion of intersubjectivity, inherent in the ethics of solicitude. On the meta-narrative level, however, the intersubjectivity at work between the reader and the text may be more promising, and I would, in this regard, argue that *The Secret Agent* profoundly calls for an ethical reading.

The Ethics of Reading

If the character of Stevie with his oversentimentality cannot qualify as the ethical centre of the novel, then the event of his death may. In fact, Stevie's death is the absent scene around which the plot revolves, and which haunts readers once they have closed the book. This death proves faithful not to the letter, but to the spirit of Mr. Vladimir's project: "'But what is one to say to an act of destructive ferocity so absurd as to be incomprehensible, inexplicable, almost unthinkable; in fact, mad?'" (33). And indeed, for the Police as for the anarchists, it remains unaccountable. Chief Inspector Heat, who discovers "the heap of nameless fragments," acts as a mediator between the reader and the horror in all its radical Otherness. His reaction is first one of utter revulsion: the shock makes him "lose his inclination for food." This is an understatement that contrasts with the following sensational descriptions. "[Fighting] down the unpleasant sensation in his throat," he is deeply affected, his feelings of "a sense of ruthless cruelty" are contradicting his reason which "told him the effect must have been as swift as a flash of lightning." Chief Inspector Heat seems pained by Stevie's fate and shows empathy for him:

> The man, whoever he was, had died instantaneously; and yet it seems impossible to believe that a human body could have reached that state of disintegration without passing through the pangs of inconceivable agony. No physiologist, and still less of a metaphysician, Chief Inspector Heat rose by the force of sympathy, which is a form of fear, above the vulgar conception of time. Instantaneous! [...] The inexplicable mysteries of conscious existence beset Chief Inspector Heat till he evolved a horrible notion that ages of atrocious pain and mental torture could be contained between two successive winks of an eye. (87-88)

In this statement, Inspector Heat seems to go through the two forms of ethical intersubjectivity analysed earlier. He offers compassion to a suffering Other and receives an intimation of his own mortality. Furthermore, he is interrupted amid his activities, summoned to a face-to-face encounter with an Other that calls him to responsibility, and the ensuing silent dialogue opens onto a philosophical deliberation on "the inexplicable mysteries of conscious existence." The absence of a face does not invalidate this hypothesis but rather substantiates it. In the Levinasian face-to-face, the Other's face is pure exteriority, an enigma that resists interpretation. The *Stanford Encyclopaedia of Philosophy* reads: the face "opposes a passive resistance to our desire for mastery wherein our freedom asserts its sovereignty."[22] The absent face is precisely what resists Inspector Heat's investigation:

> He would have liked to trace this affair back to its mysterious origin for his own information. [...] Before the public he would have liked to vindicate the efficiency of his department by establishing the identity of that man. [...] That, however, appeared impossible. The first term of the problem was unreadable – lacked all suggestion but that of atrocious cruelty. (*SA* 89)

Stevie cannot be appropriated. Paradoxically, his faceless, fragmented body, which cannot be made whole, reinstates him in a truly intersubjective relationship. Significantly, the piece of cloth Inspector Heat discovers does not bear a name but an address, a discovery he calls "a gratuitous and accidental success." Stevie's shattered body may, in this way, be said to be an address to Inspector Heat, and through him, to the reader.

Stevie's unreadable body, much like Winnie's unfathomable face, may be viewed as a metaphor for the text itself which, likewise, at once calls for and resists interpretation. As Rochelle L. Rives writes in an article devoted to the reading of faces in *The Secret Agent:*

> In particular, the hermeneutic inquiry inspired by the face [Winnie's] and the novel itself offers no final "revelation of meaning" – no clear ethical outcome. In allegorical fashion, the face then invites the reader to consider the possibility of a narrative that, according to Conrad, can be "laid hold of mentally" but as it simultaneously resists

reading, this face pronounces the meaninglessness of a narrative
that cannot centre itself in the world of "distinct, significant facts."
The narrative challenge of the face is also its ethical challenge since
an illegible face confronts the very codes through which we read and
generate fictions.[23]

The Secret Agent tends to undermine the very genres and
literary conventions it draws upon. Through its plot –
conspiracies, a violent accidental death, a murder, a deserted
woman, suicide – as well as the tone of some descriptions,
the novel seems to belong to the genre of melodrama.
There are also numerous examples of Dickensian irony, as
we have seen. However, this very overabundance and the
over-sentimentalism of some sentences often reveal parodic
undertones. This is true of the description of Winnie's
melancholy memory of Stevie and starry-eyed devotion to
deceitful Ossipon. This description is rife with hyperbolic
similes and seems all the more parodic as Winnie completely
misinterprets the latter's words and intentions: "And Mrs.
Verloc, hearing these words of commendation vouchsafed to
her beloved dead, swayed forward with a flicker of light in her
sombre eyes, like a ray of sunshine heralding a tempest of rain"
(SA 297). The episode of the cabman particularly lends itself to
this over-sentimentalism, as if the narrator were modelling his
style on Stevie's extreme emotions: "The monstrous nature
of that declaration of paternity seemed to strike the world
dumb. A silence reigned during which the flanks of the old
horse, the steed of apocalyptic misery, smoked upwards in the
light of the charitable gas-lamp" (166-67). Self-parody is also
at work when the narrator calls attention to his own devices:
"The conveyance awaiting them would have illustrated the
proverb that 'truth can be more cruel than caricature,' if such
a proverb existed" (155).

Thus, the pathos of melodrama is mitigated by a comic
effect, also present in jarring juxtapositions, as when the
narrator resorts to Virgil to describe the destitute cabman:

> His jovial purple cheeks bristled with white hairs; and like Virgil's
> Silenus, who, his face smeared with the juice of berries, discoursed
> of Olympian Gods to the innocent shepherds of Sicily, he talked to
> Stevie of domestic matters and the affairs of men whose sufferings
> are great and immortality by no means assured. (166)

Here, it is the literary convention of the omniscient narrator –
since none of the characters could possibly be thinking in such
terms – which is derided through exaggeration. The narrator
is fond of these discordant effects, as shown in the many
oxymoronic phrases disseminated throughout the novel, such
as "soft brutality," or "Mrs. Verloc, full of deep purpose, spoke in
the tone of the shallowest indifference," (181) or again "'Yes,'
answered obediently Mrs. Verloc the free woman" (261).

These simultaneous contradictions – also conveyed in the
stylistic device of antiphrasis mentioned earlier – emphasize
the treacherous nature of reality and of a text which keeps
undermining itself. Indeed, if caricature saps melodrama, it
also works against itself through its pervasiveness and inflated
nature. The caricatures pointed out at the beginning of this
study keep recurring, almost to the point of saturation. This is
particularly true of Sir Ethelred, whose obsessive refusal to hear
about details is belied by Inspector Heat's discovery of the little
label, the single clue to the resolution of the case; or again of
Ossipon: "because he had had much to do with excited women,
and he was inclined in general to let his experience guide his
conduct in preference to applying his sagacity to each special
case. His sagacity in this case was busy in other directions" (282)
… namely Mrs. Verloc's money. Undermining the very codes of
its narrative, the text functions as a secret agent, working from
within against the norms it pretends to abide by.

This disruptive effect forces the reader into an ethical reading
since, deprived of the aesthetic and moral security of accepted
literary codes, he/she must make his/her own interpretative
choices. In a sense, the distorted, unreadable face of the text
is a call to the reader's responsibility. Consequently, the writer
himself may feel like the Assistant Commissioner: "'Here I am
stuck in a litter of paper,' he reflected, with unreasonable

resentment, 'supposed to hold all the threads in my hands, and yet I can but hold what is put in my hand, and nothing else. And they can fasten the other ends of the threads where they please'" (115). Various narrative threads co-exist and are intertwined in this narrative – the political plot around the anarchists, the domestic drama, the detective story – and, in the absence of any guiding authorial moral principle, readers are eventually free to privilege whichever reading option they choose. Thus, they may string these threads together whenever they are individually called to respond ethically to the text and can do so according to their own free will and conscience. Besides, alongside this narrative's ethical open-endedness and its obvious ironies, the text invites its readers to disentangle and pick out ironic parallels that may go unobserved. This requires remaining alert to details, as Inspector Heat's "gratuitous and accidental success" encourages us to. Indeed, some words echo throughout the narrative with haunting insistence, impressing the mind with lingering hints and images. Stevie's drooping lip is mentioned in the sentence that haunts Winnie in her fear of the gallows: "The drop given was fourteen feet." Likewise, Winnie's constant terror of being hanged is proleptically present in Verloc's expostulation to his wife: "Hang it all" or "Hang everything!" It later reappears in the newspaper title announcing Winnie's drowning which haunts Ossipon: *"An impenetrable mystery is destined to hang forever ...,"* the three dots suspending it forever.

In these instances, it is the mystery of death that is evoked, as in the parallel between Chief Inspector Heat's meditation on the time of death – on the ages of agony "contained between two successive winks of an eye," as well as in the quasi-cinematic scene when Verloc sees in slow motion the knife and the arm that is about to stab him: The shadow *"flickered* up and down. Its movements were leisurely. They were leisurely enough for Mr. Verloc to recognize the limb and the weapon" (262, my emphasis). The anaphoric "they were leisurely enough," repeated four times, freezes time until the final modulation "they were not leisurely enough" – all this in a flicker. Once again, through the proliferation of these references, the text invites an ethical reading that confronts us with the mystery of death and reminds us of our vulnerability. Even the two most questionable characters that remain at the end of the narrative, the frightful Professor and the devious Ossipon, seem to be included in this melancholy intimation. Thus, although scathing irony does not spare any character in the novel, or maybe precisely because of these all-inclusive ironies, the text avoids alienating the reader from the characters. In a way, universal irony seems to succeed where Stevie's indiscriminate compassion fails. Because the narrator offers us access to the characters' thoughts, and although we can see their limitations and biases, we ultimately come to understand their motives and we are not completely estranged from them. We somehow come to feel some sympathy for their moral and existential predicaments. The kaleidoscopic picture of the various subjectivities provided in the text could almost be read in a Sternean vein, since, as in Sterne's works, the characters' idiosyncrasies in *The Secret Agent* are often gently mocked. This is more particularly true of Verloc, who is scorned for his laziness, gullibility, blindness to others and to himself, and misplaced self-confidence, while he is also partly redeemed by his generosity and his "indefatigable devotion" to his wife – a redemption that is not free from the narrator's irony, however. Thus, *The Secret Agent* adeptly combines Dickensian and Sternean irony, distance and proximity, in a double allegiance which, paradoxically, calls for an ethical reading. Claude Maisonnat analysed the various stylistic devices used to destabilize the text, such as antiphrasis, Gallicisms, capitalisation, and free indirect discourse. He argued that "[t] his allows the text of *The Secret Agent* to oscillate between effects of immediacy and distance, intimacy and extimacy, thus opening a discursive space available to the reader who is called upon to assume the responsibility of his interpretive choices."[24] I would add that this text is also ethical, inasmuch as it invites solicitude, reminding the readers of their own human condition and limitations. Indeed, if nobody in this narrative is spared Conrad's scepticism and ironies, including the narrator, why should the reader be?

Manifestly, this text, with its contradictions and double allegiances to various modes and genres, places readers in an uncomfortable position in which they cannot rely on fixed codes of conduct. It fundamentally calls for an ethical reading that requires the reader's ability to acknowledge and cope with the double bind of this text which keeps undermining itself. Like Inspector Heat, the reader may feel as a tight-rope walker focused on the difficult task of keeping his/her balance as the narrator shakes the rope. Faced with a text that is, in many ways, radically Other, the reader is called to the responsibility of his/her interpretations.

The reciprocity of the reader's intersubjective relationship with the text stems from his/her admiration for Conrad's deft handling of irony to write at once a critical melodrama and humane caricature. *The Secret Agent* also confronts the reader with *suffering*, inducing him/her to offer their compassion to an Other, and receiving, in return, an intimation of their own humane frailty. Stevie's drawing of "circles, innumerable circles, concentric, eccentric; a coruscating whirl of circles" has often been perceptively seen as a metafictional representation of the novel.[25] In its attempt at rendering "cosmic chaos," *The Secret Agent* indeed symbolizes "a mad art attempting the inconceivable" (*SA* 45): denouncing the pettiness of the world while taking it all, secretly, in "a bed of compassion."

NOTES

[1]   Pauly 49.

[2]   The original: "*Soi-même comme un autre.*"

[3]   According to Ricoeur, the aim is "[that] of a good life lived with and for others in just institutions."

[4]   The original: "*On se propose d'établir [...]*" : *1) la primauté de l'éthique sur la morale; 2) la nécessité pour la visée éthique de passer par le crible de la norme; 3) la légitimité d'un recours de la norme à la visée, lorsque la norme conduit à des impasses pratiques, qui rappelleront à ce nouveau stade de notre méditation les diverses situations aporétiques auxquelles a dû faire face notre méditation sur l'ipséité. Autrement dit, [...] la morale ne constituerait*

qu'une effectuation limitée, quoique légitime et même indispensable, de la visée éthique, et l'éthique en ce sens envelopperait la morale" (Ricoeur 200-01).

⁵ The original: *"Ensuite, l'idée d'interprétation ajoute, à la simple idée de signification, celle de signification pour quelqu'un. Interpréter le texte de l'action, c'est pour l'agent s'interpréter lui-même. Je rejoins ici un thème important de Charles Taylor dans ses 'Philosophical Papers': l'homme, dit-il, est un* 'self-interpreting animal.'" *Du même coup, notre concept du soi sort grandement enrichi de ce rapport entre interprétation du texte de l'action et auto-interprétation. Au plan éthique, l'interprétation de soi devient estime de soi. En retour, l'estime de soi suit le destin de l'interprétation. Comme celle-ci, elle donne lieu à la controverse, à la contestation, à la rivalité, bref au conflit des interprétations, dans l'exercice du jugement pratique"* (Ricoeur 211).

⁶ See Ricoeur 222.

⁷ See Atkins.

⁸ The London of *The Secret Agent* echoes Dickens' depiction of this city in his novels. Conrad, as he stated in "Poland Revisited," applied for a berth as an "Able Seaman" and went to London to meet the man to whom he sent his application. On his way to this man's office he described the streets he walked through and used the word "Dickensian" three times: "a Dickensian nook of London" (*NLL* 152); "the office I entered was Dickensian too" (152); and "Dickensian eating-house" (153). For more information on Dickens' influence on Conrad, see Caserio.

⁹ The phrase is used eight times within one paragraph (*SA* 297).

¹⁰ The phrase "He was terrified" appears five times within a few paragraphs (290-91).

¹¹ "Her object attained in astute secrecy, the heroic old woman had made a clean breast of it to Mrs. Verloc" (152).

¹² See Martinière; Wake.

¹³ Winnie, who has been urging Verloc to take Stevie with him on his walks, watches them go: "Might be father and son," an image that haunts her just before Verloc's cannibal feast.

¹⁴ Stevie being the son of a victualler who used violence against him, his remains may be seen as "the by-product of a butcher's shop."

¹⁵ The fact that Winnie's first love, whom she had to renounce for the sake of her young simple-minded brother, was a young butcher, further complicates the family's entanglement around Stevie as a sacrificial victim (Stevie could be the would-be son of Winnie's fantasy, punished for this transgression or again Winnie's unconscious revenge on her brother for ruining her hopes of a happy union).

¹⁶ Verloc's eating without bread may suggest impossible transsubstantiation.

¹⁷ The Assistant Commissioner is indeed able to sympathise with Verloc when the latter confesses to him that he would have run away, were it not for his wife's refusal to go abroad. "'Nothing could be more characteristic of the respectable

bond than that,' went on, with a touch of grimness, the Assistant Commissioner, whose own wife, too, had refused to hear of going abroad" (*SA* 221).

[18] Prickett 50.

[19] Bergo.

[20] The original: "*Quelle est alors l'autre extrémité du spectre de la sollicitude, [...]? La situation inverse de l'injonction est la* souffrance. *L'autre est maintenant cet être* souffrant *dont nous n'avons cessé de marquer la place en creux dans notre philosophie de l'action, en désignant l'homme comme* agissant et souffrant. *[...] Ici l'initiative, en termes précisément de pouvoir-faire, semble revenir exclusivement au soi qui 'donne' sa sympathie, sa compassion, ces termes étant pris au sens fort du souhait de partager la peine d'autrui. Confronté à cette bienfaisance, voire à cette bienveillance, l'autre paraît réduit à la condition seulement de 'recevoir'*" (Ricoeur 223).

[21] Paccaud-Huguet, "Winnie Verloc's Secret Passion" 123. In the scene where she stabs Verloc Winnie displays an emotional pattern which is like that of her brother. She remains silent, unable to voice her grief and rage to her husband, and then strikes a deathly blow, her face strangely looking at that moment like Stevie's.

[22] See Bergo.

[23] Rives 102.

[24] Maisonnat 105.

[25] See Paccaud-Huguet, "Economies of the Gaze"; Lothe; Martinière; Pauly.

WORKS CITED

Atkins, Kim. "Paul Ricoeur." *Internet Encyclopedia of Philosophy*. Ed. James Fieser and Bradely Dowden. Web. <https://iep.utm.edu/ricoeur/>. 3 Nov. 2020.

Bergo, Bettina. "Emmanuel Levinas." *The Stanford Encyclopedia of Philosophy*. Ed. Edward N. Zalta (Fall 2019). Web. <https://plato.stanford.edu/archives/fall2019/entries/levinas/>. 3 Nov. 2020.

Caserio, Robert L. "Joseph Conrad, Dickensian Novelist of the Nineteenth Century: A Dissent from Ian Watt." *Nineteenth-Century Fiction* 36 (1981): 337-47. Print.

Levinas, Emmanuel. *Totality and Infinity: An Essay on Exteriority*. Trans. Alphonso Lingis. Pittsburgh: Duquesne UP, 1969. Print.

Lothe, Jakob. *Conrad's Narrative Method*. Oxford: Clarendon P, 1989. Print.

Maisonnat, Claude. "Reflexivity and the Thrust of the Feminine in *The Secret Agent*." *L'Époque conradienne* 33 (2007): 95-110. Print.

Martinière, Nathalie. "Corps propre et corps du texte dans *The Secret Agent* : du morcellement des corps à la fragmentation signifiante du texte." *L'Époque conradienne* 27 (2001): 83-98. Print.

Paccaud-Huguet, Josiane. "Economies of the gaze in *The Secret Agent*." *Conradiana* 42.3 (2010): 1-16. Print.

---. "Winnie Verloc's Secret Passion." *L'Époque conradienne* 33 (2007): 111-25. Print.

Pauly, Véronique. "Le Chaos et la totalité dans *The Secret Agent.*" *Joseph Conrad: la fiction de l'autre.* Ed. Josiane Paccaud-Huguet. Paris/Caen: Lettres Modernes/Minard, 1998. 43-63. Print.

Prickett, David. "No Escape: Liberation and the Ethics of Self-Governance in *The Secret Agent.*" Simmons and Stape 49-56. Print.

Ricoeur, Paul. *Soi-même comme un autre.* Paris: Seuil, 1990. Print.

Rives, Rochelle L. "Face Values: Optics as Ethics in Joseph Conrad's *The Secret Agent.*" *Criticism* 56 (2014): 89-118. Print.

Simmons, Allan H. and J. H. Stape, eds. *"The Secret Agent." Centennial Essays.* Amsterdam: Rodopi, 2007. *The Conradian.* Print.

Wake, Paul. "The Time of Death: 'Passing Away' in *The Secret Agent.*" Simmons and Stape 13-20.

Laëtitia Crémona,
Université de Montréal,
Montréal, Canada

Alfred Hitchcock's *Sabotage*:
Ethics, Politics, and Aesthetics

In 1936, Alfred Hitchcock adapted Joseph Conrad's *The Secret Agent* into a movie entitled *Sabotage*.[1] During his career as filmmaker Hitchcock has been a long-standing adaptor of a wide variety of novels and short stories, most of his films (41 out of 54) being literary adaptations. However, as pointed out by Palmer and Boyd, "unlike his Hollywood contemporary John Huston [...][who] built a long and productive career by screening the fiction of an amazing number of celebrated authors," Hitchcock did not present himself as a literary adaptor.[2] On the contrary, he is famously known for "consider[ing] source material eminently disposable"[3] and also for being only interested in the basic idea of the story he adapts not in its plot or moral. Moreover, his literary sources were often "obscure" and "not always adequately indicated in the screen credits of the films."[4] In his famous interview with François Truffaut, Hitchcock explained why he did not want to adapt ambitious, classic literary works, such as Fyodor Dostoevsky's *Crime and Punishment*:

> Well, I shall never do that, precisely because *Crime and Punishment* is somebody else's achievement. There's been a lot of talk about the way in which Hollywood directors distort literary masterpieces. I'll have no part of that! What I do is to read a story only once, and if I like the basic idea, I just forget all about the book and start create cinema.[5]

As he suggests here, Hitchcock values his artistic autonomy and creative independence to the extent that he sees literary texts as merely sources of inspiration that he adapts to his own aesthetic and ethical purposes. It is hardly surprising, therefore, to realize that, with the notable exception of his adaptation of Daphne du Maurier's *Rebecca*, Hitchcock scarcely marketed the fictional works he screened as adaptations of these literary texts. Furthermore, he often changed the titles of his films to distance his works from the original texts and thus preserve his creative independence. This is the case with his adaptation of Conrad's *The Secret Agent*, whose title Hitchcock changed into *Sabotage* to assert his autonomy and detachment from his source material.[6] He also widely shied away from Conrad's ethical framework, as we shall see throughout this discussion.

This said, despite Hitchcock's deliberate will, as an author, to distance himself from his original literary source, several literary critics tend to see and analyze *Sabotage* through the traditional lens of the "fidelity discourse."[7] Avrom Fleishman's article *"The Secret Agent* Sabotaged?" (1997) is emblematic of this dominant critical trend: in this article Fleishman focuses on the notion of faithfulness, interpreting and evaluating the discourse of Hitchcock's movie in terms of its conformity to Conrad's work. He sees *Sabotage* as a *"medium* adaptation – capturing an important part of the original in theme and form, while sacrificing other aspects of perhaps equal value."[8] Similarly, Paula Marantz Cohen argues that Hitchcock "failed to digest and reconstitute its literary source fully"[9] and reproaches Hitchcock for failing to explore the complex incentives, desires, and ideological frameworks that fuel the characters' choices and actions in Conrad's novel.[10] By so strictly abiding by the fidelity principle, both Fleishman and Cohen fail to go beyond the essentialist vision of filmic adaptations that "posits the literary text as the essence to which the adaptation must conform."[11] They also fail to see *Sabotage* as the expression of an original cinematic authorship and a creative work on its own terms.

In *Sabotage*, Hitchcock certainly overlooks the complexity of the moral and ideological identities of some of the characters, conveyed in Conrad's novel, and sometimes even reshapes their physical appearance. For instance, Winnie Verloc is described in the novel as being plump or having a "full, rounded form" (*SA* 6), but in the film she is slender and graceful. These distortions may surely be unsettling for someone who expects a faithful rendering of event and character, but, again, it is important not to overlook that Hitchcock regards adaptations as merely a source into which he taps and from which he chooses whatever he thinks suitable for his movie. And precisely, given Hitchcock's notion of adaptation, underlined in his previous declaration, it would be excessive to view *Sabotage* as an act of "treason" or "sabotage." It is more fitting to see this film instead as an autonomous work of art which draws on an original story that he adapts and re-orients to suit his own aesthetic, ideological, and ethical goals.

As it becomes clear, in this chapter, I do not intend to offer a detailed account of the similarities and discrepancies between Conrad's novel and Hitchcock's film. Other critics have already addressed this issue. Michael Anderegg in particular offers the most detailed, nuanced, and illuminating account of the adaptation process at work in *Sabotage* in his article "Conrad and Hitchcock."[12] Besides, this article has the merit of avoiding the essentialist literary discourse to fully take into consideration the complex, multi-layered relationship between Conrad's *The Secret Agent* and Hitchcock's cinematic adaptation. Anderegg states:

> In spite of differences in tone, plot, characters, and incidents, Conrad and Hitchcock end up making nearly parallel statements. Both novel and film create a lower middle-class milieu where what appears to be tawdriness, laziness and stupidity are in fact external manifestations of genuine evil. [...] Both works reveal a claustrophobic world of limited options and stunted emotions. [...] Admittedly, a devoted reader of Conrad whose major concern is to see how "faithfully" the film reflects the novel must be disappointed with *Sabotage*. But if the two works are approached with a neutral attitude and with an appreciation for the integrity of both novels and films, the exercise of comparing the two is extremely satisfying; each enriches the other.[13]

I similarly believe that the intricate relationship between an original text and its filmic adaptation is a rich, productive process, and that the study of an adaptation such as Hitchcock's *Sabotage* can stir a new set of ethical interpretations of both Hitchcock's and Conrad's works. Thus, in this chapter, I will analyze the relationship between politics, ethics, and aesthetics in Hitchcock's film, not only to better understand Hitchcock's ethical discourse which permeates his work, but also to see how his recasting of Conrad's novel in 1930s London can enrich and extend our vision of Conrad's own work. Before delving further into Hitchcock's ethical world, let me highlight some recent developments in the philosophy of film, or what has come to be known over the last decade as "film as philosophy" or "film-philosophy," and more specifically, the interrelation of film and ethics.

Cinema, Philosophy, Morality

The history and development of cinema and films are closely related to questions of morality: as early as the 1900s and 1910s, both clergymen and politicians saw cinema, which provided entertainment at low costs to the masses, as a potential threat to morality. Soon censorship was put in place to control which films could be distributed or exhibited on screen. British film industry established as early as 1912 the independent British Board of Film Censors (BBFC, now known as the British Board of Film Classification) which authorized the official release of films in the country. Film directors and producers were, in theory, free to create any film they wanted, but, as a BBFC certificate was required to ensure exhibition, producers and directors tended to self-censor their work to ensure future distribution. In 1927, for instance, BBFC outlined seven broad categories which could justify censorship: religious, political, military, social, questions of sex, crime, and cruelty. Under these large categories, European films such as Friedrich Wilhelm Murnau's *Nosferatu* (1922) or Sergei Eisenstein's *Battleship Potemkine* (1925) were initially banned by British censors.[14]

In a like manner, Hollywood's major studios, which dominated and left a considerable and lingering imprint on the film industry, created in the 1920s a self-censorship process, that was to become the Motion picture production code, also known as Hays Code. A first independent National Board of Censorship (later renamed National Board of Review, NBR) had been put in place in the United States as early as 1908, with the aims of pushing the industry to some form of self-regulation. But the NBR did not manage to influence film production companies, and was soon considered by many lobbying groups, notably the powerful General Federation of Women's Clubs, as too permissive.[15] The NBR was thus dissolved in the early 1920s, to be soon replaced by the Hays Code, an initiative arising from the Hollywood major film studios themselves. The Code principally aimed at avoiding the implementation of a governmentally controlled film censorship. The Code's general principles promoted the idea that films should not "lower" the moral level of viewers, that natural or human law should never be ridiculed, and that its violation should not arouse sympathy. It also specified that such elements as profanity, nudity, sexuality, white slavery, or miscegenation were banned from films, and notably discouraged controversial political views.[16] The Code, which clearly stated what could and could not be shown on screen, had a major and lasting influence on film production and was closely followed by the industry from 1934 to the mid-1950s. This elitist vision of the world, wherein the censors controlled what the masses were authorized to see, clearly assigned a "moral responsibility" to cinema.[17] The establishment of these systems of censorship in the US, Great Britain, and many other European and non-European countries, aimed at ensuring obedience to established moral codes and values. By controlling the distribution process (i.e. what could and could not be shown to the public in a specific country), these monitoring agencies compelled film producers and directors to self-censorship.

Given the general context of moral scrutiny in which cinema evolved and the underlying understanding that films were conducive of morals and values, it is surprising that until very recently film theorists and philosophers alike looked with a certain disdain at the interrelation of ethics and films. Film theory has since its beginning asked several philosophical questions, predominantly on the nature of film or on its unique artistic characteristics. Many of the first influential film theorists were not philosophers, but filmmakers or thinkers. In the 1920s and 1930s, for instance, filmmaker Sergei Eisenstein's essays were particularly interested in films' aesthetics, with a notable focus on the importance of montage. Few film theorists from the twentieth century dealt explicitly with film and ethics. Some of the few film theorists integrating ethical issues in their thinking were Siegfried Kracauer and André Bazin, although they did so from a predominantly aesthetic perspective. These theorists argued that the specificity of cinema lies in its realism: for both Kracauer and Bazin, film has the aesthetic power to reveal reality and renew the spectator's engagement with the world.[18] Focusing on examples from the 1960s *Cinéma vérité* documentaries, Bazin considered realism as a condition of morality in cinematic representation. He claimed that aesthetic realism allows for a "veridical representation of social reality," and that this aesthetic realism is equated with "truth-telling" and "moral edification."[19] As Robert Sinnerbrink demonstrated, Kracauer and Bazin can, therefore, be considered as the first cinema theorists to integrate the notion of ethics in what had previously been predominantly aesthetics film theory. This interest in ethics within film-theory was, however, short-lived, since, with the development of structuralist discourses in the 1970s and, more specifically, with the strong influence of Christian Metz's semiotics writing on film theory, emphasis was once again laid on the constructed nature of cinema.

Similarly, philosophers have only recently started to see or acknowledge the philosophical relevance of films. Gilles Deleuze, who explores how, through new forms of movement-image and time-image, cinema communicates thought, has, in this respect, been very influential. He was among the first philosophers to bring into light the similarities between philosophy and cinema, and to consider cinema as a philosophical undertaking that stirs our thoughts. Writings by the philosopher Stanley Cavell have also drawn major interest and proved instrumental in highlighting the close connections between cinema, philosophy, and morality.[20] In *Pursuit of Happiness*, for instance, Cavell studied seven prominent comedies from the 1930s and 1940s, that he dubbed "Comedies of remarriage," which, according to him, are of great moral and philosophical significance. Based on the analyses of these various mainstream films, he argued that "the achievement of happiness requires not the [...] satisfaction of our needs [...] but the examination and transformation of those needs."[21] The treatment of the remarriage theme within these films drew attention to the fact that, within a relationship, happiness requires "growing up" together with one's partner.[22] Through his various studies and writings, Cavell demonstrated that the relationship between cinema and philosophy may potentially be multi-directional: philosophical concepts could, of course, be relevant and help to better understand the specific aesthetic and ontological nature of cinema. But most importantly, films could also be a valuable medium to study and directly inform philosophy, in a non-doctrinal way.[23] Cavell stated in 1996:

> to my way of thinking the creation of film was as if meant for philosophy – meant to reorient everything philosophy has said about reality and its representation, about art and imitation, about greatness and conventionality, about judgment and pleasure, about scepticism and transcendence, about language and expression.[24]

Although over the last two decades this idea of cinema as a vehicle of philosophical reflection has inspired multiple writings by philosophers in the field of "philosophy as film" or "film-philosophy," it would be incorrect to conclude that Cavell's vision has reached a consensus. There are still controversy and ongoing debates in philosophical circles over the capacity of film to provide a reliable source for philosophizing. Cavell's endeavours, however, opened new possibilities, by going beyond the relationship of film and the philosophy of aesthetics, to validate the relevance of film for ethics and ethical thought. Sinnerbrink has extensively written on the links between film and ethics over the last decade. He shows the ethical significance of film and underlines the recent growing interest in ethics within film-philosophy. He argues that cinema is a medium "evok[ing] ethical experience and invit[ing] philosophical reflection,"[25] and that "film has an ethical potential for exploring moral issues, ethically charged situations or moral 'thought experiments.'"[26] He also significantly remarks that "cinema can be understood as a medium of ethical experience: a 'cinematic ethics' that brings film and philosophy together in order to cultivate an experiential approach to ethical understanding and philosophical reflection."[27]

Hitchcock's *Sabotage*, the focus of this study, provides a good example of the close connections between film and philosophy. In his interviews and writings, Hitchcock described himself as "someone who merely provides entertainment to an interested public,"[28] thus distancing his works from philosophy and philosophical thought. However, several critics, including Irving Singer, consider Hitchcock a "philosophical filmmaker."[29] Most of Hitchcock's films, including *Sabotage*, can, indeed, be seen as philosophical in the sense that they deal with important social and moral issues – crime, guilt, justice, etc. – which call for philosophical thought and ethical judgment. In this chapter, I will particularly look at this productive connection between cinema and philosophy, and film and morality, by exploring the interrelation of ethics, politics, and aesthetics in *Sabotage*, in the light of Conrad's ethical reflection in *The Secret Agent*.

Aesthetics, Politics, and Ethics

Sabotage is set in the 1930s and starts with a close-up shot on the definition of the term *sabotage*. Hitchcock seems to consider the meaning of this word so important that he readily imparts it to the viewer. While Hitchcock's urge to define this term from the outset sets immediately the tone of the film, it most importantly also reveals his pedagogic intention, or, more exactly, his desire to instruct the common viewer on how to understand the key word on which revolves the story, and, above all, to direct the audience's gaze and moral perspective. This moral didacticism, implied in the opening of the film, runs through the entire movie and this is hardly surprising. Hitchcock is a moralist filmmaker, and this moral vision widely stems from his Catholic upbringing.

A devout Catholic, Hitchcock grew up in a strict Catholic family, attended Mass regularly, went to a Jesuit school, and even served briefly as a choir boy. This religious upbringing had a manifest impact on his handling of themes and characters in his films. Patrick McGilligan, a biographer, wrote: "Catholicism pervades his films, albeit a brand of Catholicism spiked with irreverence and iconoclasm."[30] He also remarked that Hitchcock spoke of having acquired from his Jesuit schooling "a strong sense of fear," a capacity "to be realistic" and "Jesuit reasoning power." During his interview with Truffaut, Hitchcock declared: "It was probably during this period with the Jesuits that a strong sense of fear developed – moral fear – the fear of being involved in anything evil. I always tried to avoid it."[31] Donald Spoto also points out the influence of Hitchcock's Catholic education on his moral universe and states that Hitchcock is "a profoundly Victorian Catholic, a rigid moralist."[32] Other critics, such as Palmer, Pettey, and Sanders, similarly referred to Hitchcock's moralism, but stressed that Hitchcock was not a rigid moralist but a "moralist not moralizing."[33] French filmmakers Eric Rohmer and Claude Chabrol, who helped Hitchcock to achieve the status of film *auteur*, likewise discussed the moral character of Hitchcock's movies, while they also underlined that Hitchcock did not succumb to religious mysticism or dogmatism despite his stern religious education:

> Though Hitchcock is a practicing Catholic, he has nothing of the mystic or the ardent proselyte about him. His works are of a profane nature, and though they often deal with questions relating to God, their protagonists are not gripped by an anxiety that is, properly speaking, religious.[34]

It is important to mention here that apart from "I Confess," a 1953 murder mystery, set in Quebec city and focused on a priest, Father Michael Logan, which is a clearly Catholic movie, none of Hitchcock's films can be strictly labelled Catholic.

Hitchcock nonetheless considers Christian morality of the utmost importance and although his movies are not sermons, they yet pervade with moral concerns that reflect his Catholic upbringing, psyche, and mindset. As a moralist, Hitchcock explores a wide range of issues in his movies: the notions of good and evil, the order of society and its transgression, the rightness or wrongness of the characters' conducts, reward and retribution of these conducts, sin, guilt, punishment, and redemption, etc. Through deft narrative and cinematic techniques he brings to his audience's attention these moral questions and implicitly, or explicitly, steers them to moral reflection and ethical choices.

In *Sabotage*, Hitchcock's moral canvass is vast and varied, and stands in sharp contrast with Conrad's ethical framework in *The Secret Agent*. In this film Hitchcock clearly moves away from Conrad's moral skepticism and this significant shift is perceptible on the level of both narrative and characterization. He engages in what seems like a moral rehabilitation, in his portrayal of both Mrs. Verloc and Stevie, but also in the film's overall ideological and moral intention. When he describes Winnie Verloc, for example, Hitchcock reshapes her moral and physical portrait to the extent that she reappears in the film in a completely different light. In *The Secret Agent*, Mrs. Verloc is described as dull and chubby, whereas in the movie she is of a slender and attractive silhouette. As he sheds Winnie of her protuberance, Hitchcock also upgrades her morally. In the novel, Winnie's passivity, inscrutable and blank look, and "constitutional indolence" are emphasized. In the film instead, she is described as an active, transparent, free woman in control of her destiny. In what looks like a feminist undertaking, Hitchcock thus rescues Winnie from her physical and moral mediocrity and makes her a heroine with a distinct will and moral agency. While he steadily revises and reshapes his characters' moral identity, as he does here with Winnie Verloc, Hitchcock also reshuffles some of the elements of the plot to assign them a new moral or ideological purpose. He tends to remove or elude details he considers morally suspect, by either deliberately erasing moral traits within the characters that may undermine the moral sentiment he wants to convey, or simply by resorting to an ethics of vagueness to keep the origin or moral identity of a particular character in the dark. He, for instance, does not tell us why Winnie Verloc left America nor explicitly informs us why she married Mr. Verloc. In Conrad's novel, of course, we know that Winnie married Mr. Verloc only for his money. Her marriage is merely a means to an end, moved exclusively by a pragmatic ethics of survival: she sacrifices her life and consents to marry Mr. Verloc in exchange for Verloc's support for her and her "crippled mother and a crazy idiot of a boy."

Winnie is certainly not an emblem of ethical integrity in Conrad's novel, and, by erasing this morally suspect trait in his film, Hitchcock raises her moral profile and increases the chances of seeing the audience identify sympathetically with her. Hitchcock resorts to the same process in his portrayal of Stevie. He avoids all reference to his mental deficiency and presents him as a normal boy with a generous heart and exemplary kindness. Furthermore, Hitchcock not only upgrades physically and morally Mrs. Verloc and her brother, but also rehabilitates the Verlocs' means of subsistence, by substituting what is a sordid porno bookshop in Conrad's novel for a respectable movie theatre – the *Bijou*. Clearly, marriage in *The Secret Agent* is presented as a sham, and the aridity of the Verlocs is reflected in the confined, claustrophobic atmosphere of their household. Meantime, patriarchy is prominent in Conrad's story and even when Winnie Verloc finally kills the emblem of patriarchy, Mr. Verloc, she immediately slips again into the meshes of patriarchy, by falling in love with Ossipon, "the robust anarchist" whom she ironically sees as her "saviour." This so-called saviour seduces her, robs her of her money, and leads her to suicide. In *Sabotage*, Hitchcock flattens out this overwhelming patriarchal order and goes even as far as to present Mr. Verloc as a quiet, caring fatherly figure. Moreover, he removes from the film the morally objectionable suicide to which Winnie Verloc resorts in *The Secret Agent* and thus shifts his heroine from a helpless victim of circumstances into a subject of will and power who learns to master her destiny. He even foresees for Winnie Verloc a happy matrimonial life, as suggested in Winnie's intimacy with Ted at the end of the film; a promising and morally higher relationship, based on love, as a counterpoint to Winnie Verloc's relation both with her husband and Ossipon in Conrad's novel. In the film, Winnie Verloc and Ted embody an ideal family model, characterized by serenity and tenderness. This is reflected in the scene at the restaurant where Winnie, Ted, and Stevie eat and socialize in a soothing, relaxed ambience.

Hitchcock's attempt in *Sabotage* at moral rehabilitation of Conrad's philosophical and ethical universe indicates a strong sense of moral didacticism, which reveals his endorsement of a conventional moral framework as a bulwark against Conrad's ethical skepticism. In terms of ideology and politics, too, Hitchcock seems to undertake a similar shift, as we shall see throughout. What is striking in Hitchcock's films is that, like Conrad, he does not articulate his narratives around a specific political agenda. Several of his movies of the mid and late 1930s, including *Sabotage*, are espionage thrillers. As we know, this filmic genre is generally politically oriented, and Hitchcock's use of this generic form may lead us to the belief that he was harbouring in these films a political vision he wished to convey to his audience. However, in his interviews, Hitchcock consistently insisted on his being "non-political,"[35] a disclaimer reminiscent of Conrad's assertion of his ideological and political detachment. While Conrad's novel is primarily aimed at condemning anarchism,[36] Hitchcock's adaptation does not mention the word *anarchism* at all. This may result from Hitchcock's consideration of himself as a non-political filmmaker – he does not "do" political films, as he stated. The absence in *Sabotage* of all reference to anarchism, central to Conrad's novel, seems, therefore, to conform to and confirm Hitchcock's non-political stance; it reinforces his claim to neutrality and distance from any political or ideological agenda.

Hitchcock's claim to being apolitical cannot, however, be taken at face value. Indeed, things are more complex than they seem, and to shed light on this complexity it is important to set the production of *Sabotage* in its historical context. The political and ideological climate of the 1930s was turbulent and precarious. In 1936, when *Sabotage* was released, the threat of war hovered in the air, as Hitler's aggressive Nazi ideology grew prominent. Meanwhile, in Great Britain, censorship was overwhelming and increasingly led to self-censorship at the production level. As Pam Hirsch interestingly observes:

> the British Board of Film Censors (BBFC) frowned upon politics in film, and so, in effect, supported, or at least did not challenge, the policy of appeasement. Lord Tyrrel, in 1936 President of the Board, told exhibitors that "nothing would be more calculated to arouse the passion of the British public than the introduction on the screen of subjects dealing with religious or political controversy."[37]

Like most filmmakers Hitchcock was constrained by the BBFC's norms of censorship, which, as made clear in the previous statement, targeted everything that pertained to religion or politics. The absence in *Sabotage* of any direct reference to politics or anarchism, for that matter, may thus widely result from self-censorship. Hitchcock's decision to shift the time-frame of the film to the 1930s might also indicate an attempt to redirect attention to a more diffuse, foreign threat on Great Britain.

Sabotage is, indeed, one of many espionage films that were released in Britain in the 1930s, and one among several spy movies directed by Hitchcock: from *The Man Who Knew Too Much* (1934), *The 39 Steps* (1935) to *The Lady Vanishes* (1938), these thrillers are some of the best British movies ever made.[38] The preponderance of spy movies in Great Britain at the time is, however, not fortuitous, and deserves close attention. Discussing the British cinema of the 1930s, Tom Ryall states: "it can be argued that the spy thriller genre is an indication of the growing consciousness of the political turbulence in Europe, the rise of Fascism and the troubled international situation which was to erupt into the Second World War."[39] Ryall further specifically remarked with regard to *Sabotage*:

"the middle European accents of [...] Verloc and his spymaster [...] provide a distinctive aural token of the European menace from the British point of view."[40]

Hitchcock never openly stated that he was political or expressed his political opinions in his interviews, as mentioned earlier. However, he was involved in some activities that may be called political. Before the Second World War he was part of a group of English film directors in Hollywood, including Boris Karloff, Reginald Gardiner, and Robert Stevenson, who agreed to make films that would attempt to stir the United States out of their neutrality and support Britain's and Europe's war effort against Nazi Germany.[41] *Foreign Correspondent* (1940) and *Suspicion* (1941) are examples of this political agenda. Despite his discretion about his political views, therefore, Hitchcock was, in practice, far from being apolitical or bereft of political ideals, as he declared. *Sabotage* is certainly not an overtly political movie, but it cannot be considered fully "non-political" either. Furthermore, by virtue of its affiliation to a cinematic genre that lends itself to political considerations, *Sabotage* may rightly be viewed as political, and, therefore, as a means to raise the public's awareness about contemporary political threats – sabotage in its various dimensions. In the light of this context, then, this film may be seen as responding to a tense political climate and harbouring a political standpoint with palpable patriotic goals: to open the eyes of the audience to the potential threat that the rise of Nazism in Europe represents to Great Britain and to induce the public to brace up for this threat. The film's structure, Hitchcock's aesthetic choices, and the representation of a cohesive London crowd all point to these political concerns and to Hitchcock's patriotism as well. As Hirsch observes: "The Londoners on the Underground, in the street markets, or sharing their enjoyment of watching a film in the cinema, represent a form of social cohesion, which comes under threat."[42] The threat here is the immediate power failure caused by the saboteur Verloc, and which plunges London in darkness, but it also symbolically refers to the darkness of the fascist ideology hovering over Great Britain and Europe.

Overall, when analysing the way terrorism is represented in *Sabotage*, we realize that Hitchcock, like Conrad, is, willingly or not, enmeshed in ideological and political considerations, although Hitchcock's aesthetic and ideological orientation is different from Conrad's. On the one hand, Hitchcock does not associate terrorism with anarchism: in the film, terrorism is rather implicitly related to the German threat of the 1930s and its potential effects on Great Britain. As such, *Sabotage*, alongside Hitchcock's other espionage movies from the 1930s, may be considered as a means of mobilizing crowds against the rise of Fascism and Nazism across Europe. Furthermore, Hitchcock does not identify a specific, individual threat that could be easily pinned down and crushed. He represents instead this threat as vague, and this vagueness increases the diffused and overwhelming character of this danger, leaving the spectator with the impression that the looming danger is not only uncontrollable, but could be anywhere. Even the death of Mr. Verloc at the end of the film is no guarantee that this danger is over, since the real instigators of these plots, the men behind Mr. Verloc's action, remain on the loose.

In *Sabotage*, these "masterminds" are not clearly identified; they are obscure, nameless shadows lurking in the dark backwaters, as suggested in the sequence taking place at the Aquarium. While many of Hitchcock's felons are described as "likeable" characters (they are educated, charming gentlemen, who are respected in their communities), in *Sabotage* the spymaster that Mr. Verloc meets at the Aquarium is anything but likeable; he is a mean, cold shadowy figure whose obscure identity connotes unpredictability and invisible menace. The ghostliness of this character and the dim atmosphere of the Aquarium add to the suspense and increase the ghastly nature of this encounter. The choice of the Aquarium as a meeting place between Mr. Verloc and the invisible order--giver is highly significant. It symbolizes the dark and cold "underworld," in which prowl all sorts of menacing and deadly creatures waiting for their prey; the saboteur Verloc and his mysterious companion are emblems of these dark, deadly forces. And to enhance the ominous prospects of these saboteurs' designs Hitchcock plays on the contrast between dimness and light in this scene, showing the two characters' black shadows, their backs turned to the spectator, standing out on the luminous fish tanks. The image and location are not the only elements that refer to this bleak, ill-boding universe: the spymaster's menacing voice and categorical statement also widely contribute to the gloomy and threatening atmosphere. The fact that Verloc is the spymaster's puppet, unable to release himself from his domineering grip, further reinforces the power of this mysterious man and increases the prevailing tension.

To hark back to the analogy between Conrad's novel and Hitchcock's movie, another noticeable and relevant modification that Hitchcock makes lies, of course, in the title of his film, which changes from *The Secret Agent* to *Sabotage*. It is obvious that Hitchcock had no choice but to change the film's title: his previous film, released in January 1936, a few months prior *Sabotage*, was already entitled *The Secret Agent*. At the same time, this modification is also prompted by other far more significant reasons, which, entailed, in turn, a change in the narrative perspective. Since the film's emphasis ultimately shifts from the individual "agent" to the action itself, that is the act of sabotage in its various manifestations. Furthermore, this title modification shifts the film's focus from Mr. Verloc, who is no longer the main character, to his wife who becomes the film's central protagonist. However, Conrad's novel confines Winnie to a marginal status, whereas Hitchcock puts her center stage in what looks like an endorsement of a feminist ethics: she is listed first in the credits, and the patriarchal order is unsettled: the revaluation of gender roles is subtly suggested in Mr. Verloc being identified as "Mrs. Verloc's husband," rather than Winnie being defined as "Mr. Verloc's wife." This turn of phrase gives Winnie Verloc patronymic pre-eminence and confers upon her a higher social status. Here, Hitchcock clearly dismisses Mr. Verloc as a character of secondary importance and throughout the film he portrays him in terms that both repeat and break away from Conrad's depiction of this character.

In the novel, Mr. Verloc is a protuberant, dishevelled person, with "an air of having wallowed, fully dressed, all day on an unmade bed" (*SA* 4). He is also an emblem of indolence and laziness, as the narrator mockingly states: "He was in a manner devoted to [his idleness] with a sort of inert fanaticism, or perhaps rather with a fanatic inertness" (12). In enhancing Mr. Verloc's idleness Conrad's narrator tends to undermine this character's social as well as moral worth. In *Sabotage*, Hitchcock reiterates Mr. Verloc's characteristic idleness by constantly showing him in passive postures, seated eating or slouching on the couch, but strips this character of his protuberance and scruffiness. In contrast, Winnie Verloc shines both physically and morally and is far more active and bolder than she appears in Conrad's work. At the beginning of the film, Winnie Verloc is presented as a dutiful spouse and a trusting, respectful and non-conflictual figure: when Mr. Verloc is displeased with the food at the dinner table, she ensures to fulfill promptly and unquestionably his request. In a sense, she fits into the conventional portrait of a respectable woman, aware of her responsibilities, to whom spectators could easily identify with or relate to. Winnie is also an unconventionally energetic, working woman, who takes care of her husband and brother, while her husband is idling about and sprawling on the sofa and giving orders. Throughout the film, she is often in action: unlike her husband, she is seldom seated or immobile in a shot, a way for Hitchcock to increase her dynamic role in the plot.

Another significant element worth underlining is Hitchcock's relation to action and to the ethics of efficiency within the climate of violence and sabotage he depicts. While in *The Secret Agent* Mr. Verloc is unable to organise a single successful terrorist attack, Hitchcock's film starts with a successful act of sabotage; an attack on a London power station perpetrated by Mr. Verloc, which plunges the city in darkness. Though successful, this sabotage is of limited impact, however. It does not lead to the devastating effects wished by the perpetrators but becomes instead the subject of mockery. The Londoners are shown responding stoically to the black out, laughing, lighting candles, and coming together as a calm, harmonious community. This act of sabotage is nonetheless ideologically effective, as Hitchcock suggests, and serves as a strong warning: that saboteurs are a real threat; they can act or reach their targets and cause destruction at any time, and people – and the government – should take this threat seriously. Besides emphasizing this potential threat, Hitchcock gives it a diffused and global character. The initial definition of the word sabotage acquires, in turn, renewed impetus after this act of sabotage. For, as we come to realize, Hitchcock does not only want to instruct the viewer on the meaning of this word, but through his wide-ranging definition he also sets this violence within a broader ideological and political context that transcends the specific and narrow scope of anarchism. Sabotage, as both a word and a material act, is more diverse and encompassing than anarchism, and suits better Hitchcock's implicit ideological and political considerations.

Conrad in *The Secret Agent* focuses on the specific problem of anarchism, rife in the mid- and late-nineteenth centuries in Great Britain. Hitchcock instead deals with violent activities in their diverse occurrence, regardless of the ideological or political provenance of these violent acts. And precisely, by choosing the word *sabotage* over that of *agent* Hitchcock inscribes violence within a wider global scope, thus assigning to these acts of violence a universal dimension. In a sense, by shifting the ideological field from anarchism to sabotage, Hitchcock broadens his film's ethical frame. The goal of this encompassing, universal outlook is to arouse the public's awareness about the global threats of sabotage. Moreover, in *Sabotage* Hitchcock seems more interested in highlighting the consequences that an act of sabotage may have on individuals and society, than in describing the act itself – i.e., the logistic "how" or ideological "why." Indeed, although the success of Mr. Verloc's act of sabotage is short-lived and relative (the Londoners are laughing at the situation, rather than being scared), the narrative lays emphasis on the action itself – violent action at that – rather than on discourse or ideology. This is one way for Hitchcock to suggest that the real danger lies in concrete violent actions that directly affect people's life, rather than in abstract theoretical concepts. Hitchcock is interested in the concrete aspect of violent action, in its consequences on ordinary people and society. In *Sabotage* Mr. Verloc's action aims not to wipe the ideology of anarchism in Great Britain and across the planet, but to destabilise and paralyse society by preventing people from pursuing their basic daily duties. In this, Hitchcock differs largely from Conrad.

In *The Secret Agent* Mr. Verloc is in charge of bombing the Greenwich Observatory, the symbol of universal time and emblem of elite culture, science, and intellectual power, located in an isolated suburb of peripheral importance. In *Sabotage* the final bomb explosion, which kills Stevie, targets directly ordinary people, and occurs in Piccadilly Circus in a crowded urban bus. Hitchcock thus enhances the realistic effect of a terrorist attack to shock and increase public awareness about the effects of such violence on common people. As Hirsch points out:

> Hitchcock utilised the spy story format to depict London and Londoners to create a heightened sense in the audience what might be under threat. [...] In *Sabotage* a child, a puppy, and a busload of people destroyed by an act of terror in the centre of London symbolise a threat to a whole way of life. And in 1936 this was politically significant.[13]

No doubt, that is also the reason why Hitchcock's character targets in its first sabotage act not the symbol of an ideology or cultural icon (Greenwich), but a down-to-earth, essential convenience: electricity, indispensable to every social and economic activity. The black-out of the English capital is shown as directly impacting all citizens – in their daily travel or commuting, work or even leisure time. But, as Hirsch rightly demonstrates, the inhabitants of London are shown as resilient and cohesive, displaying both confidence and empathy towards each other. The film's depiction of these ordinary residents in such a favourable light clearly aims to enhance British cohesion and solidarity in the face of adversity.

It is important to point out here the difference between Conrad's and Hitchcock's view of the masses in their works. Conrad is an elitist, with an aristocratic background and a manifest contempt for the populace. [44] Hitchcock, instead, comes from a popular social background and tends to relate sympathetically to ordinary citizens. In *Sabotage*, he provides a balanced, favourable portrait of the crowds, depicting them as boisterous and unruly, as when they rush for their ticket refund, but also as being capable of discipline when handled properly. The intervention of Ted who convinces the spectators to leave without being reimbursed illustrates, indeed, this crowd's pliancy. Social class is another key concern for Hitchcock. His positive portrayal of Winnie Verloc in *Sabotage* may, in this respect, owe to class empathy. Hitchcock comes from the same social background as Winnie Verloc. Winnie is the daughter of a licensed victualler and Hitchcock the son of a greengrocer. Just as Hitchcock shares social affinities with Winnie, he also shares kinship with the common people – the ordinary London dwellers, shown at the opening scene, who are described as models of empathy and solidarity, with whom the spectators can easily identify. Furthermore, in *Sabotage* the crowd sometimes fulfils a major moral function, as at the end of the film where it serves as a refuge for Winnie Verloc and the policeman Ted. After Winnie Verloc's murder of her husband and confession to Ted, both are shown slipping smoothly into the munificent crowd and into happy anonymity. They literally melt into this community of ordinary citizens where awaits them a quiet, anonymous existence.

In this specific scene Hitchcock shows the communion of the individual and the community. He clearly privileges communal ethics over individualistic ethics and its underlying moral nihilism, central to Conrad's novel, where all sense of community is either dissolved or bankrupt. Even suffering is given a communal dimension in Hitchcock's film. While in the novel the ethics of suffering is presented as an individual concern – Winnie Verloc solitarily lamenting and mourning her loss – in *Sabotage* mourning becomes collective. It is not just Winnie who suffers from the loss of her brother, but all the families who have a son, brother, father, or relative killed in this explosion, share in this sorrow. This communal response to grief links once again Winnie Verloc's to the rest of the community. In *Sabotage* Hitchcock steadily works against Conrad's moral nihilism, by trying to build a moral consensus, a set of common moral values that binds individuals to the community. Meantime, as he draws attention to the saboteurs' threat and efficiency, however relative, Hitchcock underlines the inefficacy of the police, which is reflected in the conduct of the undercover policeman Ted. The latter is with Stevie, eavesdropping on the saboteurs through the fanlight when he is brutally hauled down into the room by one of the saboteurs. Stevie quickly pops through the fanlight and tells the saboteurs that he was just showing Ted the back of the cinema screen. Stevie conveniently provides a convincing explanation for Ted's reckless behaviour, but this policeman's cover is compromised, as one of the plotters recognises him.

Ted is an added character; he does not exist in Conrad's novel. Besides, in *The Secret Agent* Inspector Heath is overtly blamed by his superior, the Assistant Commissioner who holds him responsible for his failure to prevent the terrorist act and later informs Sir Ethelred that this tragedy is due to Heat's inefficient methods of investigation. In *Sabotage* instead, Ted does not directly assume responsibility for what happened, nor is explicitly summoned by his superiors to account for his failure. Moreover, in *The Secret Agent* Conrad discloses the police's hierarchy and chains of command – the chief inspector, the assistant commissioner and the chief of the police, Sir Ethelred – and calls all characters to account individually for their moral responsibility. In short, Conrad both takes into consideration the responsibility of each member of the police force and condemns their inefficiency individually as well as collectively. In *Sabotage* Hitchcock treats the police as a uniform block.

He mostly refers to an individual policeman's action to highlight the inefficiency of the overall police force. Therefore, while he may be implicitly blaming Ted's inefficiency as a policeman, in practice he holds the entire police force responsible for this individual incompetence. Although not treated with similar complexity, the issue of ethical responsibility is also a prominent concern in *Sabotage*, and it is conveyed in Verloc's reaction to the bomb explosion, as well as in Stevie's death and Winnie's murder of her husband.

Action, Moral Impulse, Ethical Responsibility

Although Mr. Verloc in *Sabotage* gives to Stevie the packet with the bomb, he refuses to take full responsibility for the teenager's death. He first blames the police whose close surveillance of his quarters left him no chance but to count on Stevie for this deadly mission. He also complains to his wife that she too was responsible for what happened to her brother because she urged him to take Stevie with him on his walks. Worse still, he minimizes his spouse's loss by telling her they could have a child of their own. Mr. Verloc is an unsettling and unpredictable character. His wife calls him a "good man" and Hitchcock presents him as a descent, family man; a quiet, inoffensive, caring father figure. That is why when Ted later explains to Winnie that her husband is suspected of being a saboteur, she is flabbergasted and unwilling to believe his words. In fact, even Hitchcock seems to find extenuating circumstances for Mr. Verloc. He depicts him as a hesitant saboteur, acting from mere financial constraints, rather than for ideological reasons or from sheer love of violence. In short, Hitchcock shows this character as a victim of circumstances who is moved by an ethics of self-preservation that desperately compels him to this ruthless deed. On two occasions, indeed, Mr. Verloc explicitly declares that his act of sabotage proceeds from financial constraints over which he has no control, thus implicitly blaming these unfortunate circumstances, as well as the people who put him in this position – the givers of orders.

Hitchcock himself seems to suggest, too, that these obscure order-givers who have control over Verloc's life share a greater part of responsibility in this tragedy.

The scene where Mr. Verloc meets at the Aquarium the man who ordered the sabotage provides an enlightening example. The two men are facing large fish-tanks and we can only discern their dark shadows. The spymaster refuses to pay Mr. Verloc, stating that the previous job – the sabotage of the power station – was not properly carried out, as the targeted inhabitants of London made fun of this act of sabotage instead of being frightened and destabilized. He orders Mr. Verloc to plant a bomb in the heart of London, but Verloc complains he is not a murderer. Mr. Verloc's response reveals a sense of moral restraint that sharply distinguishes him from the man giving the order. However, in the end, he reluctantly submits to the obscure man's power and later collects a bomb at a bird shop to "finish the job."

Without absolving Mr. Verloc of his crime, Hitchcock, in this scene, nonetheless underlines that this character is not completely devoid of morals – of the notions of right and wrong, what can be done and what cannot be done – but is simply overwhelmed by circumstances which compel him to an abominable conduct. Moreover, by presenting Mr. Verloc as both a reluctant murderer and a powerless victim of contingency, Hitchcock tends to lead the audience to lay greater blame on the invisible man of the Aquarium, a merciless creature who stops at nothing to achieve his goals. This mysterious man embodies the moral nihilism of the plotters and this abject moral nihilism is also reflected in the Professor. The scene where Mr. Verloc meets the Professor is very suggestive, indeed, and has a dramatic ironic twist to it. In a debonair manner, the owner, a rotund, jovial character, refers to the bombs in the presence of his daughter and granddaughter, as if they were mere toys. Unlike the Professor or the spymaster, who both display self-confidence, Mr. Verloc is shown as increasingly nervous. Soon after the bomb explosion he is still in turmoil, visibly plagued by a mute, lingering sense of guilt. Food serves as a catalyst for this repressed guilt. With stunning insensitivity, Mr. Verloc complains twice about food – the greens, more specifically – first immediately after the sabotage of the power station and then after the bomb explosion which killed Stevie with many other victims. The two complaints may be seen as a means of diverting his wife's attention, as well as of keeping at bay his evil acts, at least momentarily.

In the final scene, Mr. Verloc's complaint about the greens, reminds his wife of Stevie: she looks at Stevie's empty place, then continues serving silently, but notices that she holds the carving knife and fork. She puts them down, looks at her husband who anxiously notices her focused attention on the knife and brusquely walks toward her. Both reach out for the carving knife, but Winnie is quicker. She snatches the weapon and stabs her husband. This murder sequence is rather short. Unlike the previous sequences in which Winnie is presented as voluble and her husband quiet and withdrawn, in this tensely dramatic sequence Hitchcock confronts a rather vocal Mr. Verloc to a silent but vigorous Mrs. Verloc. Hitchcock focuses his camera on hands and eyes, as well as on the knife to enhance action and the imminence of tragedy. As William Rothman points out:

> Hitchcock cuts to a shot of the knife a moment before [Winnie] looks at it. The camera's gesture thus appears to cue, rather than simply register, her glance [...]. But it is also as if by this cut Hitchcock calls the knife to her attention – and by this means provokes her to think of killing her husband.[45]

In this scene ethics and aesthetics blend to build tension and moral drama. The art of compactness, which Hitchcock uses admirably in *Sabotage*, is at its apex here and serves to enhance the dramatic effect and moral intensity of the action. Setting and mood are given primacy over expression and dialogue, and beyond its tragic quality, this climatic scene's expressive power comes largely from this overall mood and its aesthetic compactness.

Confession, Redemption, Moral Open-endedness

Assuming or rejecting responsibility for one's acts is a prominent concern in *Sabotage*, as well as in *The Secret Agent*. In Conrad's novel Winnie Verloc refuses to take responsibility for the murder of her husband and regards herself as a passive, helpless victim of overwhelming circumstances: "'Haven't you guessed what I was driven to do!'" (*SA* 282), she says to her new lover, Ossipon. Like Mr. Verloc, Winnie's response to her act, her justification of her murder, is grounded in an ethics of self-preservation, and all that matters to her in Conrad's novel is to escape the gallows. In *Sabotage*, instead, Winnie, stirred by a strong sense of moral obligation, fully assumes the responsibility of her act, confesses to the policeman Ted, and is ready to go to the police station to make an official statement and assume the consequences of her act. But strangely, Hitchcock spares his heroine punishment for her crime, as Ted prevents her from confessing to the police. Further still, later on, while Winnie is sitting motionless in the hallway, Ted even declares his feelings for her and convinces her to run away with him, leading her outside the apartment. From that moment on, Winnie and Ted are bound by a secret, which, while preserving their individual interests (their love relationship), violates the social contract and the communitarian values of law and justice on which society rests.

Ted's intervention is controversial and blurs the frontiers between morality and immorality. On the one hand, by dissuading Winnie from giving a public confession, Ted not only betrays his own conscience and professional duty, but also precludes the exercise of justice and the social moral norms which regulate the community's conduct. From this perspective, he may be seen as an agent of immorality; some even viewed him as a "saboteur," who "sabotages" the police investigation, thwarts the course of justice, and sets out to marry the woman who has just killed her husband. On the other hand, Ted may be considered a moral hero – a supreme ethical agent who can properly judge what is right and wrong, and good and evil, without recourse to outside social or legal norms. As the film seems to suggest, Ted tends to consider Winnie's act ethically right and justifiable because the man she killed has violated the most basic norms of human conduct. His decision to let Winnie free despite her crime is certainly problematic from a legal and social point of view, but it may also be regarded as a patriotic gesture that serves a greater justice and a grander national interest: that of definitively preventing a merciless saboteur from committing other abominable crimes on the British soil. Hitchcock further highlights the tension between established conventional moral norms of conduct and individual ethics of freedom of will and conscience through Winnie Verloc's conduct. Mrs. Verloc is shown as a retributive figure – the hand of providence that re-establishes justice and rectifies social order, thus making up for the incompetence and inefficiency of the police.

Through both Ted's moral choice and Winnie's action, as well as her subsequent immunity, Hitchcock unsettles Manichean moral prescriptions and opens the ethical scope of the film. By this ethical open-endedness he blurs the frontiers between good and evil, crime and justice, and guilt and innocence, thus highlighting the complexity of moral thought and ethical agency. As he complicates moral judgement, Hitchcock also unsettles the spectators' conventional moral expectations. The fact that Winnie avoids prison thanks to the complicity of the policeman Ted leaves the ending of the movie open. A tacit moral consensus seems to be reached by Ted and Winnie Verloc, and this moral complicity binds them forever. Hitchcock distinguishes between intimate and public confession, and in the absence of public confession Winnie Verloc escapes public condemnation. This intimate confession seems morally adequate for Hitchcock since he does not urge the policeman Ted to compel Winnie to a public confession. However, he does not seem fully comfortable with this response. Precisely, because he does not want to appear as someone bending the established moral conventions or justifying morally murder, Hitchcock in the final scene lessens the criminal charge of

Winnie's act, by presenting her homicide as a case of self-defense rather than a cold and ruthless murder.

However immoral it may seem, therefore, Winnie's act partakes of an overall ethical framework, and this act, though morally problematic, involves yet an ethics of justice through which Hitchcock tends to redeem society and bring things back into order and harmony. David Sterritt argues that Hitchcock tends toward the redemption of his central characters.[46] In *Sabotage* Hitchcock clearly engages in an ethics of redemption; he does not punish Mrs. Verloc because he deems her a victim of an abject saboteur who has no regard for her feelings or empathy for humankind. By sharply contrasting the morally repentant Winnie who kills in self-defense to her saboteur husband who kills blindly and without remorse, Hitchcock visibly seeks to persuade his audience to see Winnie Verloc as a victim rather than a murderer and thus sympathize with, if not condone her act.

Ethics of Spectatorship

The ethics of spectatorship consists of both the filmmaker's moral projections onto his audience and this audience's moral expectations from the filmmaker. Hitchcock is overly concerned with audience and uses his camera to entertain and instruct his spectators, while abiding by this tacit moral pact. The Russian filmmaker Dziga Vertov tells us that only the camera can represent events unbiasedly or objectively. We know, of course, that the eye of the camera is anything but unbiased or objective, as Vertov wants us to believe, and Hitchcock in *Sabotage* provides us with an eloquent illustration of the biased character of the camera in the scene where Mrs. Verloc murders her husband. Rather than let the characters' give free rein to their mutual thoughts or intentions through dialogue or interior monologue, as Conrad does in *The Secret Agent*, in *Sabotage* Hitchcock relies on the camera to visualize the thoughts and sentiments of Mr. and Mrs. Verloc. In this specific scene the camera is not only a means of representation but also a mirror reflecting the two protagonists' thoughts and intentions. The camera focuses particularly on Mr. and Mrs. Verloc's hands and eyes, which function here as privileged vehicles of these two protagonists' emotions and mental impulses. As he draws attention to the intense exchange of glances between Mrs. and Mr. Verloc, Hitchcock directs these characters' gaze to the knife with such intensity and wicked intention that Mr. Verloc reaches readily for the knife, which induces his wife to grasp it first. At this instant, the camera literally visualizes Mr. Verloc's vicious intention. Hitchcock insists on the fact that Mr. Verloc has noticed that just before grabbing the knife his wife was looking with focused, ominous interest at the weapon and he may have already guessed her foreboding intent, which made him brusquely reach for the knife.

A mirror of thought and sentiment, the camera acquires in this scene the status of a moral medium with a significant moral incentive: to redeem morally Mrs. Verloc in the eyes of the audience. Through his deft use of the camera Hitchcock didactically directs the gaze of his audience and steers them to a sympathetic identification with his heroine who, Hitchcock suggests, finds powerlessly herself in a situation where she either kills or is killed by her criminal husband. For one thing, Hitchcock in this murder scene does not use the camera as an objective or impartial mirror of reality but as a clearly subjective and morally oriented device through which he seeks to elicit the audience's moral complicity and condonement of his heroine's act. In short, the eye of the camera functions here as a moral gaze with a tacit moral judgment intended for the audience, and this moral message, as hinted earlier, tends to the heroine's redemption. While the devoutly Catholic Hitchcock may not condone Winnie Verloc's homicide, as pointed out earlier, he nonetheless seems to tolerate her act, and uses the camera as a moral prop to this necessary evil.

It is interesting to see how through this camera angle Hitchcock seeks to guide the spectators to see Mrs. Verloc's act in the same ethical vein. Cohen argues that "Hitchcock seeks to steer the spectator into a shared moral reaction."[47] In fact,

Hitchcock wants his audience to feel justly, to have the right or appropriate moral response. In other words, he wants his audience to know that Mrs. Verloc is a killer but not a murderer, thus endorsing what looks like an ethical relativity. Above all, Hitchcock seeks to make his audience understand that Winnie Verloc, a vulnerable, grieving woman, who impulsively reacts to secure her survival, has acted in a way that anyone in the audience might have acted in such a situation. We may further state that, in this scene, Hitchcock literally takes Mrs. Verloc by the hand and executes her sentence. As Rothman points out:

> [Mrs. Verloc's] punitive hand seems to be guided by Hitchcock himself. In *Sabotage* Hitchcock intervenes to force Mrs. Verloc's hand, to make her do what she wishes do (what Hitchcock wishes her to do, what we wish her to do). His intervention leaves her no choice but to kill, at least if she values her life, which seems threatened at that moment by her husband.[48]

However, while Hitchcock morally justifies Winnie Verloc's action, he does not absolve her of her guilt. Indeed, as he spares her prison, he lets her live forever in contrition which she shares with her new lover, Ted. Besides, rather than lead his heroine to suicide, as Conrad does in *The Secret Agent*, Hitchcock preserves her from this unpardonable sin. More still, he opens for her the doors of a promising romance and a happy union with Ted. This happy ending redeems the institution of marriage which, as shown through the relation of Mr. and Mrs. Verloc in Conrad's novel, is barren and reduced to a sham. Yet, despite Hitchcock's clear ethical distance from Conrad, despite his moral re-orientation of the film, and the attempts at the moral rehabilitation of his heroine, in particular, *Sabotage* may be said to have been a moral disappointment in the eyes of the audience.

As a reminder, when the film was released, the audience was shocked by Stevie's death. Anthony Lejeune, for example, was outraged by this terrorist act and declared in 1936: "This is the sort of thing that should get a fellow blackballed from the Crime Club. Discreet directors don't kill schoolboys and dogs in omnibuses. Believe me, it isn't done."[49] We may easily understand such extreme reactions, for no movie in the 1930s Great Britain went as far as this: "the film offended audiences, inspiring so much 'public unease' that is was banned in some places."[50] Many people were shocked and infuriated by the death of both Stevie and the puppy, symbols of universal affection and empathy. The killing of a young boy was felt by critics and audience alike as a betrayal of the moral contract between filmmaker and audience. As Adam Lowenstein clearly explains:

> Since Stevie is a sympathetic character developed with affectionate care earlier in the film, the fretting audience still assumes that he will survive – that the contract of suspense will be upheld. Instead, Hitchcock kills Stevie and a busload of innocents when the bomb explodes.[51]

Focusing on Hitchcock's later works, most notably *The Enjoyment of Fear* (1949), Lowenstein further remarks that "although [the spectators] may identify with characters placed in perilous situations in order to feel vicarious fear, they will not 'pay the price' for this identification – [...] once audience sympathy with a character is established, it is not 'fair play' to violate it."[52] By killing Stevie, Hitchcock breaks this "moral contract" between filmmaker and the audience. Truffaut went as far as to state that Hitchcock should not have killed Stevie at all. In his Interview with Truffaut, Hitchcock recognized having made a mistake and regretted having killed Stevie in this way.[53] But this later re-reading or re-evaluation of his initial scenario (Truffaut's famous interview was made in the 1960s) may be downplaying the film's political context of the 1930s. Indeed, in *Sabotage,* Hitchcock seems to be stirred by profound moral demands: he wants to demonstrate the saboteurs' blindness and abjectness stronger to vigorously condemn them and raise the audience's awareness and need to confront this evil. By presenting Stevie as a normal teenager Hitchcock certainly makes the death of this boy more unbearable. Unlike Conrad's novel, in Hitchcock's film the bomb did not kill a mentally retarded or a non-entity, who is a burden to his family and society, but an ordinary, healthy boy who is the emblem of kindness and compassion. Though Hitchcock may be trying to make an important moral statement through this tragic event – that sabotage and the destruction it occasions do not spare anyone, not even innocent children, or puppies – his audience did not seem ready to reckon with this statement. Whether it was negligence or sheer oversight, the fact remains that Hitchcock manifestly failed in his moral assessment of his public. His filming ethics in *Sabotage* has thwarted the moral expectations of his audience, and the viewing moral conventions of his time in a way that seemed unforgivable. It looks as though Hitchcock overlooked what should be shown and what should not be shown, what is morally acceptable for the audience of the 1930s and what is not. Obviously, he did not ponder sufficiently his artistic gesture and measure the moral impact that the killing of the boy may have on his audience.

Aesthetically, *Sabotage* is an unquestionable masterwork, but morally it is a clearly mixed issue. While Hitchcock may get moral approval from his audience for sparing Mrs. Verloc public confession and possible imprisonment for her murder, he was not spared his audience's wrath for having deceived their moral expectations and the ethics of spectatorship to which they are accustomed. In *Sabotage*, Hitchcock inadvertently violated his audience's sympathies and betrayed the "moral contract" which normally links a director to the audience. The impact of this betrayal was powerful enough to cause Hitchcock to rethink his moral framework in his subsequent filmic productions, to better attune his aesthetics to his ethics.

NOTES

[1] Not to be confused with Hitchcock's *The Secret Agent*, his previous film, released a few months earlier, in January 1936, and which was an adaptation from the novel *Ashenden* by W. Somerset Maugham.

[2] Palmer and Boyd 2.

[3] Palmer 91.

[4] Palmer and Boyd 6.
[5] Truffaut 49.
[6] Palmer and Boyd 2, 5-6.
[7] For a more detailed discussion of filmic fidelity in the context of Conrad's works, see Crémona 303-11.
[8] Fleishman 59.
[9] Cohen, *Alfred Hitchcock* 29.
[10] Cohen, *Alfred Hitchcock* 32.
[11] Crémona 306.
[12] See Anderegg; Cohen, "The Ideological Transformation."
[13] Anderegg 224.
[14] Petrie 52.
[15] Bordat 6-7.
[16] Bordat 9-10.
[17] In the Hays Code, films are seen either as lowering moral standards, or, on the contrary, as elevating morality through good examples. This dualistic vision is far from being restricted to the 1920s United States: it has always been pervasive since the invention of the new medium and continues to have a major impact on our understanding and analyses of the moving images. This ambivalence is persistent in film theory: as Sinnerbrink points out, "this ambivalent attitude towards cinema as potentially manipulative medium, source of moral panic, or medium for moral and aesthetic education, continues today in the digital age." "Film and Ethics" 186.
[18] Sinnerbrink, "Film and Ethics" 188.
[19] Sinnerbrink, "Film and Ethics" 199.
[20] Techio 26.
[21] Cavell, *In Pursuits of Happiness* 4.
[22] Cavell, *In Pursuits of Happiness* 136.
[23] Read and Goodenough 31.
[24] Cavell, *Contesting Tears* xii.
[25] Sinnerbrink, *Cinematic Ethics* 3.
[26] Sinnerbrink, "Film and Ethics" 191.
[27] Sinnerbrink, "Film and Ethics" 191. In a similar vein, French philosopher Hugo Clémot points out in his recent book *Cinéthique* (2018) the moral relevance of films for the spectator and its importance for the cinematographic experience.
[28] Singer 7.
[29] See Singer.
[30] McGilligan 17.
[31] Truffaut 17-18.
[32] Spoto 277.
[33] Palmer, Pettey and Sanders 8.
[34] Rohmer and Chabrol 113.
[35] Hirsch 44.

[36] See Mulry; as well as Higgins' article in this volume: "'He died for the Revolution:' Anarchism and Ethical Commitment in *The Secret Agent*."
[37] Hirsch 44.
[38] In 2018, *Time Out* magazine dressed a list of "The 100 Best British Films," in which *Sabotage* ranked 44th, *The Lady Vanishes* 31st and *The 39 Steps* 13th. See Calhoun et al.
[39] Ryall 138.
[40] Ryall 138.
[41] See Rothman.
[42] Hirsch 46.
[43] Hirsch 53-4.
[44] On Conrad's elitism, see Acheraïou; Higdon; Kermode.
[45] Rothman 54.
[46] See Sterritt.
[47] Cohen, *Alfred Hitchcock* 42.
[48] Rothman 57.
[49] Quoted by Spoto 174-75. See also Barr 172.
[50] Osteen 260.
[51] Lowenstein 186.
[52] Lowenstein 186.
[53] Truffaut 88-89.

WORKS CITED

Acheraïou, Amar. *Joseph Conrad and the Reader: Questioning Modern Theories of Narrative and Readership*. Basingstoke: Palgrave Macmillan, 2009. Print.

Allen, Richard, and Sam Ishii-Gonzáles, eds. *Hitchcock: Past and Future*. London: Routledge, 2004. Print.

Anderegg, Michael A. "Conrad and Hitchcock: *The Secret Agent* Inspires *Sabotage*." *Literature/Film Quarterly* 3 (1975): 215-25. Print.

Barr, Charles. *English Hitchcock*. Moffat: Cameron, 1999. Print.

Bordat, Francis. "Le Code Hays : l'autocensure du cinéma américain." *Vingtième Siècle: Revue d'histoire* 15 (1987): 3-16. Print.

Calhoun, Dave, et al. "The Hundred Best British Films." *Time Out*. 10 Sept. 2018. Web. <https://www.timeout.com/london/film/100-best-british-films#tab_panel_4>. 17 Jan. 2021.

Cavell, Stanley. *Contesting Tears: The Hollywood Melodrama of the Unknown Woman*. Chicago: U of Chicago P, 1996. Print.

---. *In Pursuits of Happiness: The Hollywood Comedy of Remarriage*. Cambridge: Harvard UP, 1981. Print.

Clémot, Hugo. *Cinéthique*. Paris: Vrin, 2018. Print.

Cohen, Paula Marantz. *Alfred Hitchcock. The Legacy of Victorianism*. Lexington: UP of Kentucky, 1995. Print.

---. "The Ideological Transformation of Conrad's *The Secret Agent* into Hitchcock's *Sabotage*." *Literature/Film Quarterly* 22 (1994): 199-209. Print.

Crémona, Laëtitia. "Screening Decolonization: Richard Brooks's *Lord Jim*." *Joseph Conrad and the Orient*. Ed. Amar Acheraïou and Nursel Içöz. Boulder: Social Science Monographs; Lublin: Maria Curie-Skłodowska UP; New York: Columbia UP, 2012, 303-24. Print. Vol. 21 of *Conrad: Eastern and Western Perspectives*. Ed. Wiesław Krajka. 30 vols. to date. 1992- .

Fleishman, Avrom. "*The Secret Agent* Sabotaged?" *Conrad on Film*. Ed. Gene M. Moore. Cambridge: Cambridge UP, 1997. 48-60. Print.

Higdon, David Leon. "'His Helpless Prey': Conrad and the Aggressive Text." *The Conradian* 12.2 (1987): 108-21. Print.

Hirsch, Pam. "Hitchcock's *Sabotage* (1936): Conspirators and Bombs in Actual, Literary and Filmic London." *London on Film*. Ed. Pam Hirsch and Chris O'Rourke. Basingstoke: Palgrave Macmillan, 2017. 41-56. Print.

Hitchcock, Alfred. "The Enjoyment of Fear." 1949. *Hitchcock on Hitchcock*. Vol. 1: *Selected Writings and Interviews*. Ed. Sidney Gottlieb. Berkeley: U of California P, 2015. Print.

---. *Sabotage*. Gaumont British Picture Corporation. 1936.

Kermode, Frank. "Secrets and Narrative Sequence." *The Art of Telling: Essays on Fiction*. By Kermode. Cambridge: Harvard UP, 1983. Print.

Lowenstein, Adam. "The Master, The Maniac, and *Frenzy*: Hitchcock's Legacy of Horror." Allen and Ishii-Gonzáles 179-92.

McGilligan, Patrick. *Alfred Hitchcock: A Life in Darkness and Light*. New York: Regan, 2004. Print.

Mulry, David. *Joseph Conrad among the Anarchists: Nineteenth Century Terrorism and* The Secret Agent. New York: Palgrave Macmillan, 2016. Print.

Osteen, Mark. "'It Doesn't Pay to Antagonize the Public': *Sabotage* and Hitchcock's Audience." *Literature/Film Quaterly* 28 (2000): 259-68. Print.

Palmer, R. Barton. "*Secret Agent:* Coming from the Cold, Maugham Style." Palmer and Boyd 89-101.

Palmer, R. Barton, and David Boyd, eds. *Hitchcock at the Source: The Auteur as Adaptor*. New York: State U of New York P, 2011. Print.

Palmer, R. Barton, Homer B. Pettey, and Steven M. Sanders, eds. *Hitchcock's Moral Gaze*. New York: State U of New York P, 2017. Print.

Petrie, Duncan. *Creativity and Constraint in the British Film Industry*. Basingstoke: Palgrave Macmillan, 1991. Print.

Rawls, Christina, Diana Neiva and Steven S. Gouveia, eds. *Philosophy and Film: Bridging Divides*. New York: Routledge, 2019. Print.

Read, Rupert, and Jerry Goodenough, eds. *Film as Philosophy: Essays on Cinema after Wittgenstein and Cavell*. Basingstoke: Palgrave Macmillan, 2005. Print.

Rohmer, Eric, and Claude Chabrol. *Hitchcock: the First Forty-Four Films*. Trans. Stanley Hochman. New York: Ungar, 1979. Print.

Rothman, William. *Must We Kill the Thing We Love? Emerson Perfectionism and the Films of Alfred Hitchcock*. Columbia: Columbia UP, 2014. Print.

Ryall, Tom. *Alfred Hitchcock and the British Cinema*. London: Athlone, 1996. Print.

Singer, Irving. *Three Philosophical Filmmakers: Hitchcock, Welles, Renoir*. Cambridge: MIT, 2004. Print.

Sinnerbrink, Robert. *Cinematic Ethics: Exploring Ethical Experience through Film*. London: Routledge, 2016.

---. "Film and Ethics." Rawls, Neiva and Gouveia 185-205.

Spoto, Donald. *The Life of Alfred Hitchcock: The Dark Side of Genius*. London: Collins, 1983. Print.

Sterritt, David. *The Films of Alfred Hitchcock*. Cambridge: Cambridge UP, 1993. Print.

Techio, Jônadas. "The World Viewed and the World Lived: Stanley Cavell and Film as the Moving Image of Skepticism." Rawls, Neiva and Gouveia 26-49.

Truffaut, François. *Hitchcock/Truffaut*. Paris: Gallimard, 1983. Print.

Nathalie Martinière,
Université de Limoges,
Limoges, France

Reading "Heart of Darkness" with Francis Bacon: An Ethics of Uneasiness

> I have never tried to be horrific. [...] in fact,
> I wanted to paint the scream more than the horror.[1]
> Francis Bacon

A recent exhibition[2] showed that Joseph Conrad's works, and more particularly "Heart of Darkness," had been a source of inspiration for the British artist Francis Bacon (1909-1992). Bacon's paintings represent a paroxystic image of violence in the twentieth century world of art: they abound with images of torture, dismembered bodies, distorted faces, and screaming mouths. These paintings can easily be associated with the scenes of torture or ill-treatment of natives in Conrad's novella, as well as with Kurtz's last moments or with the ghosts that haunt Marlow's return to Europe and his visit to the Intended. Such images confront the viewers and readers to things, realities, or ideas they had rather forgotten, and, in the process, create a sense of uneasiness and discomfort that lead us to question why they have such a powerful effect on us, what abysses they suggest, and what burden of guilt they may reveal. Bacon's interest in Conrad is not only an indication of the writer's wide-ranging influence; it also sheds light on the appeal of Conrad's works to modern readers as well as on the diverse readings or interpretations that his fiction lends itself to. As we know, readers of the late twentieth and early twenty first centuries, influenced by post-colonial readings of history and literature, have re-evaluated the importance of "Heart of Darkness" as a denunciation of colonial violence, while earlier generations were more sensitive to the "existential" dimension of the novella and to Kurtz's moral alienation and self-destruction.

What fascinated Bacon in "Heart of Darkness" was not so much its realistic dimension, the actual condemnation of the "horrors" of colonization, however repulsive, but the images it triggered in his mind and which echoed his own obsessions. In this, the juxtaposition of Conrad's texts and Bacon's paintings does not, therefore, only point at the way Bacon reworked such a source of inspiration. It also highlights a set of key features in the novella, including the fact that realism may not be the sole or the best method to confront readers with the "horror" or the unpalatable realities "Heart of Darkness" deals with. Thus, "derealizing" unpleasant realities, as does Conrad in this novella, may paradoxically guarantee that these realities find an echo with larger audiences and, by their haunting power, compel these audiences to face the causes of these realities' disturbing effects. In Conrad's as well as in Bacon's case, this process of derealization corresponds to a choice – the choice of aesthetic uneasiness and discomfort over direct denunciation, and such a choice endows uneasiness with a significant ethical dimension.

Francis Bacon's Fascination with "Heart of Darkness"

In his book on Bacon's painting entitled *Francis Bacon: the Logic of Sensation*, the French philosopher Gilles Deleuze establishes a parallel between Bacon's 1976 *Figure at a Washbasin* in which an immobile figure, resting his hands on a washbasin, "exerts an intense, motionless effort upon itself in order to escape down the blackness of the drain,"[3] and the scene in *The Nigger of the "Narcissus"* in which Jim Wait tries to force his way through a hole in the cabin's partition:

> that infamous nigger rushed at the hole, put his lips to it, and whispered "Help" in an almost extinct voice; he pressed his head to it, trying madly to get out through that opening one inch wide and three inches long. *In our disturbed state we were absolutely paralysed by his incredible action.* It seemed impossible to drive him away. (*NN* 69, my emphasis)

Such a scene, Deleuze says, "is one of Bacon's paintings." In both cases, it is "a scene of hysteria [...] in which the body attempts to escape from itself *through* one of its organs [...] by vomiting and excreting"[4] or, as in the case of Jim Wait, by escaping from the cabin where he is trapped. In the two examples, the scene suggests obscene bodily images that create uneasiness, not only in the viewer of the paintings but also, in Wait's case, in his shipmates – the involuntary witnesses of his attempt to get out, who were "paralysed by his incredible action." Juxtaposing Bacon's painting with this striking scene in *The Nigger of the "Narcissus"* underlines the significance of disarticulated bodies and their organs in Conrad's fiction and the importance of the grotesque[5] in his representation of human beings. To define the passage, Deleuze uses terms like "abomination" and "abject,"[6] which can also be found in "Heart of Darkness," and this suggests that what Bacon depicts in his paintings is present in an embryonic form in Conrad's fiction.

Bacon was an avid reader, with a library of more than a thousand books, most of them read, re-read, and abundantly annotated. His friendship with Michel Leiris and his admiration for T. S. Eliot and Nietzsche are well documented, as is his fascination with Aeschylus' *Oresteia. Within the Tides, The Secret Agent,* and *Chance* were found during the inventory of his library,[7] which shows that he was familiar with Conrad's fiction. "Heart of Darkness" was one of his favourite books: the biographer Michael Peppiatt contends that it was "one of the few 'narratives' Bacon admitted readily into his exclusive pantheon."[8] As the catalogue of the Pompidou exhibition points out, Bacon's interest in Conrad's novella may have been grounded in his family history. His father served as an officer in South Africa and his elder brother and two of his sisters had moved to Rhodesia.[9] Bacon himself went to South Africa in 1950 where he visited his mother who had settled and remarried there and then again to South Africa and Kenya in 1952,[10] where he was fascinated with big game hunting. In 1965, he met the photographer Peter Beard who published *The End of the Game,* a chronicle of the extinction of elephants in Kenya and Bacon himself, speaking of his *Triptych, 1976* in interviews, associated Beard's images with "Heart of Darkness." Peppiatt also identifies in Bacon's *Painting 1946* "a mood of generalized evil reminiscent of the atmosphere Joseph Conrad builds up towards the end of 'Heart of Darkness.'" Obviously, "Heart of Darkness" may have influenced more than one painting, and the atmosphere of "unspecified threat and nameless evil" that pervades Bacon's work can recurrently be related to Conrad's novella. However, *Triptych, 1976* is the painting most associated with "Heart of Darkness," for a good reason: in a letter to Leiris,[11] Bacon himself mentioned the text as a source of inspiration. The *Triptych, 1976* is a complex work, with two portraits on the side panels and a headless body devoured by what looks like a bird of prey in the central part, while two more avian forms can be seen on each side. The face on the left has been identified as Sir Austen Chamberlain, a former British wartime chancellor and "Empire-builder," wearing a monocle or looking at himself in a distorting mirror,[12] while the portrait on the left is related to a photograph of Peter Beard taken when he was released from prison in Kenya. Both individuals are linked to colonization and its effects in Africa, either as participants or witnesses.[13] Bacon, however, chose Beard, an active anti-colonialist, as a figure for his *Triptych, 1976*, thus moving away from Conrad's novella and his mode of denunciation, which is never active or unequivocal, as many critics have pointed out.[14]

The entry in the Sotheby Catalogue online provides a description of the foreground in the three panels:

> Each [figure] oversees an imbroglio of human flesh, among the best painting of the human form to be found in Bacon's oeuvre. In the foreground of the left panel, a half-clothed figure bleeds down from the portrait, a muscular forearm discernible in the organic mound of flesh. Crouched on a stool, he stoops over an open case filled with paper evocative of the torn ticket stubs of shattered dreams, crumpled newsprint created with Letraset at his feet. The bag is an echo of *Triptych Inspired by T. S. Eliot's Poem "Sweeney Agonistes"* from 1967. Its zipper is as evocative of a primal scream *as the open mouth*

– caught between pleasure and pain – in the right panel. Here, two
contorted nudes are locked in physical embrace. Whether they are
fighting or copulating, or manifestations of a psyche in conflict, is
deliberately unclear, much like in the *Sweeney Agonistes* picture. All
that can be discerned is a clenched haunch and the *open mouth
replete with teeth*, a motif that looks back to Bacon's series of Heads
and screaming Popes from the late 1940s and 1950s.[15]

What this entry makes clear is the wealth of influences which
can be traced in the *Triptych, 1976*: T.S. Eliot's poem or his
play *The Family Reunion* led Bacon to Aeschylus's *Oresteia*
and the *Furies* or *Eumenides* which became a recurring
motif in his oeuvre. The notice also identifies "K. C. Clark's
manual, *Positioning in Radiography* (1939)," "Muybridge's
photographs of animals in motion," Aeschylus's *Prometheus
Bound*, Leiris's *Frêle bruit*, and a few other references...
but not "Heart of Darkness," which Bacon himself had
nevertheless mentioned as a source of inspiration and which
is referred to in the *Catalogue Raisonné*. From a thematic
standpoint, there are obvious similarities between the two
works: the atmosphere of pagan sacrifice related to the three
Eumenides and the blood chalice in the foreground of the
central panel are highly reminiscent of Kurtz's "unspeakable
rites" ("Heart of Darkness," YS 118); the open "mouth" of
the bag on the left and those of the naked bodies on the right
prompt images of Kurtz's wide open mouth with its "weirdly
voracious aspect, as though he had wanted to swallow all
the air, all the earth, all the men before him" (134); the
sheets of paper with letraset that cannot be deciphered are
evocative of Towson's manual; the bald head of the figure on
the right vividly recalls Kurtz's head which is compared to
"an ivory ball" (115), while the blind eyes of the figures and
the raw flesh remind us of the heads on stakes around Kurtz's
compound, or of his final confrontation with "some vision"
that leads him to "craven terror," to "an intense and hopeless
despair" (149).

The presence of so many superimposed sources confirms
that Bacon almost systematically combined multiple references

and adapted them to his own artistic goals. This means that these various sources interact in his work, creating layers of potential meanings: juxtaposing elements evocative of "Heart of Darkness" with the Eumenides, for instance, suggests that what Bacon found in Conrad's novella goes beyond the topical reading of the story, even though the figures of Chamberlain and Beard evoke the imperial question – colonisation and its effects in Africa. Such an approach, therefore, complexifies our reading of "Heart of Darkness," revealing enlightening echoes between the different works Bacon superimposed in his painting: between the Furies in Aeschylus's play, for instance, and the shadows that force their way into the Intended's house with Marlow at the end of the story. As Peppiatt underlines: "separating the various layers of allusion and meaning in this complex, highly charged allegory is hazardous, however tempting it may be to suggest specific links with Conrad's haunting story or even to find a real-life model for the phantom which rises in both side-panels."[16] Bacon may have had a personal interest in "Heart of Darkness," rooted in his family history or his ties with Beard, but this was merely a superficial motivation that aroused or increased his fascination and then was cast aside. His approach as an artist was never illustrative: he appropriated the texts he liked, and these texts fuelled his imagination. This does not, however, mean that acknowledging the "influence," as he stated in a letter to Leiris, is of no interest. Bacon "absorb[ed] and reinvent[ed]"[17] what he found in "Heart of Darkness" and made it his own: "I'll tell you what I really read: things which bring up images for me [...]. They open up the valves of sensation for me," he declared to David Sylvester.[18] As he points out, what fascinated him in Conrad's "Heart of Darkness" was the text's capacity to conjure up *images* in his mind, while their context was only of secondary importance to him. There were elements in the novella that could "make [him] *see*" (*NN* x), as Conrad wrote in the Preface to *The Nigger of the "Narcissus,"* even if what he "saw" was not faithful images of what the narrators evoke in the novella. And it is quite clear that the images he found fascinating were the most violent ones, and these images were related to the body. Consequently, our reading of both the novella and painting is altered by their proximity: re-reading "Heart of Darkness" after viewing *Triptych, 1976* gives new force and more intensity to violence in the novella, by highlighting its physical dimension and the marks it leaves on bodies. Bacon's reference to "Heart of Darkness" in his letter, on the other hand, encourages us to interpret *Triptych, 1976* in the light of imperialism and its consequences on the Africans' bodies.

Didier Ottinger also remarks that what fascinated Bacon in "Heart of Darkness" was the equivalence and reversibility of civilization and savagery, which is a central theme in the novella: "one of the dark places of the earth" (YS 48) had become modern Victorian England, while colonizers in Africa resorted to the subtleties of sophisticated rhetoric to justify their barbarous, dehumanizing behaviour, calling their victims "enemies" and "criminals" (66).[19] The entanglement and interchangeability of civilization and savagery which is reflected in "Heart of Darkness" – the fact that each could morph into the other, inspired Bacon, allowing for endless variations:

> "Heart of Darkness" gave a poetic form to the collusion of progress and barbarous behaviour. For Bacon, it was one of the deepest motivations in his work: trying to reclaim the figure in a time of triumphant abstraction, sitting his popes, those venerable images of art and spirituality, onto electric chairs, placing destruction at the centre of his creative process, he gave a visible shape to the inexorably destructive power of progress, [...] producing paintings that were monuments of culture and savagery at the same time [...].[20]

Another important common feature of "Heart of Darkness" and the *Triptych, 1976* that comes out of their juxtaposition is their mutual rejection of hermeneutics. Deleuze notes that Bacon is not interested in meaning, or in the message that can be derived from his paintings; he is only interested in painting as action:

Francis Bacon's painting is of a very special violence. Bacon, to be sure, often traffics in the violence of a depicted scene: spectacles of horror, crucifixions, prostheses and mutilations, monsters. But these are overly facile detours that the artist himself judges severely and condemns in his work. What directly interests him is a violence that is involved only with colour and line: *the violence of a sensation (and not of a representation), a static or potential violence, a violence of reaction and expression.* For example, a scream rent from us by a foreboding of invisible forces: "to *paint the scream more than the horror* [...]."[21]

This interpretation is highly reminiscent of Conrad's refusal to lead us to a final revelation, as the frame narrator in "Heart of Darkness" tells his listeners about "the meaning of an episode" which is not to be found "inside like a kernel but outside, enveloping the tale which brought it out only as a glow brings out a haze" (YS 48). In both cases, the impossibility to reach a fixed, definite meaning exhorts us, readers and viewers, into a mode of interpretation of the painting or text that destabilizes, creates discomfort, and relies on it, leaving us to grope in the dark for a potential signification that keeps eluding us.

This does not mean that violence is not explicit, but as Bacon himself insisted, it is a violence that "makes the scream more that the horror" visible in both cases. While Bacon insists on the colours and textures of the flesh beneath the skin, the "grove of death" scene in "Heart of Darkness" is filled with pictures of dehumanized, dying men "crawling" and "crouching." The description of these "moribund" creatures is aestheticized, as they are transformed into "bundles of acute angles," they have become "black bones" and are "scattered" "in every pose of contorted collapse, as in some picture of a massacre or a pestilence" (66-67). The aesthetic strategy in this scene is premised on the derealisation and aestheticization of the black men's bodies to convey the "unspeakable"[22] and make it acceptable for Marlow's listeners and Conrad's readers. However, such derealisation does not only attest to Marlow's extreme shock, but also paradoxically contributes to restoring the Africans' humanity. The description is, indeed, filled with poignant details like the white worsted around one of the dying men's neck – Roland Barthes would call them "puncta" – which, because they "prick" and "bruise,"[23] force Marlow to sympathize with the victims, introduce a personal dimension and, therefore, the possibility of seeing these dying Africans as human beings and victims of colonialism rather than "criminals" or "enemies."[24]

Both Conrad and Bacon, in their distinct way, provide us with the shocking obscene image of the consequences of violence on human bodies, and the extreme pain resulting from this physical violence. And it is quite remarkable that in the works of these two artists the bodies are not only "in every pose of contorted collapse," as Marlow puts it, but also "half effaced" – their humanity challenged – as are the two side figures in Bacon's *Triptych, 1976*, not to mention the headless central one.

Aesthetic Uneasiness

What reading "Heart of Darkness" with Bacon clearly underlines is, above all, the writer's or artist's complex relation to realism. Since Chinua Achebe's diatribe against Conrad's representation of Africans in "Heart of Darkness,"[25] several studies were published and further explored the issue of race and racism in Conrad's "Heart of Darkness" and other works, highlighting Conrad's position towards colonialism and, most importantly, his ambivalent or controversial representation of Africans. While most of these studies examine Conrad's fiction mainly from a postcolonial standpoint, overall, they offer a more nuanced view of race and racism and do not share Achebe's reading of the novella and Conrad's presumed racism or perpetuation of stereotypes about Africans.[26] "Heart of Darkness" is a rich and highly evocative text, and if postcolonial readings of this novella are prominent within contemporary literary criticism, at previous periods this story was read through other critical lenses. In the 1940s and 1950s, for instance, many critics read Conrad's novella from a predominantly psychoanalytic perspective and interpreted it as a journey into man's "dark soul," thus overlooking its ideological and political dimension – the question of colonialism or exploitation, for example. In *The Political Unconscious*, Fredric Jameson for his part adopts a materialist approach to Conrad's works and contends that Conrad "derealizes the content and make[s] it available for consumption on some purely aesthetic level [...] transform[ing][...] realities into style [...]."[27]

In his book, Jameson focuses on *Lord Jim* and addresses the representation of labour (or rather what he sees as the absence of representation of labour) on the *Patna*, insisting on what he calls Conrad's "strategy to displace unwanted realities" and re-code them in "existential terms."[28] Jameson looks at the issue of labour from a Marxist perspective and his attacks are ultimately aimed at high modernism, with its unwavering confidence in science and technology, as well as aestheticist explorations, formal innovations, and detachment from society, history, and politics. Yet, the conclusion he reaches is not extremely different. For Jameson, the novels are not committed enough because they are not realistic enough. He considers the way Conrad uses language as dangerous, if not dishonest, and further argues that the "existential" dimension that relies on "aestheticization" represents a distraction from what is really important.

Bacon's approach to realism may help us to understand that Conrad's aestheticized approach to reality could, on the contrary, serve as a prompt that leads us to question our reading of his texts, exactly *because* it creates discomfort and uneasiness that stir us into reflection. Asked about the "meaning" of his paintings, which were repeatedly read as existential commentaries on man's plight in the twentieth century, Bacon kept repeating two important things: first, he was not interested in *illustrating* a story or a text (or a situation in life), second, his triptychs had *no narrative dimension*. He insisted that what he wanted to do was to convey the *ambience* of a work and the sensations it aroused in him:

> I have attempted to create images of the sensations which certain episodes have bred in me. [...] Perhaps, at its deepest level, realism is always a subjective thing. When I see grass, I sometimes want to

> pull up a clump and simply plant it on the canvas. But of course
> that would not work, and we need to invent the techniques by which
> reality can be conveyed to our nervous system without losing the
> objectivity of the thing portrayed.[29]

Or, as Deleuze suggests, representation fails to convey reality
according to Bacon:[30] "After all, it is not the so-called 'realist'
painters who manage to convey reality best."[31] Conrad's ideas
about the best way of representing reality were not so different
when he declared: "And what is a novel if not a conviction of our
fellow-men's existence strong enough to take upon itself a form
of imagined life clearer than reality and whose accumulated
verisimilitude of selected episodes puts to shame the pride
of documentary history" (*PR* 15). And Marlow is a kind of
narrative and moral filter who also tries to convey images to his
audience, "sensations[s]" that he defines as the essence of life
and experience: "the dream-sensation, that commingling of
absurdity, surprise, and bewilderment in a tremor of struggling
revolt, that notion of being captured by the incredible which
is of the very essence of dreams...." ("Heart of Darkness," *YS*
82). Shifting the focus of interest in the novella from the dying
men in the grove of death to Kurtz – the "remarkable man [...]
[who] had stepped over the threshold of the invisible," with his
voracious mouth and ivory head – can certainly be regarded
as a way of "derealizing the content" and leaving the Africans'
plight or perspective in the background. However, this neither
means that the "content" is erased, nor that it is necessarily
weaker. Bacon insisted that:

> [t]hings are not shocking if they have not been put into memorable
> form. Otherwise, it's just blood spattered against a wall. In the end,
> if you see that two or three times, it's no longer shocking. It must be
> a form that has more than the implication of blood splashed against
> a wall. It's when it has much wider implications. It's something
> that reverberates within your psyche, it disturbs the whole life cycle
> within a person. It affects the atmosphere in which you live.[32]

This declaration is also reminiscent of Conrad's 1917 Author's
Note where he stated that "Heart of Darkness" was "experience

pushed a little (and only very little) beyond the actual facts of the case *for the perfectly legitimate, I believe, purpose of bringing it home to the minds and bosoms of the readers*" (YS vii, my emphasis). Again, both Conrad and Bacon highlight the necessity of transforming reality, of giving it a "form," to turn it into something memorable. For both, "[d]erealizing the content" is a way of making it even more disturbing and "bringing it home to the minds and bosoms of the readers," because it rests on a series of images that remain branded in the readers' minds and create persisting discomfort, questioning their spontaneous response to the work and their aesthetic and ethical expectations.

One way of producing images capable of inducing uneasiness and discomfort, shared by Conrad and Bacon, lies in their capacity to generate and question aesthetic pleasure at the same time. A characteristic of Francis Bacon's painting is the contrast systematically established between backgrounds, on the one hand, and figures, on the other hand. The "large fields of bright, uniform and motionless color [...] on which the Figure detaches itself – fields without depth, or with only the kind of shallow depth that characterizes post-cubism,"[33] also contribute to "derealizing" the figures and what may have remained of a possible narration, while creating a violent tension within these images. Ottinger states that Bacon's technique is characterized by its "chromaticism," "complex geometry," and "lightness and transparency" – aesthetically seducing and gratifying features that clash with the tortured figures: "Another indicator of the work's artificiality is a dichotomy between the handling of figures and that of settings: the figures are realized with highly visible brushmarks, the settings with a flat layer of thin paint."[34] This is particularly obvious in *Triptych, 1976* which is characterized by an entirely subjective choice of almond green, a very smooth background, unexpected colour associations, and a considerably precise geometric organisation (orange and purple straight lines create an impression of depth, as if the "portraits" at the back could slide on rails; pools of pink and orange liquid can be seen under the figures in the foreground). This background contrasts heavily with the contorted figures on each side panel and with the headless figure in the centre, its spine and flesh made visible, with three birds preying on him: "Hyper-refined lines and bright colours create an impression of dematerialisation. Far from weakening Bacon's works, [...] it accentuates the gap between the cruelty in the treatment of the figures and the plastic refinement that is an asset of the paintings."[35] The whole scene is outside time and place, the links with "Heart of Darkness" (or any other literary work) are far from obvious and not immediately accessible, nothing is familiar, nothing is explained. The result for the viewers is a mixture of attraction and repulsion, aesthetic enjoyment, and horrified disgust, which is close to Marlow's fascination with "the change that came over [Kurtz's] features" ("Heart of Darkness," YS 149) in his last moments ("I stood over him as if transfixed"). This gives Marlow the impression that "[i]t was as though a veil had been rent" (149), as if he were suddenly given access to a mystery, a tragic epiphany.

Though, unlike Marlow, for the viewer of the triptych or the reader of the novella the "veil" may not be "rent," the upsetting impression created by these artworks certainly still lingers on. Or, to paraphrase Jameson, in "Heart of Darkness" the realities of colonization and its atrocities are re-coded as a tragic experience for Kurtz and Marlow,[36] and are transformed into a source of enjoyment for the readers for that reason. Yet, tragedy traditionally has a cathartic function that is absent from "Heart of Darkness," as Marlow underlines at the end of his narration: "It seemed to me that the house would collapse before I could escape, that the heavens would fall upon my head. But nothing happened. The heavens do not fall for such a trifle" (162). In other words, reality may be re-coded as a tragic (and therefore enjoyable) experience, but the incapacity of the tragic to perform its traditional task of purification or healing clearly indicates that there is something amiss, that we cannot easily free ourselves from the grip of reality. And, because the failure of this recoded tragic experience keeps, as Bacon puts it, "reverberat[ing] within [our] psyche," creating enduring uneasiness, it forces us to acknowledge the role and value of "derealisation" in the novella. Like Bacon's refusal of narration and illustration, "derealisation" is the reason why "Heart of Darkness" has remained so powerful: it keeps haunting us, though the topical dimension of the story has faded, and even readers initially not interested in colonialism are forced to take into consideration the images of its most unpalatable manifestations.

The way discomfort is mediated by Conrad's aesthetic choices and compels us to question our spontaneous response to his fiction is also illustrated in the differences between works like "Heart of Darkness" and "An Outpost of Progress," two stories that Conrad, as he declared in his Author's Note, "brought out from the centre of Africa" (YS vii) and which are characterised by many similarities, both from a thematic and ethical point of view. A major difference between these two stories however lies in the narrative method, and there are ethical consequences: "An Outpost of Progress" is narrated by an omniscient narrator, while Marlow's "inconclusive experiences" (YS 51) are filtered by a succession of narrators – and remain "inconclusive," largely because of these filters.[37] Consequently, there is never any doubt about what we should think of Kayerts and Carlier: from the very beginning the director calls them "imbeciles" and, as if this was not enough, the narrator further refers to them as "two perfectly insignificant and incapable individuals" ("An Outpost of Progress," TU 89). Throughout the story the narrator operates as an authoritarian guide, telling us how to interpret every event and behaviour. Through this direct, explicit intervention, he secures a comfortable ethical distance for readers who become mere spectators of the two characters' stupidity and downfall.[38] Words have a firm meaning in "An Outpost of Progress" and this meaning does not change. Even if irony is present, as when, for example, Kayerts and Carlier read about "the rights and duties of civilization, [...] the sacredness of the civilizing work, and [...] the merits of those who went about bringing light, and faith and commerce to the dark places of the earth" (94), this ironic charge is signposted and its targets obvious. In "Heart of Darkness," on the other hand, Marlow relentlessly keeps us in an uncomfortable verbal ambiguity. He, for instance, defines Kurtz equivocally as "a remarkable man" on several occasions, while he progressively modifies the connotations of this phrase, thus highlighting the unreliability of language:

> Kurtz was a remarkable man. He had something to say. He said it. Since I had peeped over the edge myself, I understand better the meaning of his stare, that could not see the flame of the candle, but was wide enough to embrace the whole universe, piercing enough to penetrate all the hearts that beat in the darkness. He had summed up – he had judged. 'The horror!' He was a remarkable man." ("Heart of Darkness," YS 151).

In "Heart of Darkness" language often proves incapable of adequately rendering the reality it depicts; it may also be used to disguise unpalatable realities, as when Marlow lies to the Intended supposedly to "spare" her pain and disillusionment: "'And you admired him,' she said. 'It was impossible to know him and not to admire him. Was it?' 'He was a remarkable man,' I said, unsteadily" (158). The same word is used for two incompatible facets of Kurtz's personality or behaviour, which points out that language can easily distort reality.

The question of language's duality in this novella has received extensive critical attention: an excellent linguist, Marlow is never fooled and systematically draws attention to the degeneration of language into cliché, pointing out that words have become the signs of a social and ethical dysfunctioning.[39] Critics agree that, rather than plainly denouncing crimes, it is the imperialist and colonialist discourse of the nineteenth and early twentieth centuries that "Heart of Darkness" exposes: like the mist and fog, which are essential to the atmosphere of the novella, the vocabulary chosen by Marlow systematically hints at what remains in the shade, what cannot be clearly conveyed through words and sentences about the colonial situation, or what language obfuscates: "No, it is impossible; it is impossible to convey the life-sensation of any given epoch of one's existence – that which makes its truth, its meaning – its subtle and penetrating essence" (82). Hence the choice of a diction that consistently underlines the limits of language, its distortion, the famous "adjectival insistence,"[40] and the "central obscurity"[41] leading to no revelation, but insisting instead on what cannot be grasped by language, what lays beyond its scope:

> it occurred to me that my speech or my silence, indeed any action of mine, would be a mere futility. What did it matter what anyone knew or ignored? [...] One gets sometimes such a flash of insight. The essentials of this affair lay deep under the surface, beyond my reach, and beyond my power of meddling. (100)

What Marlow identifies here is a crisis of language, which cannot account for reality anymore[42] or is susceptible to convey two contradictory things at the same time. This crisis destabilizes the readers' expectations, leading them to persistent discomfort. What Marlow's lie to the Intended shows, however, is that he himself is not immune to the general hypocrisy he denounces, or maybe that he cannot disentangle himself from it. As Acheraïou points out, "Marlow audaciously forces into the open the horrors of colonialism [...] but his bold critique of imperial horrors does not lead to the ethical imperative to end definitively imperialism and its inhuman practices."[43] Marlow's ambiguity, his lie, it should be noted, occurs at the end of the narrative and therefore remains embedded in the readers' minds after they have closed the book. It may be interpreted as a way for Conrad to confront the readers with their own small arrangements with the truth and ethics, their own weaknesses, and difficulties in facing and fighting unwanted realities. Hence the symptomatic image of the mouth that lets out a voice which, in the end, has only "The horror! The horror!" to say – the scream that signals and conceals what it refers to at the same time, the irreducible contradictions at the heart of colonialism.[44]

No wonder that such "flash[es] of insight" resonated within Francis Bacon, who also acknowledged a crisis of (pictorial) language after the second world war and became famous for the silent screams of his figures. They have come to symbolize his refusal of both abstraction in a period in which abstraction acquired a prominent status, and of narration, since the story behind the scream remains enigmatic. This refusal led him to constant experimentation; it also drew him to writers like Conrad who was also sceptical about traditional realism that "fails to convey reality" and believed that images may be more powerful and create more persistent or haunting effects on the readers' minds. In the end, it seems that what Jameson calls "derealisation" is a more effective source of uneasiness than the direct confrontation with the worst aspects of reality.

An Ethics of Discomfort

For both Bacon and Conrad, discomfort or uneasiness takes on an ethical dimension, forcing the viewers or readers to question their response to the work and realize that what they are looking at or reading concerns them directly, despite their spatial and temporal distance from these representations. The presence of the Eumenides in *Triptych, 1976* connects "Heart of Darkness" with Aeschylus's *Oresteia*. Threatening figures, the Eumenides relentlessly punish and are linked to the theme of expiation and guilt. This connection with the *Oresteia* and myth[45] hints at the universal dimension of the novella that transcends the context of the Congo in the nineteenth century and seems to function as a confirmation of the "derealisation" underlined by Jameson. It also "evoke[s] in a new language ancient notions of despair."[46]

In the light of the contemporary reconsideration of the political and moral message behind "Heart of Darkness" (legitimate or not, valid or flawed) and its poetic expression, reading this novella with Francis Bacon may look like a movement backwards; an impulse toward the universal, toward the impersonal and the self-centred that obfuscates or evades power issues. It is true that Francis Bacon was not interested in the possible social or political dimension of his works and did not care for the viewers' interpretation of his paintings or for what these paintings might "signify." His own emotions or impressions, the images in his mind were all that mattered to him. But this does not mean that his works are mere artistic objects devoid of all ideological or philosophical content. As Peppiatt remarks, his work "cries out urgently, like an oracle, to be interpreted,"[47] and his fascination with the Furies "was regarded as a visceral reaction to the horrors of war, or more universally still, of man's inhumanity to man."[48] To a twenty-first century reader of "Heart of Darkness," what the timeless Eumenides in *Triptych, 1976* suggest is that guilt and the need for expiation are not over but remain obstinately with us, haunting us even though we did not personally take part in the process of colonization. Our discomfort in front of both the paintings and the novella shows that "the past is not dead, it is not even over," as William Faulkner stated in *Requiem for a Nun* (1950). It gloomily glides over our conscience and forces us to reconsider our response to the novella, and this leads me to several concluding remarks.

First, discomfort is different from revolt and while we may feel repelled by the description of the colonizers' horrific treatment of Africans, our position is no longer that of 1901 readers. The Congo Free State has long been dismantled. So, to lament the situation retrospectively does not make sense any longer and, in any case, this is not why the novella still concerns us, although acknowledging the evils of the past is necessary and does make a difference. Unlike Achebe, who thought that writers and literature should be vehicles of social transformation, Conrad did not believe that literature could change society. But he knew and believed that it could open people's eyes and urge them to acknowledge their own contradictions, even if he somewhat disingenuously contended that he "was only a wretched novelist inventing wretched stories" (*CL* 3: 102) and declined to directly take part in the fight against the Congo Free State. At the time, the novella was nevertheless regarded by E. D. Morel, one of the leaders of the campaign against King Leopold's rule over the Congo, as "the most powerful thing ever written on the subject," as Allan Simmons reminds us.[49] Its persisting power has obviously changed. Nowadays it largely lies in its capacity to highlight the contradictions and inconsistencies in Marlow's response to colonialism; it lies in the ethical difficulties raised by his problematic oscillation between the denunciation of its "horrors" and the lies to the Intended that preserved the myth of colonial benevolence; it also lies in our response to such ambiguities.[50] If "Heart of Darkness" is still talking to us today, making us uncomfortable and raising questions for us, it is precisely because, as Bacon puts it, it is "not just blood splattered against a wall." This novella is more than just a pamphlet against colonialism, it is a text that fundamentally questions the coherence between our moral certainties and the way we adhere to them.

Which is why our discomfort is probably highest when we realize that Marlow's attitude or reaction towards Kurtz (or the Intended or the Africans) cannot always be justified from a moral point of view, that he cannot even justify it in his own eyes. Conrad does not provide us with clear ethical solutions, he only asks us questions and prompts us to the realization that we must constantly grope our way through irreconcilable contradictions. How can we account in a morally satisfactory manner for his "choice of nightmares" ("Heart of Darkness," YS 147)? How can we explain the fact that he "laid the ghost of [Kurtz's] gifts at last with a lie" (115) while earlier he boasted that his speech "was the speech that cannot be silenced" (97)? How can we account for his declaring that "they were not inhuman. Well, you know, that was the worst of it – this suspicion of their not being inhuman" (96). Marlow's constant wavering between clear-sightedness and honesty on his own motivations in some cases, and dubious self-justifications and excuses in others generates repeated discomfort that cannot easily be dispelled, and which may lead us to question our own reactions, assumptions, and certainties regarding the way the story is narrated.

Then, this uneasiness and the questions it raises for us involve aspects of colonialism that are still with us today and should probably be renegotiated by each new generation: the fantasies we still project onto Africa without even realizing it, as Achebe puts it, the fact that "[w]omen [...] are out of it – should be out of it" ("Heart of Darkness," YS 115) when in reality they are not, the fact that the opposition "civilized/savage," prominent in Conrad's novella, echoes ecological concerns which have become prevalent in the age of the anthropocene. It is because of, not despite, this uneasiness that "Heart of Darkness" still speaks to us: it makes it clear for us that the past is still with us and that we still must confront its consequences.

In the end, the discomfort generated by "Heart of Darkness" and *Triptych, 1976* shows that both Conrad and Bacon rejected the idea that literature or art should provide comforting answers or moral certainties. They clearly indicate instead that they would not leave us to enjoy peacefully their works. For this, they kept raising uneasy questions about the function of art and literature, challenging our preconceived ideas. And precisely, because they reject plain realism, they also urge us to re-consider what we look for in texts or paintings and the way they affect us.

NOTES

[1] Sylvester, *The Brutality of Facts* 55, 57.
[2] *Bacon: Books and Paintings.*
[3] Deleuze 15.
[4] Deleuze 16.
[5] Why Deleuze does not seem to perceive or be interested in what critics like Albert Guerard and Marianne DeKoven underlined (i.e., the birth metaphor that runs through the whole passage and likens Jim to a baby being born from the Narcissus's womb/cabin) is an interesting question that has more to do with Bacon than Conrad: while Conrad conflates birth and death in the scene, Bacon clearly disregards what this association might suggest.
[6] Deleuze 16, 17.
[7] Ottinger 213.
[8] Peppiatt 138.
[9] Ottinger 6.
[10] Ottinger 225.
[11] Letter from Bacon to Leiris, 3 April 1976. Peppiatt 343. See also "Francis Bacon: Letters to Michel Leiris, 1966-1989." Castellani et al 23.

¹² Sotheby Catalogue online. See also Harrison 11. Chamberlain had been awarded the Nobel prize for peace (1925), yet he later encouraged Mussolini's colonial ambitions.

¹³ Ottinger 29. Peppiatt 343n13. "In the right panel the distorted head emulates the same photograph [of Chamberlain], but it is fused with a photograph of Peter Beard. Peter Beard had sent Bacon photographs of himself shaven-headed on his release from prison in Kenya, following his arrest for allegedly assaulting a poacher. Thus, in *Triptych, 1976* Beard functions as a cipher of the experience of the white man in Africa." See Daniels and Harrison 1096.

¹⁴ On Conrad's elusive, ambivalent position towards colonialism, see Collits; Acheraïou, *Rethinking Postcolonialism*, especially 138-55; Rancière.

¹⁵ My emphasis. Sotheby Catalogue online.

¹⁶ Peppiatt 343.

¹⁷ Sotheby Catalogue online.

¹⁸ Sylvester, *Looking Back at Francis Bacon* 236.

¹⁹ Ottinger 28.

²⁰ My translation. Ottinger 29.

²¹ My emphasis. Deleuze x. See also Sylvester *The Brutality of Facts* 55-57.

²² Simmons 188-89. See also Martinière.

²³ Barthes 26.

²⁴ On this question, see Acheraïou, "Ethics and Horror," in which he argues that "Marlow's ethics of the gaze exhorts him not just to look into and empathize with the Africans' suffering, but also to acknowledge their humanity that the colonizer denied them" (60).

²⁵ Achebe 336-49.

²⁶ For more insights into both Conrad's complex position toward colonialism and to the controversial issue of race, see Firchow; Collits; Acheraïou, *Rethinking Postcolonialism*.

²⁷ Jameson 202.

²⁸ Jameson 205, 204.

²⁹ Letter to Leiris, 20 Nov. 1981. Peppiatt 379-80.

³⁰ Ottinger 181.

³¹ Peppiatt 379.

³² Peppiatt 377-78.

³³ Deleuze xi.

³⁴ Sylvester, *Looking Back at Francis Bacon* 189.

³⁵ My translation. Ottinger 18.

³⁶ Jameson 204. Jameson contends that Conrad re-codes the realities of capitalism in *Lord Jim* as existential melodrama.

³⁷ See Delesalle-Nancey 251-72.

³⁸ See Watts 30.

³⁹ See Hawthorn; Baxter and Hampson.

⁴⁰ Leavis 216.

⁴¹ Qtd. in Simmons 315.

[42] From this point of view, Marlow is often seen as some sort of mouthpiece of modernism who acknowledges the collapse or the duplicity of meaning. For a detailed study of the crisis of language in Conrad's fiction, see Greaney.

[43] Acheraïou, "Ethics and Horror" 54.

[44] Rancière 127.

[45] Philippe Lacoue-Labarthe gives the following definition of myth: "a spoken word [parole] (neither simply a discourse, nor simply a narrative) which offers itself, by means of some testimony as a bearer of truth, an unverifiable truth, prior to any demonstration or logical protocol. Too difficult to enunciate directly, too heavy or too painful – above all, too obscure" (113-14). Acheraïou points out that Conrad's use of the notion in "Heart of Darkness," however, encompasses the modern sense of false assumptions and that he plays on the ambiguity of the term. For more information on the issue of myth in this novella, see Acheraïou, "Ethics and Horror" 50-54.

[46] Peppiatt 282.

[47] Peppiatt 138.

[48] Peppiatt 110.

[49] Simmons 192.

[50] See Acheraïou, *Rethinking Postcolonialism*; Collits; Ross.

WORKS CITED

Achebe, Chinua. "An Image of Africa: Racism in Conrad's *Heart of Darkness*." *Hopes and Impediments: Selected Essays, 1965-67*. By Achebe. Oxford: Heinemann, 1988. Print.

Acheraïou, Amar. "Ethics and Horror in *Heart of Darkness*." *Critical Insights: "Heart of Darkness*." Ed. Robert C. Evans. New York: Salem, 2019. Print.

---. *Rethinking Postcolonialism: Colonialist Discourse in Modern Literatures and the Legacy of Classical Writers*. Basingstoke: Palgrave Macmillan, 2008. Print.

Aeschylus. *Oresteia*. Trans. C. Collard. Oxford: Oxford UP, 2003. Print.

---. *Prometheus Bound*. Trans. A. J. Podlecki. Oxford: Aris and Phillips, 2005. Print.

Bacon, Books and Paintings Exhibition. 11 Sept. 2019 – 20 Jan. 2020. Paris: Centre Georges Pompidou.

Bacon, Francis. *Figure at a Washbasin*, 1976. Oil and dry transfer lettering on canvas, 78 x 58 in. (198 x 147.5 cm). Museo de Arte Contemporáneo, Caracas. The Estate of Francis Bacon. Web. <https://www.francis-bacon.com/artworks/paintings/figure-washbasin#technical-data>.15 Nov. 2020.

---. *Painting 1946*. Oil and pastel on canvas, 77⅞ x 52 in. (198 x 132 cm). Museum of Modern Art, New York. CR number 46-03. The Estate of Francis Bacon. Web. <http://www.francis-bacon.com/

artworks/paintings/painting-1946#technical-data>. 15 Nov. 2020.

---. *Triptych, 1976*. Oil, pastel and dry transfer lettering on canvas. Each panel: 78 x 58 in. (198 x 147.5 cm). Private collection. CR number 76-05. The Estate of Francis Bacon. Web. <https://www.francis-bacon. com/artworks/paintings/triptych-1>. 15 Nov. 2020.

Barthes, Roland. *Camera Lucida. Reflections on Photography*. Trans. Richard Howard. New York: Hill, 1981. Print.

Baxter, Katherine Isobel, and Robert Hampson. *Conrad and Language*. Edinburgh: Edinburgh UP, 2016. Print.

Beard, Peter. *The End of the Game. The Last Word from Paradise: a Pictorial Documentation of the Origins, History & Prospects of the Big Game in Africa*. San Francisco: Chronicle, 1988. Print.

Castellani, Valentina, Mark Francis, and Stephan Ratibor, eds. *Francis Bacon Triptychs*. London: Gagosian Gallery, 2006. Print.

Clark, Kathleen C., Louis Kreel, and Ann Paris. *Clark's Positioning in Radiography*. London: Heinemann Medical, 1979. Print.

Collits, Terry. *Postcolonial Conrad*. London: Routledge, 2005. Print.

Daniels, Rebecca, and Martin Harrison, eds. *Francis Bacon. Catalogue Raisonné*. Vol. 4. 1971-92. London: The Estate of Francis Bacon, 2016. Print.

DeKoven, Marianne. *Rich and Strange: Gender, History, Modernism*. Princeton: Princeton UP, 1991. Print.

Deleuze, Gilles. *Francis Bacon. The Logic of Sensation*. Trans. Daniel W. Smith. London: Continuum, 2003. Print.

Delesalle-Nancey, Catherine. "Essence et évanescence: l'alchimie du langage dans 'An Outpost of Progress' et 'Heart of Darkness.'" *Joseph Conrad: l'écrivain et l'étrangeté de la langue*. Ed. Josiane Paccaud-Huguet. Caen: Lettres Modernes Minard, 2006. 251–72. Print.

Eliot, T. S. *The Complete Poems and Plays: 1909-1950*. New York: Harcourt, 1980. Print.

Faulkner, William. *Requiem for a Nun*.1950. New York: Vintage, 1975. Print.

Firchow, Peter E. *Envisioning Africa: Racism and Imperialism in Conrad's "Heart of Darkness."* Lexington: UP of Kentucky, 2000. Print.

Greaney, Michael. *Conrad, Language and Narrative*. Cambridge: Cambridge UP, 2009. Print.

Guerard, Albert. *Conrad the Novelist*. Cambridge: Harvard UP, 1958. Print.

Harrison, Martin. *In Camera. Francis Bacon, Photography, Film and the Practice of Painting*. New York: Thames, 2005. Print.

Hawthorn, Jeremy. *Joseph Conrad, Language and Fictional Self-Consciousness*. London: Arnold, 1979. Print.

Jameson, Fredric. "Romance and Reification. Plot Construction and Ideological Closure in Joseph Conrad." *The Political Unconscious, Narrative as a Socially Symbolic Act*. By Jameson. 1981. London: Routledge, 2002. Print.

Lacoue-Labarthe, Philippe. "The Horror of the West." *Conrad's "Heart of Darkness" and Contemporary Thought: Revisiting the Horror with Lacoue-Labarthe*. By Lacoue-Labarthe. Ed. Nidesh Lawtoo. London: Bloomsbury, 2012. 111-22. Print.

Leavis, F. R. *The Great Tradition*.1948. New York: Doubleday, 1954. Print.

Leiris, Michel. *Frêle bruit*. Paris: Gallimard, 1992. Print.

Martinière, Nathalie. "'He had tied a bit of white worsted round his neck': Focusing on Details in 'Heart of Darkness.'" *FATHOM* 6 (2019). Web. <http://journals.openedition.org/fathom/1062 ; DOI : 10.4000/fathom.1062>. 21 Jan. 2021.

Muybridge, Eadweard. *Muybridge's Animals in Motion*. Mineola: Dover P, 2007. Print.

Ottinger, Didier, ed. *Bacon en toutes lettres*. Paris: Centre Pompidou, 2019. Print.

Peppiatt, Michael. *Francis Bacon. Anatomy of an Enigma*.1996. London: Constable, 2008. Print.

Rancière, Jacques. "L'Inimaginable." *Joseph Conrad*. Ed. Josiane Paccaud-Huguet and Claude Maisonnat. Paris: L'Herne, 2014. 125-30. Print.

Ross, Stephen. *Joseph Conrad and Empire*. Columbia: U of Missouri P, 2004. Print.

Simmons, Allan H. *Joseph Conrad: Critical Issues*. London: Palgrave Macmillan, 2006. Print.

Sotheby Catalogue online. "Francis Bacon, Triptych, 1976." Sotheby's. Web. <https://www.sothebys.com/en/auctions/ecatalogue/2008/contemporary-art-evening-auction-n08441/lot.33.html?>. 12 March 2020.

Sylvester, David. *The Brutality of Facts: Interviews with Francis Bacon*. London: Thames, 2016. Print.

---. *Looking Back at Francis Bacon*. London: Thames, 2000. Print.

Watts, Cedric. *Conrad's "Heart of Darkness": A Critical and Contextual Discussion*. 1971. Amsterdam: Rodopi, 2012. Print.

Subhadeep Ray,
Bidhan Chandra College, Kazi Nazrul University,
Asansol, India

"After such knowledge what forgiveness?" Nature, Community and Individual Ethics in Joseph Conrad's "Because of the Dollars" and Adwaita Mallabarman's "A River Called Titas"

The twentieth-century French philosopher Emmanuel Levinas has exerted a strong influence on the development of poststructuralist and postcolonial thought. In his works, written against the backdrop of two World Wars, he undertakes a sustained critique of Western metaphysics and ontology based on the opposition between war and ethics. In *Totality and Infinity: An Essay on Exteriority* Levinas states: "the visage of being that shows itself in war is fixed in the concept of totality, which dominates Western philosophy."[1] In response to the threat of totalitarianism that the above thesis associates with the imperial domination, Levinas invokes the concept of the Other, by which he means "exteriority, transcendence, and alterity." He argues that in the "ethical relation with the Other, the freedom of the Self is not the first priority but is overtaken and surpassed by the demands of the relation."[2] Significantly, the historical events that led to Levinas' critique are also, to varying degrees, at work in Joseph Conrad's later texts. These texts cover a wide range of global geopolitical realities and highlight the ethical anxiety of the Western subject in material and conceptual encounters with what is posited as the Other. Levinas' claim that the Self's ethical dialogue with the Other does not assimilate the latter's thought and expression but refers to them as exceeding and surpassing the Self's pre-conceptions may, in this respect, be compared with Conrad's Author's Note to *Within the Tides* (1915), which deals with complex ethical issues related to the individual's role and responsibility in a radically shifting world. Conrad's specific purpose in this Note is to clarify his position toward his "Eastern" tales, repeatedly labeled as "exotic":

> [T]hat origin of my literary work was very far from giving a larger scope to my imagination. On the contrary, the mere fact of dealing with matters outside the general run of everyday experience laid me under the obligation of a more scrupulous fidelity to the truth of my own sensations. The problem was to make unfamiliar things credible. To do that I had to create for them, to reproduce for them, to envelop them in their proper atmosphere of actuality. (WT viii)

Here, Conrad promises his readers to describe this exotic, unfamiliar world as realistically as possible in order to remain faithful to his own creative sensations. His "scrupulous" obligation of narrative fidelity involves an ethical responsibility both for his own readers and for the people depicted in this unfamiliar world, whom he pledges to show in their authenticity, and "envelop" in "their proper atmosphere of actuality."

How far Conrad remains true to this narrative pact is open to debate. What is, however, manifest is his fundamental ambivalence toward his fictional material and, particularly, to the notion of fidelity or truth itself. His colonial tales offer an eloquent illustration of this ideological inconsistency. Not only these tales cannot be easily pinned down to one single message or moral truth, but they are often overdetermined by the contradictions in imperial ideology which they explore. Wiesław Krajka states that the Conradian narrative has often been interpreted as being determined by "the repressed kernel of imperialist ideology" that "resurfaces and disturbs the imperial world and destroys its salutary and artistic pretexts."[3] In *Rethinking Postcolonialism* Amar Acheraïou examines in depth this cultural determinism to account for Conrad's ambivalence toward imperialism and colonial ideology.

Conrad's relation to imperialism is complex and involves, indeed, repression, as well as ambivalence and narrative mystification, which further complicate his vision of imperialism itself. According to Terry Collits, Conrad's "deepest knowledge" about the interaction between Europe and its Others "derives not so much from authentic life experiences" of the non-European Others "as from despair at the impossibility of achieving them"[4] because of the burden of the imperial ideology. Collits further asserts that "[t]his edge of despair aligns him with the great tragedians, who also have complicated relationships to formal knowledge."[5] Conrad's works thus examine the limitation of any single ideological stance in relation to imperialism. Though a European author, his narrative particularly evokes the contradictory nature of the Western system of knowledge itself. His fictional universe is a place of shifting perspectives and ideological inconsistencies, resulting from his own complex relationship with European imperialism. In *Rethinking Postcolonialism* Acheraïou points out the double-sidedness of the colonial relation to explain the source of Conrad's peculiar sensibility:

> The core of his contradiction in relation to imperialism lies precisely in his being a hybrid figure that combines the colonized and colonizer, the once subjected native and now (marginal) member of the imperial dominant centre. By virtue of his complex history, Conrad belongs at once to the periphery and the centre, caught like Nina and Marlow, in the tangles of the imperial drama. He is at once a detached critic of imperialism and a helpless participant in the imperial game.[6]

While "this hybrid cast" results in multiple levels of tensions, it also provides Conrad with a privileged literary tool to investigate the conflicting and intersecting worlds of the Self and Other across socio-cultural borders. As Acheraïou shows in "Colonial Encounters," "Conrad sets Orientalist and Occidentalist discourses in a productive dialectical relationship."[7]

Though Conrad's attitude to colonialism is ambivalent primarily because of his allegiance to both the world of the colonizer and colonized, as many critics have pointed out, he criticizes the colonial ideology's excesses in his works and calls for moral restraint.[8] Marlow in "Heart of Darkness," for instance, clearly admits that the whole imperial business never happens to be "a pretty thing when you look into it too much" (*YS* 50-51).

As he describes the colonial context, he thus calls for the end of the imperial horrors of which he is a direct witness, without, however, seeking to abolish this criminal colonial enterprise, because, as a British citizen, he is profoundly determined by the colonial ideology he criticizes.[9] In the face of these conflicting urges, Marlow tends to promote "fortitude and restraint" that "make possible," as Debra Romanick Baldwin observes, a "humanizing element in the Conradian cosmos: work."[10] Marlow – by extension Conrad – understands work in terms of the classical conception of human action: "human beings are active beings who fulfill themselves and the concrete particulars of the world around them."[11] We shall discuss below how the humanizing potential of concrete actions or activities is set against the precarious condition of human interactions within the imperial social organization as delineated in Conrad's fiction.

The imperialist system, as Acheraïou points out in *Rethinking Postcolonialism*, was first and foremost a capitalist enterprise, based on the exploitation of foreign people and resources. It considered colonized people as mere tools in the service of its materialist interests. Furthermore, imperialism did not exploit only the colonized populations, but also the colonial agents themselves who were similarly turned into mere instruments of imperial expansion and profit. Stephen Ross explains how the empire's "transition from a disciplinary regime to a regime of control becomes relevant as a means of describing the ways in which Conrad's characters experience the constraints (both internal and external) of their worlds." He further argues that "[a]n understanding of this transition – and the means that it affords global capital to produce subjectivities – is crucial for reading [...] often enigmatic [...] sketches [...] of his key characters."[12]

Kurtz is a good case in point. Despite the supreme power he exerts over the African tribes, he, too, is merely an obedient and efficient servant of the imperial system. This reification shows how the "freedom" of the European agent in distant worlds soon becomes a delusion within the imperial framework itself, and Conrad's fiction sheds light on this colonial aberration.

It reveals how "the imperialist project of transforming the human world" is extended further by "redefining the individual's social and moral responsibilities in terms of his/her efficiency serving the mechanism of dominance."[13] However, by depicting Kurtz's absolute isolation – "[t]here was nothing either above or below him" ("Heart of Darkness," YS 144) – Conrad's narrative stresses the value of meaningful human communication undermined by the imperial scheme to exploit and dehumanize the Other. As Romanick Baldwin remarks in her discussion of "Heart of Darkness," "[r]ecognizing the claims of other human beings not only connects [...] us to them, but keeps us human ourselves."[14]

In *Totality and Infinity*, Levinas associates the individual's relation to the "other being" with a demand for justice. In *Otherwise than Being or Beyond Essence,* on the other hand, he shows how this justice also requires the subject's admission of his/her own Otherness. In literary texts the narrative project generally tends to emphasize the question of alternative choices of character and action involving different modes of responsibility. This obligation to do justice and welcome those who – for several reasons – turn out to be beyond the Self's perceptible functions as a redemptive human force in many of Conrad's tales, particularly those written during and after the First World War. Even the bleak narrative of "Heart of Darkness," a product of the early phase of Conrad's writing career, acknowledges this "vision of shared humanity,"[15] in what involves, as Acheraïou remarks in *Rethinking Postcolonialism,* a twofold humanist project: "to reconcile colonization with its utopianism and restore the Africans' humanity in the name of cultural relativity and solidarity with humankind's condition."[16]

In Conrad's later works the Self's attempt to reach out to the Other is explored through complex narrative instances, where the central character sometimes takes the most impractical and un-*self*ish decisions in respect to his own position. For instance, in *The Rescue,* Captain Tom Lingard sets out to help his Malayan friend Hassim but finds Mrs. Travers on the deck of a stranded yacht near an island of the Eastern archipelago inhabited by hostile tribes involved in community conflicts. Mrs. Travers is a woman from a completely different world with an equally different sense of commitment. Lingard's sense of honor and duty, as well as involvement in complex native politics, are increasingly guided by his urge to remain faithful to Mrs. Travers, the object of his forbidden and unexpressed love that stimulates him to find his true Self: "It seemed to him that till Mrs. Travers came to stand by his side he had never known what truth and courage and wisdom were" (*Res* 341). The course of action chosen by a Conradian protagonist often involves tragic suffering and moral dilemmas. Lingard, in this case, is caught between the cusp of honor and that of passion, though, for obvious reasons, he must take leave of Mrs. Travers at the end of the narrative. Actions often lead to unpredictable consequences, and in Conrad's works, as we shall see in "Because of the Dollars," an individual agent's apparently "irrational" choice of action may turn out to be a powerful gesture that undermines established moral norms or totalitarian forms of power.

In colonial contexts, this omnipotent power generally operates through free-floating agents who seem to satisfy their "self-interest" only on the condition that they contribute to the maximization of the profits of the empire which they loyally serve. Conrad's works describe this imperial power and further explore more complex human relationships and ideological concerns that Amartya Sen, a leading Indian philosopher and economist of the late-twentieth and twenty-first centuries, discusses in *On Ethics and Economics*. In this book Sen proposes a revaluation of "modern rationality," as he brings to light this rationality's limitations in assessing human nature:

> Why should it be *uniquely* rational to pursue one's own self-interest to the exclusion of everything else? [...] The self-interest view of rationality involves *inter alia* a firm rejection of the "ethics-related" view of motivation. Trying to do one's best to achieve what one would like to achieve can be a part of rationality, and this can include the promotion of non-self-interested goals which we may value and wish to aim at. To see any departure from self-interest maximization as

> evidence of irrationality must imply a rejection of the role of ethics
> in actual decision taking [....]. Universal selfishness as *actuality* may
> well be false, but universal selfishness as a requirement of *rationality*
> is patently absurd.[17]

In *Nostromo*, Charles Gould stands for a figure of "universal selfishness," hiding behind a universal idealistic rhetoric of progress and planetary love. From the outset, he promises to turn the re-opened silver mine of Sulaco into a moral force and convert "the very paradise of snakes" (*N* 105) into a source of order and justice which would improve the destiny of the population of Sulaco. However, this idealistic project is, in truth, driven mostly by material profit and power on which, as Gould egotistically believes, the fate of the South American republic of Costaguana "can continue to exist" (84).

Gould is corrupt and manipulative. He is involved in political intrigue and has partly financed the revolution which brought dictator Ribiera to power. His "cold and overmastering passions" (245), concealed in a prolific philanthropic discourse, are further subtly challenged by Antonia, who sarcastically tells him that "[i]t is your character that is the inexhaustible treasure which may save us all yet; your character, Carlos, not your wealth" (361). Significantly, in "Autocracy and War" Conrad warns, "democracy, which has elected to pin its faith to the supremacy of material interests [in which Gould also puts his faith as stated in *Nostromo*], will have to fight their battles to the bitter end" (*NLL* 107).

It is important to remember that in Conrad's fiction the revelation of an individual's moral character and his specific actions or conduct in imperial contexts often occurs amidst continuously changing natural surroundings and contact zones which involve communities with varied cultures and histories. This creates intriguing relations between Nature, community and individual ethics which, as Keith Carabine states in "No Action is Simple," "always complicate human actions and choices, and raise fundamental questions of identity."[18] Set in the totalized, dehumanizing context of late-nineteenth and early-twentieth century imperialism, Conrad's fiction addresses, among other things, the fundamental existential question of being with oneself and the Other, namely "how should one live?" – a philosophical inquiry which is believed to be initiated by Socrates and widely echoed in Stein's famous speculative phrase in *Lord Jim*: "how to live." And akin to Levinas' analysis in *Totality and Infinity*, Conrad, too, represents in his works what may be termed a discursive "intractability," that is "the difficulty of mastering or controlling the expression of the Other in conversation."[19] The issue of mediation and control is prominent in Conrad's narratives. In "Heart of Darkness," for instance, notwithstanding his inquisitiveness and willingness to disclose the reality of empire to his audience, Marlow is afraid of unearthing "[t]he inner truth" that is "hidden – luckily, luckily" (*YS* 93). This fear is tinged with a feeling of guilt and shame, which links Marlow and, through him, Conrad to the postcolonial experiences of moral crisis wrought by modernity and empire.

Discourse, as Levinas observes, is always relational and Conradian aesthetics reveals further implications when compared with similar narrative preoccupations in postcolonial texts, particularly those which, though written under the shadow of colonization and European cultural movements, unapologetically and inherently articulate the ethos of Europe's Other. Such works question the "totality" and "sovereignty" of any value system, while they uphold the heterogeneous worlds of ethical rights of what Conrad, in his other "Eastern" story "Falk: A Reminiscence," pithily refers to as "the organization of mankind" (*TS* 198).

This chapter mainly explores Conrad's narrative of the tragic loss faced by his protagonist, Davidson in "Because of the Dollars." It shows how Conrad's sense of ethical motivation in this Malay tale is ultimately defeated by an unforgiving fate, in a world dominated by the terms and relationships of imperial trade on the banks of intersecting waterways amidst the dark tropical rainforest. To tease out these thematic connections, this chapter compares Conrad's treatment of the conflicting and tragic relationship between the individual,

Nature, and community in "Because of the Dollars" to Adwaita Mallabarman's depiction of an individual character's ethical struggle, as part of the struggle for survival of a riverine community in "A River Called Titas."[20] It explores the journey of literary modernism from Conrad to Mallabarman, and examines the fluctuant times and spaces of these two tales by following the narratives of human relationships which they depict. Meanwhile, it offers an "inter-discursive" analysis of the complex theme of justice and the individual's moral struggle against changing circumstances, physical as well as cultural, which are distinctly delineated in these two important twentieth-century texts.

"A River Called Titas" is a post-Tagore Bengali modernist novella in its right, rather than merely an imitation derived from a specific European literary tradition. It revolves around the life of a young Malo fisherman and his failure to do justice to the girl whom he marries and impregnates only to be violently separated from her. When the narrative brings them together, the man has already turned insane and a helpless object of social coercion. On the verge of a mutual recognition, the young couple becomes the cause of their respective destruction, which dooms their child to premature orphanhood.

Written on the cusp between the political independence and the emergence of the post-colonial state of India, Mallabarman's narrative describes this rural community's struggle for subsistence and dependence on the Titas and draws attention to the changing socio-economic conditions which erode these people's social foundations. It charts the lives of three generations of Malo fishermen, a community living in a perennial relationship with nature on the bank of the river called the Titas, which flowed through north-eastern India and Bangladesh. Mallabarman was a member of this community and his story addresses the relationship between humans and Nature. In the course of history, the Malo community, who, for generations, subsisted mostly on hunting and fishing, lived in harmony with their environment and adapted to the natural changes. However, this community is gradually threatened with extinction as the water in the river decreases, whereas the agrarian population becomes stronger with the rise of land on the heart of the parching up water-tracts. This tale interrogates the colonial structure of dominance and subjection. It also significantly provides an illuminating context for re-reading Conrad's tale from the perspective of marginalized native people compelled into a life dictated by oppressive socio-economic structures and ecological changes.

Both "A River Called Titas" and "Because of the Dollars" deal with rivers and share thematic and ideological patterns, although they are produced at different times and spaces. In "Because of the Dollars" Davidson displays an unflinching sense of human empathy and responsibility, which is framed within a clear Conradian ethical structure that characterizes sea communities or ship communities. His struggle against a group of European ruffians to save someone else's mistress and her child radically disrupts Victorian bourgeois social compromises. Davidson succumbs, however, to a suspicious and insensitive social order and his ordeal is imbued with the typical Conradian duality that Hugh Epstein identifies with reference to "Youth" as a "vision of man as belittled and as exalted."[21] He powerlessly sees his individual ethical conduct flagrantly belittled, which suggests an overruling sense of injustice. This duality between Davidson's surrender to external pressure and his personality's indelible goodness is implied by the narrative introduction to Davidson's "story":

> "Who on earth has paid him off for being so fine by spoiling his smile?"
> "That's quite a story, and I will tell it to you if you like. Confound it! It's quite a surprising one, too. Surprising in every way, but mostly in the way it knocked over poor Davidson – and apparently only because he is such a good sort. [...] You musn't suppose that Davidson is a soft fool." ("Because of the Dollars,"*WT* 171-72)

Mallabarman's "A River Called Titas" bears notable affinities with Conrad's treatment of justice with regard to human actions. This Bengali story uses the dissolution of the socio-economic foundations of the Malo community and the steadily shrinking river as the backdrop for the tragic destiny of a young fisherman and his family. As in Conrad's fiction, the fishermen's fraternal bonding in Mallabarman's story is violently destroyed by a human and physical environment that gradually becomes insensitive and leads its dwellers to the brink of extinction. In both works the notion of the "good," that is, human fellowship is played out through a series of registers and resonances. "A River Called Titas" provides a re-reassessment of the anxieties surrounding the sense of "goodness" underlying friendship, love, and human communion across physical and psychological distances. In "Because of the Dollars," instead, it is provided from a contrasting perspective to suggest the impossibility of imposing absolute control over human motives.

Both "Because of the Dollars" and "A River Called Titas" relate significant experiences of fellowship. The ethical dimension involving the interrelation between the individual and society can, in this regard, be adequately assessed by extending Levinas' understanding of the individual's capacity to apprehend and accept the Other, whether human or otherwise, in spite of all the differences between Self and Other. The philosophical and political implication of such fellowship or bonding between two or more individuals is suggested by Jacques Derrida's *The Politics of Friendship*, whose ideas on "friendship" are widely influenced by Levinas. This text, which gives priority to human actions, is relevant to the argument developed in the present discussion:

> In all good sense [...] friendship consists in loving, does it not; it is a way of loving, of course. Consequence, implication: it is therefore an act before being a situation; rather, the *act* of loving, before being the state of being loved. An action before a passion. [...] This is an irreversible order. [...] It would be in itself declared, given order to knowledge or to consciousness.[22]

In the light of Derrida's thought, Conrad's and Mallabarman's narratives reveal the multiple possibilities created by the Self's arduous effort to relate to the Other's exteriority. Regarding the central man–woman relationship in each of these two texts, more specifically, these narrative possibilities do not lead to full realization but suggest instead an endless interplay between the Self and Other. In *The Politics of Friendship*, Derrida extends Aristotle's ideas to evoke the role of events in this interplay: "It may be, then, that the order is the other – *it may well be* – and that only the coming of the event allows, after the event [*après coup*], *perhaps*, what it will previously have made possible to be thought."[23]

As the Author's Note to *Within the Tides*, mentioned earlier, suggests, the romantic employment of the exotic East is reconsidered by Conrad in the form of more positive aesthetic commitment to human communication and truthfulness, which involves the relentless struggle of the responsible artist, a feature that links Conrad's ethics to that of the postcolonial artists:

> To render a crucial point of feelings in terms of human speech is really an impossible task. Written words can only form a sort of translation. And if that translation happens, from want of skill or from over-anxiety, to be too literal, the people caught in the toils of passion, instead of disclosing themselves, which would be art, are made to give themselves away, which is neither art nor life. Nor yet truth! At any rate, not the whole truth; for it is truth robbed of all its necessary and sympathetic reservations and qualifications which give it its fair form, its just proportions, its semblance of human fellowship. (*WT* x-xi)

In this statement Conrad expresses language's inadequacy to render feelings or truth in their fullness. Meantime, he also seems to suggest that it is the inability of complete disclosure of truth or sentiment within human relationships which, paradoxically, allows for a semblance of human fellowship. Giving oneself away, even partially, constitutes a step towards this precarious human fellowship.

In "Because of the Dollars" Conrad shows Davidson giving himself away beyond all sorts of "rational" control of profit--seeking self-interest and bourgeois domestic codes, as the sequel of events allows Davidson to realize what Derrida calls in *The Politics* "the meeting" of human fellowships' "presence in act."[24] However, Conrad's protagonist is caught in an intricate situation which challenges his "ethics of fellowship," as Acheraïou has pointed out in "Ethics and Horror."[25] He is an isolated and vulnerable honorable gentleman, threatened by ruthless villains, and feels a sense of responsibility towards a woman, Laughing Anne. Because of his genuine feeling of fellowship with this defenseless woman, Davidson is universally regarded as "a good man." So, the tale functions, in this respect, as a cautionary reminder that even good men may suffer misfortune and injustice in pursuit of doing "The Right Thing."

The narrative characteristically begins with the group of sailors sharing specific codes of fellowship. This close-knit community seems, at the same time, always on the verge of dissolution, as its members are steadily threatened by external forces, namely the imperial trade lurking on the shore: "we were hanging about near the water's edge, as sailors idling ashore will do" ("Because of the Dollars," *WT* 169). As in most of his works, Conrad in this story shows how the sailor's sense of fellowship and discipline is continuously in conflict with the capitalist ethics or material interests which lead to the alienation and suffering of "thoroughly humane" individuals such as Davidson: "I don't imagine there can be much of any other sort of goodness that counts on this earth. And as he's that with a shade of particular refinement, I may well call him a '*really* good man'" (171).

The characteristic Conradian irony becomes evident in the description of Davidson as both singularized and an identifiable case of common goodness. In *The Politics of Friendship* Derrida reminds us that in the modern human civilization "[t]here is no virtue without this tragedy of number without number. This is perhaps even more unthinkable than a tragedy" – a fact that Derrida in *The Politics* links back to Aristotle's "counsel [...]: my friends, if you want to have friends, do not have too many."[26] The singularity of Davidson is "forever wounding,"[27] as made clear in the narrator's attempt to explain this protagonist's feeling of pain, only because "his goodness was of a particularly delicate sort" ("Because of the Dollars," *WT* 190).

In "Hospitality" Kaoru Yamamoto points out that though Conrad's "The Secret Sharer" is mostly interpreted as a metaphorical rediscovery of the inner self, this story "also reveals an external gesture of [...] [the young captain's] self, to meet with the other person." She further states that if read from this alternative perspective, the text seems "less as a story of self-reflection than as that of externally oriented desire to go beyond the self to speak and give to the other."[28] Yamamoto shows how the captain's "roaming eyes" prompt him to look for the unconventional "beyond the horizon of his Western self-sameness."[29] The captain's action may, in this respect, be contrasted with the old English teacher's narrative motive in *Under Western Eyes* "who has lost himself and the otherness of the other in 'a wilderness of words.'"[30] On another ethical level, *Under Western Eyes* provides us with a Conradian version of "hospitality" in the character of Tekla who unconditionally takes care of the wounded Razumov. In each case, the individual's urge to welcome a stranger whose "[c]rossing the threshold is entering and not only approaching or coming," as Derrida states in *Of Hospitality*, is meant to go beyond the mechanical set of ethical norms formally sanctioned by social authority.[31]

In "Because of the Dollars" Davidson perhaps represents the most critical case of this human urge to reach out to the unreachable with an inner ethical integrity at the backdrop of a complex network of Nature and community, both threatened by the encroaching economic modes of transactions introduced by the colonial power in the Eastern islands[32]:

> But I had better begin at the beginning. We must go back to the first time the old dollars had been called in by our Government in exchange for a new issue. [...] Every trader in the islands was thinking of getting his old dollars sent up here in time, and the demand for empty French wine cases [...] was something unprecedented. The custom was to pack the dollars in little bags of a hundred each. I don't know how many bags each case would hold. A good lot. Pretty tidy sums must have been moving afloat just then. (*WT* 172)

In a typically Conradian gesture, Davidson's effort to embrace the unknown is in stark opposition to all these above-mentioned interests. Broadly speaking, the priority given to the presence of the Other, or the stranger, in the individual subject's life in Conrad's narrative may be explained by what Edward Said considers "an extraordinarily persistent residual sense of [Conrad's] own exilic marginality."[33]

With continuously shifting notions of the *home* and the *world* the primary question, "how should one live?,", is addressed by the exiled, the migrant, the sailor, and the colonized in ways different from those who are accustomed to permanent homes. Furthermore, the special bonding between the sailor and the ship in a story like "Because of the Dollars" can be viewed as Conrad's response to the decline of humanity in the First World War, whose sudden outbreak he described in his essay, "First News," 1918: "Four years ago, on the first day of August, in the town of Cracow, Austrian Poland, nobody would believe that the war was coming. [...] This incredulity was so universal amongst people of intelligence and information, that even I, who had accustomed myself to look at the inevitable for years past, felt my conviction shaken" (*NLL* 174). Therefore, what Conrad calls "memories of my sea-life" in "Poland Revisited" (173) helps him to conceive of the organic tie between the ship and her sailor: "Davidson then was commanding the steamer *Sissie* – the little one which we used to chaff him about. He ran her alone" ("Because of the Dollars," *WT* 172-73).

Davidson's penetration into the farthest points of the island, whose purpose consists of collecting old dollars from local traders, enables him to move through uncharted territories and learn how to actively experience the Other in its infinity, which in Conrad's outlook always carries an ethical dimension. This journey toward the Other reminds people of the existence of a world beyond the self-enclosed bourgeois universe with its unethical classification of humans and the environment into fixed and impermeable categories: "His steamer, being so small, could go up tiny creeks and into shallow bays and through reefs and over sand-banks, collecting produce, where no other vessel but a native craft would think of venturing" (173).

Such ventures into the world of the unfamiliar Other introduce Davidson into various native communities inhabiting the banks of numerous waterways. Through individual wanderers, such as Davidson, Conrad explores the cultural plurality and relationality created by the imperial trade. In *The Politics of Friendship* Derrida explains that in relation to "friendship," which involves the sense of fellowship,

> there is no more just category for the future than that of the 'perhaps'. Such a thought conjoins friendship, the future, and the *perhaps* to open on to the coming of what comes – that is to say, necessarily in the regime of a possible whose possibilization must prevail over the impossible.[34]

Therefore, the kind of Victorian code of conduct Davidson is reported to abide by in his marriage with "a meek, shy little thing" ("Because of the Dollars," *WT* 176) and his distance from native girls are momentarily unsettled; a temporary disruption that largely steers him towards action: "here comes the only moment in this story where accident – mere accident – plays a part" (174). The accidental nature of impressionistic writing, which in Conrad is linked to what Ian Watt calls "delayed decoding,"[35] also helps to establish the importance of the unexpected, notwithstanding the shock created by its presence, or even by brushing aside all previous assumptions about that specific existence:

> He stared about with his mouth open [....]. "Try to imagine the shock: in that wild place that you couldn't find on a map, and more squalid than the most poverty-stricken Malay settlement had a right to be, this European woman coming swishing out of the long grass in a fanciful tea-gown thing, dingy pink satin, with a long train and frayed lace trimmings [...]. The woman came forward, her arms extended, and laid her hands on Davidson's shoulders, exclaiming: "Why! You have hardly changed at all. The same good Davy." And she laughed a little wildly. [...] "Davidson looked up at the sky; but there was to be seen no balloon from which she could have fallen on that spot. When he brought his distracted gaze down, it rested on a child holding on with a brown little paw to the pink satin gown. [...]. "No more paint and dyes for me, Davy," she struck in, "if only you will do what he wants you to do." (182-83)

In a rare occasion in Conrad's works, therefore, a European man is made to face a European woman with whom he was formerly familiar and who has presently become a topic of gossip because of her association with several male companions. Anne now appears a stranger both in time and space. Considering Conrad's own alienation as an exiled author, this situation takes a particular significance with regard to the ethics of writing in general and, more specifically, to Conrad's own marginality. In a sense, both Davidson and Conrad ultimately tend to redraw the map of fellowship and belongingness in their own ways. Interestingly, the "pleasant silvery laugh always at [Anne's] disposal" (179) is a sort of pretention that conceals her anxieties about her son's future: "She was stranded in Saigon with precious little money and in great trouble about a kid she had" (178). The narrator claims that "[h]is pity for Laughing Anne was no more than her case deserved. But his goodness was of a particularly delicate sort" (190).

The "delicacy" of Davidson's humanity, which is also evident in his fellow feeling towards other characters, and his "earnestness" (183) regarding what Anne "deserves" – not just as an object of "pity" but as a subject with distinct experiences – expose both Anne and Davidson to exploitation, violence, and robbery induced by the imperial business scheme. The cruel loss of Anne reconfirms the logic of the colonial power, for, as Jeremy Hawthorn notes in "Power and Perspective," "initiating an interactive mutuality [...] dissolves power and hierarchy" which, therefore, cuts "the individual wielding power off from what may be a desired intimacy."[36] The devilish Frenchman who seems to control other robbers psychologically exhibits the wickedness that underlies colonial practices: "He's a devil. He keeps them going. Without him they would have done nothing but talk" ("Because of the Dollars," *WT* 194). But Davidson's goodness is further manipulated by social reservation and suspicion that intrude on his private life and turns him into a "remorseful" person (208).

In his study on James Joyce's *Ulysses* Fredric Jameson points out that "[g]ossip is indeed the very element in which reference

– or, if you prefer, the 'referent' itself – expands and contracts, ceaselessly transformed from a mere token, a notation, a short-hand object, back into a full-dress narrative."[37] In the same way, Davidson becomes the subject of a gossip of enjoyable scope as exploited by Ritchie, who provides sufficient clues to Mrs. Davidson by hinting at her husband's close and long-term relationship with Laughing Anne. In this story gossip establishes a sort of social solidarity, achieved at the cost of the individual's integrity and inner hope as reflected in Davidson's smile. As an early cosmopolitan artist, with all his reservations about social change in the collective action, Conrad expands our view of the range of possibilities within human encounters, in opposition to the over-determining state authority and systems of oppression such as colonialism, which unjustly categorize people and nature to serve their own aims.

Strikingly, the frame narrator of "Because of the Dollars" enquires into the loss of Davidson's smile at the tale's closure: "Hollis ceased. But before we rose from the table I asked him if he knew what had become of Laughing Anne's boy" (*WT* 211). The ultimate ethical concern of the bond between Davidson and Anne is the "boy" who also embodies a dire need for survival on the part of his mother: "'Davidson was attempting a veiled warning as to Bamtz, but she interrupted him. She knew what men were. She knew what this man was like. But he had taken wonderfully to the kid. […] 'It's for the kid, Davy – it's for the kid'" (185). It is around the illness of Anne's son that the story's climatic action revolves. Children as the living force of a community are not a common occurrence in Conrad's works. However, in London – far away from the Malay Archipelago – Winnie in *The Secret Agent* desperately attempts to protect her mentally retarded brother, Stevie, by surrendering her body and individuality to Mr. Adolf Verloc, only to find herself betrayed at the heart of the empire. In a similar way, Laughing Anne sacrifices her liberty: "'if the kid hadn't been in this state I would have run off with him – to you – into the woods – anywhere. […] she cried aloud suddenly" (194). Children deserve the sort of relationship described by Derrida in *The Politics of Friendship*, where he states: "it is to love *before* being loved."[38]

Like *The Secret Agent* or "Because of the Dollars," Mallabarman's story is centrally concerned with the ethical questions involving the relation between parent and child in a community life where communal bonds are disintegrating under the pressure of economic and social forces. Widely considered as Mallabarman's most notable work, "The River Called Titas" is one of the finest literary pieces of mid-twentieth century Bengali modernism.[39] Supriya Chaudhuri examines the growth of the Bengali novel after the era of Bankimchandra Chattopadhyay, Rabindranath Tagore and Saratchandra Chattopadhyay, who are regarded as the main founders of Bengali fiction:

> The great novelists of this period, Bibhutibhusan Bandyopadhyay (1894-1950), Tarashankar Bandyopadhyay (1898-1971) and Manik Bandyopadhyay (1908-56), as well as Satinath Bhaduri (1906-65) and Advaita Mallabarman (1914-51), all focus on the Bengal countryside, but see it under the lens of change, wasted by poverty and dearth, unsettled by migration to the ruthless, all-consuming city. The project of modernity had been the principal concern of the Bengali novel from its inception in the nineteenth century [...]. In the twentieth century, despite its hard-fought gains of the independence movement, that project loses its aura of hope. A new kind of social realism, drawing upon modernist techniques of representation as well as upon the anger, confusion, and despair of the rural poor and the urban unemployed, leaves its imprint in fiction.[40]

Another interconnected development of this cultural production may be summarized in the following way:

> The colonizers' particular anxiety over the insidious elements in Bengali literary practices, violating the norms of "normalcy" and "progress" and the institutionalized reservations imposed upon them were simultaneously internalized by the English educated elitist intellectuals of the second half of the 19th century. Thus, bare corporeality and crude violence, once central themes in pre-colonial literature, were encoded within the model of "nineteenth century positivist sociology and utilitarian political economy" [...]. Countering this essentialising tendency of colonial knowledge and its derivative discourses, the

modernist works [of the mid twentieth century] [...] revived unclear
and "irrational" utterances, nightmares and illusive dreams [...] rooted
deep in the country soil.[41]

The tortured body of both human subject and Nature is an
essential narrative trope in Mallabarman's story which entails
specific ethical components. In a central narrative moment that
links the individual, the community, and Nature, a small boy,
Ananta, recently orphaned and a vagabond, is seen returning
from the river Titas after performing his mother's funeral
rituals. No "forgiveness" is permitted to Ananta in the course of
his tragic history against the backdrop of the inevitable decline
of the values and beliefs of his Malo community. According to
Chaudhuri,

if [Manik Bandyopadhyay's] *Padmanadir Majhi* [or, *The Boatman of
the Padma*] is the greatest example of the "river novel" in Bengal, in
large part a deltaic plain defined more by water than by land, that
genre is consolidated by [...] [the] classic chronicle of fishermen's
lives, *Titas Ekti Nadir Nam* [*A River Called Titas*].[42]

It can be further argued here that there are significant
topographical similarities between the setting of Conrad's Malay
stories and that of "A River Called Titas."[43] Mallabarman's
narrative begins by connecting the river with a specific way of
life. Both the river and the community are separated from the
grand-narratives of the outside world:

she doesn't have the terrible look of the Meghna or the Padma. [...]
Thus, comparatively the Titas is a river of medium length and width.
Yet, the naughty village boy cannot swim across her. On the other
hand, the sailor is not frightened of her modest tides when trying
to reach its other bank on his canoe with his young bride on board.
("A River Called Titas" 399)

The river's changing course and decreasing tide over the years
are directly related in the narrative to Malo people's mores and
modes of life. Similarly, their lyrical speech tries to grasp the
rhythm of the stream till the river itself dries up, leading to the
loss of everything these fishermen stand for. It is also this very

pattern that both creates and constrains, or even destroys, the individual in the novel through the conflict between the residual and the emergent elements of his/her life. Within this narrative treatment of individuality, the "I," as Derrida declared, struggles and *"finds itself* comprised and determined in advance by the fact that it belongs to the most suspended '*we.'"*[44] Though demographically more limited than the global scope of Conrad's works, Mallabarman's narrative makes a powerful statement against the homogenizing tendency of socio-cultural structures of power.

Thus, the life on the Titas is initially characterized by a sense of stability that is not found in any fishing community residing elsewhere, as the river provides this community with physical sustenance and ethical authority:

> The Titas is brimming with water! So many boats! She is generous in every way! [...] Malos who have visited the bank of another river, called Bijoy, know how the river shrinks in the month of *Chaitra*. They have dreaded the thought that if the river Bijoy instead of the Titas would have been flowing by their villages, they would not be able to breathe freely. ("A River Called Titas" 401-02)

Malo women, on the other hand, are not anxious when male members of their family earn their living from fishing on the river, for they are not to be afraid of the Titas's small waves. The river's centrality is confirmed in the narrative in obvious terms:

> All the paths of the Malo village start from courtyards of the cottages and end at the Titas. But they are narrow paths: a child's cry from any cottage can easily be heard by another's mother inside another cottage on the other side of a road; the main path, however, passes through the river herself. (410)

This waterway is also celebrated in the riverside clans' rituals, as suggested by the great rowing competition.

As in Mallabarman's story, in Conrad's fiction, too, there is a consistent attempt to recover lost organic communities with their set of principles guiding the individual subject's behavior and activity. This is usually enacted through a narrative reconstruction of the sailors' community, as it is poignantly stated at opening of the narrative of "Heart of Darkness":

> their home is always with them – the ship; and so is their country – the sea. One ship is very much like another, and the sea is always the same. In the immutability of their surroundings the foreign shores, the foreign faces, the changing immensity of life, glide past, veiled not by a sense of mystery but by a slightly disdainful ignorance; for there is nothing mysterious to a seaman unless it be the sea itself, which is the mistress of his existence and as inscrutable as Destiny. (YS 48)

Comparatively, the first part of Mallabarman's narrative relates the persistent efforts of a close-knit organic community which derives its strength from the river's waters. For Conrad's European sailors and traders, the boat represents a social microcosm with its values and codes of conduct shared by seamen living in rough, alien environments. These seamen's communal bonds and values are often undermined from inside, by crew members, for various reasons. *Lord Jim* and *The Nigger of the "Narcissus"* offer, in this respect, eloquent examples of internal violation of these fundamental codes of conduct. In Mallabarman's story, the native fishermen helplessly experience the breakdown of the mutual understanding that held them together. It is this kind of value system which, for example, allows Subal, the son of an impoverished fishing family to be brought up, after his father's death, with his friend Kishore, a boy from relatively affluent family of the same community.

Raymond Williams' following observation can be applied here to both Conrad and Mallabarman: "a personal breakdown was a genuinely social fact, and a social breakdown was lived and known in direct personal experience. But then to take breakdown as an illustration of this continuity is itself a mark of a very deep kind of change."[45] Urged by the village elders, Subal and Kishore sail to the river Meghna, for greater fishing profits. This undertaking implies the unviability of the Malo mode of sustenance, already unsettled and on the verge of yielding to encroaching agrarian interests, which reshape the existing socio-economic conditions, by reversing the earlier prevalence of water over land.

Terry Eagleton notes in *The English Novel* that Conrad's fiction "threaten[s] to subvert" the European sense of cultural "supremacy at exactly the point where it is most urgently needed" in a "sea of doubts and indeterminacies" which result from an encounter between different cultures.[46] Mid-twentieth century Bengali fiction involves the modernist questioning of the aesthetic "impulse to moralize reality, that is, to identify it with the social system that is the source of any morality that we can imagine" by another set of doubts and indeterminacies regarding the stability of the so-called native cultural formations.[47]

This aesthetic and ethical preoccupation in both Conrad and Mallabarman is established by the latter's use of a series of unpredictable events that happen to Kishore and Subal, in which the former meets a girl from a distant village with a different cultural upbringing. Significantly, Kishore is primarily received as a friend by the girl's family: "Friendships. Let there be friendship between you and me" ("A River Called Titas" 434). Their wedding is arranged by the bride's relatives according to their custom. Kishore seems to reinvent himself psychologically and physically. But the marital life of the young couple is cut short as Kishore's pregnant wife is kidnapped by a group of pirates during their return journey. Kishore is unable to stand the shock. In her absence, Kishore suffers from what Derrrida calls "dissymmetry and tensions," which cause his own Self to become "thus out of joint with its own existence."[48]

Significantly, the adolescent Kishore grows into a man while he is away with a different community that has been enjoying a steadier source of sustenance which is reflected in their cultural practices. For instance, in the narrative of *dol utsab*, a festival of color and love, the beauty of a dancing woman being identified with the beauty of Nature catches Kishore's eyes. But in Mallabarman's narrative the union between the Self and an enchanting Other can take place only at the cost of the two individuals' violent separation. Failing to defend his newly wed wife, Kishore's own obligation to do justice is thwarted, as he primarily holds himself responsible for the tragic incident. The ensuing shame and guilt lead to Kishore's absolute isolation from every kind of human communion: "Kishore's eyes had turned unnaturally large and red like hibiscus flowers. A monstrous look could be seen on his face. [...] 'O Subal, come instantly! See, Kishore has gone insane!'" ("A River Called Titas" 440). Subjected to tortuous social abuses in his native village, Kishore's condition seems to represent the disjointed state of Malo modes of living in the final part of the text.

Ironically, Kishore's wife and their son Ananta, who are rescued by two kind-hearted Muslim brothers, arrive in the Malo village after much wandering. As marriage is the central institution of the community life, celebrated by social gathering and a set of rituals to uphold social norms, the collapse of Kishore's marital life raises serious questions about the child's legitimacy. In "Because of the Dollars" Davidson suffers because of his compassion towards Anne. In a more extreme situation, where human relationships are disrupted, Kishore turns into an object of physical and mental humiliation, and even occasional thrashing. Both texts refuse to consider the man-woman bonding in simple moral terms. The question of social acceptance becomes crucial with the arrival of Ananta and his mother, who are significantly offered shelter by Basanti, once Kishore's betrothed but ultimately married to Subal:

> "Sister, when did your son's father pass away?"
> "I do not know."
> "Is he really dead?"
> "I have no idea."
> "Where do your in-laws live?"
> "I don't know."
> "I say, have you been married at all?"
> "I am not sure, sister." (448)

Though unable to recognize each other, Ananta's parents nevertheless feel an uncanny mutual attraction which finally leads to their demise. Kishore finds scope to madly embrace his beloved and hurt her fatally. The woman dies and Kishore is also beaten to death. Once the protection normally secured by marital bonding is violently destroyed by the coercive external forces, which cause social marginalization and injustice, the couple turns out defenseless. Kishore tries to overcome this situation by exerting his love in the most "asocial" manner. After the couple's death, Basanti, whose character displays similarities with Tekla in Conrad's *Under Western Eyes*, takes care of Ananta. But Mallabarman's narrative does not provide any easy or definite solution. Both the river and the boy lose their sense of direction, and this suggests lack of adequate caring, evident in Ananta's brief relationship with another girl, who lives near Basanti's paternal home and who also dejects Ananta.

Conrad and Mallabarman, with distinct but overlapping worldviews, explore an unequal fight between the unjust and totalitarian forms of power and the individuals' ethical orientations towards strangers. As a result of this fight, Davidson in "Because of the Dollars" and Kishore in "A River Called Titas" inevitably lose their mental and physical strength. However, the individual characters make concrete and continuous efforts to relate to others amidst all sorts of hostility and continue their search for alternative meanings in life that would find expression in a variety of human conduct and give significance to the inconsistency of human experiences, even in a seemingly limited context. Conrad's and Mallabarman's tales, with their characteristic inclination towards the dignity of the individual's tragic suffering, challenge easy surrendering of human fellowship to a monologic frame of achievement and profit-driven materialist interests. The narratives' emphasis on empathy and responsibility in "Because of the Dollars" and "A River Called Titas" provides the ethical foundation for a world yet to come. Significantly, both tales suggest the unfinished nature of reality by introducing two orphan kids, who seem to look forward to an unpredictable future. Thus, in both Conrad's and Mallabarman's narratives, uncalculated actions that cross the border of self-preservation in a largely deterministic world anticipate the radical affirmation of differences in human perceptions regarding their relation to the rest of the world. Reading modernist authors such as Conrad and Mallabarman thus becomes an ethical responsibility of the contemporary world.

Acknowledgements

I wish to express my sincere gratitude to Professors Laëtitia Crémona and Amar Acheraïou, the editors of *Joseph Conrad and Ethics* for exploring such a fascinating area of Conrad studies. This book chapter is indebted to the suggestions of Ashok Sengupta, Retired Professor of English from the University of Kalyani, India. I also sincerely thank Professors Wiesław Krajka of Maria Curie-Skłodowska University, Poland and Mark D. Larabee, executive editor of *Joseph Conrad Today*, for enabling me to interact with Conradians from different parts of the world; and Nandini Saha, Professor, Department of English, Jadavpur, Kolkata, India, for encouraging me to work on Bengali modernism.

NOTES

[1] Levinas 21.
[2] Hiddleston 17-18.
[3] Krajka 10.
[4] Collits 24.
[5] Collits 24.
[6] Acheraïou, *Rethinking Postcolonialism* 154.
[7] Acheraïou, "Colonial Encounters" 153.
[8] See Collits; Acheraïou, *Rethinking Postcolonialism*; on the issues of humanity and moral restraint, see Acheraïou, "Ethics and Horror" 63.
[9] For a detailed analysis of ethics and empire in "Heart of Darkness," see Acheraïou, "Ethics and Horror."
[10] Romanick Baldwin 196.
[11] Romanick Baldwin 197.
[12] Ross 24.
[13] Ray, "Modernism's Footprints" 162.
[14] Romanick Baldwin 194.
[15] Romanick Baldwin 202.
[16] Acheraïou, *Rethinking Postcolonialism* 151.

[17] Sen 15-16.
[18] Carabine 240.
[19] Hiddleston 18.
[20] Although "A River Called Titas" ("Titas Ekti Nadir Nām") is available as a separate text, I have, for the purpose of this article, translated relevant sections of Adwaita Mallabarman's Bengali text included in the single volume *Rachanasamagra* (*Complete Works*) 2000. All references to the novella "Titas Ekti Nadir Nām" ("A River Called Titas") in this article are to my translation.
[21] Epstein 12.
[22] Derrida, *The Politics of Friendship* 8-9.
[23] Derrida, *The Politics of Friendship* 18.
[24] Derrida, *The Politics of Friendship* 18.
[25] Acheraïou, "Ethics and Horror" 49.
[26] Derrida, *The Politics of Friendship* 22.
[27] Derrida, *The Politics of Friendship* 22.
[28] Yamamoto 253-54. In one of the endnotes to the quoted essay Yamamoto, too, points out that "Emmanuel Levinas's argument of welcoming of the infinity of the other, the face-to-face relation, is especially illuminating in thinking about the relationship between the captain and Leggatt" in "The Secret Sharer." Yamamoto 265.
[29] Yamamoto 257.
[30] Yamamoto 256.
[31] Derrida, *Of Hospitality* 123.
[32] Carabine's introduction to the Wordsworth Classics edition of *Joseph Conrad's Selected Short Stories* provides an illuminating study on the gradual complexity of Conrad's narrative technique in his early Malay tales. See Carabine.
[33] Said 27.
[34] Derrida, *The Politics of Friendship* 29.
[35] Watt 317. For an understanding of Conrad's impressionistic technique, the present essay is indebted to Watt's "Impressionism and Symbolism in 'Heart of Darkness.'"
[36] Hawthorn 277.
[37] Jameson 145.
[38] Derrida, *The Politics of Friendship* 8.
[39] The cultural reception of "Titas Ekti Nadir Nām" is partly dependent on a 1973 major Bengali movie adaptation of the novella by one of the pioneers of the modern Bengali Cinema, Ritwik Ghatak.
[40] Chaudhuri 116.
[41] Ray, "Fighting against Multiple Bodies!" 134.
[42] Chaudhuri 118.
[43] Bengal, being the largest delta of the world, shares with the Malay Archipelago tropical rain forest intersected by numerous water ways, heavy rain, and hot weather.
[44] Derrida, *The Politics of Friendship* 77.
[45] Williams 139.

[46] Eagleton 236-37.
[47] White 269.
[48] Derrida, *The Politics of Friendship* 24.

WORKS CITED

Acheraïou, Amar. "Colonial Encounters and Cultural Contests: Confrontation of Orientalist and Occidentalist Discourses in 'Karain: A Memory.'" *Conradiana* 39 (2007): 153-67. Print.
---. "Ethics and Horror in 'Heart of Darkness.'" *Critical Insights. "Heart of Darkness"*. Ed. Robert C. Evans. New York: Salem P, 2019. 49-71. Print.
---. *Rethinking Postcolonialism: Colonialist Discourse in Modern Literatures and the Legacy of Classical Writers*. New York: Palgrave Macmillan, 2008. Print.
Carabine, Keith. Introduction. Joseph Conrad. *Selected Short Stories and "The Rover."* Ware: Wordsworth Classics, 1997. Print.
---. "'No Action is Simple': Betrayal and Confession in Conrad's *Under Western Eyes* and Ngugi's *A Grain of Wheat*." Fincham and De Lange with Krajka 233-71.
Chaudhuri, Supriya. "The Bengali Novel." *The Cambridge Companion to Modern Indian Culture*. Ed. Vasudha Dalmia and Rashmi Sadana. Cambridge: Cambridge UP, 2012. 101-23. Print.
Collits, Terry. *Postcolonial Conrad: Paradoxes of Empire*. New York: Routledge, 2005. Print.
Derrida, Jacques. *Of Hospitality*. Trans. Rachel Bowlby. Stanford, CA: Stanford UP, 2000. Print.
---. *The Politics of Friendship*. Trans. George Collins. London: Verso, 2005. Print. Radical Thinkers Series.
Eagleton, Terry. *The English Novel: An Introduction*. Malden: Blackwell, 2012. Print.
Epstein, Hugh. "The Duality of 'Youth': Some Literary Contexts." *The Conradian* 21.2 (1996): 1-14. Print.
Fincham, Gail, and Attie De Lange, with Wiesław Krajka, eds. *Conrad at the Millennium: Modernism, Postmodernism, Postcolonialism*. Introduction Gail Fincham. Boulder: Social Science Monographs; Lublin: Maria Curie-Skłodowska U; New York: Columbia UP, 2001. Vol. 10 of *Conrad: Eastern and Western Perspectives*. Ed. Wiesław Krajka. 30 vols. to date. Print. 1992- .
Hawthorn, Jeremy. "Power and Perspective in Joseph Conrad's Political Fiction: The Gaze and the Other." Fincham and De Lange with Krajka 275-307.
Hiddleston, Jane. *Understanding Postcolonialism*. Jaipur: Rawat, 2012. Print.
Jameson, Fredric. *The Modernist Papers*. New Delhi: ABS, 2007. Print.
Krajka, Wiesław. "Introduction." Krajka, *"Wine in Old and New Bottles"* 1-12.

Krajka, Wiesław, ed. *"Wine in Old and New Bottles"*: *Critical Paradigms for Joseph Conrad*. Lublin: Maria Curie-Skłodowska UP; New York: Columbia UP, 2014. Print. Vol. 23 of *Conrad: Eastern and Western Perspectives*. Ed. Wiesław Krajka. 30 vols. to date. 1992- .

Levinas, Emmanuel. *Totality and Infinity: An Essay on Exteriority*. Trans. Alphonso Lingis. The Hague: Martinus Nijhoff, 1969. Print.

Mallabarman, Adwaita. "Titas Ekti Nadir Nām" [A River Called Titas]. *Rachanasamagra [Complete Works]*. Kolkata: Dey's, 2000. 399-562. Print.

Ray, Subhadeep. "Fighting against multiple bodies! Translating 'Nāri o Nāgini' and 'Tamoshā' Tarashankar Bandyopadhyay and 'Bonjhi Gunjomālā' by Jagadish Gupta." *Disability in Translation: The Indian Experience*. Ed. Someshwar Sati and G. J. V. Prasad. London: Routledge, 2020. 133-45. Print.

---. "Modernism's Footprints: World, Text and Ideology in Joseph Conrad and Manik Bandyopadhyay." *Some Intertextual Chords of Joseph Conrad's Literary Art*. Ed. Wiesław Krajka. Lublin: Maria Curie-Skłodowska UP; New York: Columbia UP, 2019. 161-202. Print. Vol. 28 of *Conrad: Eastern and Western Perspectives*. Ed. Wiesław Krajka. 30 vols. to date. 1992- .

Romanick Baldwin, Debra. "The Horror and the Human: The Politics of Dehumanization in *Heart of Darkness* and Primo Levi's *Se questo è un uomo*." *Conradiana* 37 (2005): 185-204. Print.

Ross, Stephen. *Conrad and Empire*. Columbia: U of Missouri P, 2004. Print.

Said, Edward. *Culture and Imperialism*. London: Vintage, 1994. Print.

Sen, Amartya. *On Ethics and Economics*. New Delhi: Oxford UP, 1990. Print.

Watt, Ian P. "Impressionism and Symbolism in 'Heart of Darkness.'" Joseph Conrad. *"Heart of Darkness"*: *An Authoritative Text, Backgrounds and Sources, Criticism*. Ed. Robert Kimbrough. New York: Norton, 1988. 311-36. Print. Norton Critical Edition.

White, Hayden. "From 'The Value of Narrativity in the Representation of Reality.'" 1987. *Modern Literary Theory: A Reader*. Ed. Philip Rice and Patricia Waugh. 4th ed. London: Oxford UP, 2001. 266-72. Print.

Williams, Raymond. *Modern Tragedy*. London: Hogarth, 1992. Print.

Yamamoto, Kaoru. "Hospitality in 'The Secret Sharer.'" Krajka *"Wine in Old and New Bottles"* 253-68.

Harold Ray Stevens,
McDaniel College,
Westminster, MD, USA

The Cross of Christ as Afterthought: Killing the Christian Ethic at "An Outpost of Progress"

> And this is the condemnation, that light is come into the world, and men loved the darkness rather than light, because their deeds were evil. (3 John 19)

The director of the great trading company erected "a tall cross much out of the perpendicular" as an afterthought on the elevated grave of the station master of an outpost of progress before Kayerts and Carlier arrived at the station in the heart of darkness to continue the work of civilization. Kayerts, the new station master, and his subordinate brother-in-exploitation Carlier were employed, like the previous station master, to devote their brief stay in central Africa to gather ivory to be shipped back to Europe for the gimcracks of colonialism – bibelots, bracelets, dominoes, piano keys, cutlery handles, and sundry ornaments – for the parlors of the gentlefolk of empire. Seldom mentioned in those parlors were the requirements of the slaughter of thousands of elephants[1] and the enslavement of the indigenous people of Africa to bring the trinkets of conquest to fruition. The cross predominated in the mists that engulf "An Outpost of Progress," but never mentioned in the narrative is Christ or Christianity. Also never mentioned in the narrative is a reference to Christian missions or missionaries like those that Joseph Conrad had met travelling up the Congo River, some of whose names he recorded in the "Congo Diary."[2]

Conrad kept that penciled record during his seven months stay in the Belgian Congo in 1890,[3] beginning at Matadi, where he spent days weighing, sorting, and packaging ivory for shipment to Europe. Later he began his trip up the Congo in central Africa, first by inland trek around the Livingstone Falls to Kinshasa, where he boarded as a supernumerary the *Roi des Belges*, a Congo River steamer for a trip to Stanley Falls and return. Later Conrad became its temporary pilot and returned, ill with malaria and dysentery, to Matadi and later to Europe. Kayerts and Carlier – like Conrad – spent less than a year in Central Africa. Unlike Conrad, however, Kayerts and Carlier were unable to return to the civilized world, because both died irreverently in the presence of the mist-enshrouded cross: Carlier was killed by Kayerts; Kayerts hanged himself from the arm of the cross, "a dark smudge, a cross-shaped stain, upon the shifting purity of the mist" ("An Outpost of Progress," *TU* 116).

The mist-enshrouded cross is the ironically conceived pervasive ethical image at the outpost, and is predominant, used four times, first, when Kayerts and Carlier arrived at the outpost and saw the cross that had been erected incorrectly by a representative of the Great Trading Company and not by Christian missionaries. Second, Carlier strengthened the cross by setting it upright, as oppressive incidents in the mists of central Africa began to disturb him, both mentally and physically, typified by Carlier complaining that the mist-enshrouded out of perpendicular cross caused him to squint. Third, shortly after, Kayerts – with the assistance of the Sierra Leone station hand Makola – began to negotiate under the cross with African ivory traders, which led to exile, death, rapine, and enslavement of people who worked for the Great Trading Country, in return for ivory. Finally, Kayerts hanged himself from the arm of the upright cross after having shot Carlier in a fit of anger.

Seldom has the rejection of the meaning of the cross been so vividly presented. Contrast the mounts of Judeo-Christian belief with the cross-topped elevated grave where Kayerts committed suicide: on Mount Sinai God communicated the 10 commandments to Moses (Exod. 20); on a mount by the Sea of Galilee Jesus delivered his Sermon (Matt. 5-7); and on Golgotha – the hill of skulls above Jerusalem where Jesus was crucified – Christ died so that all who believe, Christian ethics affirms, will merit salvation (3 John 16). On the cross of an elevated grave in the mists of a river in the heart of darkness, however, Kayerts hangs himself ingloriously, crying out, in Conrad's ironic vision: "*Help! .... My God!*" ("An Outpost of Progress," *TU* 115). Kayerts' valediction comes not from 3 John 16, but from 3 John 19: "And this is the condemnation, that light is come into the world, and men loved darkness rather than light, because their deeds were evil."[4]

"An Outpost of Progress" did not spring whole cloth from Conrad's thought when he began writing it in June 1896. Rather, it was a logical as well as aesthetically developed creation that evolved over years. His affirmation of the truth of colonial denial of the Christian ethic is evident not only in his experience in the Congo and many years he spent at sea where he met many people from various cultural traditions, but also in several letters, such as his denial of the miracles of Christ's birth, which "irritates" [him]" and his disdain for Christianity's "impossible standards [that] has brought an infinity of anguish to innumerable souls."[5] Conrad also questioned Leo Tolstoy's over-indulgent incorporation of the Christian ethic in his fiction (*CL* 5: 358). Elsewhere Conrad questioned the excesses of some Roman Catholic practitioners, at the same time contrasting, genially, some of the practices of the Anglican Church (8: 190). Conrad also recorded experiences with the crucifix in his life – at the burial of his father, Apollo Korzeniowski, and at the birth of his children. The cross was also present at Conrad's burial. Especially notable in Conrad's life is the cross present near Apollo's death bed, and the ivory crucifix that survived the ransacking at the home of Nicholas Bobrowski, a relative in Ukraine, who was notably mentioned in *A Personal Record*. He would also have been aware of the heavy stone monument with a stone cross atop his father's grave at Rakowicki Cemetery in Kraków. Finally, also significant is the prominence of the cross in "An Outpost of Progress" and its complete absence in "Heart of Darkness." As Conrad commented in the Author's Note to *Tales of Unrest*: "An Outpost of Progress" was "the lightest part of the loot I carried off from Central Africa, the main portion being of course 'The Heart of Darkness'" (*TU* vii).

This discussion contrasts Conrad's overt use of the cross in "An Outpost of Progress" with the much more aesthetic incorporation of the denial of European abandonment of the Christian ethic in "Heart of Darkness." Compare for example the final moments of the lives of Carlier, Kayerts, and Kurtz. Carlier cries out, shortly before Kayerts kills him: "You are a Slave-dealer. I am a slave-dealer. There's nothing but slave dealers in this cursed country" ("An Outpost of Progress," *TU* 110). Denouement continues quickly: Kayerts kills Carlier, and shortly before hanging himself from the cross, he cries out with a final ironic afterthought: "'*Help!* ... *My God!*' A shriek inhuman, vibrating and sudden, pierced like a sharp dart the white shroud of that land of sorrow" (115–16). Finally heard at the mist-enshrouded cross with Kayerts hanging by his belt is the screeching of the Congo steamer's whistle calling, ironically, Kayerts and his ivory back to civilization. Less tumultuous is the death of Kurtz, a manager of another great company in the heart of darkness who made it to a steamboat with the hope of escaping Africa. Kurtz's final utterance is prefaced by Marlow[6]: "He cried in a whisper at some image, at some vision - he cried out twice, a cry that was no more than a breath – 'The horror! The horror!'" ("Heart of Darkness," *YS* 149, see also 161). "Heart of Darkness" concludes not with the screeching whistle of a "tin-pot steamboat," but more aesthetically in the dark- -enshrouded parlor of the Intended with ivory keys encoffined by a closed grand piano keyboard cover, while the Intended is comforted by Marlow's lie about Kurtz, including a reference to Kurtz's belief inscribed in his magnum opus for the International Society for the Suppression of Savage Customs. The conclusion of "Heart of Darkness" cannot meliorate, however, the cry of Kayerts – "*Help!... My God!*" – before he desecrated the solitary cross at an outpost of progress by hanging himself from the arm of the upright cross, as Judas had hanged himself elsewhere after receiving thirty pieces of silver (rather than ivory) by betraying Jesus; neither can ivory piano keys enclosed in a mute grand piano replace the whispered cry of Kurtz: "The horror! The horror!" Neither did Conrad forget the meaning of the Cross as he concluded his tale of an outpost of progress in the heart of darkness, because the final words of Kayerts and Kurtz echo Christ's words as He died on the cross at Golgotha, the place of skulls: "'Eli, Eli, lama sabachthani?' that is to say, My God, my God, why hast thou forsaken me?" (Matt. 27:46).

The contrast of the death on the cross of Christ with the death of Kayerts on the cross and Kurtz on his way out of the Congo is stark. Matt. 27:51 records that, as Christ died, "the veil of the temple was rent in twain [...] and the earth did quake," intoning, among other things in Christian ethical narrative: the rending of the veil opens God's presence to all who believe. In contrast, immediately before Kurtz dies, Marlow comments, echoing the biblical phrase: "It was as though a veil had been rent" ("Heart of Darkness," YS 149), presenting "eternal condemnation" (157) and "eternal darkness" (159). Kayerts' earthbound death, on the other hand, concludes without Christ as he hangs from the cross elevated on a "high and narrow" grave, "irreverently [...] putting out a swollen tongue at his Managing Director" ("An Outpost of Progress," TU 117). In addition, in "Heart of Darkness" the word *Christian* appears only as allusion, as when Marlow comments that the rolling drum beats often heard in the distance is "perhaps with as profound a meaning as the sounds of bells in a Christian country" ("Heart of Darkness," YS 71). Furthermore, Marlow swears "By Jove" (76, 114, 117, 157), with occasional references in passing to the commonly used "God knows" and "Good God," not in a Christian ethical context but as afterthoughts. Finally, "soul" and "prayer," commonly associated with Christian thought, are transformed malevolently as Kurtz succumbs to evil in his heart of darkness: "the wilderness [...] sealed his soul to its own by the inconceivable ceremonies of some devilish initiation" (115); and the word "ivory" is in the air everywhere: "You would think they were praying to it" (76).[7]

Two Conrad Letters:
The Virgin Birth, the Commercialization
of Christmas, and the Christian Ethic in Literature

Among the thousands of letters that Conrad wrote to family, friends, and literary associates, two relate especially to the present discussion of the Christian ethic in the fiction that Conrad brought out of Africa. Written to Edward Garnett, his mentor, editor, and friend, Conrad's first letter doubts the narrative of the birth of Jesus, especially within the context of celebrating the Bethlehem legend with books primarily written to capitalize on gift-giving during the Christmas season: Conrad wrote that the "Bethleem legend" – primarily presented in the gospel of Luke 2:1-20 – is a fable that has become more a time for trade rather than worship, especially in the publishing business. His attitude is confirmed in "An Outpost of Progress" where the cross is substituted for "Christ," the latter of which is not mentioned in the lust for ivory. In the letter of 22 December 1902 Conrad complained that fiction more superficial than serious would curtail the sales of *Youth: A Narrative, and Two Other Stories*, which contains "Heart of Darkness." "Youth" was published in Edinburgh and London on 13 November 1902, and the publisher James Blackwood had "sent me word that the thing "Youth" sells decently if the Christmas does not kill it."

> It's strange how I always, from the age of fourteen, disliked the Christian religion, its doctrines, ceremonies and festivals. Presentiment that someday it will work my undoing. I suppose. Now it's quite on the cards that the Bethleem [Bethlehem] legend will kill the epic [...]. Hard. Isn't it. And the most galling feature is that nobody – not a single Bishop of them – believes in it. The business in the stable isn't convincing; whereas my atmosphere (vide reviews) can be positively breathed. (*CL* 2: 468-69)

In the second letter to Garnett, dated 23 February 1914, shortly after Garnett had just completed *Tolstoy: A Study*, and while his wife Constance was translating Tolstoy into English,

Conrad explained his critique about Tolstoy's over-indulgence in using Christianity.[8] He also returned to what he considered Christianity's mixed blessings.

> Dislike as definition of my attitude to Tolst:[oy] is but a rough and approximate term [...]. Moreover the base from which he starts – Christianity – is distasteful to me. I am not blind to its services but the absurd oriental fable from which it starts irritates me. Great, improving, softening, compassionate it may be but it has lent itself with amazing facility to cruel distortion and is the only religion which, with its impossible standards, has brought an infinity of anguish to innumerable souls – on this earth [...]. Why I should fly out like this at Xtianity which has given to mankind the beautiful Xmas pudding I don't know [...]. (5: 358)

Illness, Dying, and Death in Conrad's Life, Before and After "An Outpost of Progress"

Conrad's interest in death did not originate in the mists of the Congo in 1890; and it continued throughout his life and letters. His 1890 experience in the Congo was prefaced by illness and death – first with family members, and second, anticipating illness and death in the Congo in letters to Polish acquaintances. Two letters, among others, to Polish relatives and friends mention Conrad's concern about illness and death after he decided to leave the sea and assume command of a Congo river steamboat involved with the ivory trade. One letter, to Karol Zagórski, commented that the *Société Anonyme Belge pour le Commerce du Haut-Congo* often returned employees to Europe within six months because of illness: "Fever and dysentery! There are others who are sent home in a hurry at the end of a year, so that they shouldn't die in the Congo. God forbid. It would spoil the statistics which are excellent, you see" (1: 52). Again, in a letter to his aunt Marguerite Poradowska, he wrote, with a touch of melodrama:

> Dismal day [...]. Some haunting memories, some vague regrets, some still vaguer hopes. One doubts the future [...]. A little illusion,

many dreams, a rare flash of happiness, followed by disillusionment,
a little anger, and much suffering, and then the end. Peace! That is
the programme, and we must see this tragi-comedy to the end [...].
The screw turns. (51)

Not that he had been immune from death, even as a boy. In 1862,
at the age of five Conrad (né Korzeniowski) accompanied his
father, Apollo, and mother, Ewa, into exile from Poland to Vologda,
Russia. Harsh living conditions brought illness, resulting in
Ewa's death from tuberculosis in 1865, frequent illness with the
young Joseph, and Apollo's death in 1869. Obviously, Conrad's
childhood was not filled with Christmas happiness; rather the
cross of Christ, not the birth of Jesus, was more evident, as
for instance, when he followed the cross down the aisle of the
Church of St. Peter and Paul on the Grand Square in Kraków
at his father's funeral. And Conrad remembered the crucifix
in Apollo's sickroom, which Conrad's father memorialized in
a letter to a friend in 1866, referring to his chaotic life: "I have
lived through them [bad situations] with God given strength, not
my own [...]. By looking continually at the Cross I kept fortifying
my enfeebled soul."[9] One should not forget also Conrad's brush
with death by attempted suicide in 1878, shortly before he left
Marseilles to go to sea.[10]

Dying and death followed Conrad into the Congo. As he
began his trek from Matadi, Conrad had to care for Prosper
Harou,[11] providing quinine for Harou who was carried by
porters, slung from a hammock, as they skirted the Livingstone
Falls heading up-river; he looked after Georges-Antoine Klein,
too, the agent of the *Société Anonyme Belge pour le Commerce
du Haut-Congo* who died on the *Roi des Belges* on the down-
river journey. Conrad also recorded the horrors of colonial
exploitation of the natives and noted them in the "Congo
Diary": on 3 July 1890, he wrote: "Met an off[icer] of the State
inspecting; a few minutes afterwards saw at a camp[ing] place
the dead body of a Backongo. Shot? Horrid smell" (*LE* 163).
The next day, 4 July, he "saw another dead body lying by the path
in an attitude of meditative repose" (165). Again, on 29 July:

"On the road today passed a skeleton tied-up to a post. Also white man's grave – no name – heap of stones in the form of a cross" (169). Conrad, also ill with dysentery and malaria, was carried in a hammock part of his way back to Matadi. He also witnessed the abandoned villages along the Congo, a product of slavery and depraved conditions brought by the exploitation of the native residents by colonial enterprises, expressed fully in "An Outpost of Progress" and "Heart of Darkness." Conrad memorialized death and dying in the Congo in his literary record with the illnesses and deaths of Carlier, Kayerts, Kurtz, and the many African natives who, among other things, had their heads mounted on staves surrounding Kurtz's compound.

Dying and death also entered Conrad's life at sea, where he witnessed burials at sea, especially on the *Torrens,* where three people died on board during his tours of duty as first mate on the Australia run. Given his difficulties with spoken English, however, he might have let others read the ritual of burial that included passages from the *King James Bible.* Such an incident entered Conrad's fiction, because Captain Allistoun of *The Nigger of the "Narcissus"* turned the reading of the scripture over to Mr. Baker at James Wait's burial. Conrad's knowledge of burials at sea contributed to the creation of immediacy of scene at Wait's burial, like the detail as the sailmaker sewing the canvas shroud, weighted at the foot with an "anchor-shackle without its pin" and other pieces of scrap metal to assure proper descent to the bottom after he was dropped overboard (*NN* 157). Tossing men overboard was not always so ritualistic: the helmsman of the steamer carrying Marlow in the heart of Africa was tossed overboard quickly, lest cannibals who served on the steamboat began to eat him; casting the pilot overboard was followed by a hurried burial service later, involving the pilgrims who had earlier been firing their rifles into the African bush. Conrad carried his knowledge of the scripture included in ship-side burial services with him throughout life: Jessie Conrad reported that, when her husband was seriously ill for two months in 1910, the burial service was on his lips: "He seemed to breathe once [...] a cold sweat came over him, and he lay on his back faintly murmuring the words of the burial service" (144).[12] Among the scripture committed to Conrad's memory were the "De Profundis" (Ps. 130), and 1 Cor. 15, which address the resurrection of the dead both from the depths of the ocean and on earth, accompanied by the promise of eternal life. In contrast, the silence accompanying the lack of any Christian reference when Kayerts hangs himself from the cross in "An Outpost of Progress" speaks eloquently to Christians who read Conrad's account. And for any Christian who might believe in a literal meaning of the resurrection of the dead, note that the cross capable of carrying Kayerts' weight is on top of an unopened grave, not as a headstone.

Congo Missionaries, Converting Africans, Caring for the Ill, Charting Rivers, Killing Elephants, and Using a New Testament on Conrad

Conrad met Christian missionaries occasionally as he travelled in central Africa because missionaries had preceded him there, having established stations along the Congo – often at villages previously occupied primarily by the Backongo people, and which were later pillaged and denuded by colonial exploiters like those of the *Société Anonyme Belge pour le Commerce du Haut-Congo*. For example, George Grenfell became a primary representative of the Baptist Missionary Society in central Africa. He established mission stations along the Congo, at or near native Bakongo villages.[13] On the way, Grenfell charted the Congo River and its estuaries – such as the Kasai River; and others made charts associated with Grenfell's maps to assist in navigating up and down the river.

Conrad's "Up-River Book," published with "Conrad's Diary," is primarily a series of notes that Conrad made to assist when he assumed command of a river steamer on subsequent journeys – voyages that he did not make. Conrad also identified locations of missions once he boarded the *Roi des Belges* as supernumerary for the up-river journey. A reference in "Up-River Book" to a Catholic mission on the north bank of the river – in the

French Congo at Kwa Mouth – indicates how mission stations rather than missionaries fit into Conrad's Congo experience.[14] Conrad at this point was travelling north of Stanley Pool, and stopped at the Catholic mission for an hour and a half on the up-river passage. By doing so, the steamboat's crew took a break from the turbulence of Bankap (Bankab) point at Kwa Mouth. Conrad identifies the river as the "Kassai" in "Up-River Book," noting the location with a series of roman numerals keyed to charts belonging to the *Société*, and which were developed from Grenfell's maps.[15] A portion of the entry on page 21 of "Up-River Book" indicates the complexity of Conrad's attempt to learn quickly the minutiae of Congo travel necessary for a commander of a river steamer to know. The "XII" refers to a chart created from Grenfell's map-making excursions:

> XII Entrance to Kassai rather broad. On S[th] side a bright beach with
> a spreading dead tree above it mark the mouth.
> At the Cath[oli][c] mission moor along-side the head of the beach. –
> From P[oin]t S' to Mission – NNE. 1[h] [hour]
> Made fast at 1[h] pm.
> Point XX bore N 5°
> Left the mission at 2 ½ --
> In the bight between the miss[ion]
> And P[oin][t] XX a rocky ledge – Of[f]
> P[oin]t XX a stony ridge partially
> Cover[e][d]
> From XX at high water –
> P[oin][t] TOff P[oin][t] XX at 3 [h] 20[m] [minute] making it
> Bore about 2h from the P[oin]t S'
> NbyE 1/2E
> At 3[h] 20[m] pm.[16]

Notations like these continue in pencil for 93 pages in the small notebook that Conrad kept with the "Congo Diary." Page 21 of "Up-River Book" is included here to indicate what might have been, at least in part, on Conrad's mind when he met the Reverend Samuel Norvell Lapsley, a Southern Presbyterian Church missionary attached to the American Baptist Mission in the Congo. Conrad met the Reverend Lapsley on his down-river voyage when he was concerned not only about navigating the Congo, but also hoping to save his life from the dysentery and malaria that were ravaging his body. The Reverend Lapsley had other things on his mind, because he had been sent to central Africa to save the heathens. During that effort, he met Conrad, on whom Lapsley apparently wanted to try his Presbyterian and Baptist prayer group expertise. But more about that after two additional missionaries are introduced.

Conrad knew the first reverend, Percy Comber – stationed at the Sutuli Baptist mission located inland beside a cataract on the Livingstone Falls – only because Mrs. Annie Comber entertained Conrad at an overnight stop on 26 June: "Hospitable reception by Mrs. Comber – All the missio[naries] absent." Annie Comber, incidentally, a recent arrival at the Sutili mission would be dead before Conrad returned to Europe: contracting fever quickly, she died at Banana (19 December 1890) while awaiting a ship to carry her away from Africa.[17]

The second, the Reverend Charles E. Ingham, stationed at Banza Manteka, represented the Livingstone Inland Mission (otherwise, American Baptist Mission) and was one of the first missionaries who reached Stanley Pool (December 1881). Among other things Ingham converted Africans to Christianity, translated Christian hymns into the Kikongo language and was – according to a report that the Reverend Lapsley[18] sent back to his sponsors in America – a great killer of elephants who had bagged fifty for ivory by the time Lapsley arrived in 1890. Cosmic irony must have accompanied Conrad's use of irony in central Africa: Ingham was killed by an elephant (456n124:21) on an expedition to Lukunga. If reports back to America like Lapsley's are true – Ingham combined hymn singing with killing elephants for ivory – they give credence to Conrad's observation in "Heart of Darkness": "The word ivory rang in the air [...]. You would think they were praying to it" ("Heart of Darkness," YS 76).

Conversion, not ivory, was the primary commitment to missionaries in the Congo, especially the Reverend Lapsley, an evangelical Presbyterian of Scottish-Irish descent.[19] Lapsley arrived in Africa proclaiming the message of evangelical

Presbyterian clergy and singing constantly hymns of faith. He reported from Manyanga, a village on the path around Livingstone Fall: "I managed to get a small and somewhat interested audience to listen to a summary of gospel truth. They took more kindly to me singing. 'Sing them over again to me' and 'Nothing but the blood of Jesus'. 'Menga ma Jesus Kaka.'"[21] Lapsley also reported from Banza Manteka: "The church [...] has between three hundred and four hundred members, though nearly a thousand have claimed conversion. The interest, *though not at revival heat*, [italics mine] continues."[22] An evangelical Presbyterian's "revival heat" approach to convert hearers to Christianity might not have appealed to a Polish Catholic gentleman recently naturalized as a citizen of the United Kingdom who had served briefly as the captain of a Belgian Congo River steamer, had participated in and knew well Anglican rituals for the burial of the dead at sea, and had travelled and communicated with many people from various cultural traditions for more than two decades. The Reverend Lapsley knew about Conrad only what he communicated to an aunt in America; but some of that was wrong. Lapsley did know, however, that Conrad was ill, and suspected that he might need to be converted. As the tone of Lapsley's letter suggests, he was willing to try "revival heat" on Conrad: "[a] captain of an English (*sic.*) steamer, is sick in a room at the other end of the court [...]. I look across the fruit and palm trees right into his window. He is a gentlemanly fellow. An English Testament on his table furnishes a handle I hope to use on him."[23] Whether or not Conrad had to endure Lapsley's proselytizing, Conrad knew the routine from somewhere. Witness the immediacy of scene when the religious fanatic Podmore tries to save the immortal soul of James Wait in *The Nigger of the "Narcissus."*[24] Without hesitation Podmore fell to his knees to pray and – when Wait was too ill to join Podmore on his knees – Podmore arose to pray for Wait. Podmore believed that he was doing God's will when he saved the crew by providing coffee for the *Narcissus'* crew during the storm. But most of all Podmore wanted to save the soul of James Wait who, shortly before dying and anticipating burial at sea, cried out "Overboard ... I ... My God" with an intensity like Kayerts crying "Help! My God!", and Kurtz whispering "The horror! The horror!" Note the phrases with "revival heat" that are associated with Podmore: "Providence," "born again" (*NN* 63); "contemplated the secret of the hereafter" (115).

Disgusted by Podmore, Wait says "Don't care damn!" And Podmore admonishes: "Swear! [...] in the very jaws [of hell]! Don't you see the everlasting fire ... don't you feel it? Blind, chockfull of sin! [...]. Jimmie, let me save you" (116). Finally exasperated, Wait cries out: "Keep him away from me" (119). Conrad expressed ironically and judgmentally the problem with Podmore, who believed that he was "the object of a special mercy for the saving of our unholy lives. Fundamentally he was right, no doubt; but he need not have been so offensively positive about it" (83).

Christianity "has lent itself with amazing facility to cruel distortion"

In his letter to Garnett in 1914, Conrad expressed his disgust with approaches to Christianity demonstrated by people like Podmore, and perhaps also by people like Lapsley: Christianity "has lent itself with amazing facility to cruel distortion and is the only religion which, with its impossible standards, has brought an infinity of anguish to innumerable souls – on this earth" (*CL* 5: 358). Conrad's approach to Christianity differed greatly on 8 October 1923, when his letter to Gordon Gardiner confronted the question about Christian belief with humorous and ironic attention. Gardiner was the secretary of the National Club in Whitehall Gardens, an organization that required acceptance of the discipline of the Church of England to become a member. It would be impossible to join, Conrad wrote, because it required, among other things, an affirmation of "the Protestant principles of the Constitution," that the "Holy Scriptures" be maintained in British education, and that the *Authorized Bible* is "the only infallible standard of faith and morals" (8: 190n2). Conrad declined the invitation genially and ironically: "I cannot very well belong to this Club by the mere fact that I was born a R[oman] C[atholic] and though dogma sits lightly on me I have never renounced that form of Christian religion." He continued that the requirement stated in the rules of the National Club – to be a member of the Protestant Church of England – would mean that signing membership papers "would be like renouncing the faith of my fathers."

Conrad continued that he had also declined an invitation to join a Roman Catholic club in England, which required its members to "engage themselves with all their might and power to work for the restoration of the temporal power of the Pope. Conceive you that imbecility!" That imbecility, probably like additional imbecilities that he had witnessed in the Congo, prompted him to conclude with an ironic lament about his eternal life:

> I am afraid that I am a lost soul [...]. So you can see now I have got to stand between the two [Protestantism and Catholicism], a prey to the first inferior devil that may come along. My only hope of escaping the eternal fires is my utter insignificance. I shall lie low on the Judgment Day, and will probably be overlooked. (190 91)

There is no cross, perpendicular or otherwise, at Conrad's grave to mark where he is buried in consecrated ground after a Catholic funeral mass at St. Thomas Church in Canterbury. Rather, inscribed on the granite obelisk are two verses from Edmund Spenser's *The Faerie Queene:* "Sleepe after toyle, port after stormie seas, / Ease after warre, death after life does greatly please." As Frederick Karl notes, Conrad selected the passage with "grim irony," because "it is spoken by Despair, and counsels suicide."[25] Two verses in the nine-line Spenserian stanza precede the inscription on Conrad's tombstone: "Is not short payne well borne, that bringes long ease, / And layes the soule to sleep in quiet grave?" Spenser's lines neither affirm nor imply an afterlife. Conrad's selection of the inscription from Spenser perhaps connotes skepticism about the significance of Christ's crucifixion and the promise of resurrection as he had connoted doubt in the letter to Garnett about the meaning of the Virgin birth of Jesus.

In selecting the passage from *The Faerie Queene* spoken by Despair in the context of Despair's reference to suicide, Conrad was perhaps also thinking about the traditional Catholic approach to suicide that Conrad attempted in Marseilles in 1878, and which he alludes to in passing in "Heart of Darkness" about suicide among Africans who were forced into slavery or servitude. He had written to Garnett about "cruel distortion" by Christians whose "impossible standards" have "brought an infinity of anguish to innumerable souls." His skepticism in 1902 about the Virgin birth – when he was concerned about the marketing of the "Heart of Darkness" volume during the Christmas season, beginning with the Feast of the Immaculate Conception on 8 December – was tempered by his affirmation in the letter to Gardiner in 1923 that he will not abandon the faith of his fathers. Finally, as Conrad's life ended, he accepted last rites, a funeral with a Catholic mass, and burial in consecrated ground with a granite obelisk identifying his grave. Christianity survives in Conrad's world despite the excesses of evangelists like Podmore and Lapsley, the failures of Kayerts and Kurtz, and the afterthoughts of people like the director of the great trading company at outposts of progress.

NOTES

[1]   England imported about 500 tons of ivory annually. Tusks ranged up to 165 pounds each, but a pair of tusks averaged 28 pounds. About 40,000 elephants were slaughtered annually for English needs. Cutlery production alone required 12,000 elephants. Statistics come from *Stanley and Africa* (381-82). See also Stevens "A tall cross" 100n8.

[2]   The word "Congo" is not stated in "An Outpost of Progress," but is implied everywhere, not only by context in common knowledge of European recollection, especially recorded by Henry Stanley in *Through the Dark Continent* and various volumes – a series of reports originally published in news journals throughout the Western world, and which Conrad read as they were initially published. The location of the Congo is also confirmed by the life of Conrad, explicitly recorded in the "Congo Diary."

[3]   Conrad arrived at Boma, on the African coast, on 12 June 1890, and left Africa on 4 December 1890.

⁴   Quotations are from the *Authorized* (*King James*) *Bible*, the official biblical text of the Church of England during Conrad's lifetime. As will be noted below, Conrad had the New Testament of the English Bible by his bed as he was cared by a Presbyterian missionary in the Congo in 1890.

⁵   Letters cited here are to Edward Garnett, a friend and editor for many years, dated 22 December 1902 and 23 February 1914. They are discussed with more context below (*CL* 2: 468-69; *CL* 5: 358).

⁶   Marlow is, of course, in the opinion of many, an alter ego of Conrad, whose experience in central Africa is transformed into fiction in "Heart of Darkness."

⁷   For a further discussion of this, see Stevens "A tall cross," especially 88-92.

⁸   Constance Garnett (1861-1946) was a prolific translator of Russian literature – especially Leo Tolstoy, Fyodor Dostoevsky, and Anton Chekhov – into English, and was central in introducing their works to many English readers. Among other Tolstoy's works, she had published *War and Peace* (1904) and *The Kingdom of God is Within You* (1894). The latter volume is devoted to Tolstoy's religious and philosophical thoughts.

⁹   For a more extensive discussion of the cross in Conrad's life, see Stevens "A tall cross" 82. Conrad would return to a crucifix – an ivory crucifix – in *A Personal Record*, when he refers to the sacking of the residence of a relative, Nicholas B – in a Ukrainian rebellion: "the only one solitary thing [...] left whole was a small ivory crucifix, which remained hanging on the wall" (*PR* 62). Conrad was also aware of the heavy stone cross on his father's grave in the Rakowicki Cemetery in Kraków.

¹⁰   Stevens' "A tall cross" (82-83) provides a discussion of the context of Conrad's attempted suicide.

¹¹   Prosper Harou (1855-1893) was a minor officer for the *Société Anonyme Belge pour le Commerce du Haut-Congo* who had travelled with Conrad to Africa and accompanied him on the trek from Matadi to Kinshasa. Harou's illness delayed Conrad's arrival at Stanley Pool.

¹²   Dwight Purdy also mentions this in the context of Conrad's presence at burials at sea (197).

¹³   The Bakongo, a branch of the Bantu African people, were the primary occupants of the lands along the lower Congo River.

¹⁴   A French government station existed near the Catholic mission at Kwamouth, where the Kasai River joined the waters of the Mbihé and Mfini rivers to form the Kwa. The turbulent waters at Bankap (Bankab) Point required more than usual care negotiating the current. Conrad's attention to detail in his notes referring to the charts based on Grenfell's Congo River maps are fascinating in their complexity, if confusing in their interpretation. See Stevens and Stape's edition of Conrad's *Last Essays* 144-46.

¹⁵   Grenfell was also active in other ways: an early Congo riverboat, *Peace*, sponsored by the Baptist Missionary Society, was used primarily for charting the Congo River and its estuaries and servicing Baptist missions along the Congo. *Peace* was once appropriated by colonial interests to wage war against

the Bakongo. Grenfell, who also commissioned two additional river steamers, has been the subject of various studies, and is mentioned here in passing to suggest his presence in Conrad's experience in central Africa.

[16] Copied as it appears in Stevens and Stape's edition of Conrad's *Last Essays* 146. Conrad's original notebook is housed in the Houghton Library at Harvard. Capital letters, of course, refer to directions: NNE is north/north/east.

[17] Death haunted missionaries as well as Conrad. The Reverend Percy Comber lived only 30 years (1862-92); his brother, the Reverend Thomas James Comber, died at 33 (1852-87). Accompanying Comber at Sutuli was the Reverend Holman Bentley, who had translated the New Testament into the Kikongo language, and wrote *Pioneering on the Congo* (1900). Bentley lasted fifty years (1855-1905). See Stevens and Stape's edition of Conrad's *Last Essays* (130n458; n514; n515).

[18] See Lapsley 82. Lapsley is an excellent source for the life of evangelical Christians in the Congo. He joined the ranks of missionaries who did not live long, dying during his 26th year (1866-92), after two years in the Congo. Lapsley was one of the many missionaries who sent reports back to sponsoring organizations in America and Europe – similar, perhaps to the one Kurtz prepared for the International Society for the Suppression of Savage Customs. Another report from Africa, presenting an affirmative record of Congo missionaries, is that by Edmund F. Merriam, *The American Baptist Missionary Union and Its Mission* (1897).

[19] Lapsley 12-13.

[20] Lapsley 88. Letters and reports recorded in Lapsley's hastily written and edited volume are filled with errors in dating and, while Lapsley's evangelical fervor is evident throughout the volume, some dates and other details inserted within the time frames cited in chapter headings are suspect. In a letter to his aunt, Lapsley identifies Conrad as Russian, not Polish. Adam Hochschild relies on Lapsley's narrative in *King Leopold's Ghost* (1998, 140), where he records Lapsley's contact with Conrad. "Nothing but the blood of Jesus" was written by Robert Lowry in 1876. Perhaps "Menga ma Jesus Kaka" was a translation by Ingham.

[21] Hochschild reports that Lapsley and Conrad crossed paths two times in 1890 (153).

[22] Lapsley 66.

[243] Lapsley 83.

[24] For a further discussion of Conrad's association with Christian missionaries in the Congo, see Stevens ("A tall cross" 86), with its references to annotations to the "Congo Diary" in *Last Essays* and several records to journals kept by Christian missionaries who staffed various outposts of progress along the Congo.

[25] Karl 911.

WORKS CITED

Bentley, Holman. *Pioneering on the Congo*. 2 vols. Oxford: Religious Tract Society, 1897. Print.

Conrad, Jessie. *Joseph Conrad and His Circle*. New York: Dutton, 1935. Print.

Conrad, Joseph. *Last Essays*. Ed. Harold Ray Stevens and J. H. Stape. Cambridge: Cambridge UP, 2010. Print.

Hochschild, Adam. *King Leopold's Ghost: A Study of Greed, Terror, and Heroism in Colonial Africa*. Boston: Houghton, 1998. Print.

Karl, Frederick. *Joseph Conrad: The Three Lives*. New York: Farrar, 1979. Print.

Lapsley, Samuel Norvell. *Life and Letters of Samuel Norvell Lapsley. Missionary to the Congo Valley, West Africa. 1866-1892*. Richmond: Whittet, 1892. Print.

Merriam, Edmund F. *The American Baptist Missionary Union and Its Missions*. Boston: American Baptist Missionary Union, 1897. Print.

Purdy, Dwight H. *Joseph Conrad's Bible*. Norman: U of Oklahoma P, 1984. Print.

Scofield, C. J., ed. *Scofield's Reference Bible*. 2nd ed. Oxford: Oxford UP, 1917. Print.

Stanley and Africa. London: Scott, [n.a.]. Print.

Stanley, Henry Morton. *Through the Dark Continent*. London: Sampson, 1878. Print.

Stape, J. H. *Conrad's Congo: Joseph Conrad's Expedition to the Congo Free State, 1890*. London: The Folio Society, 2013. Print.

Stevens, Harold Ray. "Conrad, Slavery, and the African Ivory Trade in the 1890s". *Approaches to Teaching Conrad's "Heart of Darkness" and "The Secret Sharer."* Ed. Hunt Hawkins and Brian W. Shaffer. New York: Modern Language Association, 2002. 22-30. Print.

---. "'A tall cross much out of the perpendicular': Some Christian Contexts in Conrad's Life, Letters, and 'Heart of Darkness.'" *Joseph Conrad's Authorial Self: Polish and Other*. Ed. Wiesław Krajka. Lublin: Maria Curie-Sklodowska UP; New York: Columbia UP, 2018. 79-104. Print. Vol. 27 of *Conrad: Eastern and Western Perspectives*. Ed. Wiesław Krajka. 30 vols. to date. 1992- .

Index of Non-Fictional Names

Achebe, Chinua 90, 91, 96, 99, 111, 112, 145, 164, 166, 245, 254, 256-58
Acheraïou, Amar 8, 9, 14, 82-85, 111-13, 140, 142, 149, 150, 156, 164-66, 233, 252, 257, 258, 262-65, 273, 286-88
Ackroyd, Peter 165, 166
Addyman, Mary 115
Adorno, Theodor W. 7, 8, 10, 145, 163, 164, 166
Aeschylus 239, 241, 242, 253, 258
Allen, Richard 233
Anderegg, Michael 203, 232, 233
Arens, William 100, 112, 113
Aristotle 1, 3, 14, 97, 272, 273
Atkins, Kim 197, 198
Austen, Jane 118, 139

Bacon, Francis 7, 12, 237-50, 252, 253, 255-59
Bakhtin, Mikhail 46, 83, 85
Bakunin, Mikhail 8
Bandyopadhyay, Bibhutibhusan 279
Bandyopadhyay, Manik 279, 280, 289
Bandyopadhyay, Tarashankar 279, 289
Barker, Francis 114
Barr, Charles 233
Barthes, Roland 245, 257, 259
Batchelor, John 83, 85
Baxter, Katherine Isobel 257, 259
Bazin, André 206
Beard, Peter 239, 240, 242, 257, 259
Bennett, Gillian 112, 113
Bentley, Holman 308, 309
Bergo, Bettina 198

Bernstein, Joshua 10
Bhaduri, Satinath 279
Białas, Zbigniew 86
Bismarck, Otto von 84
Blackburn, William 139, 142
Blackwood, James 296
Blackwood, William 142
Bobrowski, Nicholas 293
Bohlmann, Otto 139, 142
Bordat, Francis 232, 233
Bourdin, Martial 147, 148, 151, 152, 154-56, 161-65
Bowlby, Rachel 288
Boyd, David 201, 232, 234
Brillat-Savarin, Jean Anthelme 110, 113
Brudney, Daniel 139, 142
Buddha 58, 109
Busza, Andrzej 81, 85
Butte, George 82, 85

Caesar, Julius 93
Calhoun, Dave 233
Carabine, Keith 82, 85, 140, 142, 267, 287, 288
Carretta, Vincent 113
Carroll-Najder, Halina 87, 144
Carter, Alan 146, 164, 166
Caserio, Robert L. 197, 198
Castellani, Valentina 256, 259
Cavell, Stanley 206, 207, 232, 233
Chabrol, Claude 209, 232, 235
Chamberlain, Austen 240, 242, 257
Charlesworth, James 112, 113
Chattopadhyay, Bankimchandra 279
Chattopadhyay, Saratchandra 279
Chaucer, Geoffrey 118, 139, 144

Chaudhuri, Supriya 279, 280, 287, 288
Chekhov, Anton 115, 307
Christ, Jesus 291, 293, 295, 296, 298, 303, 306, 308
Clark, Kathleen C. 241, 259
Clark, Samuel 146, 164, 166
Clarke, Randolph 139, 142
Clémot, Hugo 232, 233
Cohen, Paula Marantz 202, 228, 232, 233
Colebrook, Claire 112, 113
Coleridge, Samuel Taylor 101
Collins, George 288
Collits, Terry 257-59, 262, 263, 286, 288
Comber, Annie 302
Comber, Percy 302, 308
Comber, Thomas James 308
Conrad, Jessie 82, 121, 140, 142, 299, 309
Cooper, Christopher 140, 142
Crémona, Laëtitia 11, 12, 232, 234, 286
Crisp, Roger 119, 139, 142
Critchley, Simon 112, 113
Cronin, Ciaran P. 15
Cunninghame Graham, Robert Bontine 75, 112, 132
Curle, Richard 82, 123, 147, 164, 166

Dąbrowski, Marian 81, 85
Dalmia, Vasudha 288
Damrosch, David 114
Daniels, Rebecca 257, 259
Darwin, Charles 92, 93
DeKoven, Marianne 256, 259
Delesalle-Nancey, Catherine 11, 82, 85, 140, 142, 257, 259
Deleuze, Gilles 5, 7, 14, 206, 238, 239, 243, 247, 256, 257, 259
DeMille, Barbara 118, 142
Derrida, Jacques 1, 4, 7, 8, 11, 13, 14, 36, 39, 92, 93, 103, 108, 110, 111, 113, 115, 271-74, 276, 278, 281, 287, 288
Dickens, Charles 115, 174, 197
Diderot, Denis 7, 80
DiSanto, Michael John 136, 141, 142
Domsky, Darren 137, 139, 142
Dostoevsky, Fyodor 122, 140-43, 201, 307
Dowden, Bradley 198
Duncan, David 114

Eagleton, Terry 283, 288
Eisenstein, Sergei 204, 206
Eliot, T. S. 1, 15, 89, 111, 113, 152, 165, 166, 239-41, 259
Ellison, David 1, 14
Enoch, David 139, 142
Epstein, Hugh 270, 287, 288
Equiano, Olaudah 89, 107, 112, 113
Erdinast-Vulcan, Daphna 33, 34, 82, 85, 140, 142
Eribon, Didier 5
Evans, Robert C. 113, 258, 288

Faulkner, William 254, 259
Feinberg, Joel 119, 139, 142
Fielding, Henry 7, 80
Fincham, Gail 288
Firchow, Peter 90, 91, 99, 111-13, 257, 259
Fisher, M. F. K. 113
Fleishman, Avrom 202, 232, 234
Ford, Ford Madox 82
Foucault, Michel 1, 5, 7, 15, 112
Francis, Mark 259

Gardiner, Gordon 304, 306
Gardiner, Reginald 214
Garnett, Constance 142, 296, 307
Garnett, Edward 122, 123, 142, 296, 304-07
Gauguin, Paul 117, 120, 125
Ghatak, Ritwik 287
Gibbard, Paul 165, 166

Gill, David 99, 111-13
GoGwilt, Christopher 133, 141, 143
Goldman, Emma 160
Gomulicki, Wiktor 81, 85
Goodenough, Jerry 232, 234
Gottlieb, Sidney 234
Gouveia, Steven S. 235
Greaney, Michael 84, 86, 111-13, 258, 259
Grenfell, George 300, 301, 307
Griffin, Nicholas 140, 143
Guerard, Albert 256, 259
Guest, Kristen 112, 113
Guimond, James 152, 165, 166

Habermas, Jürgen 14, 15
Haggard, Henry Rider 89
Hampson, Robert 257, 259
Hanna, Nathan 139, 143
Haraway, Donna 91-93, 97, 111, 113
Hardy, Thomas 118, 139
Harou, Prosper 298, 307
Harpham, Geoffrey Galt 5, 14, 15
Harris, Robert 153, 154, 165, 166
Harrison, Martin 257, 259
Hawkins, Hunt 309
Hawthorn, Jeremy 84, 86, 257, 259, 277, 287, 288
Hawthorne, Nathaniel 105
Hay, Eloise Knapp 84, 86
Heidegger, Martin 4
Hiddleston, Jane 286-88
Higdon, David Leon 84, 86, 233, 234
Higgins, Thomas 10, 11, 233
Higgitt, Rebekah 152, 165, 167
Hirsch, Pam 213, 214, 219, 232-34
Hitchcock, Alfred 7, 11, 12, 152, 201-04, 208-31, 232-35
Hochman, Stanley 235
Hochschild, Adam 308, 309
Hollander, Rachel 14, 15, 82, 86, 118, 143
Holquist, Michael 85
Hopkins, Robert 139, 143
Howard, Richard 259

Howe, Irving 141, 143, 147, 164, 167
Hulme, Peter 114
Hunter, Allan 15, 83, 86, 93, 111, 113, 141, 143
Huston, John 201

İçöz, Nursel 85, 87, 234
Ingham, Charles E. 302, 308
Irwin, Terence 14, 15, 83, 86
Ishii-Gonzáles, Sam 233, 234
Iversen, Margaret 114

James, Henry 97, 113, 123
Jameson, Fredric 246, 249, 253, 257, 259, 277, 287, 288
Jean-Aubry, Georges 82, 86
Jowett, Benjamin 114
Joyce, James 277

Kaczynski, Theodore John 152, 153, 166
Kant, Immanuel 25, 39, 82, 86, 102, 112, 113
Kaplan, Carola 141, 143
Karl, Frederick 305, 308, 309
Karloff, Boris 214
Kermode, Frank 84, 86, 233, 234
Kilgour, Maggie 112, 113
Kimbrough, Robert 289
Kipling, Rudyard 82, 113
Klein, Georges-Antoine 298
Knowles, Owen 118, 140, 143
Korzeniowski, Apollo 293, 298
Kovaleski, Serge 153
Kracauer, Siegfried 206
Krajka, Wiesław 14, 15, 81, 83, 85, 86, 234, 262, 286, 288, 289, 309
Kropotkin, Peter 8, 146, 159-61, 163, 165-67
Kurczaba, Alex S. 81, 86

Laches (General) 28
Lackey, Michael 118, 143

Lacoue-Labarthe, Philippe 258, 260
Laden, Osama bin 153, 154, 166
Lange, Attie De   85, 288, 289
Lapsley, Samuel Norvell   301-04, 306, 308, 309
Larabee, Mark D. 286
Larson, Jil 139, 143
Latus, Andrew 126, 128, 139, 140, 143
Lawtoo, Nidesh   260
Leavis, F. R. 89, 111, 113, 257, 260
Lee, Michael 112, 113
Leopold II (King) 254, 308, 309
Levi, Primo 289
Levinas, Emmanuel 1, 4, 7, 8, 13-15, 36, 38, 39, 44, 82, 86, 93, 94, 96, 97, 103, 109-12, 114, 118, 144, 171, 181-83, 198, 261, 265, 268, 271, 286, 287, 289
Lingis, Alphonso 15, 114, 198, 289
Lispunov, Vadim 85
Lombroso, Cesare 153, 165, 175
Lothe, Jakob 84, 86, 140, 143, 147, 150, 164, 167, 198
Lowenstein, Adam 230, 233, 234
Lowry, Robert 308

Macfie, A. L. 144
Madden, Fred 15, 83, 86
Maisonnat, Claude 195, 198, 260
Mallabarman, Adwaita 7, 269, 279, 282, 283, 285, 289
Mallet, Marie-Louise 113
Mallios, Peter 122, 140, 143, 153, 165, 167
Marmor, Andrei 139, 142
Martinière, Nathalie 12, 197, 198, 260
Maugham, William Somerset 231
Maurier, Daphne Du 202
Maynard, Katherine Kearney 153, 165, 166
McGilligan, Patrick 209, 232, 234
McKay, Ian 167
Meldrum, David S. 142

Merriam, Edmund F. 308, 309
Meyers, Jeffrey 82, 86, 125, 140, 143
Mickiewicz, Adam 81
Mitchell, J. Allan 139, 144
Mooney, Timothy 114
Moore, Gene M. 234
Moran, Dermot   114
Morel, E. 254
Morf, Gustav 81, 86
Moser, Thomas   141, 144
Mulry, David 147, 151, 164, 165, 167, 233, 234
Murnau, Friedrich Wilhelm 204
Muybridge, Eadweard 241

Nagel, Thomas 119, 120, 125, 130-32, 139, 141, 144
Najder, Zdzisław 81, 86, 121, 125, 140, 144
Neiva, Diana 234, 235
Nelkin, Dana K. 117, 120, 126, 132, 133, 137, 140-42, 144
Nettlau, Max 162, 166, 167
Newbolt, Henry 82
Ngugi wa Thiong'o 85, 288
Nicias (General) 28
Nietzsche, Friedrich 82, 85, 87, 118, 142, 239
Niland, Richard   140, 144, 167
Noble, Edward   97
Norcia, Megan 112, 114

O'Rourke, Chris   234
Oser, Lee 1, 15
Osteen, Mark 233, 234
Ottinger, Didier 243, 248, 256, 257, 260

Paccaud-Huguet, Josiane 188, 198, 199, 259, 260
Palmer, R. Barton 201, 209, 231, 232, 234
Panagopoulos, Nic 83, 87, 165, 167
Panichas, George A. 14, 15, 82, 87, 140, 144, 147, 164, 167

Park, Mungo 89
Pauly, Véronique 170, 196, 199
Peppiatt, Michael 239, 240, 242, 254, 256-58, 260
Petrie, Duncan 232, 234
Pettey, Homer B. 209, 232, 234
Phillips, Jerry 112, 114
Phillips, Temple 139, 144
Pinker, J. B. 121, 149
Plato 1, 3, 14, 15, 28, 83, 86, 102, 105, 112, 114
Poradowska, Marguerite 297
Prasad, G. J. V. 289
Prickett, David 181, 198, 199
Purdy, Anthony 114
Purdy, Dwight 307, 309

Quincey, Thomas de 110

Rabinow, Paul 15
Raja, Masood Ashraf 90, 114
Rancière, Jacques 257, 258, 260
Raphael, D. D. 144
Ratibor, Stephan 259
Rawls, Christina 234, 235
Ray, Subhadeep 12, 13, 286-89
Read, Rupert 232, 234
Rice, Philip 289
Richards, Norvin 133, 134
Ricoeur, Paul 1, 5, 7, 11, 14, 15, 36, 39, 170, 171, 181, 183, 186, 187, 189, 196-99
Rives, Rochelle L. 165, 167, 191, 198, 199
Rizzuto, Nicole 141, 144
Roberts, Andrew Michael 14, 15, 83, 87, 141, 144
Rohmer, Eric 209, 232, 235
Romanick Baldwin, Debra 83, 87, 90, 111, 114, 264, 265, 286, 289
Ross, Stephen 258, 260, 264, 286, 289
Rossetti, Christina 110
Rothman, William 224, 229, 233, 235
Russell, Bertrand 123-25, 140, 143

Ryall, Tom 213, 214, 233, 235

Sadana, Rashmi 288
Sagan, Eli 112, 114
Saha, Nandini 286
Said, Edward 102, 112, 114, 275, 287, 289
Sanders, Steven M. 209, 232, 234
Sanderson, E. L. 84
Sartre, Jean-Paul 89, 111, 114, 163
Sati, Someshwar 289
Sceats, Sarah 114
Schneider-Rebozo, Lissa 141, 144
Schopenhauer, Arthur 14, 15, 42, 83, 87, 118
Scofield, C. J. 309
Sen, Amartya 266, 287, 289
Sengupta, Ashok 286
Sewlall, Harry 83, 87, 100, 112, 114
Shaffer, Brian W. 309
Shakespeare, William 114
Shelley, Mary 101
Sherry, Norman 140, 144
Shulevitz, Judith 153, 165, 167
Simmons, Allan H. 85, 96, 105, 112, 114, 143, 198, 199, 255, 257, 258, 260, 261
Singer, Irving 208, 232, 235
Sinnerbrink, Robert 206, 207, 232, 235
Slemon, Stephen 112, 114
Słowacki, Juliusz 81
Smith, Adam 119, 139, 144
Smith, Daniel W. 259
Smith, David R. 124, 140, 144
Socrates 28, 29, 268
Spencer, Herbert 92, 93, 100, 112, 114
Spenser, Edmund 305
Spivak, Gayatri Chakravorty 82, 87
Spoto, Donald 209, 232, 233, 235
Stanley, Henry Morton 89, 107, 114, 306, 309
Stape, John H. 85, 114, 144, 199, 307-09

Statman, Daniel 144
Sterne, Laurence 7, 80, 140, 195
Sterritt, David 227, 233, 235
Stevens, Harold Ray 13, 306-09
Stevenson, Robert 214
Stoker, Bram 110
Sylvester, David 242, 256, 257, 260
Szittya, Penn R. 84, 87, 128, 140, 144

Tagore, Rabindranath 279
Taylor, Charles 196
Techio, Jônadas 232, 235
Tenenbaum, David 83, 87
Tiedemann, Rolf 166
Tolstoy, Leo 293, 296, 307
Truffaut, François 201, 209, 230, 232, 233, 235
Tyrrel, William 213

Vertov, Dziga 227
Virgil 192

Wake, Paul 197, 199
Watt, Ian 83, 87, 141, 144, 198, 276, 287, 289
Watts, Cedric 257, 260
Waugh, Patricia 289

Wells, H. G. 82
White, Andrea 143
White, Hayden 288, 289
Williams, Bernard 8, 15, 117-21, 125, 137-39, 141, 144
Williams, Raymond 102, 114, 287, 289
Wills, David 113
Wolf, Susan 137-39, 142, 144
Wolfrey, Julian 111, 112, 115
Wollaeger, Mark A. 14, 15, 83, 87,
Wood, Allen W. 86
Wood, Laura 112, 115
Woolf, Virginia 1, 15, 125, 174
Wray, Helena 165, 167

Yamamoto, Kaoru 274, 287, 289
Yiannitsaros, Christopher 115

Zagórski, Karol 297
Zalta, Edward N. 144, 198
Zhang, Chengping 139, 144

Index of Conrad's Works and Letters

Almayer's Folly 19, 83, 84
"Amy Foster" 8, 18, 21, 54, 55, 60, 82
"Autocracy and War" 82, 84, 103, 267
"Because of the Dollars" 12, 261, 266, 268-279, 284-86
Chance 239
Collected Letters 1 76, 84, 97, 297, 298
Collected Letters 2 83, 112, 132, 296, 307
Collected Letters 3 148, 149, 151, 254,
Collected Letters 4 72, 84, 122
Collected Letters 5 122, 293, 297, 304, 307
Collected Letters 7 122
Collected Letters 8 293, 304, 305
"Congo Diary, The" 96, 291, 298, 301, 306, 308
"Falk: A Reminiscence" 268
"Geography and Some Explorers" 96
"Heart of Darkness" 6, 8, 9, 12-15, 18, 29, 35, 43, 50-60, 66-68, 73, 76, 77, 83, 87, 89-96, 98-111, 113, 114, 116, 136, 141, 143, 145, 170, 237-60, 263, 265, 268, 282, 287-89, 293-96, 299, 302, 306, 307, 309
"Karain: A Memory" 8, 18, 54, 59, 60, 73
Last Essays 96, 298, 307-09
Lord Jim 6, 8, 14, 15, 18, 21, 23, 24, 26-31, 45, 54, 56, 60-68, 73, 76-78, 83, 84, 87, 119, 139, 142, 234, 246, 257, 268, 282

Nigger of the "Narcissus, The 19, 20, 80, 84, 238, 239, 242, 282, 299, 303, 304
Nostromo 8, 18, 26, 43-50, 60, 73, 83, 85, 121, 132, 267
Notes on Life and Letters 82, 84, 103, 197, 267, 275
"Outpost of Progress, An" 13, 96, 250, 259, 291-96, 299, 300, 306
Outcast of the Islands 84
Personal Record, A 2, 39, 40, 81, 247, 293, 307
"Poland Revisited" 197, 275
Rescue, The 265, 266
Secret Agent, The 8, 10, 11, 26, 63, 84, 121, 145-61, 163-65, 167, 169-99, 201-03, 210, 211, 216-19, 221, 225, 227, 229, 231, 233, 234, 239, 278, 279
"Secret Sharer, The" 8, 18, 21, 22, 64, 65, 83, 274, 287, 289, 309
Tales of Unrest 59, 250, 292-95
Twixt, Land and Sea 22
Typhoon and Other Stories 55, 268
Under Western Eyes 6, 8, 10, 14, 18, 21, 31-43, 48, 54, 61, 68-71, 73-77, 82-87, 117-19, 121-45, 274, 285, 288
Victory 8, 18, 45, 54, 77
Within the Tides 239, 261, 262, 270, 272, 274-78,
Youth: A Narrative, and Two Other Stories 106, 270, 295

The published volumes of the series
Conrad: Eastern and Western Perspectives
Editor: Wiesław Krajka

I 1992 Carabine, Keith, Owen Knowles, and Wiesław Krajka, eds. *Conrad's Literary Career*

II 1993 Carabine, Keith, Owen Knowles, and Wiesław Krajka, eds. *Contexts for Conrad*

III 1994 Morzinski, Mary. *Linguistic Influence of Polish on Joseph Conrad's Style*

IV 1995 Lothe, Jakob, ed. *Conrad in Scandinavia*

V 1996 Kurczaba, Alex S., ed. *Conrad and Poland*

VI 1998 Carabine, Keith, Owen Knowles, with Paul Armstrong, eds. *Conrad, James and Other Relations*

VII 1998 Davis, Laura L., ed. *Conrad's Century: The Past and Future Splendour*

VIII 1999 Krajka, Wiesław, ed. *Joseph Conrad: East European, Polish and Worldwide*

IX 2000 Lucas, Michael A. *Aspects of Conrad's Literary Language*

X 2001 Fincham, Gail, Attie de Lange, with Wiesław Krajka, eds. *Conrad at the Millennium: Modernism, Postmodernism, Postcolonialism*

XI 2002 Lange, Attie de, Gail Fincham, with Wiesław Krajka, eds. *Conrad in Africa: New Essays on "Heart of Darkness"*

XII 2003 Carabine, Keith, and Max Saunders, eds. *Inter-Relations: Conrad, James, Ford and Others*

XIII 2004 Krajka, Wiesław, ed. *A Return to the Roots: Conrad, Poland and East-Central Europe*

XIV 2005 Krajka, Wiesław, ed. *Beyond the Roots: The Evolution of Conrad's Ideology and Art*

XV 2006 Paccaud-Huguet, Josiane, ed. *Conrad in France*

XVI 2007 Göbel, Walter, Hans Ulrich Seeber, and Martin Windisch, eds. *Conrad in Germany*

XVII 2008 Bobrowski, Tadeusz. *A Memoir of My Life*. Trans. and ed. Addison Bross

XVIII 2009 Krajka, Wiesław, ed. *Joseph Conrad: Between Literary Techniques and Their Messages*

XIX 2010 Krajka, Wiesław, ed. *In the Realms of Biography, Literature, Politics and Reception: Polish and East-Central European Joseph Conrad*

XX 2011 Sokołowska, Katarzyna. *Conrad and Turgenev: Towards the Real*

XXI 2012 Acheraïou, Amar, and Nursel Içöz, eds. *Joseph Conrad and the Orient*

XXII 2013 Krajka, Wiesław, ed. *From Szlachta Culture to the 21st Century, Between East and West. New Essays on Joseph Conrad's Polishness*

XXIII 2014 Krajka, Wiesław, ed. *"Wine in Old and New Bottles": Critical Paradigms for Joseph Conrad*

XXIV 2015 Curreli, Mario, ed. *Conrad in Italy*

XXV 2016 G. W. Stephen Brodsky. *Joseph Conrad's Polish Soul. Realms of Memory and Self.* Ed. George Z. Gasyna

XXVI 2017 Claude, Maisonnat. *Joseph Conrad and the Voicing of Textuality*

XXVII 2018 Krajka, Wiesław, ed. *Joseph Conrad's Authorial Self: Polish and Other*

XXVIII 2019 Krajka, Wiesław, ed. *Some Intertextual Chords of Joseph Conrad's Literary Art*

XXIX 2020 Krajka, Wiesław, ed. *Various Dimensions of the Other in Joseph Conrad's Fiction*

XXX 2021 Acheraïou, Amar, and Laëtitia Crémona, eds. *Joseph Conrad and Ethics*